Vergil's Empire

Vergil's Empire

Political Thought in the *Aeneid*

Eve Adler

ROWMAN & LITTLEFIELD PUBLISHERS, INC.
Lanham • Boulder • New York • Oxford

ROWMAN & LITTLEFIELD PUBLISHERS, INC.

Published in the United States of America
by Rowman & Littlefield Publishers, Inc.
A Member of the Rowman & Littlefield Publishing Group
4501 Forbes Boulevard, Suite 200, Lanham, Maryland 20706
www.rowmanlittlefield.com

PO Box 317
Oxford
OX2 9RU, UK

British Library Cataloguing in Publication Information Available

Library of Congress Cataloging-in-Publication Data

Adler, Eve.
  Vergil's empire : political thought in the Aeneid / Eve Adler.
     p. cm.
  Includes bibliographical references and index.
  ISBN 0-7425-2166-4 (alk. paper) — ISBN 0-7425-2167-2 (pbk. : alk. paper)
    1. Virgil, Aeneis. 2.   Political poetry, Latin—History and criticism.
3. Epic poetry, Latin—History and criticism. 4.   Aeneas (Legendary
character) in literature. 5.   Virgil—Political and social views. 6.
Politics and literature—Rome. 7.   Imperialism in literature. 8.
Rome—In literature.   I. Title
  PA6825 .A68 2003
    873'.01—dc21
                                    2002014231

Printed in the United States of America

⊗™ The paper used in this publication meets the minimum requirements of
American National Standard for Information Sciences—Permanence of Paper for
Printed Library Materials, ANSI/NISO Z39.48-1992.

~

Contents

Part III: *Pietatis Imago*

~

Acknowledgments

I am grateful to Harvey C. Mansfield Jr., the William R. Kenan Jr. Professor of Government at Harvard University, for his princely support and encouragement in bringing this work to publication. Middlebury College gave me the leave from teaching that enabled me to complete the writing of this book.

~

Introduction

The most controversial question in contemporary interpretation of Vergil's *Aeneid* may be said to be the question whether Vergil in this poem is pro-Augustan or anti-Augustan, pro-imperial or anti-imperial, pro-Roman or anti-Roman.[1] The argument of the following study claims for Vergil an intention that goes far beyond the terms of this controversy: Vergil aims neither to advocate nor to oppose Augustus' Roman Empire, but to found his own empire; Vergil's poem is a "foundation poem" not because its subject matter is the Aenean first foundation or the Augustan refoundation of Rome, but because it itself claims to be the foundation of an altogether new and greater order of things, *maior rerum ordo* (*Aeneid* 7.44). The political problem that animates Vergil's founding ambitions is the conflict between scientific enlightenment and religion. The specific form in which this problem was given to Vergil was the form of Lucretius' poem *De Rerum Natura*, in the theoretical argument of the poem on the one hand, and in the literary or political fact of its publication on the other.

Lucretius teaches that we human beings are accidental, mortal, and alone without gods—without gods to provide for us, to protect morality, to reward and punish us, to govern nature or guide the government of cities, to preserve our country, our posterity, our world itself from inexorable dissolution and oblivion. According to Lucretius, full knowledge of our unprotected situation in the universe, bitter or frightening as it may appear at first, is the source of the highest and most secure happiness attainable by a human being. Lucretius' astonishing project, his presentation in beautiful poetry of

ix

the comprehensive Epicurean doctrine, not only presents the argument for the truth of Epicureanism but also aims to make this argument accessible to a far wider audience than Epicurus himself, or Epicurus' followers, had ever thought good to address.[2] Thus while the argument of the *De Rerum Natura* is theoretical, its literary form—its presentation as beautiful and ingratiating poetry—is a practical or political deed of the greatest moment. And thus a thoughtful reader who was persuaded by Lucretius' argument that we live in a godless world must nevertheless have directed to Lucretius' poem the question: granted that this is true, is it desirable that this truth be publicly, not to say poetically, propagated? Granted that knowledge of this truth is the greatest happiness attainable by a human being, is it attainable by the general run of human beings who read poetry? Can Lucretius' poem transform the general run of human beings who read poetry into a race of philosophers? If so, then what is the error that Lucretius has found in the opinion of all antiquity that the philosophers are always and necessarily few? And if not, then on what grounds does Lucretius believe it is desirable for nonphilosophers to be taught that we live in a godless world?

The thoughtful reader whose questions I have sketched here is Vergil. His questions are alive for us too because we too live in a world in which materialist or atheistic science claims to offer a general improvement of human life, not only in the provision of comforts and conveniences, not only in the development of great insights into the nature of things, but also in the reformation of the human spirit, the dismantling of religious fears and comforts in favor of human autonomy, human courage and prudence in the face of our unprotectedness.

In this study I have argued that Vergil is indeed persuaded by Lucretius' argument that we live in a godless world, but is also persuaded by other things that the propagation of this truth is harmful to human life. That the truth is harmful to human life is somehow a sad teaching, which goes far towards illuminating the famous melancholy of Vergil's *Aeneid*. In Vergil's view, all of human natural sociability, human laws, human force, and human education are insufficient, without widespread belief in provident and punishing gods, to sustain human life at all, not to speak of cultivating the good life or enabling the few, like Lucretius, to philosophize. Lucretius' deed, his public propagation of Epicurean doctrine in poetry, reflects according to Vergil a grave error in Lucretius' understanding of human nature, and thus a grave defect in Lucretius' account of the whole nature of things. Vergil's own project[3] may be described as the public rectification of Lucretius' error in such a way as to lay the foundation for his own "greater order of things." As Lucretius' poem has both a theoretical argument and a practical effect, so Vergil aims to both correct Lucretius' theory—thereby perfecting the true doctrine of the whole nature of things—and undo the harmful practical effect of Lucretius' poem by outshining it utterly and forever with the brilliant attractions of his own.

That Vergil's poetry is profoundly influenced by or imitative of or responsive to Lucretius' poetry is felt at once by all readers in Vergil's massive echoing of Lucretius' words. The detailed chronicling of these echoes by scholars[4] has brought vividly to sight the full extent of them.[5] But interpretation of the brute fact of this literary phenomenon has been scanty,[6] and most of it has assumed that Vergil's elaborate reverberations of Lucretius arise from the attractions rather of Lucretius' style than of his substance.

Thus the view of Sellar, in his influential essay on the "Relation of the Georgics to the Poem of Lucretius,"[7] is that Vergil was imaginatively attracted to the thematic grandeur but spiritually repelled by the philosophic "attitude" of the De Rerum Natura:

> The influence, direct and indirect, exercised by Lucretius on the thought, the composition, and the style of the Georgics was perhaps stronger than that ever exercised, before or since, by one great poet on the work of another. This influence is of the kind which is oftener seen in the history of philosophy than in that of literature. It was partly one of sympathy, partly of antagonism. Virgil's feeling and conception of Nature have their immediate origin in the feeling and thought of Lucretius; while at the same time his religious convictions and national sentiment derive new strength by reaction from the attitude assumed by his predecessor. This powerful attraction and repulsion were alike due to the fact that Lucretius was the first not only to reveal a new power, beauty, and mystery in the world, but also to communicate to poetry a speculative impulse, opening up, with a more impassioned appeal than philosophy can do, the great questions underlying human life,—such as the truth of all religious tradition, the position of man in the Universe, and the attitude of mind and course of conduct demanded by that position.[8]

According to Sellar, Vergil's poetic imagination was kindled to emulate the grandeur of Lucretius' cosmic and speculative themes, while Vergil himself was not only repelled by Lucretius' "attitude" but unequal to a sober understanding of the meaning of Epicureanism:

> Certain results of a philosophic system affect his imagination, but he does not seem to feel how these results necessarily exclude other conclusions which he will not abandon. Hence arises his prevailing eclecticism,—the existence of popular beliefs side by side in his mind with the tenets of the Epicureans, Stoics, and Platonists,—of some conclusions of the Lucretian science along with

the opposing doctrines expressed in the poetry of Alexandria. Even in the arrangement of his materials and the grouping of his landscapes, some chance association or rhythmical cadence seems to guide his hand, more often than the perception of the orderly connexion of phenomena with one another.[9]

Vergil was imaginatively enchanted by Lucretius' poetry but understood neither Lucretius nor, for that matter, himself:

> Probably not even the poets themselves, and least of all Virgil, could have given an explanation of their real state of mind. The dreams of an older faith were still haunting them, though its substance was gone.[10]

Sellar's essay provides an insightful and sensitive account of the poetic connections of many passages in the Georgics with their Lucretian sources. In the present study I have argued, however, that Vergil understood very well both Lucretius and himself; in fact, Vergil claims, with some reason, to have understood Lucretius' doctrine better than Lucretius did, and thus to be in a position not to shrink away in dreamy uneasiness from the furthest implications of that doctrine but to provide a magisterial critique and correction of it.

Among critics who have given Vergil more credit than Sellar does for understanding Lucretius, the most widespread view has been that Vergil had been an Epicurean in his youth, had later turned away from Epicureanism to some form of Stoicism or Platonism, but nonetheless continued to reflect in his poetic language the Lucretian language of his rejected youthful enthusiasm. This is the view of Pease:[11]

> I believe that Virgil had come to see that, pleasant as hedonistic philosophies are for the individual—and λάθε βιώσας (Epic. fr. 551 Usener) would have been very congenial to him—yet no state has been raised by them to greatness.[12]

In Pease's view, Vergil in the Aeneid represents the Epicureanism that he himself has rejected by attributing it to Dido:

> We may not unreasonably find in the contrast between Dido, for whom he feels sympathetic understanding but no real approval, and Aeneas, whom his sober thought commends, a suggestion of his own passage from an Epicureanism which he once cherished and for which he still feels sympathy and regard to other beliefs which now seem to him of greater value for the state and deeper comfort to the individual. This thought had already been expressed in the Georgics, in the contrast between the intellectual pride of the Epicurean philosopher—like Lucretius—and the simple, sturdy faith of the Italian coun-

trymen, and this, I believe, we may see more clearly developed in the characters of the *Aeneid*.[13]

Pease's view that in Dido and Carthage Vergil has represented Epicureanism
is adopted and developed in detail in Part I of the present essay, and indeed
is central to my interpretation of the *Aeneid*. But his view that the mature
Vergil had himself rejected Epicureanism is found inadequate for reasons already hinted at, but not pursued, in Pease's own account of the matter. For to
see that "no state has been raised by [Epicureanism] to greatness," and that
"other beliefs . . . seem . . . of greater value for the state and deeper comfort
for the individual," is rather a different thing from rejecting Epicureanism as
false in itself.

In his study of the *Aeneid*, *Darkness Visible*, W. R. Johnson[14] presses beyond
Pease's view. Agreeing that Vergil's understanding of Lucretius' poem was a
philosophic understanding of Lucretius' teaching, Johnson proposes that Vergil
may never have decisively rejected that teaching, but may rather have been
permanently and profoundly torn between acceptance and rejection of it:

> Vergil's reading of [*De Rerum Natura*] was probably the most important thing
> in his life as a poet (to call that reading an event would be misleading since it
> is clear that the reading was habitual and unending). Our problem, then, was
> Vergil's. Why should a man who read *De Rerum Natura* so passionately and ab-
> sorbed it so thoroughly undertake to write a poem that is not merely about
> what happens in history but is also about the vindication of the meaning of his-
> tory in general and the meaning of the City in particular (in Epicurean terms,
> about how illusion is vindicated by illusion)? Why should an Epicurean at-
> tempt to write not merely a foundation epic but *the* Foundation Epic (imagine,
> if you will, a Shaker who "believed in the green light" at work on the Great
> American Novel)?
>
> These questions admit of no exact answer, but they invite speculation. Sup-
> pose Vergil's heart was divided. Suppose he read and reread his Lucretius as a
> religious atheist might peruse his Saint Paul. . . . But suppose that, unpersuaded
> that the objects of his dread were unreal, he kept turning toward a belief in a
> divinely rational design. . . . I would suggest . . . that . . . continuing in this vac-
> illation and indecision, he wrote a great epic which succeeds partly because its
> author has the honesty to admit not only the intensity and durability of his
> fears but also the depths of his weakness and indecision.[15]

Johnson's brief but penetrating remarks have the virtue of recognizing that
Vergil is, like Lucretius, a philosophic thinker;[16] and thus his question, "Why
should an Epicurean attempt to write *the* Foundation Epic?", goes to the heart
of the interpretation of the *Aeneid*. But in the present study I have argued

that the Epicurean Vergil composed "*the* Foundation Epic" not in "vacilla-tion and indecision" but in the deliberate intention of completing and cor-recting Lucretian Epicureanism.

While my argument differs in the ways indicated from most modern in-terpretation of the *Aeneid*, its fundamental premise is by no means new. Servius describes Vergil's practice in this way:

> He mixes poetic fictions with philosophy and thus shows forth both what is vulgar and the contents of truth and natural reason.
>
> (*ad* 6.719)

Servius' view[17] is that Vergil is a philosophic poet, that Vergil's poetry con-tains both a philosophic argument and vulgar fictions, and that Vergil is the master and manipulator of the artful mixing of the two in accordance with his own purposes. Servius' understanding of what Vergil's purposes are may be sketched as follows. Vergil is an Epicurean philosophic poet who at times finds it prudent to speak, when he is speaking philosophically, not as an Epi-curean philosopher but in accordance with "general" philosophy:

> Knowing that [the philosophers'] opinions about the rule of the gods are vari-ous, he has very prudently held to a generality; though for the most part he fol-lows Siro, his Epicurean teacher;
>
> (*ad* 6.264)

and at times, when he is speaking poetically, not as a philosopher at all but in accordance with "public opinion":

> He said this [that falling stars trail their hair behind them] poetically, in ac-cordance with public opinion; for as Lucretius says [2.206 ff.], the wind, when making for the higher places, pulls the aetherial fire along with it, so that its path gives the appearance of falling stars.
>
> (*ad* 5.527)

Vergil finds it prudent to speak in these ways because Epicurean doctrine baldly stated is both offensive and harmful to non-Epicureans; Vergil speaks so as to protect both Epicureanism from public opinion and public opinion from Epicureanism. Vergil's prudence however lies not in suppressing Epi-curean doctrine altogether—since he is interested in transmitting it to those few who will be neither offended nor harmed by it—but in making his ap-proval of it tantalizingly difficult, though not impossible, to discern. Vergil achieves this difficulty by "mixing poetic fictions with philosophy." For example, Servius indicates, Vergil appears to contradict himself when he says in Book 10, "everyone's day [of death] is fixed for him" (467), while in Book 4 he had said that Dido died "neither by fate nor by a due death, but wretchedly before her day" (696). Servius' comment on this indicates that one must study the dramatic contexts of Vergil's contradictions in order to find his true opinion:

> What he says in Book 4.696, *sed misera ante diem*, is according to the Epicure-ans, who attribute all things to chance [*casibus*]; but what he says now, *stat sua cuique dies*, is according to the Stoics, who say that the decrees of the fates are preserved. Vergil acted very prudently in attributing the weak and vague opin-ion of the Epicureans to a human being—that is, to himself (for that phrase was spoken in the person of the poet)—while attributing this strong opinion to Jupiter; for the Stoics are both very virtuous and worshipers of gods.
>
> (*ad* 10.467)

Vergil, that is, prudently attributes to his poetic fiction, Jupiter, the "strong" opinion that accords with the worship of Jupiter, while reserving to himself, as merely human, the "weak" opinion that undermines the worship of Jupiter: Vergil's prudence lies in seeming to subordinate his own disbelief in Jupiter to Jupiter's belief in Jupiter, while simultaneously calling attention to his own disbelief as his own.

Servius, then, read the *Aeneid* with attentiveness both to Vergil's Epicure-anism and to the prudent manner of his obscuring it with poetic fictions and accommodations to public opinion.[18] Servius' comprehensive reading of the *Aeneid* as *latenter secundum Epicureos*,[19] "secretly in accordance with the Epi-cureans," underlies the cool confidence of his infamous judgment on Vergil's account of the Underworld as concluded by the "twin gates of Sleep":

> Poetically, the meaning is manifest: he wishes it to be understood that every-thing he has said is false. Indeed, physiology indicates that the gate of horn sig-nifies the eyes . . . and the ivory gate signifies the mouth (from the teeth). And we know that the things we say can be false, while the things we see are true without doubt.[20]

The interpretation of the *Aeneid* offered in the present study takes its bear-ings by the key insight of Servius' interpretation: Vergil's poem is an Epi-curean book whose pious or poetic fictions are artfully calculated to protect his full teaching from the many and the many from his full teaching. In mod-ern Vergil scholarship, the closest approach to this interpretation has been made by A. K. Michels.[21] Starting from a consideration of the linguistic

echoes of Lucretius in Book 6 of the *Aeneid*, the book "which seems to contradict the Epicurean doctrine of the mortality of the soul . . . and may be interpreted as a rebuttal of Lucretius,"[22] Michels argues that Vergil in the
Aeneid "still accepted" Epicurean physics:

> I feel sure that Vergil meant Aeneas' journey to Hades to be interpreted as a
> dream by those versed in the Epicurean theories of dreams and visions, while
> he left it to be taken as a real episode by the uninitiated. . . . The introduction
> of the tree of dreams at the entrance to Hades and its association with the the-
> ory of images must have been meant as the clue to the interpretation.[23]

Michels' reading follows Servius' in distinguishing a philosophic content from
a vulgar fiction; but it also claims that while Vergil in the *Aeneid* still accepted
Epicurean physics, he had "discarded its ethics;" for otherwise why (as Johnson asks) should an Epicurean attempt to write a foundation epic? Michels
suggests that the "one cardinal point" on which Vergil rejected Epicurean
ethics amounts to a rejection of Epicurean politics: it is the status of "participation in public affairs" on which Vergil "sets forth his challenge to Lucretius." But how is it possible for one who follows the Epicureans in physics
to reject "the principle on which their secure and peaceful lives were founded"
in favor of "a dream,"[24] without thereby sinking into the mists of confusion attributed to Vergil by Sellar? This question Michels does not address.

The present study has three parts. In Part I, "The Foundations of Carthage
and of Rome," Vergil's founding intentions are discussed in connection with
his portrayal of Carthage and Rome as ideal types of the two alternative foundations of cities, atheistic science and ancestral religion. Dido, the founder of
Carthage, is as it were the pupil of Lucretius, and Carthage is the enlightened
city founded according to the unrevised teaching of Lucretius' *De Rerum
Natura*; in the tragedy of Dido and Carthage, Vergil has indicated how Lucretius' teaching would need to be revised both practically, in order to serve
as a secure foundation of human souls and cities, and theoretically, in order to
capture the truth of the whole nature of things. Vergil's critique of Lucretius
centers upon Lucretius' analysis of the passions and particularly of anger; the
error in Lucretius' understanding of the nature of anger is responsible for the
error in his political understanding. This is the key to the question how Vergil
can consistently accept Lucretius' physics while rejecting his politics: Vergil
in fact corrects Lucretius' physics, his physiology of the passions, in a way that
strictly requires a corresponding correction of Lucretius' politics.

While Part I analyzes Vergil's critique of the defect of Lucretian doctrine,
Part II, "The Greater Order of Things," treats Vergil's positive teaching on

the relation of the nature of things to the nature of a well founded city. Here I have taken up the question of what Vergil understands by *imperium sine fine*, universal and eternal empire. The argument of this part is that Vergil has composed his mythical or vulgar account of this Vergilian Empire in such a way as to link his revolutionary political program simultaneously to Roman ancestral religion and to Epicurean science; or, to state it more bluntly, in such a way as to put Roman ancestral religion at the service of Epicurean science so as to lead towards the foundation of a world-state. This part contains a detailed analysis of Vergil's myth of Rome as Universal Empire and restored Golden Age; the results of the analysis show how Vergil has artfully assimilated his myth at every point to the truth that the atoms, the void, and the unordered All are the only universal and eternal beings. Our own practical interest in the diverging paths leading, on the one hand, from ancestral religion to the multiplicity of nations, and, on the other, from atheistic science to the world-state, make reflection on Vergil's teaching conspicuously relevant to our own situation.

Part III of this study, "The Image of Piety," treats Vergil's portrayal of Aeneas, or Vergilian heroism. Heroism is the domain of the poets' formation of the people, their establishment of popular agreement as to what is noble or praiseworthy. In this part, I have discussed Vergil's rivalry not only with Lucretius but also with Homer in seeking to win the hearts of men to a poetic model of human greatness and thus to a common object of praise and imitation. The argument of this part is that Vergil has constructed the character of Aeneas in such a way as to smash the foundations of Achillean immortal glory, Odyssean domestic bliss, and Epicurean contemplative felicity as objects of popular imitation, and to erect in their stead an "image of piety," the image of *pius Aeneas*. Images are "real" in the sense of being composed of atoms, but not necessarily "real" in the sense of corresponding to existing compound beings. Men's false beliefs in the existence of gods and the survival of the dead are based on the false interpretation of images. In harmony with the overall plan of the *Aeneid* as a certain mixture of philosophy and poetic fictions, Vergil's portrayal of Aeneas shows how the formation of Aeneas' own heroic character, his piety, is itself accomplished through images, and most notably through the images of divine reward and punishment in the Underworld whose cognitive status Servius has so forcefully indicated. Aeneas, the hero whose imitation by the general run of readers of poetry would be most desirable for Vergil's universal and eternal empire, the man who represents the highest happiness attainable by most men, is a man whose happiness is rooted in ignorance of the nature of things and lively responsiveness

to marvelous images: "He marvels and, ignorant of the things themselves, rejoices in an image" (8.730). Ignorance of the things themselves, of the truth
of things, is for most men the necessary condition of their rejoicing; herein
lie the "tears of things," the sad truth of human life. But with a properly
formed ignorance most men can, at any rate, properly rejoice; and their
proper rejoicing can so harmonize them as to provide the condition for the
felicity of the few, the universal peace prayed for by Lucretius, in the invocation to the *De Rerum Natura*, as the condition of his own philosophizing:

> Bring it to pass that the savage works of war may be stilled to rest throughout
> all seas and lands!
>
> (1.29–30)

Vergil proposes in the *Aeneid* to grant Lucretius' prayer. Whether it was a
wise prayer for one philosophic poet to pray or another to perform is a question that calls for the most sober reflection.

PART ONE

THE FOUNDATIONS OF CARTHAGE AND OF ROME

CHAPTER ONE

~

The Theme of the *Aeneid*

i. Rome (1.1–7)

Arma virumque cano, "Arms and a man I sing." In the first three words of the *Aeneid* Vergil indicates his rivalry with Homer: the *Aeneid* will outdo the *Iliad* and the *Odyssey* by including both, by making a unity of them.[1] *Arma* stands for Achilles and the *Iliad*, *virum* for Odysseus and the *Odyssey*: the *Aeneid* will show as one both the Iliadic warring hero and the Odyssean wandering hero. The unity of these two, and the superiority of this unity to Homer's duality, is shown by their common end, the foundation of Rome:

> arma virumque cano, Troiae qui primus ab oris
> Italiam fato profugus Lavinaque venit
> litora—multum ille et terris iactatus et alto
> vi superum, saevae memorem Iunonis ob iram,
> multa quoque et bello passus, dum conderet urbem
> inferretque deos Latio—genus unde Latinum
> Albanique patres atque altae moenia Romae.

> Arms and a man I sing, the first who came from the shores of Troy, an exile by fate, to Italy and the Lavinian shores—that man was much tossed about on land and sea by the power of gods, through the unforgetting anger of savage Juno; and he suffered many things in war, until he could found the city and bring his gods into Latium—whence the Latin race, the Alban fathers, and the walls of lofty Rome.

(1.1–7)

Homer began his poems by invoking the Muse to sing of the anger of Achilles and to tell of the man of many ways; Vergil begins his poem by declaring that he himself sings *arma virumque*. Vergil appears to do and outdo by his own powers what Homer had relied on the Muse to do; apparently Vergil has within himself, or is for himself, the source of song about arms and a man, and therewith about the foundation of Rome.

Vergil, however, revises Homer's account of the theme of the *Iliad*. Homer had said it was "anger," but Vergil says it is "arms." Perhaps Vergil has been able to appropriate and unify the two themes of Homer's Muse only at the cost of omitting one of them.

ii. Anger (1.8–11)

The reason why Vergil has replaced "anger" with "arms" as the Achillean theme, and the reason why he has replaced Homer's Muse with himself as the singer of *arma virumque*, come to light together in lines 1.8–11:

> Musa, mihi causas memora, quo numine laeso
> quidve dolens regina deum tot volvere casus
> insignem pietate virum, tot adire labores
> impulerit. tantaene animis caelestibus irae?

> Muse, recall the causes for me: how injured in her divinity, or by what embittered, did the queen of the gods drive that famously pious man to undergo so many misfortunes, to enter upon so many travails: Is there such anger in celestial spirits?

Vergil invokes the Muse not, like Homer, to "sing" or "tell" of the hero's deeds and sufferings, but to recall to the poet *the causes of divine anger*. Vergil has replaced "anger" with "arms" as the Achillean theme in order to promote the theme of anger from the human to the divine level: Vergil's theme is the anger of the goddess, not the anger of the hero. Divine anger is the highest theme of the *Aeneid*, the theme for which Vergil is dependent on the aid of the Muse; knowledge of the causes of divine anger is a higher theme than Homer ever aspired to. Arms and a man, and with them the founding of Rome, are secondary themes of the *Aeneid*.

Vergil himself knows the story of Juno's anger against the hero; this is part of what he will sing without the Muse's aid (4). What he wishes to learn from the Muse are the *causes;* and the sense in which he wonders about these causes is that the known history of Juno's anger seems incredible: *tantaene animis caelestibus irae?* (is there such anger in *celestial* spirits?)

As Servius observes, the key word here is *caelestibus:* Vergil's question has regard to the supposed division or difference between the infernal world, where anger is said to have its rightful place in the order of things (the Furies), and the celestial world, where the omnipotent wisdom of Jupiter is said to rule.[2] The world is thought to be constituted by the separation of the infernal from the celestial in such a way that the celestial governs the infernal; but Juno is a celestial god who seems to be governed by infernal anger; perhaps the unintelligible misfortunes and travails of the pious man at the hands of the angry goddess show a rent in the foundation of the world, a point of ungoverned irruption of infernal fury into the world above? The cities and souls of men are thought to be constituted like the world itself by the ordering of their celestial and infernal parts in such a way that their own infernal furies are governable from above; but if the celestial gods themselves are anarchically angry, if the world itself is disordered at its foundations, what foundation is there for the foundation of Rome?

The particularly shocking thing about Juno's angry persecution of Aeneas is that Aeneas is a man famous for his piety (10). When Aeneas meets in battle a young man who deserved to be happier in his father's rule and whose father indeed was hardly a father to him (7.653–654), and yet who is willing to defend his father even at the price of his life, Aeneas says to him, "Your piety is deceiving you unawares" (10.812). What if the cause of divine anger is a fundamental disorder in the constitution of the world, such that pious men deserve to be happier in their gods' rule and their gods are hardly gods to them? Thus the *Aeneid*, which praises the armed man Aeneas for his piety above all things, takes for its highest theme the question of the *causes* of divine anger.

iii. Carthage (1.12–33)

Vergil begins to speak of the causes of divine anger by beginning to speak of Carthage:

> Urbs antiqua fuit (Tyrii tenuere coloni)
> Karthago, Italiam contra Tiberinaque longe
> ostia, dives opum studiisque asperrima belli.

> There was an ancient city (settled by Tyrian colonists), Carthage, far away facing against Italy and the Tiber's mouth, rich in wealth and very harsh in the pursuits of war.

> (1.12–14)

Vergil begins to speak of Carthage as at the time of the Punic Wars, when she was an ancient city and had also become very warlike. At the time of Aeneas' wars and wanderings, Carthage was a new city without an army; but "already then" (18) Juno favored Carthage for kingship over the nations, and wished to prevent the foundation of Rome because she had heard that Rome would one day overthrow Carthage and become king over the nations (15–22). Juno's anger against Aeneas springs from her opposing Rome and favoring Carthage, together with her remembering the judgment of Paris, the honors done to Ganymede, and everything connected with the war against Troy that she had waged on behalf of her beloved Greeks (23–28). Inflamed by all these things, Juno harried the remnant of Troy all over the seas for many years, keeping them far from Latium; so massive a task it was to found the Roman nation (29–33).

iv. Rome vs. Carthage

The proem of the *Aeneid* proposes, then, a complex triadic theme: Rome, anger, Carthage. The connection among the three parts of Vergil's theme may be roughly sketched as follows: the *Aeneid* proposes to present and to decide the contesting claims of the two types of city to be the well-founded city—the city that has the key to the rule of anger in the souls and cities of men; the city, therefore, that has the rightful claim to be king of the nations. "Rome" and "Carthage" are Vergil's poetic types of *the* two foundations of cities; and knowledge of the causes of divine anger, which is the highest theme of the *Aeneid*, is the compelling factor in a wise decision between them.

Rome is founded on the arms and piety of Aeneas, as appears already from the proem;[3] Carthage on the gold and science of Dido, as emerges from the narrative of Book 1. "Rome" and "Carthage" in the *Aeneid* are the alternatives that Vergil shows to be facing his own contemporaries, or perhaps even all men of the future for whom the founding or refounding of a regime is at issue. According to Jupiter's prophecy (1.257–296), Rome was originally well founded in accordance with his providential design for bringing Furor permanently under rule and securing peace; this design will need to be completed by Caesar's refounding in the fullness of time (286 ff.), that is, in Vergil's time. Vergil's *Aeneid* poetically presents the rival claim of Carthage to be the well-founded city, and the defect of her claim, in order that the descendants of Aeneas may not be diverted at the last moment from the refounding of Rome to the refounding of Carthage, as Aeneas himself was almost diverted at the beginning from the first founding of Rome to the first founding of Carthage. The love of Vergil's contemporary Romans for the foundations of Carthage—for gold and especially for science—is prefigured or symbolized in the *Aeneid* by the love of Rome's founder for the founder of Carthage.

CHAPTER TWO

~

The Song of Iopas
and the Song of Vergil

According to the myth of the *Aeneid*, the teacher of the founder of Carthage was Iopas, whom Vergil introduces, at the end of Book 1, at the feast given by Queen Dido to welcome the shipwrecked Trojans to her city:

> cithara crinitus Iopas
> personat aurata, docuit quem maximus Atlas.
> hic canit errantem lunam solisque labores,
> unde hominum genus et pecudes, unde imber et ignes,
> Arcturum pluviasque Hyadas geminosque Triones;
> quid tantum Oceano properent se tingere soles
> hiberni, vel quae tardis mora noctibus obstet.

> Long-haired Iopas, whom great Atlas taught, sounded the golden lyre. He sang of the wandering moon, the labors of the sun, the origin of the human race and of the beasts, of water and of fire, Arcturus and the rainy Hyades and the twin Triones, why the winter suns so hurry to dip themselves in Ocean, and what delay holds back the long nights.

> (1.740–746)

The pious Trojans did not spontaneously applaud this Carthaginian song, the likes of which had never been heard at Troy;[1] but observing the Carthaginians themselves break into resounding applause, the Trojans followed their lead (1.747). What delay holds back the Trojans' applause?

For the Trojans, the song of Iopas is the climax of a long day of coming to understand the Carthaginians. The shipwrecked Trojans' first encounter with

9

the Carthaginians, whose coast guard, instead of assisting their disabled fleet, had tried to prevent their landing by torching the ships, had raised in the Trojans the suspicion that the Carthaginians despised the human race and regarded the gods as indifferent to right and wrong (1.542–543). Although the Carthaginians' subsequent turn from firing the ships to feasting the shipwrecked has made that suspicion less urgent, it has not laid it to rest. The song of Iopas, which the pious Trojans ever so briefly hesitate to applaud, reveals finally the basis of the Carthaginians' suspicious conduct: Iopas teaches them the nature of things without reference to any gods at all. Hearing for the first time a natural account of the causes and origins of heavenly and earthly things, the Trojans were momentarily behindhand in their response. They may have been reflecting that, if Iopas' account of things is true, then the piety for which they have been recommending themselves and their king to Carthage would need to be reassessed. Or they may have been reflecting that if the Carthaginians fear no gods, then their sudden turn from hostility to hospitality may be unreliable, and may turn back to savagery or treachery without regard for what is required by piety between guest and host. In any case, moved finally whether by the dawn of enlightenment or by polite manners, they follow the lead of the Carthaginians in applauding Iopas' song.

The meaning of Iopas' song, and its relationship to Vergil's song, is laid out in the central section of the *Georgics*, the section comprising the closing of Book 2 and the opening of Book 3 (2.458–3.48). Here Vergil claims that his own first poetic aspiration would be to sing of the nature of things:

Me vero primum dulces ante omnia Musae,
quarum sacra fero ingenti percussus amore,
accipiant caelique vias et sidera monstrent,
defectus solis varios lunaeque labores;
unde tremor terris, qua vi maria alta tumescant
obicibus ruptis rursusque in se ipsa residant,
quid tantum Oceano properent se tingere soles
hiberni, vel quae tardis mora noctibus obstet.

But as for me, first before all things may the sweet Muses receive me, smitten as I am with an enormous love and bearing their sacred things, and show me the paths of the heaven and the stars, the various eclipses of the sun and labors of the moon; the source of earthquakes; the force by which the deep seas swell and burst their barriers, then subside into themselves again; why the winter suns so hurry to dip themselves in Ocean, or what delay holds back the long nights.

(Geo. 2.475–482)

But Vergil renounces this highest aspiration,[2] to physiologic poetry, on physiologic grounds: the blood around his heart is too cold.[3] He hopes therefore, as his second, "inglorious" aspiration, to love the rural things:

> sin has ne possim naturae accedere partis
> frigidus obstiterit circum praecordia sanguis,
> rura mihi et rigui placeant in vallibus amnes,
> flumina amem silvasque inglorius. o ubi campi
> Spercheusque et virginibus bacchata Lacaenis
> Taygeta! o qui me gelidis convallibus Haemi
> sistat, et ingenti ramorum protegat umbra!

But if the cold blood around my heart holds me back from being able to gain access to these parts of nature, then may the rural things and the running streams in the valleys delight me, may I love, without glory, the rivers and the woods. O for the fields, and Spercheus, and Taygeta with its Spartan virgins celebrating Bacchic rites! O who will put me in the cool valleys of Haemus, and protect me under the great shade of the boughs!

(Geo. 2.483–489)

In the next lines Vergil shows that the ranking of poetry he has made, the placing of physiologic poetry first and ruralist poetry second, is based on a judgment about happiness: the physiologist is happy, *felix*, while the ruralist is fortunate, *fortunatus:*

> felix qui potuit rerum cognoscere causas,
> atque metus omnis et inexorabile fatum
> subiecit pedibus strepitumque Acherontis avari.
> fortunatus et ille does qui novit agrestis
> Panaque Silvanumque senem Nymphasque sorores.

Happy was he who was able to come to know the causes of things, and trampled under foot all fears and inexorable fate and the din of greedy Acheron. Fortunate also is he who knows the country gods, Pan and old Silvanus and the sister nymphs.

(Geo. 2.490–494)

In these beatitudes Vergil clarifies two important aspects of his account of the two kinds of poetry. First, the master of the physiologic poetry he has in mind is Lucretius, as he shows by encapsulating in Lucretian language the core of Lucretius' teaching: knowledge of the causes of things is the cure of man's fear of punishing gods.[4] Second, while the description of the two kinds of poetry might suggest that the chief difference between them is that the highest poetry speaks of sublime nature (the heavens, earthquakes, and sea storms) while the second-highest speaks of mundane nature (the pleasant countryside), the beatitudes show that the chief difference is that physiologic poetry tramples under foot religion, conceived as fear of angry underworld gods, while ruralist poetry promotes religion, conceived as familiar intercourse with mild local gods.[5]

Finally, while the physiologist and the ruralist enjoy different kinds of happiness,[6] what they have in common is that their happiness is emphatically unpolitical:[7] they are unaffected by *res Romanae perituraque regna*, "Roman affairs and perishable kingdoms" (498), and by all the passions and distracted actions that go with these things (495–512). Vergil's division of poetry and happiness in this passage would appear therefore both to exclude the *Aeneid* from the ranks of poetry and to deny that any kind of happiness belongs to political life. But the incompleteness of this division is already suggested at the end of the second *Georgic* by Vergil's allusion to the time when "Remus and his brother" lived the golden life under Saturn, and Rome became the most beautiful of things (532–540). It is decisively supplied at the beginning of the third *Georgic* by Vergil's symbolic description of his future poem that will have Caesar at its center (3.1–48).

Of his future poem Vergil says here it is the way by which he will be able to raise himself above the earth and fly as victor through the mouths of men (3.8–9).[8] He will be the first to lead the Muses in triumph down from the Aonian peak to his fatherland, and the first to bring the palm to Mantua (10–12). The poem with Caesar at its center, in which Vergil will conquer the Greek Muses on behalf of his fatherland, will itself represent Rome's conquest of Britain, Ganges, Nile, and the cities of Asia (25–33); in it there will be breathing statues of the Trojan ancestors (34–36); climactically,

Invidia infelix furias amnemque severum
Cocyti metuet tortosque Ixionis anguis
immanemque rotam et non exsuperabile saxum.

Unhappy Envy will be cringing in terror before the Furies and the grim stream of Cocytus, the twisted snakes of Ixion and the huge wheel and the insuperable stone.

(Geo. 3.37–39)

In addition, then, to physiologic and ruralist poetry, there is a third, political genre, whose subject matter is the "Roman affairs and perishable kingdoms" excluded from the other two kinds; of this third kind, Vergil's *Aeneid* is to be the supreme exemplar. This political poetry will be characterized by taking for its highest theme the opposite of the physiologic theme: whereas physiologic poetry tramples under foot all fears of punishment in the Underworld by showing the natural causes of things, Vergil's future political poetry will triumphantly revive those fears so as to secure Roman conquests (Caesar's conquest of the nations and Vergil's conquest of the Muses) by terrorizing unhappy Invidia into submission. In physiologic poetry, felicity arises from the conquest *of* fear; in political poetry the source of infelicity, Invidia, will be conquered *by* fear. According to physiologic poetry, nature has three parts: earth, sky, and ocean (2.477–482); but according to political poetry it has, as Homer taught, four parts: earth, sky, ocean, and Underworld.[9]

According to the *Georgics*, then, there are three genres of poetry and three spheres of happiness. Ruralist poetry, connected with the fortunateness of the farmers, who would be all too fortunate if they were to know their own good (*Geo.* 2.458–459), is inglorious (486); both physiologic and political poetry are glorious. When Vergil's renunciation of physiologic poetry is viewed in the light of his practicing ruralist poetry, his renunciation appears to be the necessary result of his defect, the insufficient warmth of his heart-blood; but when it is viewed in the light of his practicing political poetry, the possibility arises that this renunciation is a choice based on some defect of physiologic poetry itself. Which of the two glorious poetries is the more glorious? Vergil acknowledges in the *Georgics* the inferiority of the *Georgics* to the *De Rerum Natura*,[10] but asserts in the *Aeneid* the superiority of the *Aeneid* to the *De Rerum Natura*.

The contest between physiologic and political poetry that Vergil sketches in the center of the *Georgics* is represented in the *Aeneid* as a contest[11] between the song that Iopas sings to Dido[12] and the Carthaginians and the song that Vergil sings to Augustus and the Romans.[13] That Iopas stands for Lucretius is evident from the essential identity of Iopas' song with the Lucretian song that Vergil renounces in the *Georgics*. The differences in detail between Iopas' song and the Lucretian song of the *Georgics* are related to the difference between physiologic poetry as aspired to by Vergil and as practiced by Lucretius. For example, in the *Georgics* Vergil longs to be instructed in natural science by the Muses, whereas Iopas has been instructed by Atlas.[14] This difference reflects the thought that, if Vergil had been able to become a physiologic poet, his inspiration and instruction would have arisen from a poetic source, namely Lucretius' poetry; whereas Lucretius' own teacher was the unpoetic Epicurus, represented by Iopas' unpoetic teacher Atlas. Atlas, the mythic inventor of astronomy,[15] stands for Epicurus, the inventor of wisdom. That Atlas is a Titan who resisted the regime of Jupiter[16] recalls Epicurus' being the first to stand up against the thunder-threatening gods (*DRN* 1.66–70). Like Lucretius, and for the same reason, Iopas independently added poetry to the truth about the nature of things that he learned without poetry from his teacher: as Lucretius wishes to make Epicurus' teaching attractive to the political man Memmius,[17] so Iopas wishes to make Atlas' teaching attractive to Dido, the preeminently political woman,[18] and the founder of a new city with a new claim to rule all the nations.[19] As Lucretius reasoned that a man like Memmius would need to be attracted at first by the deceptive sweetness of poetry to drink the bitter healing cup of Epicurean doctrine (4.11–25), so Iopas, addressing a woman given over to the activities and cares of founding a new city, sweetens the cup for her and her court.[20]

Both Iopas' song and the Lucretian song of the *Georgics* begin, in slightly different words, with the motions of the heavenly bodies and end, in identical words, with the causes of the lengthening of nights in winter. In their central lines, the Lucretian song speaks of the origin of earthquakes while Iopas' song speaks of the origin of the race of human beings, beasts, water, and fire; the Lucretian song speaks of the force that makes the seas swell while Iopas' song speaks of the constellations. The subjects Vergil represents himself as desiring to sing about in the *Georgics* are the subjects of the fifth and sixth books of Lucretius' *De Rerum Natura*; when Vergil represents Iopas he limits the performance to Book 5.[21] Iopas' speaking of the origin of the human race is in contrast to Vergil's speaking of the origin of the Latin race (1.6) and with Aeneas' speaking of the origin of the Greeks' treachery against Troy (1.753–754): Iopas' Lucretian poetry ignores the origins of the differences among nations as if the human race were simply or already one,[22] while the *Aeneid* begins from the origins of the different nations, of Carthage and of Rome, with the unification of the human race in view as a question (the question of which city will become king over the nations). Iopas' speaking of the origin of the human race and of beasts, water, and fire reminds us of the Trojans' suspicion that the Carthaginians despise the human race (1.542): Iopas' song teaches them that the human race has the same origin as beasts,[23] water, and fire, while Vergil's *Aeneid* teaches the Romans that the Roman race is descended from Jupiter.

Vergil began the first book of the *Aeneid* by indicating his rivalry with Homer in singing of arms and a man; he ends it, as promised by the account of poetry in the *Georgics* and by the elevation of anger to the place of the central theme of the *Aeneid*, by indicating his rivalry with Lucretius in singing of the causes of divine anger. The heart of the contest between Iopas' song in the *Aeneid* and the *Aeneid* itself is that Iopas' song stamps out human fear by denying the existence of the Underworld and of angry gods, while the *Aeneid* takes for its central subject (Books 6–7) the character and activity of the Underworld, and for its highest theme the causes of divine anger. The defect of physiological poetry, and thus the reason why political poetry is more glorious than physiological poetry and the *Aeneid* more glorious than the *De Rerum Natura*, is brought to light in the *Aeneid* by this contest. Iopas' song has the defect that, by freeing its listeners from fear of angry gods without making them into philosophers, it disarms them against the irruptions of ineradicable fury that do in fact occur in men and cities; whereas Vergil's song has the merit that, while making its listeners subject to the greatest awe of the Underworld Furies and the angry gods, it arms them against the infernal fury that arises in their souls and cities.[24] In the myth of the *Aeneid*, Vergil shows dramatically in the souls of Dido and Aeneas and in the cities of Carthage and Rome[25] these effects of the song of Iopas and the song of Vergil: he shows why the claims of Carthage and Rome to be the well-founded city must be decided in favor of Rome in the light of knowledge of the causes of divine anger; why it is the *Aeneid* and not the *De Rerum Natura* that ought to be the founding poem of the well-founded city; why it is Vergil and not Lucretius who is the true teacher of the founder of Rome. Vergil shows that the intention of Lucretian poetry to replace the harsh threats of divine punishment with the gentle impulses of philosophic friendship is unrealizable, because it is based on a fundamental error of Lucretius regarding anger in particular and the passions in general ("furor"). Lucretius' error was twofold: first, he overlooked the problematic character of the passions, imagining they were much easier to disarm than in fact they are; then, as a result of this, he mistook the effect of "honeying the cup," or of freeing men from religious fears without turning them, without being able to turn them, completely to the practice of the Epicurean or philosophic life. In the beatitudes of the *Georgics*, "he who knows the country gods" is the timeless class of those who know the country gods, but "he who was able to come to know the causes of things" was uniquely Lucretius.[26] Lucretius in his philanthropy aimed to enable the human race to share his philosophic felicity; he failed to appreciate the reasons why his felicity must necessarily be solitary.

In the following pages, it will be argued that Vergil's Dido and Carthage are portrayals of a soul and a city formed by Lucretian poetry (chapter 3, "The Carthaginian Enlightenment"). Vergil's fictional Carthaginian Enlightenment projects into poetic myth some aspects of an actual late Republican "Enlightenment" connected with Roman Epicureanism (chapter 4, "Was there a Roman Enlightenment?"); and Lucretius' poem indeed appears to lend philosophic support to enlightenment as an active founding principle in competition with religion (chapter 5, "Lucretius' Teaching"). In chapters 6 and 7, "Furor" and "Dido in Love," Vergil's myth of Carthage will be analyzed as a critique of the political project of enlightenment—a critique that points both practically to the disastrous consequences of such enlightenment and theoretically to the fundamental error in Lucretian doctrine from which they spring.

CHAPTER THREE

~

The Carthaginian Enlightenment

i. Aeneas' First View of Carthage

After hearing from his mother Venus an account of how Dido has come to be founding Carthage, Aeneas ascends a high hill from which he sees the new city for the first time. Because of his elevated vantage point, his first view is a comprehensive one: he sees the principal activities and artifacts that constitute the founding of Carthage:

> miratur molem Aeneas, magalia quondam,
> miratur portas strepitumque et strata viarum.[1]
> instant ardentes Tyrii: pars ducere muros
> molirique arcem et manibus subvolvere saxa,
> pars optare locum tecto et concludere sulco;
> iura magistratusque legunt sanctumque senatum.
> hic portus alii effodiunt; hic alta theatris
> fundamenta locant alii, immanisque columnas
> rupibus excidunt, scaenis decora alta futuris.

Aeneas was amazed at the massiveness, where lately there had been huts; he was amazed at the gates and the din and the breadth of the roads. The Tyrians were ardently at work: some drawing up walls and erecting a citadel and rolling in the stones by hand, some choosing a place for a building and surrounding it with a trench; some selecting laws and magistracies and a sanctioned senate. Some were excavating a harbor; elsewhere, some were laying the deep foundations of a theatre, and cutting out huge columns from the rocks, to be the lofty adornments of a future stage.

(1.421–429)

Aeneas might well have been amazed at the massiveness of these build-ings; but more amazing still than this visible architecture is that Carthage, even from so well-placed a vantage point as Aeneas' hill, gives no visible evidence of its gods. Visible are gates, roads, a port, a theatre, but no tem-ple; the appointing of laws and political offices is, strangely, perfectly vis-ible to Aeneas, but no sacrifices or religious solemnities.

Servius, taking it for granted that the invisibility of the Carthaginians' gods must somehow be accounted for, reports that some say the gates and roads in this scene are not to be understood *simpliciter*. According to Etruscan lore, the legitimate founding of a city requires the dedication of three gates, three roads, and three temples (to Jupiter, Juno, and Minerva); so Aeneas was rightly full of admiration at the sight of this *legitima civitas*, "for he saw the gates and the roads, and was soon to see the temple of Juno."[2]

Farfetched as Servius' appeal to Etruscan lore may be, it has the merit of calling attention to Vergil's silence about the Carthaginians' gods as some-thing amazing and in need of explanation. The modern commentators are silent about Vergil's silence. But since it is not possible to understand Vergil's portrayal of Carthage without first achieving Servius' amazement at its ap-parent defect or omission, we need to reconstruct that amazement for our-selves by noticing the difference within the *Aeneid* between Aeneas' first sight of Carthage and his first sight of every other city he approaches.

The first visible thing in every other city approached by Aeneas, promi-nent either in front of it or at its summit, is the temple of the local god[3] or an activity of the local worship. Except for Carthage, there is no exception to this narrative rule in the *Aeneid*. For example, when Aeneas' men were passing through the Ionian islands on the journey from Troy,

> mox et Leucatae nimbosa cacumina montis
> et formidatus nautis aperitur Apollo.

> Soon the cloudy peaks of Mount Leucata, and Apollo, terror of sailors, came into view.

(3.274–275)

Approaching Buthrotum:

> progredior portu classis et litora linquens,
> sollemnis cum forte dapes et tristia dona
> ante urbem in luco falsi Simoentis ad undam
> libabat cineri Andromache manisque vocabat
> Hectoreum ad tumulum, viridi quem caespite inanem
> et geminas, causam lacrimis, sacraverat aras.

I set forth from the harbor, leaving ships and shore. In a grove in front of the city, it happened that Andromache was performing a solemn feast and making sad offerings beside a false Simois, and summoning the shades to Hector's tomb which, with its green sod, she had consecrated as a cenotaph with two altars, the cause of her tears.

(3.300–305)

At the Trojans' first landfall in eastern Italy:

> portusque patescit
> iam propior, templumque apparet in arce Minervae.

The port came nearer into view, and a temple of Minerva appeared on the citadel.

(3.530–531)

On the Trojans' arrival at Cumae:

> at pius Aeneas arces quibus altus Apollo
> praesidet . . . petit. . . .

But pious Aeneas made for the citadel over which lofty Apollo held sway. . . .

(6.9–11)

At the approach of the Trojan embassy to King Latinus' city:

> Tectum augustum, ingens, centum sublime columnis
> urbe fuit summa, Laurentis regia Pici,
> horrendum silvis et religione parentum.

At the summit of the city was an august hall, huge, raised up on a hundred columns, the palace of Laurentine Picus, shuddering with woods and ancestral religion.

(7.170–172)

At the approach to Pallanteum:

> ocius advertunt proras urbique propinquant.
> Forte die sollemnem illo rex Arcas honorem
> Amphitryoniadae magno divisque ferebat
> ante urbem in luco.

they set to oars and approached the city. It happened that on that day the Arcadian king was offering solemn sacrifice to great Hercules and the gods, in a grove in front of the city.

(8.101–104)

Carthage at first sight is characterized by amazing wealth, art, industry, and apparent godlessness; the Carthaginians appear unlike any other human community in not giving immediate evidence of the common worship by which they are constituted a community; indeed, they appear to be like a community of bees:

> qualis apes aestate nova per florea rura
> exercet sub sole labor, cum gentis adultos
> educunt fetus, aut cum liquentia mella
> stipant et dulci distendunt nectare cellas,
> aut onera accipiunt venientum, aut agmine facto
> ignavum fucos pecus a praesepibus arcent;
> fervet opus redolentque thymo fragrantia mella.

As bees are engaged in their labors under the sun in early summer throughout the flowery countryside, when they lead forth the grown offspring of the race, or pack in the liquid honey and distend the cells with sweet nectar, or take in the loads of those returning, or draw up a battle line and bar the drones, that lazy herd, from the hives; the work seethes, and the fragrant honey is redolent of thyme.

(1.430–436)

This account of the division of labor among the bees is taken almost verbatim from *Georgics* 4.162–169, where it forms part of Vergil's exposition of the uniqueness of the bees' natures:

> Nunc age, naturas apibus quas Iuppiter ipse
> addidit expediam. . . .
> solae communis natos, consortia tecta
> urbis habent, magnisque agitant sub legibus aevum,
> et patriam solae et certos novere penatis;
> venturaeque hiemis memores aestate laborem
> experiuntur et in medium quaesita reponunt.

Come now, I shall set forth the natures which Jupiter himself bestowed upon the bees. . . . They alone hold their offspring in common, and the houses of their city jointly, and lead their lives under great laws; they alone know a fatherland and fixed penates; mindful of winter coming, in summer they undertake labor and deposit their provisions into the common store.

(*Geo.* 4.149–150, 153–157)

The nature that Jupiter has bestowed upon the bees turns out to be their natural love of having, *innatus amor habendi* (4.177).[4] Like the bees, the

Carthaginians manifestly cooperate in the provision of houses, laws, and a port for bringing in goods; unlike all other human societies, Carthage displays its manifest difference from bee society not in a temple but in a theater.[5]

ii. Dido's Temple to Juno

Only after Aeneas has entered into the interior of the city does he come upon a grove where a temple is under construction by Dido:

> Lucus in urbe fuit media, laetissimus umbrae,
> quo primum iactati undis et turbine Poeni
> effodere loco signum, quod regia Iuno
> monstrarat, caput acris equi; sic nam fore bello
> egregiam et facilem victu per saecula gentem.
> hic templum Iunoni ingens Sidonia Dido
> condebat, donis opulentum et numine divae,
> aerea cui gradibus surgebant limina nexaeque
> aere trabes, foribus cardo stridebat aënis.

There was a grove in the midst of the city, very rich in shade, the place where the Carthaginians, tossed by waves and wind, first excavated the sign which royal Juno had shown, the head of a keen horse; for thus the nation would be outstanding in war and easy of livelihood throughout the ages. Here Sidonian Dido was founding a huge temple to Juno, opulent with gifts and the divinity of the goddess, whose brazen threshold rose up on its steps, whose lintel was worked with bronze, and whose hinge screeched on its brazen door.

(1.441–449)

Juno's purpose in leading the sea-tossed Phoenicians to excavate this spot was to promote her plan for the foundation on this site of a city that would come to rival Rome for sovereignty over the nations; her hope was to avert or overshadow the rise of Rome through the wealth and warlike power of Carthage (1.12–22), and to insure the adoration of herself by displaying her power to punish and confound the Trojans (1.37–49). Juno elected the self-exiled Phoenicians as the nation through which she would accomplish her purpose, and led them to the sign of the horse's head. "For thus the nation would be outstanding in war and easy of livelihood throughout the ages." Vergil does not indicate whose speech or thought is represented by this indirect discourse. It may have been an old belief of the Phoenicians that the excavation of a horse's head would have this meaning for them; Vergil may mean that Juno provided the sign that she knew would cause them to choose this site for their settlement. Or it may have been Juno's thought to herself, that Carthage would become the wealthy and warlike nation of her hopes if the Phoenicians would settle on this site. Or it may have been Juno's speech to the Phoenicians, as through a prophet or augur, instructing them that the sign of the horse's head was an omen of their success in war and wealth, and that they should therefore settle the site where this sign would appear to them. However this may be, Juno's election of the Phoenician refugees as her new Carthaginian nation is reflected in Dido's establishment, on the site where the horse's head was found, of a huge temple to Juno, the patron goddess of Carthage. The temple that Dido was founding for Juno was "opulent with gifts and with the divinity of the goddess," but in such a way that Aeneas, standing in front of it and inspecting it in detail, sees no clue that it is a temple of Juno:

> hoc primum in luco nova res oblata timorem
> leniit, hic primum Aeneas sperare salutem
> ausus et adflictis melius confidere rebus.
> namque sub ingenti lustrat dum singula templo
> reginam opperiens, dum quae fortuna sit urbi
> artificumque manus intra se operumque laborem
> miratur, videt Iliacas ex ordine pugnas
> bellaque iam fama totum vulgata per orbem,
> Atridas Priamumque et saevum ambobus Achillem.

> In this grove a strange thing brought before him first relieved his fear; it was here that Aeneas first dared to hope for safety and to have more confidence in his troubled affairs. For as he went about under the huge temple inspecting each detail while awaiting the queen, as he admired the city's fortune, the hands of the craftsmen in cooperation with each other, and the labor of their works, he saw the Trojan battles one after the next, and the war published by fame throughout the whole world, the Atreides, and Priam, and Achilles, savage to both.

> (1.450–458)

The strange thing that relieves Aeneas' fears and gives him more confidence in his troubled affairs is the sight of the temple of that goddess who led the sack of Troy and has now troubled his affairs by shipwrecking him in a strange land.[6] The strange thing to us is that Aeneas is oblivious of the *numen* of Juno in this place. What amazes him as he gazes at the temple is not the discovery on closer view of the Carthaginians' god, but, as earlier in his more comprehensive view of the city, the artistry and industry of the Carthaginian builders, together with the surprising fact that this building is

decorated with scenes from the Trojan War in such a way as to give due praise
to Trojan heroism.

constitit et lacrimans 'quis iam locus' inquit 'Achate,
quae regio in terris nostri non plena laboris?
en Priamus. sunt hic etiam sua praemia laudi;
sunt lacrimae rerum et mentem mortalia tangunt.
solve metus; feret haec aliquam tibi fama salutem.'

He halted and said, weeping, "What place now, Achates, what region of the
earth is not full of our labor? Behold Priam. Even here, praise has its own rewards; the tears of things exist, and mortal things do touch the mind. Put away
your fears; this fame will bring you some safety."

(1.459–463)

The way in which the fame of the Trojan War appears to Aeneas in these pictures is such as to show praise for the heroism and sympathy for the defeat of
the Trojans.[7] Seeing this evidence of admiration and compassion for Troy in
this foreign land, Aeneas for the first time dares to hope for safety. Neither
Venus' reassurances (1.387–401)[8] nor Aeneas' first view of the city had raised
this hope; the thing in Carthage that appears to Aeneas friendliest to the
Trojans is the temple where the Carthaginians honor the goddess who is the
Trojans' greatest enemy.

In the proem Vergil has explained that Juno's persecution of the pious Aeneas had two causes: anticipation of the Punic Wars and memory of the Trojan War (19–27). How, then, can the Carthaginian artisans have decorated
their temple to their patron goddess Juno with such a representation of the
Trojan War as can be comforting to Aeneas? Is Aeneas foolishly blind to the
hostility toward Troy that is expressed in a triumphant Junonian representation of Troy's defeat? Does he somehow misread as Carthaginian sympathy
for Troy what is truly Carthaginian gloating over the destruction of Troy? Or
have the Carthaginians so represented the war as to suppress or ignore the
way in which that war reflects the might and the interests of the goddess—
as if on a temple of Jupiter one had represented the Gigantomachy in such a
way as to give hope and comfort to Giant hearts. Aeneas does not recognize
that he is in a temple of Juno. For example, although he will that very night
tell Dido of Helenus' prophetic injunction to him (3.435–440) that the foremost requirement for the Trojans' passage to Italy is to adore the divinity of
Juno and make offerings to her *numen*, Aeneas, arrived at the perfect place
to do this, has no apprehension of any divinity at all; he sees only human acknowledgment of human glory, a sign that the mortal things of Troy touch

the minds of even a distant nation unknown to him. He sees no indication of those aspects of the Trojan War that reflect Juno's interests and her hatred of the Trojans—in other words, those aspects that would make a representation of the war honorable to Juno. Nothing here so much as alludes to that view of the fall of Troy granted to Aeneas himself by his mother Venus on the fatal night:

> hic Iuno Scaeas saevissima portas
> prima tenet sociumque furens a navibus agmen
> ferro accincta vocat.

Here most savage Juno is the chief in occupying the Scaean Gates; raging, armed with the sword, she summons her allied forces from the ships.

(2.612–614)[9]

If Aeneas interprets correctly the attitude towards the Trojans expressed in these pictures,[10] then Juno would seem to have elected in the Carthaginians, as the people that should honor her divinity and rout her enemies, a people that dishonors her and loves her enemies.

The possibility that Aeneas misinterprets the pictures on the temple is excluded by Dido's account later in Book 1 of the admiration in which she has held the Trojans ever since, as a girl in Sidon, she first heard about the Trojan War from Teucer, the Greek hero who himself so admired his defeated Trojan enemy as to have proudly claimed common ancestry with their race:

> tempore iam ex illo casus mihi cognitus urbis
> Troianae nomenque tuum regesque Pelasgi.

Ever since that time the misfortune of your city has been known to me, as well as your name and the Pelasgian kings.

(1.623–624)

Juno's hatred of Troy is shared neither by Troy's Greek enemy, so dear to Juno, nor by the queen whom Juno has elected to represent her, so to speak, in promoting her hatred of the Trojan race. To judge by the Carthaginian temple to Juno, Juno's purpose in her election of Carthage is not acknowledged by Carthage; it does not seem to be known in Carthage.[11] After Aeneas' tearful speech to Achates, encouraging hopes of safety on the basis of the sympathy for Troy expressed in the pictures, Vergil remarks that Aeneas was feeding his spirit or fueling his grief with an empty image, *pictura inani* (464). Dido's temple to Juno itself turns out to be an empty image: it has the shape of a temple, but is empty of any worship of the goddess whose temple it has the shape of.

While Aeneas is gazing in stupefaction at the amazing scenes on the temple (*dum . . . miranda videntur, / dum stupet*, 494–495), Dido finally enters it in regal pomp, surrounded by a dense crowd of young men and appearing like the huntress Diana when she "outshines all the goddesses," *deas supereminet omnis* (501). She proceeds at once to seat herself on the central throne and begins giving laws and distributing labors.

> tum foribus divae, media testudine templi,
> saepta armis solioque alte subnixa resedit.
> iura dabat legesque viris, operumque laborem
> partibus aequabat iustis aut sorte trahebat.

> Then at the doors of the goddess, under the central vault of the temple, hemmed about by an armed guard and supported on a lofty throne, she sat down. She went about giving laws and statutes to the men, and was making fair division of the labor of their works with just distributions and by drawing lots.
>
> (1.505–508)

The most striking thing in Vergil's portrayal of Dido's manner of legislating for Carthage is the thing that is omitted from it. In the parallel scene in Book 7 where the Trojans approach King Latinus in his temple-palace, Vergil includes what he omits in the Dido scene:

> hic sceptra accipere et primos attollere fascis
> regibus omen erat; hoc illis curia templum,
> hae sacris sedes epulis; hic ariete caeso
> perpetuis soliti patres considere mensis.

> Here it was sanctioned for kings to take the sceptre and lift the supreme fasces; this temple was their assembly, this the hall for their sacrificial feasts; here the elders were accustomed to sit at regular feasts after sacrificing a ram.
>
> (7.173–176)

Dido makes no prayers or sacrifices; she does nothing to acknowledge the presence of Juno's *numen* here; certainly she does nothing to suggest that her own authority or the laws she now gives have any divine origin or sanction.[12]

Juno's ambition in her war against the Trojan people and their Roman destiny was to gain adoration of her *numen* as demonstrated by altars laden with the sacrifices of suppliants:

> ast ego, quae divum incedo regina Iovisque
> et soror et coniunx, una cum gente tot annos

bella gero. et quisquam numen Iunonis adorat
praeterea aut supplex aris imponet honorem?

I, who walk as queen of the gods, both sister and wife of Jupiter, have been waging war for so many years with this one nation; can anyone adore the *numen* of
Juno any more, or lay suppliant sacrifice on her altar?

(1.46–49)

Immediately before Aeneas' entry into Carthage, Vergil reminds us of Juno's
jealous ambition for the honor of sacrifice by narrating how her rival Venus
departs for Paphos,

ubi templa illi, centumque Sabaeo
ture calent arae sertisque recentibus halant.

where she has a temple, and a hundred altars burning with Sabaean incense
and breathing forth the scent of fresh wreaths.

(1.416–417)

Vergil's description here of the adoration of Venus' *numen* at Paphos would
seem to be answered by his assertion at 1.447 that the temple of Juno at
Carthage was "rich with gifts and the *numen* of the goddess," but the meaning of this assertion is made utterly mysterious by the invisibility to Aeneas
and thus to us of Juno's presence here, to say nothing of any adoration of
Juno's *numen* on the part of Dido and her people.

iii. Dido's Speech to Ilioneus

From within the cloud that makes him invisible to the others, Aeneas sees
and hears with Vergil's reader the first action and speech of Dido in the
Aeneid. The beautiful queen, having taken her seat within the temple and
having taken up her work of legislation, is interrupted by the entrance of a
group of Trojan ambassadors pleading that she call off her men from attacking and burning the Trojans' ships.

Ilioneus speaks for the Trojans. Like Aeneas earlier, he fails to recognize
that he is standing in a temple of Juno; so when he wishes to begin his speech
by appealing to Dido's respect for the gods, he makes the pious presumption
that she at any rate looks up to Jupiter as disposing of the foundation of
cities:[13]

o regina, novam cui condere Iuppiter urbem
iustitiaque dedit gentis frenare superbas. . . .

O queen, to whom Jupiter has granted the foundation of a new city and the restraint of haughty peoples under justice. . . .

(1.522–523)

Ilioneus, who later in his speech will express the suspicion that Dido and her
people despise the gods altogether, here tactfully attributes to Dido a responsibility to Jupiter for restraining the "haughtiness" of her peoples; he suggests
that the men's unspeakable attempt to burn the Trojan ships is a rebellious
or, at any rate, unrestrained act of Dido's subjects, which she herself will wish
and be able to prohibit as soon as she knows the Trojans:

Troes te miseri, ventis maria omnia vecti,
oramus: prohibe infandos a navibus ignis,
parce pio generi et propius res aspice nostras.
non nos aut ferro Libycos populare penatis
venimus, aut raptas ad litora vertere praedas;
non ea vis animo nec tanta superbia victis.

We unhappy Trojans, storm-tossed over all the seas, supplicate you: prohibit
the unspeakable fire from our ships, be gracious to our pious race, and look
more closely at our affairs. We have not come to destroy your Libyan penates
by the sword or to take stolen booty to the shores; our spirit has no such force,
we conquered men have no such haughtiness.

(1.524–529)

Ilioneus proceeds to explain how the conquered Trojans were attempting to
reach Italy when a storm cast them up on the Libyan shore (530–538). Then
in the central lines of his speech, surrounded and thus softened by his more
tactful words, Ilioneus directly implicates Dido in the impious conduct of the
Carthaginians; as Servius observes, "these words are placed very opportunely
after the soft opening words; for sometimes it is expedient to be subtle about
blaming the one you are appealing to."[14]

quod genus hoc hominum? quaeve hunc tam barbara morem
permittit patria? hospitio prohibemur harenae;
bella cient primaque vetant consistere terra.
si genus humanum et mortalia temnitis arma,
at sperate deos memores fandi atque nefandi.

What race of human beings is this? Or what so barbarous fatherland permits this
custom? We are prohibited from the hospitality of the shore; they raise war and
prevent us from reaching the land's edge. If you despise the human race and mortal arms, be assured nonetheless that the gods are mindful of right and wrong.

(1.539–543)

Here Ilioneus speaks of the Carthaginian *patria* itself, and thus of its ruler Dido, as *permitting* the barbarous usage of its guards; then, speaking directly in the second person plural, he wonders whether Dido and her people despise the human race, and sternly warns her that the gods are mindful of right and wrong.[15] After this direct reproach, Ilioneus returns to his account of "our affairs," attributing to "our king Aeneas" both the greatest piety and the greatest force of arms:

> rex erat Aeneas nobis, quo iustior alter
> nec pietate fuit, nec bello maior et armis.

> Our king was Aeneas; no one has been more just in piety than he, or greater in war and arms.

> (1.544–545)

Here Ilioneus likens Aeneas to the version of Dido he had tactfully presumed in his opening words on her justice and might under Jupiter; but after his accusation of 1.539–543, his account of Aeneas is also a reproach and a warning to Dido: she is wrong to despise human arms such as those of Aeneas, and, the gods being mindful of right and wrong, she must take into account that these gods are likely to support the pious Aeneas by punishing Carthaginian impiety. In the second half of his speech, Ilioneus' account of "our affairs" moves back away from his blame of Carthage to his assurance of Trojan gratitude for a more peaceable reception.

Dido's first speech, in response to Ilioneus, is as amazing as Carthage's first appearance to Aeneas, and for the same reason: even under the pressure of Ilioneus' public accusations, and even under the central vault of Juno's temple, Dido is absolutely silent about the gods. So far from either acknowledging or extending to Juno Ilioneus' suggestion that she is founding her new city under Jupiter's authority, so far from agreeing that her subjects' unspeakable impiety is against her will, Dido asserts outright that her subjects' conduct is in accord with her own considered policy:

> solvite corde metum, Teucri, secludite curas.
> res dura et regni novitas me talia cogunt
> moliri et late finis custode tueri.

> Put away fear from your hearts, Teucrians; lay aside your worries. Hard circumstances, and the newness of my kingdom, compel me to engineer such things, and to put my borders widely under guard.

> (1.562–564)

No commentator on Vergil has brought out the character of these lines so lucidly as Machiavelli, who asserts in chapter 17 of *The Prince* ("Della Crudeltà e Pietà") that Vergil has here put "in the mouth of Dido" an expression of Machiavelli's own argument that, whatever the uses of *pietà* may be for an established prince, it is *crudeltà* that must take precedence for the new one: "And of all princes, it is impossible for the new prince to escape a name for cruelty because new states are full of dangers. And Virgil says in the mouth of Dido: [*Res dura . . . tueri*]."[16] Dido forthrightly expresses to Ilioneus that the compelling consideration for her is not the justice of Jupiter but the newness of her kingdom; this newness compels her to set aside any considerations of piety. Dido knows very well that "people say" (as, for example, the Trojans say) that Jupiter is the giver of the laws of hospitality (*hospitibus nam te dare iura loquuntur*, 1.731), and she is quite prepared to honor what people say when it is prudent to do so. It would, however, be imprudent for a new queen founding a new city among hostile neighbors and haughty subjects to be hospitable to strangers, while it is quite necessary for her to be summarily harsh to strangers. This she declares frankly to the embassy of pious Trojans before her.[17]

Nevertheless, though Dido owed these strangers no consideration on merely god-fearing grounds, her discovery that they are the Trojans—that they are the remnant of that nation portrayed on the walls of her temple with such admiration for their valor and sympathy for their defeat—changes from the ground up her view of what is prudent for her in their case. As if Ilioneus' charge of barbarous *mores* had reference not to impiety but only to geographical isolation and uninformed provincialism, she assures him that she and her people are fully aware of the Trojans, their virtues, their heroes and their war; then, promising them aid in moving on to Italy or Sicily if they will, she suggests that the best event would be that they remain in Carthage and settle down as fellow citizens with her Carthaginians:

vultis et his mecum pariter considere regnis?
urbem quam statuo, vestra est; subducite navis;
Tros Tyriusque mihi nullo discrimine agetur.

Or do you wish to settle this kingdom equally with me? The city I am establishing is yours. Draw up your ships; Trojan and Tyrian will be treated without distinction as far as I'm concerned.

(1.572–574)

Like the first appearance of Carthage, like the first appearance of Dido's temple to Juno, like the first response of the Carthaginian coast guard to the shipwrecked Trojans and like Dido's justification of it, so Dido's extraordinary proposal here startles by its absence of any reference to the gods. From first to last, the *Aeneid* envisions the founding project of Aeneas and the Trojans as the introduction of the Trojan gods into a new land ("to found a city and introduce his gods into Latium," 1.5–6). The central obstacle to this project is the hostility of Juno to those gods:

> gens inimica mihi Tyrrhenum navigat aequor
> Ilium in Italiam portans victosque penatis.
>
> A people hateful to me is sailing the Tyrrhenian Sea, bringing Troy and its conquered penates into Italy.
>
> (1.67–68)

The myth of the *Aeneid* as a whole elaborates the obstacles to the resettlement of the Trojan gods arising generally from the repulsion of all peoples and their gods from one another and particularly from the repulsion of Juno and the peoples she favors from Troy and the Trojans' gods. The whole *Aeneid* looks toward the climactic overcoming of these obstacles in a greater order of things, *maior rerum ordo* (7.44), through the establishment of a novel principle of union between the Italian peoples and the Trojans, and a novel principle of reconciliation between Juno and the Trojans' gods.

The narrative rule of the *Aeneid* is that the alliance of nations is viewed by the nations as reflecting the alliance of their gods, and that common citizenship is viewed by the citizens as common worship; to speak of cities and the relations between cities is to speak of gods and the relations between gods.[18]

When Aeneas, immediately after the flight from Troy, contemplates founding his new city in Mavortian territory, it is because of the "ancient tie of hospitality and allied penates" that that land shared with Troy (*hospitium antiquum Troiae sociique penates*, 3.15). When Aeneas prepares to celebrate the funeral games for Anchises in the friendly city of Acestes, he exhorts his men,

> adhibete penates
> et patrios epulis et quos colit hospes Acestes.[19]
>
> Bring to the feast both our ancestral penates and those whom our guest-friend Acestes worships.
>
> (5.62–63)

When Ilioneus requests from King Latinus a small territory for "our ancestral gods" (*dis patriis*, 7.229), Latinus responds in the light of the oracle of his divine ancestors:

Hunc illum fatis externa ab sede profectum
portendi generum paribusque in regna vocari
auspiciis. . . .
     'di nostra incepta secundent
auguriumque suum!'

This, then, was the man portended by the fates as the one who would come
from a foreign land as son-in-law, and be summoned into this kingdom under
equal divine auspices. . . . "May the gods favor our undertakings and their own
augury!"

(7.255–257, 259–260)

When Aeneas approaches Evander to seek with him the alliance recommended by the god Tiber, he declares,

sed mea me virtus et sancta oracula divum
cognatique patres, tua terris didita fama,
coniunxere tibi et fatis egere volentem.

The things that unite me with you are my own virtue, the sacred oracles of the
gods, the common ancestry of our forebears, and your fame spread throughout
the world.

(8.131–133)

Evander accepts this alliance by expounding to the Trojans the local worship
of Hercules and inviting them to share it:

quare agite, o iuvenes, tantarum in munere laudum
cingite fronde comas et pocula porgite dextris,
communemque vocate deum et date vina volentes.

Come, young men, in celebration of these so glorious deeds, wreathe your
heads and raise the cups in your right hands: invoke the god in common with
us,[20] and make libation with a will.

(8.273–275)

The alliance is sealed by Aeneas on the next day by his joint worship of Hercules together with the Trojan penates: "Evander equally, the men of Troy
equally" made the customary sacrifice (8.542–545). And finally, when Aeneas
goes to take command of Tarchon's Lydian armies as recommended by Evander (8.496), Tarchon joins forces and exchanges oaths with him promptly,
since the Lydian people has been "entrusted to a foreign commander by the
orders of the gods" (10.155–156).

Dido's proposal to the Trojans that they simply become fellow Carthaginians without further ado is one of the most extraordinary moments of the *Aeneid*. Sitting in the temple of the Carthaginian patron goddess Juno, Dido speaks of herself alone as the settler of her own kingdom (*mecum*, 572), the independent establisher of her own city (*statuo*, 573), and the self-sufficient disposer of its citizenship (*mihi*, 574). Dido conceives common citizenship as depending not on the sharing of gods but on the ignoring of gods. The great climax of the *Aeneid*, the novel principle of unification by which Trojans and Latins will become the common founders of the long-sought city for the Trojan penates, is here anticipated by Dido as if it presented no difficulty at all. She neither asks after the Trojans' gods nor mentions her own; it is not under the auspices of *any* gods that she is founding her city.

What makes Dido decide, while listening to Ilioneus' speech, to change her policy from burning the Trojans' ships—not simply to leaving them in peace, not simply to helping them resume their journey, not simply to proposing some alliance with them—but to offering them fellow citizenship with her people in Carthage? Her Carthaginians, intended by Juno to become not only rich but also warlike, have at present the means of wealth but not of war; Dido keeps a bodyguard, and sentries on the coast, but no army. Her coast guard is able to burn the ships of unarmed and shipwrecked strangers but not to defend Carthage against her local enemies or against reprisals from Pygmalion's forces at Tyre (4.40–44). The *res dura* Dido speaks of has reference especially to this. When Dido learns that the strangers are the Trojans, those same Trojans whose heroic valor is represented on her temple walls, she indicates to Ilioneus that everyone knows of the virtues and heroes of his people (*virtutesque virosque*, 1.566). If the wealth of Carthage could be combined with the arms of Troy, the way would be clear to a city "rich in wealth and very harsh in the pursuits of war" (*dives opum studiisque asperrima belli*, 1.14), a nation "outstanding in war and easy of livelihood" (*bello / egregiam et facilem victu*, 1.444–445). Or as Anna puts it,

> Teucrum comitantibus armis
> Punica se quantis attollet gloria rebus!

With the arms of the Trojans accompanying us, in what great affairs will Punic glory raise itself!

(4.48–49)

In accordance with Juno's own intentions for Carthage, Dido thinks of wealth and arms, but she does not think of Juno.

At the end of her speech, Dido moves from the idea of uniting the Carthaginian and Trojan peoples to the wish that Aeneas himself might yet show up:

atque utinam rex ipse noto compulsus eodem
adforet Aeneas!

And if only your king Aeneas himself might appear here, blown in by the same storm!

(1.575–576)

This wish delicately suggests the unspoken thought that, just as the Trojan people may be united with the Carthaginian people, so the Trojan king may be united with the Carthaginian queen: if the two peoples are to be one, surely they will be ruled by King Aeneas and Queen Dido.[21] Before her love for the man Aeneas brings disaster upon herself and her people, she thinks of a dynastic marriage that would bring completion to herself and her people— a royal consort, an heir, an army; the actual love affair that follows is an infernal reversal of this prudent plan.[22] Dido's prudent plan does not take account of Juno.

Dido in her first speech is silent altogether about all the gods, except possibly for her reference to the sun. Her locution for the sun's orbit, "Sol harnesses his horses" (Sol equos iungit, 568), is quite a bit more poetic than the phrase her teacher Iopas uses in his song, solis labores (742). Perhaps her mythological manner of speaking here is simply fanciful, or popular, like saying "Bacchus" when one means wine,[23] or other instances of poetic usage permitted by Lucretius as long as the user does not actually infect his mind with foul religion (DRN 2.655–660)[24]. Or perhaps Vergil suggests that Dido, in the newness of her enlightenment, has more easily or fully abandoned belief in the divinity of the Olympians than in the divinity of the heavenly bodies. In Book 4, when Dido has returned to a kind of religion, Sol heads her great prayer for vengeance against Aeneas and his descendants: "Sol, who traverse with your flames all the works of the lands" (Sol, qui terrarum flammis opera omnia lustras, 4.607).[25]

iv. Dido's Speech to Aeneas

As in the first conversation between Ilioneus and Dido, so in the first between Aeneas and Dido: he appeals to the gods and she is silent about them. Acknowledging Dido's unique compassion for the unspeakable labors of Troy (o sola infandos Troiae miserata labores, 597; these would include most recently the unspeakable fires, *infandos ignis* [525], with which the Carthaginians had received the Trojans), and her offer to unite the Trojans with her city and house,[26] Aeneas expresses the complement to Ilioneus' warning that the gods will punish Carthaginian wrongdoing even if the Trojans cannot: may the gods, prays Aeneas, reward Dido's piety and justice even though the Trojans cannot:

> grates persolvere dignas
> non opis est nostrae, Dido, nec quidquid ubique est
> gentis Dardaniae, magnum quae sparsa per orbem.
> di tibi, si qua pios respectant numina, si quid
> usquam iustitia est et mens sibi conscia recti,[27]
> praemia digna ferant.

To repay worthy thanks, Dido, is not within our power, nor in the power of whatever is left of the Dardanian nation dispersed throughout the great world. May the gods—if any divinities care for the pious, if justice is something anywhere, and mind conscious within itself of the right—may the gods give you worthy rewards.

(1.600–605)

Whether Aeneas' "ifs" in this prayer indicate his doubt, his openmindedness, his wish,[28] or his certainty ("so surely as"), in any case he prays that the gods may reward her. Aeneas congratulates the times and parents that have brought to birth such a prodigy of generous and compassionate right-doing as Dido; she seems to belong to a new era of happiness, *tam laeta saecula* (1.605–606). At the same time, he deprecates the opinion of Trojan "virtues and heroes" that had led Dido to offer city and house: he calls the Trojans "remnants left by the Danaans" (*reliquias Danaum*, 598) and "destitute of all things" (*omnium egenos*, 599), and emphasizes the resourcelessness of the men with him and the dispersedness of the rest of the Dardanian people (601–602). Having thus made himself out to be as helpless and as useless to Carthage as possible, Aeneas, with great tact, concludes his grateful speech by nevertheless declining Dido's most noble offer of Carthaginian citizenship:

> semper honos nomenque tuum laudesque manebunt,
> quae me cumque vocant terrae.

Your honor, your name and your praises will endure always, whatever the lands that summon me.

(1.609–610)

Aeneas is bound to take the Trojans on to another land. He will carry the praises of Dido's generosity to the land on account of which he cannot accept that generosity; the reward of human praise that Dido has given to the Trojans in her temple murals (*sunt hic etiam sua praemia laudi*, 461) will be reciprocated in the reward, admittedly insufficient, of praise[29] that Aeneas will bring to Dido's name.

Dido is dumbstruck first by the appearance of the man (*viri*, 613), then by his great misfortune (*casu tanto*, 614). Like Achates (582), Dido addresses Aeneas as *nate dea*, 615; she knows that Aeneas is called Venus' son, but, as her opening words show, she does not think that Aeneas' misfortune is caused by any god:

> quis te, nate dea, per tanta pericula casus
> insequitur? quae vis immanibus applicat oris?

> What misfortune, goddess-born, pursues you through such dangers? What force drives you onto dread shores?

> (1.615–616)

Vergil has so constructed Dido's question as to require us to think at first that the answer to her *quis?* will be "Juno;" when it turns out that *quis* modifies *casus*, and thus excludes Juno from the range of possible answers, we are struck once more by Dido's obliviousness to the powers and purposes of Juno. In his invocation to Book 1, Vergil had asked the Muse to recall the causes why Juno compelled the pious hero to undergo so many misfortunes (*casus*, 9), and he had referred to the force that hounded Aeneas as the force of gods (*vi superum*, 4); Dido, however, does not trace misfortunes and forces to the will of gods.

> tune ille Aeneas quem Dardanio Anchisae
> alma Venus Phrygii genuit Simoentis ad undam?

> Are you then the Aeneas whom life-giving Venus bore to Dardanian Anchises by the waters of Phrygian Simois?

> (1.617–618)

Aeneas to Dido is *ille Aeneas*, the renowned or storied Aeneas, whose story she knows; like Lucretius, she begins with a reference to Venus' generation of Aeneas:[30]

> Aeneadum genetrix, hominum divumque voluptas,
> alma Venus . . .

> Mother of the Aeneids, pleasure of men and gods, life-giving Venus . . .

> (*DRN* 1.1–2)

Dido then recounts to Aeneas how she first came to know of the Trojans and in what way she feels connected with them:

> atque equidem Teucrum memini Sidona venire
> finibus expulsum patriis, nova regna petentem
> auxilio Beli; genitor tum Belus opimam
> vastabat Cyprum et victor dicione tenebat.
> tempore iam ex illo casus mihi cognitus urbis
> Troianae nomenque tuum regesque Pelasgi.
> ipse hostis Teucros insigni laude ferebat
> seque ortum antiqua Teucrorum a stirpe volebat.

> Indeed I remember how Teucer came to Sidon, expelled from his ancestral ter-
> ritories, seeking a new kingdom with the help of Belus; at that time my father
> Belus was reducing rich Cyprus and holding it under his authority as victor.
> From as far back as then I have known the misfortune of the Trojan city, and
> your name, and the Pelasgian kings. Teucer himself spoke of you, his Teucrian
> enemy, with outstanding praise, and claimed that he himself was descended
> from the ancient stock of the Teucrians.
>
> (1.619–626)

From Teucer Dido first learned how to evaluate the virtue of the Trojans even in misfortune; and she now uses Teucer as an example to Aeneas of how a homeless refugee, expelled from his fatherland, was able to get a new king-dom with the help of her father. Why must Aeneas be summoned by other lands? What her father gave to Teucer, she can give to Aeneas.

> quare agite, o tectis, iuvenes, succedite nostris.
> me quoque per multos similis fortuna labores
> iactatam hac demum voluit consistere terra.

> Come therefore, young men, enter my house. A fortune similar to yours has
> tossed me too through many labors and ultimately willed that I settle in this
> land. Not ignorant of evil, I am learning to succor the unfortunate.
>
> (1.627–630)

According to the myth of the *Aeneid*, the agent of the will that Dido settle in this land, and that also, "similarly," the Trojans be shipwrecked here, is Juno; but the "similar fortune" that Dido thinks of is the flight or exile of her-self and Aeneas from their fatherlands.[31] The point Dido makes in her speech to Aeneas is the same point made by her temple murals: that the valor of the Trojan army is manifest even in spite of the misfortune of their city's defeat, and is praised even or especially by their enemies. Dido's opinion of the Trojans was formed long before Juno elected her to be the scourge of Troy, and has not been revised in the least by Juno's intentions. When Dido calls the Trojans *miseri* (630, answering to Aeneas' *miserata*, 597), she has in mind their present accidental misfortune, not their proper character: her interest in succoring these unfortunate men arose only when she learned that they were the Trojan army.

v. Dido's Feast

After her speech, Dido leads Aeneas into her royal house while ordering that "honor"[32] be done to the "temples of the gods" (631–632). She does not say what gods she has in mind, or who should honor them since she herself does not. Just as Dido builds a temple to Juno in which she herself conspicuously refrains from honoring Juno, so she makes provision for sacrifice by others to gods to whom she herself conspicuously does not sacrifice; the tone of Carthaginian *mores* set by the enlightened queen is gently all-embracing. As for Dido's royal house, it is decked out in royal luxury without any evidence of any god:

> at domus interior regali splendida luxu
> instruitur, mediisque parant convivia tectis:
> arte laboratae vestes ostroque superbo,
> ingens argentum mensis, caelataque in auro
> fortia facta patrum, series longissima rerum
> per tot ducta viros antiqua ab origine gentis.

> But the splendid interior of the house was decked out in regal luxury, and they were setting out a feast in the midst of the hall: coverlets wrought with art and haughty purple, massive silver on the tables, and, chased in gold, the brave deeds of her ancestors, a very long series of events traced down through so many men from the ancient origins of the race.

> (1.637–642)

The courageous deeds of Dido's ancestors remind us that, unlike the latest of them, her father Belus who recently reduced Cyprus, Dido is without an army and without apparent means of raising one from her Carthaginians, though most urgently in need of one because of her hard conditions and the newness of her kingdom; as Venus has pointed out to Aeneas (339), Dido's city borders on a "race intractable in war." Belus generously shared with Teucer the land he had conquered with Phoenician arms; Dido generously wishes to share with the Trojans the land she had bought with Phoenician gold (*mercati . . . solum*, 367), and thus to acquire arms with which to secure that purchase. Whatever it was that enabled her ancestors to achieve those valorous deeds of war is lacking to her. She has the gold itself on which their deeds are recorded, and that enabled her to buy the site of Carthage; and she has with her the Trojan army whose valor is recorded on her temple walls and who, according to Aeneas, are "destitute of everything;" can she unite them?

After the meal, Dido, wishing to mark the occasion honorifically, performs a peculiar ceremony. She calls for the mixing bowl, "heavy with gems and gold," which the original Belus and all his descendants had been accustomed to use, and makes this invocation:

> Iuppiter, hospitibus nam te dare iura loquuntur,
> hunc laetum Tyriisque diem Troiaque profectis
> esse velis, nostrosque huius meminisse minores.
> adsit laetitiae Bacchus dator et bona Iuno;
> et vos, o coetum, Tyrii, celebrate faventes.

> Jupiter—for people say you give the laws of hospitality—may it be your will that this day be happy for the Tyrians and those who have come from Troy, and that our descendants may remember this. May Bacchus, giver of joy, be with us, and good Juno; and as for you, o assembly, Tyrians, celebrate auspiciously.
> (1.731–735)

When Dido wishes to solemnize a state occasion she knows how to follow what "people say," but she also frankly, not to say gratuitously, distances herself from what they say by emphatically calling attention at the outset to the fact that she invokes Jupiter not because he gives the laws of hospitality but because "people say" he does so. What people say about Jupiter was dismissed by Dido out of hand when it was a matter of calculating Carthaginian policy toward strangers in view of the newness of her kingdom. But at this feast where she has decided in any case, and for her own reasons, to receive the Trojan warriors hospitably, she is willing to take account also of what people say about Jupiter's promotion of hospitality; she knows that the Trojans themselves, whom she wishes to bind to her by this feast, "say" that Jupiter gives the laws of hospitality (522–523, 540–543).[33]

Dido follows her invocation to Jupiter with a summons to Bacchus and Juno. Because she wishes to be hospitable, she invokes "Jupiter;" because she wishes to have the joy of wine, she invokes "Bacchus;" and because she wishes to marry Aeneas, she invokes "Juno" (whose concern is the marriage bonds, *cui vincla iugalia curae*, 4.59). Austin says she "unconsciously" invokes

Juno in this role;[34] but has she not been somehow quite conscious of her wish to marry Aeneas ever since, immediately after offering equal citizenship to the Trojans at large, she expressed the wish that their king too would be included (575–576)? According to Venus, the hospitality offered by Dido to Aeneas is in any case not Jovian but peculiarly Junonian hospitality:

> nunc Phoenissa tenet Dido blandisque moratur
> vocibus, et vereor quo se Iunonia vertant
> hospitia.

> Now Phoenician Dido holds him and detains him with seductive speeches, and I am afraid of the direction in which this Junonian hospitality is tending.
>
> (1.670–672)

And of course by the time of Dido's first reference to "Juno" here she has begun, as a result of Venus' scheme, not only to think Junonianly of marrying Aeneas but also to fall Venereally in love with him.

Dido follows her odd prayer with an impromptu libation, using the dinner table in the conspicuous absence of an altar (*dixit et in mensam laticum libavit honorem*, 736). The peculiar effect of this is brought out admirably by Macrobius in the *Saturnalia*, where Praetextatus, defending Vergil's knowledge of pontifical law, takes up the question why libation is made on a table at Evander's feast in *Aeneid* 8:[35]

> I admit that you have grounds for questioning the pouring of a libation on a table; and you would have added to the apparent difficulty, had you chosen to refer to Vergil's reference to a similar act by Dido in the line: "She spoke, and on the table poured an offering of flowing wine," for even Tertius, in his long discourse on sacred rites, says that this passage seems to him to raise a difficult question and that he has found no explanation to satisfy the doubts which he feels about it. However, with my reading to instruct me, I will tell you what I have discovered, for it is clearly declared in the Papirian legal code that a table which has been dedicated can serve the purposes of an altar. . . .
>
> And so, then, the libation made at Evander's feast was made as prescribed by law; for it was made at the table which had been dedicated, together with the Ara Maxima, in accordance with customary religious usage; it was made, too, in a consecrated grove and in the course of the ceremonies at a sacred banquet. On the other hand, at Dido's banquet, which assuredly was no more than a royal feast and not a religious occasion as well (*quod tantum regium constat, non sacrum fuisse*), the libation was made at a table designed for human use, in a banqueting hall and not in a temple; and, since Dido's libation was not a religious but a discretionary act (*quia non erat religiosa sed usurpata libatio*), Vergil

represented it as made by the queen alone, as one whose person was bound to the observance of no obligatory rites but was free and able to adopt what procedure she pleased (*multa ad usurpandum in potestate permissio*).[36]

After making this libation, Dido raises the cup just so as to touch her lips to it,[37] and passes it on to Bitias, who swills it down, and so to the other lords (737–740). The peculiarities that Vergil has so emphasized at Dido's feast— the extreme luxury of her court, her difference from her ancestors, her gratuitously skeptical invocation to the gods, her irregular libation—are explained finally by what this whole odd ceremony is leading up to, the song of Iopas (740–746),[38] which is so far from what "people say" that the Trojans are briefly dumbfounded by it (747).

Vergil's portrait of Carthage is connected somehow to the well-known historical Carthage characterized by commerce, luxury, military softness, and perfidy;[39] Vergil's poetic innovation is to collect and reorder these characteristics as flowing from the teachings of "Atlas,"[40] or more particularly as flowing from the inclination of Carthage's founder towards Epicurean science[41] as taught by Lucretian poetry. Thus, the historical characteristics of Carthage become, in the *Aeneid*, part of a poetic presentation not of the historical Carthage, which was in the past the greatest enemy of the historical Rome,[42] but of an ideal "Carthage," the city of science, which is permanently the greatest enemy of an ideal "Rome," the city of piety, and whose enmity to "Rome" is expressed accidentally by its aggressiveness towards "Rome" but essentially by its seductiveness to "Rome." The most striking characteristic of the ideal "Carthage" is its godlessness, which is the cause of both its peculiar harshness and its peculiar mildness. Its harshness arises from its not being restrained by fear of angry gods and by its not having a higher opinion of human beings than of beasts;[43] its mildness arises from its not being impressed by the grounds of the division of the human race into separate tribes.

Within the myth of the *Aeneid*, Dido's founding of Carthage is promoted by Juno, who is said to have cultivated or cared for (*coluisse*, 1.16) this one land above all others. Juno's attachment to Carthage becomes more and more strange in Book 1 as it emerges that Carthage has no answering attachment to Juno. Juno, the causes of whose unremitting anger are the highest theme of the *Aeneid*, cultivates, as the human or political vehicle of her intention to rule the world, a city that does not cultivate her, a city founded indeed on the most thoroughgoing denial of the existence of angry gods. Juno's infernal purpose of releasing Furor upon the world is to be executed through the dissemination of Lucretian doctrine because the dissemination of Lucretian doctrine is the way of undermining the fragile defenses of the world against infernal Furor.

CHAPTER FOUR

~

Was There a Roman Enlightenment?

Vergil . . . assumed the toga virilis at the age of 17 . . . and it happened that the poet Lucretius died on that very day.

Donatus, *Life of Vergil*, 6

But what a mockery of Lucretius' great hope. Vergil, in the next generation, the disciple, too, of Lucretius in poetry, became the true high priest under Augustus in a nationwide revival of worship.

W. E. Leonard[1]

The ancient tradition making Vergil somehow the successor of Lucretius is reflected in the modern view that Vergil, though his mature opinions had turned from the Epicureanism of his youth to Stoicism or Platonism, nonetheless remained always heavily indebted to Lucretius for his poetic language.[2] The "great hope" of Lucretius that Leonard refers to was to make "an attack on the state religion, as conceived in the tradition of Plato and adopted by Rome and the Stoics;"[3] Vergil's "mockery" of this hope was his restoration, in somehow Lucretian poetry, of that very "state religion" that Lucretius' poetry had set out to demolish.

As Leonard also recognizes, Lucretius in fact does not speak of the existence of any such thing as a "state religion," much less of any intention to attack it. Lucretius' account of the causes of religion does not refer to any political source or use of religion. If Lucretius had a "great hope" of attacking political religion, it is not expressed directly by any argument in the poem itself. Indeed it is widely held that Lucretius, like Epicurus, does not present any political teaching at all.

Nevertheless, Vergil makes of Lucretius *the* great opponent or rival of his own indubitably political teaching. In all his major poetry Vergil emphatically represents Rome as being on the verge of a greater political order—*maior rerum ordo* (Aen. 7.44), *magnus saeclorum ordo* (Ecl. 4.5)—and himself as the inaugurator and guide of that new order: the guide of the Romans in general and of Augustus in particular. The refounding of Rome is imminent; Vergil is the poetic teacher of the refounder; the burden of his teaching is that the hope for the new Rome depends on the Romans' uncertain choice between two alternative founding principles: "science" as represented by Lucretius and "piety" as represented by himself. In the *Georgics*, the issue between science and piety is summed up in the question whether the world has three parts or four: the teaching of science is that heaven, earth, and ocean are the only constituents of the world, while the teaching of piety is that the world is constituted by heaven, earth, ocean, and Underworld. Vergil begins the *Georgics* by attributing the view of science to Augustus and recommending to him the claims of the Underworld.[4] He invites Augustus to join him in compassion for the countrymen who are "ignorant of the way" (*ignaros viae*, Geo. 1.41), but he also shows that Augustus is ignorant of the way of compassionating the countrymen until instructed by Vergil in the claim of the Underworld to be considered the fourth quarter of the world. In the *Aeneid* Vergil presents again the crucial alternative facing the Romans on the verge of a new order: this time, science is represented by "Carthage," piety by "Rome." Again the issue between the two founding principles may be said to be the status of the Underworld: "Carthage" is founded on the song of Iopas that presents heaven, earth and ocean as the whole world, while "Rome" is founded on the song of Vergil, the *Aeneid* itself, which presents the Underworld at its center as the foundation of the world. Both the *Georgics* and the *Aeneid*, then, make this contest between a three-part and a four-part world stand for the contest between Lucretius and Vergil as the proper educator of the Romans for the proper founding of the new order. That is, Vergil presents the fundamental political alternative facing his fellow Romans not as republic versus principate, not as *optimates* versus *populares*, but as Lucretian science versus Vergilian piety.

On the face of it, Vergil's presentation of Lucretius' teaching as *the* rival to his own political teaching may seem to imply a strange distortion or exaggeration of any plausible intention or effect of Lucretius' poem; for "politics is not his theme at all."[5] Lucretius' account of the nature of things, so far from recommending any regime or political good or founding principle, denies to political life any good at all and is utterly indifferent to questions of political arrangements; in accordance with the general intention of Epicureanism, it seeks to dismantle the political passions altogether and to turn men from justice to friendship, from the city to the Garden, from public to private life. What, then, is the meaning of Vergil's making the contest between Lucretius and himself, in the form of a contest between "Carthage" and "Rome," stand for the fundamental political alternative facing the actual Rome? Can Vergil have thought that Lucretius' poem had either an intention or an effect (or both) of such practical efficacy as to warrant so concerted a counter-attack? Must not a sensible man have regarded the strange and difficult teachings of a natural philosopher as affecting no one but a few philosophers and thus, for practical purposes, no one at all?

The question of Lucretius' practical intention or effect is ultimately identical with the question of his intended or actual audience; the question is, as Farrington puts it, "What was the class for which Lucretius wrote?"[6] If Lucretius wrote for the class of the few philosophers, then his book would be in harmony with the well-known indifference of Epicureanism to political arrangements; but if Lucretius wrote for the multitude, then this deed would itself be the "attack on the state religion" that Lucretius does not mention his hope of making, and it must therefore arise either from a most far-reaching political vision of remaking human society from the ground up, or from a most thoroughgoing political blindness to the role of political religion in human society as it actually is. In either case, though, whatever Lucretius' intention may have been, could the teachings of Epicurus in any form have had any such practical effect on the Romans as Vergil appears to attribute to them?

Sober students of Roman politics have indeed argued that Roman Epicureanism had an altogether anomalous practical effect on the political life of the Romans. In his analysis of the ruin of the Republic, Montesquieu attributes to "the sect of Epicurus" as powerful a practical effect as to the unchecked growth of private wealth.[7] "I believe," he says, "that the sect of Epicurus, which was introduced at Rome towards the end of the Republic, contributed a great deal to corrupting the heart and spirit of the Romans."[8] Montesquieu supports this belief with evidence drawn from Plutarch, Polybius, and Cicero, in such a way as to sketch three stages in the corruption of the Romans. First, to show their original uncorrupted condition, he cites Plutarch's account[9] of Fabricius' first exposure to the opinions of Epicurus: "When Cyneas discoursed of them at Pyrrhus's table, Fabricius expressed the hope that Rome's enemies would adopt the principles of such a sect."[10] Then, to illustrate the first beginning of the corruption, he cites Polybius' comparison of Greek contempt for and Roman awe of oaths among his own contemporaries, with Polybius' comment that "It was therefore wise to establish the fear of the Underworld; and it is unreasonable of people to combat it today."[11] Montesquieu, in other words, imputes to Polybius the view that the unreasonable combat "today" against the wisely established fear of the Underworld was Epicurean combat. The most that Polybius himself suggests is that it was the work of men who failed to grasp the permanence or ineradicability of the difference between the few philosophers and the many nonphilosophers, or who wished to address the many as if they could be transformed into philosophers: "If it were possible to form a state wholly of philosophers, such a custom would perhaps be unnecessary. But seeing that every multitude is fickle and full of lawless desires, unreasoning anger, and violent passion, the only resource is to keep them in check by mysterious terrors and scenic effects of this sort."[12] Polybius does not say who the men today are who act so unreasonably. Finally, to illustrate the utmost contribution of the sect of Epicurus to the corruption of the Romans, Montesquieu cites Cicero's account of the corrupt doings of Memmius in his bid for the consulship in 54 B.C.:[13] Memmius and his partner agreed to pay the consuls 400,000 sesterces each "if they did not produce three augurs who would depose that they were present at the carrying of a lex curiata—which had never been passed; and two ex-consuls who would depose to having been present at the drafting of a decree for the fitting out of the consular provinces—though there had never been any meeting of the senate about it at all."[14] Cicero does not say how Memmius came to be so corrupt, but Montesquieu, by choosing for his example of complete corruption the addressee of the De Rerum Natura, implies that it was the teaching of Lucretius that completed the contribution of the sect of Epicurus to the corruption of the Romans.

Montesquieu believes then that it was by combating the state religion that the sect of Epicurus began to corrupt the Romans in the time of Polybius and completed that corruption near the end of the time of Cicero. Can philosophers have contributed so much to the ruin of the Republic?

Montesquieu's belief about the astonishing public efficacy of Roman Epicureanism is amply supported by Cicero's treatment of this subject.[15] According to Cicero, Epicureanism was distinguished from all other philosophical schools precisely by its popularity,[16] by both its intention of and its success in enlisting the multitude in the overthrow of virtue and its replacement by pleasure as the foundation of Roman morality.

In his sketch of the history of Roman philosophy at the beginning of *Tusculans* 4, Cicero contrasts the silence of Roman authors on the "true philosophy derived from Socrates" with the noisy and effective appeal to the multitude made by the Epicureans:

Meanwhile, while these [Peripatetics, Stoics, and Academics] kept silence, C. Amafinius came out talking, and the multitude, stirred up (*commota*) by the publication of his books, turned chiefly to that doctrine—whether because it was so very easy to get acquainted with, or because they were attracted by the enticements of sweet pleasure, or because, since nothing better had been offered, they held on to what there was. After Amafinius, when many emulators of the same reasoning (*rationis*) had written many things, they took possession of all Italy (*totam Italiam occupaverunt*); and they consider the very thing which is the greatest evidence that their words are not clearly reasoned, viz. the fact that they are so easily absorbed and approved by the unlearned (*ab indoctis probentur*), to be the foundation of their doctrine.

(Tusc. IV 6–7)

Amafinius "came out talking" in the time of Polybius; perhaps he was the one who began the corruption of the heart and spirit of the Romans. Cicero's account of the literary activity of the Epicureans is developed by way of contrast with the reasons he suggests for the "silence" of the Socratics: the latter may have been prevented from writing by "greatness of affairs and the business of human beings" (*magnitudinem rerum occupationemque hominum*), or dissuaded from writing by the judgment that "these things cannot be approved by the ignorant" (*imperitis probari*). The taking possession of Italy before the time of Scipio and Laelius was a human *occupatio* in great affairs that the Romans chose above literature: "as for this greatest of all the arts, the study of living well, they pursued it in life rather than in letters." But for the Epicureans the *occupatio* of all Italy is literary business: the Epicureans somehow take possession with letters of the country the Romans had taken with lives; the Epicureans are somehow the emulators, not to say the enemies, of the Romans. Their occupation of all Italy appears to have taken place by their supplying the multitude with philosophic doctrines, a thing judged impossible by the Roman Socratics but made possible by the Roman Epicureans, who replaced the subtlety and difficulty of philosophic speech with loose and easy talk about pleasure.[17] Cicero calls for a concerted defense of all Italy against these Epicureans who have with such unforeseen efficacy armed the multitude with words:[18] "Against these we must struggle 'with foot and horse,' as the saying is, if our intention is to guard and maintain morality" (*si honestatem tueri ac retinere sententia est*) (*De Officiis* III 116).

Cicero characterizes the Epicurean writers not only as the generals of an invading army but also as the leaders of a popular faction:

And indeed the Epicureans, those best of men—for no group is less malicious[19]— complain that I speak as a partisan (*studiose*) against Epicurus. I suppose, then, that we are contending for office or for rank (*de honore aut de dignitate*)! To me the highest good seems to be in the soul, to him in the body; to me in virtue, to him in pleasure. But they're the ones who fight about it and appeal to the loyalty of their neighbors and indeed there are many who promptly come flying to their side. I'm the one who says that I'm not making a to-do about it; I'll take for done what they have done. For what is at issue here? Is it a question of the Punic War? Even on this matter M. Cato and L. Lentulus, though they had different viewpoints, never made it a contest between themselves. But these people carry on with too much anger (*nimis iracunde*), especially as the opinion defended by them is hardly a spirited one (*non sane animosa*), but one on whose behalf they would not dare to speak in the Senate, in the assembly, before the army or before the censors.

(*Tusc.* III 50–51)

The many neighbors to whose party loyalty the Epicureans so effectively appeal are the many whom they claim to make into the philosophic many, as Epicurus "appears to go after disciples" with the suggestion that "those who would be rakes need only first be made philosophers" (*De Fin.* II 30). According to Cicero, this professedly most apolitical or anti-political of philosophies was actually the only philosophic school that had the character of a political movement, proselytizing among the unlearned and seeking the allegiance of the multitude. When he calls the Epicureans *plebeii philosophi* (*Tusc.* I 55), he appears to mean not only that they are the plebs of the philosophers but also that they are the philosophers of the plebs, the philosophers who address the multitude and use them to take possession of all Italy. But Epicurus emphasizes the necessary distinction between philosophizing for oneself and philosophizing for Hellas;[20] "one must release oneself from the prison of affairs and politics."[21] Lucretius declares that it is much more satisfactory to obey quietly than to wish to rule with *imperium* and hold kingdoms.[22] What could the Epicureans have wanted with all Italy?

If Cicero is correct in his view that the doctrine of the Epicureans was so widely popular among the Romans as to have constituted a practical threat to the Roman order, one must wonder how this situation was related to the intention of the Epicurean philosophers themselves. It might be that the vulgar Epicureanism whose popularity Cicero describes was not Epicureanism as understood by Epicureans, but rather an "unintended effect" of genuine Epicureanism, in the way suggested by Nichols: "The genuine Epicureanism presented by Lucretius requires . . . a difficult transformation of ordinary opinions, concerns, and passions—a transformation of which few men are capable. On the other hand, because of its clear argument that pleasure is the good for man, and its clear rejection of ordinary opinions that restrain men, such as those of religion, Epicureanism can bring about an unintended effect. Without basically altering the passions of men, Epicureanism can free men from the usual restraints and undermine devotion to family and country."[23] But if this is the case, if the genuine Epicureans presented genuine Epicureanism in such a way that, while intending only to transform the few potential genuine Epicureans, they unintentionally raised an army of vulgar Epicureans threatening the existing Roman order, then one would have to wonder if there was not some defect in their understanding of the practical effect of literature on public life, or some defect in their ability to direct this practical effect in accordance with their own intentions. Why didn't they present genuine Epicureanism in such a way as to protect it more successfully from popular misunderstanding and vulgar misuse? Did they have sound reasons for regarding the prospect of widespread vulgar Epicureanism as indifferent and therefore not worth protecting against? Or had they forgotten to think about it?

But perhaps the intention of the genuine Epicureans is discernible not in their words of disdain for politics but in their deed of raising an army of vulgar Epicureans threatening the Roman order. This is, in effect, the view of Farrington: Epicurus was "the first champion of popular enlightenment, the first organizer of a movement to free mankind at large from the fetters of superstition,"[24] and the Roman Epicureans were captains of his movement: "The composition of the De Rerum Natura was the culmination of an effort of Epicurean propaganda in Italy, which had lasted more than 100 years. The propaganda had been unwelcome to the Senate from the start. Nevertheless, it had made headway, such headway, indeed, that the philosophic effort of Cicero was mainly directed to stemming the tide of its popularity. He hoped, by routing the Epicureans in the field of philosophy, to complete the victory he had achieved in the political field by crushing the Catilinarians."[25] It was thus the intention of the genuine Epicureans not only to bring down the rule of the Senate in favor of the plebs but beyond this, with a hope leaving far behind the old-style aspirations of a Catiline, to bring down the political teaching of all antiquity in favor of popular enlightenment, of human life purged forever of the fear of gods.

Farrington's view does not take into account Epicurus' own rejection, in word and deed, of popular forms of writing. The popular influence that Cicero attributes to the Epicureans' writings does not necessarily mean that these writings were deliberately calculated to achieve that influence. Cicero leaves it open whether the Epicureans' appeal to the multitude resulted from a thoughtless mistake on their part or whether, on the other hand, they deliberately taught, however obscurely or indirectly, an utterly novel truth about the nature of human things and therewith an utterly novel political doctrine. A decision of this question would have to rest on an understanding of both the philosophic matter and the literary form of the Epicurean writings, so as to show whether their literary form is indeed calculated to enlighten the multitude and, if so, how that form is required or justified by the content of their teaching.

Cicero's writings, in fact, raise a perplexing complication about the literary form of the Epicurean writings, which at first seems to obscure what he took to be the true means of the successful propagation of vulgar Epicureanism at Rome. On the one hand, in his discussion at the beginning of *Tusculans* 4, he attributes great popular influence to the writings of Amafinius and his successors who "took possession of all Italy." On the other hand, he characterizes the writings of both Epicurus himself and his Greek and Roman followers as so repulsive in style that no one would read them who was not already a member of their school:

> There is a certain group of those who wish to be called philosophers whose books in Latin are said to be very many. I don't despise them, indeed I have never read them; but since those who write them themselves declare that they write neither distinctly nor methodically nor elegantly nor ornately, I forego reading what is without any delight. But as for what the members of this school say and what they think, there is no one of even middling education who is unaware of it. Therefore, since they themselves take no pains with their manner of speaking, I see no reason why they should be read except among themselves, who are already in agreement. For, whereas everyone reads Plato and the rest of the Socratics and those who have followed them—even people who either don't approve them or aren't their most zealous followers—hardly anyone except their own people ever takes in hand Epicurus or Metrodorus; and so also the only people who read these Latin ones are those who already think that what they say is right. To us on the other hand it seems that whatever is committed to writings ought to commend itself to the reading of all the learned. (*Tusc.* II 7–8)

Cicero's account is paradoxical: Epicureanism has been propagated at Rome by means of books written in such a way as to be repulsive to all those who are not already Epicureans. The explanation of this paradox is not far to seek, though: Cicero contends that the real core of the Epicureans' doctrine is so simple-minded and (spuriously) attractive that "what they say and what they think" is very easily known without reading what they write; Epicureanism gets adherents by being popularly and loosely talked about, or getting to be "in the air."

As for the question that is often asked, why so many are Epicureans, there are other causes as well, but the thing that most powerfully attracts the multitude is that people think that Epicurus says that the upright and honorable things themselves produce joy, that is, pleasure.

(*De Fin.* I 25)

What attracts the multitude is what people think about what Epicurus says without having read and understood what he says: they think he speaks well of the honorable (*honestum*) while making pleasure the standard; and since they like (since they are accustomed) to hear the honorable well spoken of but in such a way as to permit everything in deed (cf. *De Fin.* II 21), "the unlearned are taken in by these things, and because of that kind of views there is a multitude of people of that sort" (*Tusc.* V 28). The Epicureans say, when pressed by philosophic critics, that their standard of pleasure, or perhaps their usage of the word *voluptas*, is very different from what the vulgar understand by pleasure (*De Fin.* II 12; *Tusc.* III 37, 41–46, 49); but in sober fact, as an acute reasoner can see if he actually examines their arguments (*Tusc.* V 28; this might require a certain patience with or immunity to their repellent style), the Epicureans count as good and bad the same things as the vulgar (*eadem quae vulgus in malis et bonis numerare*)—strength, health, beauty, riches, honors, wealth and their opposites (*Tusc.* V 30–31).

Epicureanism then is actually propagated by loose talk; the vulgar understanding of Epicureanism is the truth of Epicureanism; the Epicurean philosophers' pretensions to a morality distinguishable from common criminality are empty; let Epicurus' own pleasures have been as austere as you like, his philosophy can make nothing of that austerity (*Tusc.* V 46). The writings of the Epicureans are not the means of propagating Epicureanism but the means of supplying a few of the converts—the ones with pretensions to the name of philosophy—with high-sounding but specious arguments for the vulgar doctrine. The Epicureans write repulsively in order to discourage those who are not already of the faith from grasping the philosophical bankruptcy of the Epicurean teaching. Epicureanism is the unreformed opinion of the multitude deployed against the Roman order by the "plebeian philosophers;" only for the sake of respectability does it masquerade as a philosophical doctrine.

In all of Cicero's extant works the name of Lucretius occurs but once, in a letter to his brother Quintus (II.xi.5), where he refers to the art and genius of Lucretius' poetry but puts off further discussion "until you come." From his silence about Lucretius[26] in all his published writings, one might have imagined that he regarded the propagation of Epicureanism as having relied entirely on attractive loose talk and repulsive prose writings, and that he had never heard of the philosophic poet. Cicero's suppression of public reference to Lucretius has been attributed to his reluctance to be associated by its enemies with a book that "may well have become politically disreputable,"[27] but might rather be attributed to his unwillingness to contribute, even by criticism, to the currency of the book among its potential friends.[28]

For if the propagation of Epicureanism at Rome had already been so successfully conducted by means of alluring loose talk and repulsive theoretical writings, what can have been the effect of the summons to Epicureanism by an alluring writing? The Roman order has been desperately undermined by the ambitious rivalries of the greatest men appealing against each other to the plebs; in this extremity, the "plebeian philosophers" too step in, ambitious to attach the multitude to atheism and pleasure as against the Roman order constituted by religion and virtue. The campaign of these philosophers has the defect of a great gap between its literary underpinnings and its popular manifestations; now into this gap steps a poet whose self-proclaimed mission is to replace the repulsiveness and obscurity of all former Epicurean writings with the sweetness and clarity of a gorgeous poem. "No tree can be planted by any agriculture so enduring as one planted by the verse of a poet" (Cicero, De Legibus I.1). This poet, seeing in Epicurus' doctrine something necessarily abhorrent to the vulgar, proposes for this very reason to disguise its bitterness with the honey of the Muses; he aims on the one side towards the fullest theoretical exposition of the Epicurean teaching, and on the other side toward the most attractive communication of this teaching to the widest possible audience. Lucretius' poem is composed, in Cicero's judgment, with genius and art. Cicero, who was composing his De Republica at the time of the publication of Lucretius' De Rerum Natura, introduces it with an elaborate argument in his own name against the claims of the Epicureans,[29] particularly against their combination of contempt for politics and confidence in their competence to rule "if necessary;" and he opens the dialogue itself with a discussion among his characters of the proper relationship between physics and politics (De Rep. I 10–11). Vergil's making the contest between Lucretius and himself stand for the political alternative facing the Romans has become at least far more intelligible in the light of Cicero's analysis of Roman Epicureanism.

Cicero's account of Roman Epicureanism gives a great deal of support to Montesquieu's belief that "the sect of Epicurus . . . contributed much to corrupting the heart and spirit of the Romans." Nevertheless, Cicero's view that the practical danger of vulgar Epicureanism is such as to require resistance "with foot and horse" has the practical consequence that Cicero himself takes in the first place a polemical stance toward it; his polemics include his affectation always to be addressing what the Roman Epicureans are known by everyone to say and think, and never what they themselves have written. Therefore, since Cicero's polemics begin by collapsing Epicureanism into vulgar Epicureanism, it is not at once apparent whether his account does justice to the thought of genuine Epicureans as opposed to the deeds of vulgar Epicureans. It would be reasonable to think that Vergil, like Cicero, saw with alarm the practical dangers of vulgar Epicureanism to the Roman order and sought, like Cicero, to avert or overcome these dangers practically in his writings; in taking issue with Lucretius, Vergil would be seeking to defend Rome against vulgar Epicureanism. But this thought could never lead to more than a partial interpretation of the *Aeneid*, for Rome—the founding and refounding of Rome—is only a partial, and indeed secondary, theme of the *Aeneid*; its primary theme is the causes of celestial anger, that is, a universal theme no more bound to Vergil's contemporary Rome than to any other time or place. Thus, in order to give an adequate interpretation of Vergil's taking Lucretius as his chief adversary in the *Aeneid*, it is not enough to consider whether there was in fact a "Roman Enlightenment" in the late Republic; it is altogether necessary to turn to Lucretius' poem itself in order to discover its teaching on Vergil's highest and most comprehensive theme. What does Lucretius himself understand by the project of making Epicureanism more attractive to the vulgar, or (to use a modification of Farrington's formulation of the question) what is the class for which Lucretius writes? What kind of transformation does Lucretius intend to bring about in what audience? Most important, what is Lucretius' account of celestial anger, and in what sense does his view of the potential transformation of his audience depend upon the truth of this account?

~

CHAPTER FIVE

Lucretius' Teaching

Lucretius' intention in the *De Rerum Natura* is to enable men—we do not know at the outset whether few, many, or all men—to live happy lives, lives "worthy of gods." Men are not living happy lives already because their souls are sick, suffering from the fear of death. Lucretius' book can cure the souls of at least some men because the cause of their souls' sickness is ignorance, ignorance of the nature of things in general and of the nature of death in particular. The aim of Lucretius' book is to replace at least some men's ignorant fear, which prevents them from being happy, with knowledge of the nature of things, which will enable them to become as happy as gods.[1]

Lucretius' intention appears to be fully in accord with Epicurus' teaching on the true intention of philosophy:

> Empty is the logos of that philosopher by whom no suffering of the human being is cared for; for just as there is no use in medicine if it does not expel diseases from the bodies, so there is none in philosophy if it does not expel the suffering of the soul.[2]

In accordance with Epicurus' precept, Lucretius has for therapeutic reasons composed his own logos (*haec ratio*, 4.18; *rationem nostram* 4.21) in the form of a poem:

> For just as physicians, when they are trying to give bitter wormwood to boys, first touch the rim all around the cup with the sweet golden liquor of honey, so that the boys' improvident youth may be tricked as far as the lips and

meanwhile drink down the bitter juice of the wormwood, and though deceived not be cheated, but rather by this means be restored and become healthy,—so now, since this reasoning (*ratio*) seems for the most part too harsh to those by whom it has not been handled, and the multitude (*vulgus*) shudders away from it (*abhorret*), I wanted to expound our reasoning to you in sweet-speaking Pierian song and to touch it, so to speak, with the sweet honey of the Muses, in hopes that perhaps I might be able to hold your mind (*animum*) in our verses with such reasoning until you fully perceive the whole nature of things and fully feel the advantage.

(4.11–25)[3]

Lucretius' logos has a salutary bitter part that is masked by a sweet part. The bitter part is the knowledge that has the property of curing souls of their ignorance and fear; the sweet part is the poetry that makes the knowledge palatable.

The "you" whom Lucretius addresses is Memmius: he wishes to expound "our reasoning" in sweet poetry for "you" because this reasoning usually seems too harsh to those for whom it is unfamiliar, and the *vulgus* shudders away from it. "You" are then one for whom this reasoning is unfamiliar; "you" are a member of the *vulgus* that shudders away from it. Lucretius' sweet disguise of his reasoning is for the sake of "you" as representing the *vulgus*. The *vulgus*, like the young boys, are sick and improvident: having no experience of this reasoning, they are unable to foresee its advantage (*utilitas*) for themselves; it must be provided for them by one who both knows its advantage and knows how to trick the improvident into getting that advantage. But in what sense of *vulgus* is Memmius representative of the *vulgus*?[4] Apparently Lucretius makes the *vulgus* include the class of the nobles or the class of the educated to which Memmius belongs: all human beings who are unfamiliar with the Epicurean reasoning are thereby the *vulgus*; the class distinction that is so visible and impressive from the point of view of most men entirely collapses from the point of view of Epicureanism: the *vulgus* are the non-Epicureans. But then does Lucretius mean, while demoting Memmius to the status of a representative of the *vulgus*, thereby to promote the *vulgus* to the class of potential Epicureans? If all non-Epicureans are a homogeneous class, and Lucretius proposes to provide for Memmius as representative of this class, does he thereby propose to provide for all non-Epicureans, that is, for all improvident human beings?

The possibility that Lucretius might mean to address all Latin-speaking non-Epicureans, i.e. that he might understand his reasoning as potentially beneficial to the generality of men, is raised by many other things as well, but in the first place and most generally by Lucretius' presenting himself as the rival of Homer; for this poet has been the educator of Greece[5] and Greece has been the educator of Rome, and to be the rival of Homer is to contend with Homer for the hearts and minds of Homer's pupils.

Lucretius' hexameters are conceived not only in the tradition of the pre-Epicurean poetizing physiologists but also and emphatically in the tradition of Homer,[6] as Lucretius makes evident from the very opening of the *De Rerum Natura*. In his invocation to Venus he takes up the scandalous song of the Homeric bard Demodocus ("opinion of the *demos*") on the illicit love of Aphrodite and Ares (*Od.* 8.266–366) and recasts it as a lofty symbolic plea for the pacification of war by love:

> hunc tu, diva, tuo recubantem corpore sancto
> circumfusa super, suavis ex ore loquellas
> funde petens placidam Romanis, incluta, pacem.

> You, goddess, pouring yourself about him from above with your sacred body as he lies recumbent, pour forth sweet speeches from your mouth, entreating tranquil peace, renowned goddess, for the Romans.

> (1.38–40)

Lucretius' rivalry with Homer is sustained and intensified at intervals throughout the *De Rerum Natura* and does not cease until, with the end of the poem, Lucretius has come full circle, as it were, to the beginning or principle of the *Iliad*, the principle that the plague is caused by an angry god (*Il.* 1.64). Apparently the execution of Lucretius' intention to cure men's sick souls requires the imitation of Homer because the actual form of their sickness—their ignorance, fear and unhappiness—stems from their having been badly educated by Homer in the first place. Men's ignorant beliefs that they are subject to the favor and anger of powerful gods and that their shades are destined to a sad afterlife in the house of Hades—beliefs by which they are so frightened that they live like pathetic madmen—are the beliefs taught by Homer; it is from Homer that men have acquired the opinion that their lot is lamentable. Even the great Ennius, who was the first to bring down the crown of poetry from Greek Helicon to the Italian peoples (1.117–119), was thereby a pupil of Homer and a teacher of Homer's sad error. In his eternal verses Ennius taught that the realm of Acheron exists, where neither our souls nor our bodies survive but only certain wondrously pale semblances of us, and recounted that the ghost of ever-flourishing Homer rose up to him from there and began to pour forth salty tears as he set out the nature of things in words (1.120–126). For this reason, concludes Lucretius—because Homer's error about the nature of things, and especially about the fate of men's souls, has been the prevalent poetic education first of the

Greeks and now of the Romans—Lucretius must finally give a rational account both of the things above and of the things that are done in the lands (127–130), but chiefly of the soul (*anima*) and the nature of the mind (*animus*) (130–131), so as to explain the true cause why a man like Ennius can have seemed, either when awake or when asleep, to see and hear Homer, who is dead (132–135). In this rational account Lucretius will far outdistance Ennius' own poetic achievement by becoming the first to bring from its Greek source into Latin verses not the error taught by Homer but the truth discovered by Epicurus; this will be more difficult than Ennius' feat because the Latin language is poor in the vocabulary required by the novelty of Lucretius' Epicurean teaching (136–139). In achieving this most difficult feat, Lucretius will replace Ennius as the Roman Homer and Homer as the poetic teacher of the best life for men.

For men's characters and opinions are formed by poets, especially by the poets' beautiful praise of heroes; Homer's praise of Achilles and Odysseus has made men long to emulate these heroes. Because Homer mistook the nature of things, he presented in Achilles and Odysseus two mistaken versions of the best life for men; because Lucretius knows the truth about the nature of things, he knows that the philosophic life and not the heroic life is truly praiseworthy. It was Epicurus who discovered this, but because he rejected poetry he was able to reform the opinions and aspirations of only such few men as are able to be reformed by reasoning. But because most men are formed rather by poetic images than by reasoning, it is necessary, in case one wishes to replace Homer as the teacher of most men, not only to reason with them but in the first place to provide for them an image of human greatness more charming than Homer's images of Achilles and Odysseus.

One who could replace Homer as the teacher of men might be able to induce men to transform their lives.

> si possent homines, proinde ac sentire uidentur
> pondus inesse animo, quod se grauitate fatiget,
> e quibus id fiat causis quoque noscere et unde
> tanta mali tamquam moles in pectore constet,
> haut ita uitam agerent, ut nunc plerumque uidemus
> quid sibi quisque uelit nescire et quaerere semper
> commutare locum, quasi onus deponere possit. . . .
>   morbi quia causam non tenet aeger.
> quam bene si uideat, iam rebus quisque relictis
> naturam primum studeat cognoscere rerum.

If human beings, as they seem to sense that there is a burden in their spirit which wears them down with its heaviness, were likewise able to find out from what causes this occurs, and from what source so great a mass of evil, as it were, abides in their breast, they would not lead their lives like this, as now in most cases we see that no one knows what he wants for himself and each one is always seeking to change his locations as if he would be able in this way to lay aside the weight. . . . Being ill, he does not grasp the cause of his illness. If he should see it well, each would leave all other things aside and strive first of all to get knowledge of the nature of things.

(3.1053–1059, 1070–1072)

In this passage Lucretius twice formulates the condition of the possibility that human beings could be induced to change their lives. The first formulation suggests that this condition is unfulfillable: human beings are in fact not able to find out the causes of the burden in their spirit; their inability may be incorrigible. But after stating the chief cause—the fact that men are trying to flee from what is in no way possible to escape (1068–1069)—Lucretius reformulates more optimistically the condition of the possibility of men's transformation: if each should see the cause well, each would be turned from all other things to getting knowledge of the nature of things, and thus each would be cured. The second, more optimistic formulation is separated from the first by Lucretius' own statement of the cause in question; the condition of the possibility of men's transformation is Lucretius' poetic ability to make each human being see what he is otherwise unable to see. Human beings' ability to know what they want and to move toward it is consequent not directly upon reasoning but upon the impulsion of images, *simulacra*, which move the *animus*—as an image of walking striking our mind is what we call our "will," *voluntas*, to walk; no one begins to do anything until the mind foresees the image of what it wills (4.877–885).[7] Men's will to transform their way of life, to leave everything else aside and seek first to learn the nature of things, likewise does not follow from a merely rational demonstration of the superiority of Lucretius' Epicurean wisdom to Homer's Achillean glory and Odyssean love; an impelling *image* is required, and since men are already habituated (ultimately by Homer) to being moved by the image of a hero as a man whose greatness verges on divinity, Lucretius has in this image a ready-made resource for his therapy of human souls: he makes of Epicurus an image of the greatest hero.

The true principle of Lucretius' contest with Homer is the truth about the nature of things, and preeminently the truth about Hades. From Homer's error about Hades springs men's indignation at their mortal lot (3.870, 1045), and from this indignation the senseless striving for glory or love; because of this error, men take Achilles and Odysseus as exemplars of the best life for

men. From Lucretius' true teaching about Hades springs a reasonable acceptance of men's lot, and from this springs the striving to get knowledge of the
nature of things; because of this truth one can know that Epicurus is the exemplar of the best life for men. But in order to replace Homer as the teacher
of human beings, Lucretius begins, in accordance with the truth about men's
will to change, not from reasoning about the nature of things but from the
provision of images of the best human life: Lucretius poetically presents Epicurus' way of life as a kind of heroism, his greatness as the outdoing of
Achilles' and Odysseus' heroism. The poetic praise of heroes is the honey of
poetry by which Lucretius seeks to make "this reasoning" more palatable to
the *vulgus;* but it is "this reasoning" itself that, by demonstrating the consequence of men's will on images, suggests how "this reasoning" may at first be
masked by the poetic images that may ultimately lead men to the will to pursue "this reasoning" directly. Because he is addressing men who are accustomed to being moved by the images of Homer's heroes, Lucretius first sets
out to dim the impressiveness of their heroic images by outshining them with
his own images of Epicurus' heroism.[8] Lucretius begins this project with his
first introduction of Epicurus:

> humana ante oculos foede cum vita iaceret
> in terris oppressa gravi sub Religione,
> quae caput a caeli regionibus ostendebat,
> horribili super aspectu mortalibus instans,
> primum Graius homo mortalis tendere contra
> est oculos ausus primusque obsistere contra.
> quem neque fama deum nec fulmina nec minitanti
> murmure compressit caelum, sed eo magis acrem
> inritat animi virtutem, ecfringere ut arta
> naturae primus portarum claustra cupiret.
> ergo vivida vis animi pervicit, et extra
> processit longe flammantia moenia mundi
> atque omne inmensum peragravit mente animoque.
> unde refert nobis victor quid possit oriri,
> quid nequeat, finita potestas denique cuique
> quanam sit ratione atque alte terminus haerens.
> quare Religio pedibus subiecta vicissim
> opteritur: nos exaequat victoria caelo.

When human life lay vile before the eyes, oppressed on earth under heavy religion, which used to show forth its head from the regions of the sky, looming
down over mortals with horrible aspect, a Greek human being was the first
who dared to direct his mortal eyes against it, the first to take a stand against

it; neither the reputation of the gods nor thunderbolts nor the sky with its threatening growl restrained him, but rather it excited all the more the virtue of his mind, so that he desired to be the first to break open the fast bolts of the gates of nature. Thus the lively force of his mind gained complete victory, and he set forth far beyond the flaming walls of the world and traversed the bound-less whole in mind and spirit; whence he victoriously brings back to us knowl-edge of what can come into being and what cannot, by what reason, in fine, the power of each thing and its deeply inhering boundary has been delimited. Thus religion in its turn has been trampled beneath the feet and is being crushed out; the victory makes us equal to heaven.

(1.62–79)

In the days when the heroes fought at Troy, human life as a whole was being lived "before the eyes" in craven submission to the tyranny of religion: the siege of Troy and the defense of Troy could look heroic only because one averted one's eyes from the true condition of human life, or from the true en-emy of human beings. It was as if in a conquered city the enslaved citizens should ignore the invader and carry on as if minor contests among them-selves were the whole sphere of heroism. In this world, while the *viri* were carrying on their contests, a Greek who was precisely not a *vir*, *Graius homo*, became the first nevertheless to display true virtue of spirit, *animi virtutem:* he dared to direct his eyes against the oppressor. The "mortal eyes" of Epicu-rus were the eyes "before" which human life was being vilely lived; the half-god heroes did not see the vileness of human life, but this mortal Greek hu-man being saw it, and his daring to see it with his mortal eyes was at the same time his counterattack upon the oppressive gods, made with the weapons of his eyes.[9] While Achilles was being celebrated for his siege of walled Troy on behalf of Greece, Epicurus conceived the project of being the first to besiege the walled city of nature[10] on behalf of human life. While Odysseus was be-ing celebrated for travelling far beyond the cities of Greece and reaching the house of Hades at the boundary of the world, Epicurus was travelling far be-yond the walls of the world through the boundless All. And while Odysseus brought back to Ithaca, from the victory at Troy and the great travels, stories claiming that everything can become anything—in particular that human beings can become on the one hand pigs and on the other hand immortal gods[11]—Epicurus "brings back to us" knowledge of the fixed limits on the power of each thing.[12]

For Epicurus far outshines the Homeric heroes not only because of the courage of his deeds but also because his deeds are a present benefit, indeed the greatest conceivable benefit, to "us": his victory makes "us" the equals of heaven. Each of the heroes was in his time the champion of a human city against other human cities, but this human being is now the champion of human life against the gods. Thus to eyes that can see the true human situation, not only does Achilles' siege of Troy pale before Epicurus' siege of nature, not only do Odysseus' sea travels pale before Epicurus' mental travels, but the local and temporal particularity of the war between Greeks and Trojans pales before the universal and permanent war between human life and religion. Indeed a little later in Book 1 (449 ff.), when Lucretius is setting forth the difference in status between the beings, their properties (*coniuncta*), and their accidents (*euenta*), the deeds of the Trojan War are his prime examples of mere accidents of matter and void: when people speak of Helen raped and of the Trojan races conquered in war, "we" must see to it that they do not compel us to affirm that these things "are,"[13] since irrevocable past time has carried off those generations of human beings whose accidents these were. War and peace, slavery and freedom, poverty and riches, did not affect the nature of the past beings whose accidents they were, not to speak of us now; but Epicurus' victory then makes us now the equals of heaven.

Lucretius provides, then, in his poetic representation of Epicurus as a hero, an image of the best—most courageous and most beneficent—human life, an image calculated to win men over from the Homeric images of Achilles and Odysseus. The poetic metaphor of "heroic action" for "philosophic knowledge" permeates the praises of Epicurus in the *De Rerum Natura*[14] in accordance with the project of reeducating Homer's audience to imagine Epicurus' philosophic life as the exemplar of a greater than Homeric heroism. This poetic language is the Lucretian honey; the harsh truth it masks is that heroism belongs altogether to the vile pre-Epicurean way of leading human life; Epicureanism is not the summit or perfection of Homeric heroism as of something great but the rejection of it as something vile. The summit of human life is human thought, not manly deeds. Epicurus is a *homo*, not a *vir* (1.66, 5.51); it is his mind, not his body, that is godlike (3.15); it is his words, not his deeds, that are deserving of perpetual life (3.12–13); it is by expelling men's fears with words, not arms, that this human being shows his godlikeness—and especially since those words tell the truth about the immortal gods and the nature of things:

> haec igitur qui cuncta subegerit ex animoque
> expulerit dictis, non armis, nonne decebit
> hunc hominem numero divum dignarier esse?—
> cum bene praesertim multa ac divinitus ipsis
> inmortalibus de divis dare dicta suerit
> atque omnem rerum naturam pandere dictis.

He, therefore, who conquered all these fears and expelled them from the soul with words, not arms—will it not be fitting that this human being be deemed worthy to be of the number of the gods?—especially since he habitually uttered many words, and that in godlike fashion, about the immortal gods themselves, and set forth the whole nature of things in words.

(5.49–54)

That the true sphere of "godlikeness" is human thought, not manly deeds, is known to reason and shown by Lucretius in his rational account of the whole nature of things, but to make this truth efficacious in swaying men to *desire* the life of thought, to redirect their will or aspiration from the heroic to the philosophic life, Lucretius presents the life of Epicurus in poetic terms that contest on their own ground Homer's praises of the heroes.

Lucretius' physicianly use of poetic honey goes beyond picturing Epicurus as a hero to picturing him as "a god." The harsh truth about the gods that is masked by this honey is that there are no gods, or at any rate no gods who are immortal, who inhabit our world, who help or harm human beings, or who rule anything. Nevertheless, Lucretius regularly invokes the idea of "godlikeness," "equality with the gods," "a life worthy of gods," as the poetic expression of the idea of "the best human life," "the philosophic life." As it emerges, in the course of the poem, that the traditional belief in the Olympian gods is an entirely erroneous belief arising in the first place from the faulty interpretation of images and maintained subsequently by the verbal bullying of priests and poets, Lucretius nevertheless continues to hold up "the life of the gods" as the object of human striving, and the life of Epicurus as the one life that can truly be called divine:

nam si, ut ipsa petit maiestas cognita rerum,
dicendum est, deus ille fuit, deus, inclyte Memmi,
qui princeps vitae rationem invenit eam quae
nunc appellatur 'sapientia,' quique per artem
fluctibus e tantis vitam tantisque tenebris
in tam tranquillo et tam clara luce locavit.

For if one must speak as the known majesty of things requires—he was a god, illustrious Memmius, a god, who was the first to discover that rational account of life which is now called wisdom, and who through his art removed life from such billows and shadows into such tranquil and clear light.

(5.7–12)

Lucretius' speaking in this manner is in accordance with his rivalry with Homer for the allegiance of men's hearts. Homer had displayed heroism as the striving to burst the constraints of human weakness and become godlike. Lucretius does not imagine that men educated to look up to the immortal gods, through the heroes, as objects of human aspiration will be easily induced to replace those beautiful gods in their hearts with what is in truth immortal, the atoms and the void. Rather than teaching directly that the imitation of the Homeric gods is a delusion that causes men to lead their lives vilely, Lucretius' physicianly strategy is to sublimate the traditional Homeric idea of the gods, which is enchanting and harmful to men, into a symbolic idea that should retain the power of enchantment while avoiding harmfulness and even becoming helpful to men's souls.

Lucretius proceeds by a curious combination of denying the Homeric teachings outright and indicating the method of sublimating those teachings through interpretation, as in Book 1 Demodocus' song of the love of Aphrodite and Ares is sublimated into a prayer for peace (1.29–40), and in Book 3 the Underworld as seen by Odysseus is sublimated into a symbol of the sufferings undergone by unenlightened men in this life (3.978–1023). In Book 2, Lucretius explains the method of sublimation very clearly (598–660). The ancient Greek poets sang of the earth as the "mother of the gods," who is carried in a chariot drawn by a team of lions, wears a mural crown, and is attended by eunuch priests. Lucretius on the one hand sublimates this ancient piece of Greek poetic flummery by interpreting it as symbolic of physical truths: by assigning the Great Goddess her chariot the poets "taught" that the earth is suspended in the air; by assigning her the mural crown they "taught" that the earth has walled cities in it, and so on. On the other hand, he asserts outright that these poetic tales are far from true reason (645)[15] and that the earth in fact is not even a living being, to say nothing of a god. Thus, he concludes, anyone who prefers employing the names "Neptune," "Ceres," "Bacchus," when he really means sea, grain, and wine, is just as much entitled to call the earth "mother of the gods"

> dum vera re tamen ipse
> religione animum turpi contingere parcat.

provided that he refrain from actually infecting his mind with foul religion.
(2.659–660)

Lucretius suggests then that therapeutic poetry, in seeking to impel or educate men to desire knowledge of the nature of things, allures them in their initial weakness by using the lovely old divine names for natural things, while showing them how to understand those names symbolically, and thus to excise the harmful content of religion while retaining its sweet vocabulary.

Lucretius uses the vocabulary of the gods in precisely the way he recommends interpreting the ancient poets, as a symbolic language that can impart to the rational truth the imaginative power to move men's souls. Lucretius speaks as if he concedes to Homer that the best human life is a life of striving after the condition of gods,[16] while silently correcting Homer's idea of "gods" to remove from it the infection of foul religion. Thus he speaks of Epicurus as having made "us" "equal to heaven" (1.79), as having a divine mind (3.15), and, simply, as having been a god (5.8),[17] in order to represent Epicurus as surpassing the specifically heroic achievements of Achilles and Odysseus while at the same time shifting the reference of "divinity" from the immortal Olympians to the mortal (indeed, dead) philosopher, and the reference of "heroism" from the Homeric heroes' active life to Epicurus' contemplative life. The enlightened man doubtless would not prefer to use the name "Neptune" when he means ocean, or the name "god" when he means "philosophic man;"[18] but the De Rerum Natura is not addressed to enlightened men; it is the teaching that should guide unenlightened men, Homerically educated men, toward philosophy. Nothing is immortal but the atoms and the void; there are no immortal gods to emulate, there is no immortal glory to strive for, there is no beloved for whom our longing is other than a senseless delusion. The harsh truth of Lucretius' therapy is that the heroes with their dependence on the gods are vile, and that the only way to human health is science; the "honey" with which he rims the cup of this teaching is Homeric honey, the poetic image of the philosopher as superhero and god rather than the reasonable presentation of the philosopher as the scourge of heroes and gods.

The possibility raised by the honeyed-cup simile that Lucretius means to address Memmius as a representative of the vulgus in the sense of the universality of non-Epicureans, who shudder away from the harshness of the undisguised doctrine, seems to be borne out by the heroic and Olympian imagery with which Lucretius has disguised it, since this imagery is aimed at men whose opinions and aspirations have been formed by the most popular and traditional poetry. The shuddering of the vulgus at Epicurean doctrine is in the first instance a symptom of their subservience to the seers (vates), with their terror-talking words about eternal punishments, and the poets, whose tales of the afterlife are famous among the nations of human beings, as Ennius' Homeric tales are famous among the Italian nations of human beings (1.102–126). It is these seers and poets who maintain the hold of religious fears on the vulgus. Thus if it is possible for Lucretius to displace the hold of the poets and seers on the vulgar, it would seem to be possible for him to transform human life universally from its vile pre-Epicurean form and to make "us" in the sense of "us human beings" equal to heaven; it would seem to be possible and desirable for Lucretius to extirpate religion from human life. However, such a conquest of the poets and seers would in fact overcome only the means by which religious terrors are presently maintained among human beings; for the poets and seers are not the cause of religion but only its upholders. If religion can be extirpated from human life, breaking the authority of its present upholders could only be a first step; it would be necessary finally to go to the cause that brought religion about in the first place, and to reverse or overcome that first cause.

> nunc quae causa deum per magnas numina gentis
> pervulgarit et ararum compleverit urbis
> suscipiendaque curarit sollemnia sacra,
> quae nunc in magnis forent sacra rebus locisque
> (unde etiam nunc est mortalibus insitus horror,
> qui delubra deum nova toto suscitat orbi
> terrarum et festis cogit celebrare diebus),
> non ita difficilest rationem reddere verbis.

> Now what cause communicated the divinities of the gods to the *vulgus* throughout great nations and filled the cities with altars and saw to it that solemn rites would be undertaken, rites which now flourish in great affairs and places, as a result of which even now there is implanted in mortals a horror which raises up new shrines of the gods all over the circuit of the lands and compels mortals to frequent them on festal days—it is not very difficult to give a rational account of this in words.

> (5.1161–1168)

Lucretius speaks here as if the cause of religion operated once and universally in the past, and so efficaciously that its results continue and indeed flourish "even now." If this cause was then some event that took place in the past, and that had the power to implant in the many, universally, the horror of gods, then it would seem that the reversal of that cause would require another event with an even stronger power to uproot from the many, universally, the horror of gods. In his praise of Epicurus in the proem to Book 5 Lucretius appears to say that this counterevent has taken place: it was Epicurus' invention of the rational account of life that is "now" called wisdom (5.9–10); unlike the gods' reputed invention of grain and wine, Epicurus' invention was the necessary and universal condition of living well, for it is reported that there are "some nations even now" (*aliquas etiam nunc . . . gentis*, 17) that live without grain and wine, but because of Epicurus' invention "the sweet solaces for life, having been spread abroad throughout the great nations, even now are soothing the spirits" (*nunc etiam per magnas didita gentis / dulcia permulcent animos solacia vitae*, 20–21). The great nations throughout which the cause of religion operated appear to be answered by the great nations throughout which Epicurus' invention was disseminated: Epicurus' invention appears to be the counterevent to the original cause of religion. The cause of religion appears to have been outmatched by the cause of irreligion; it appears to be possible, indeed it appears to be actual, that human life can be lived well by human beings universally, or that religion can be extirpated from human life.

This result cannot be the whole truth, however, for the following reason. The event that was the original cause of religion turns out to be a two-part cause: on the one hand, the early generations of mortals used to see distinguished forms of gods (*divum . . . egregias . . . facies*, 5.1169–70); on the other hand, they used to observe the annual cycle of the heaven without being able to find out by what causes this happened. Both parts of this original cause operated by misleading the early generations into erroneous attributions: to the "distinguished forms of gods" that they saw, they erroneously attributed sensation, eternal life, invincibility, and outstanding good fortune (1172–1182), and to the power of these erroneously imagined gods they then proceeded to attribute the control of all the phenomena in the heaven; finally, to these attributions they added bitter anger, thus completing their legacy of misery for the future generations:

o genus infelix humanum, talia divis
cum tribuit facta atque iras adiunxit acerbas!
quantos tum genitus ipsi sibi, quantaque nobis
vulnera, quas lacrimas peperere minoribus nostris!

O unhappy human race, when it attributed such deeds to gods, and then added also bitter angers! What great groanings they themselves then brought into being for themselves, what great wounds for us, what tears for our descendants!

(5.1194–1197)

Now of this two-part original cause of religion it must be observed that both parts are in fact not unique past events, or even occasional or frequent past events, but present and perhaps permanent conditions of the human race. The distinguished forms of gods that early men saw in their minds "even then," *iam tum*, are the same ones seen also by contemporary men, nor is there any reason to doubt that these forms will always be seen by men (6.76–77, 4.722–748, 5.146–152, 3.18–24); and the observation of the heavenly phenomena without being able to know their causes is also a permanently recurring situation for the generations of mortals, as Lucretius goes on to make clear in 5.1204–1240: whenever "we" look up at the heaven, want of reasoning attacks our doubtful mind and leads us along a train of thought starting from anxiety about the beginning and end of the world and leading inexorably to imaginations of powerful and angry gods. Indeed this train of thought is so inexorable as to affect even those who have already learned well the truth about the gods; they too, if at times they wonder by what means things are managed in the heavens, are carried back again into the old religions and take on harsh lords who they, in their wretchedness, believe have power over all things (6.58–64).

Thus the two-part cause of religion, though presented at first as a past event, is in fact a cause that operates now and always among human beings; while the invention of wisdom by Epicurus, though presented at first as the past cause of present irreligion, is in fact a thing that needs to be continuously recovered and continuously applied against the continuously operating causes of religion. The "prize" that Epicurus "left to us" (5.5) when he invented wisdom is after all ours not by inheritance but only by our own laborious acquisition; Epicurus left us a prize in the sense that he demonstrated that this prize exists by manifestly acquiring it for himself.

Epicurus' accomplishment, then, is a benefit to us only in a very qualified sense; we ourselves would first have to come to perceive fully the whole nature of things before being able to acquire for ourselves Epicurus' prize. And while the cause of religion emphatically communicated religion to the vulgar (pervulgarit) around the world, the invention of wisdom was not itself able to overcome the abhorrence of the vulgar from the contents of wisdom; the Epicurean solaces for life have been spread abroad, didita, but not thereby communicated to the vulgar, pervulgata, throughout the great nations; the universality of Epicurus' benefit to human life lies in its being accessible to human beings of all nations, but not thereby to all human beings of any nation. Indeed Epicurus' achievement, while benefiting human life as a whole by demonstrating that humanness in itself is not an insurmountable obstacle to living well, did not thereby enable any other human being, simply as a human being, to live well. This is at least partly because he did not present his teaching in a way that could overcome the abhorrence of the vulgar; but it may also be because, regardless how attractively this teaching is presented, it is too difficult—not too ugly, but too difficult—for all but the keenest intellects.[19]

Perhaps Lucretius, while modestly claiming that he cannot even fashion praises adequate to Epicurus' benefit to the human race (5.1–4), in fact gives an even greater benefit to the human race: Epicurus gave the human race the satisfaction as a race of seeing that humanness does not preclude withstanding the gods and being equal to heaven; but Lucretius brings to the individual members of the human race the satisfaction of acquiring for themselves the ability to live well; and he does this by overcoming the initial abhorrence of the vulgar through the "honey" of his poetry. Perhaps then Lucretius means to transform human life on a scale far beyond anything ever conceived by Epicurus:[20] Epicurus could not extirpate religion from human life generally, but Lucretius both can and means to. Lucretius would have then either greater benevolence towards the human race than Epicurus did, or greater understanding of how to enable human beings to know the nature of things, or both. But granting that Lucretius' invention of poetic honey is capable of overcoming through physicianly deceit the initial abhorrence of the vulgar from the salutary truth and thus awakening in any and all human beings the will to be quit of the sickness of their souls, is it capable also of supplying for this will an ability of any and all human beings to grasp the whole nature of things? Would it be a benefit to a human being to awaken him to his vile sickness without being able to make him able to carry out his will to cure himself? Would it be a benefit to the human race to make the generality of its members regard fear of gods as a vile sickness to which they are nonetheless subject, thus removing from the fear of gods whatever dignity it now has without being able to replace it with the sweet tranquillity of the healthy Epicurean soul? Apparently Lucretius must hold that any human being who can be attracted by sweet poetry can also grasp the whole nature of things for himself.

For while the honeyed-cup simile evokes very powerfully the connection between the sick body and the ignorant soul, the ministering physician and the philanthropic philosopher, nevertheless the force of the simile must finally break down upon the reflection that while the body can be cured of disease by medicine whose operation it does not consciously perceive, and thus be "tricked" into health by the skillful physician, the soul does not seem able to be cured of ignorance by knowledge that it does not consciously perceive. If people could be duped into philosophic enlightenment without their own knowledge or their own effort, it would indeed be irrelevant how difficult the teaching is and how well or ill equipped any given human being is for learning it. But is it not, rather, likely that men will not become philosophers unless they come not only with desire but also with singular preparation, alertness, intelligence, and conscious resolve to the quest for the truth, however harsh? Men will never fully perceive the whole nature of things and fully feel the advantage merely by allowing Lucretius to hold their minds in his verses; the cure of men's debilitating ignorance requires in fact that they throw over everything else in order to devote themselves singlemindedly to learning the causes of things, and particularly the causes of their own illness (3.1055 ff.). Does Lucretius make a case for the ability of human beings to make the transition from being objects of a sweet deception to being autonomous agents of the quest for truth?

Cicero's charge that the Epicureans sought to address and transform the many certainly appears to be borne out by Lucretius' account of his own methods and intentions, and Vergil's rivalry with Lucretius as the poetic teacher of the many takes on a sharp meaning in this light. But we are still left with the questions what defense Lucretius has to offer against Cicero's charge of the political folly of propagating vulgar hedonism, and how Lucretius' expectation of transforming his audience is supported by his account of the human soul and especially of the relationship between reason and the passions. If Lucretius is proposing, against the opinion of all antiquity, that there is no essential difference between the few and the many, no natural obstacle to transforming the many into philosophers, the foundations of this view will have to appear in his account of human psychology. The issue is well defined with reference to Polybius' defense of Roman political religion:

> If it were possible to compose a polity of wise men, perhaps such a course would not be necessary; but since every multitude is lightminded and full of lawless desires, irrational anger, and violent spiritedness, the only way is to restrain the multitudes by means of invisible terrors and that sort of tragedy.
>
> (VI.56.10–11)

What Lucretius seems to suggest is that it *is* possible to compose a polity of wise men by making the multitude wise, and thus that political religion, so far from being the only way to restrain the harmful passions of the many, is a way inferior to the dissemination of philosophy or the fruits of philosophy.

According to Lucretius' account, the use of religion by political society to control the passions through invisible fears, while not entirely ineffectual (e.g., 5.1151–1157), is both harmful to men and unnecessary to society. The moderation of men's excessive passions is altogether necessary both for society and for the happiness of each man; but this necessity can be met more effectively by exposing the irrationality of invisible terrors than by cultivating their hold on men.[21] This is because fear of death, the invisible terror par excellence, is itself the root of the excessive passions. Political society, in using that fear to restrain the passions, is by that very use preserving the cause of those passions and of the need to restrain them, while also depriving its terrorized members of the possibility of living well. Lucretius' improvement on this scheme is, rather than first arming the passions with invisible terrors and then suppressing the armed passions with the same terrors, to disarm the passions altogether and thus eliminate once and for all the need to suppress them, thus preserving society while at the same time opening to every man the possibility of happiness.

Lucretius' account of the soul and the passions is set forth in Book 3. In the proem Lucretius shows how the most comprehensive philosophic vision demonstrates the nonexistence of Acheron (25–27), and in introducing the contents of the book he makes clear at the outset that knowledge of the truth about the human soul is tantamount to the expulsion of the invisible terror par excellence: "the nature of the *animus* and of the *anima* must be made clear by my verses, and the notorious fear of Acheron driven out headlong" (35–37). For men's fear of death is not a fear of death rightly understood but a fear of "Acheron," a fear of the punishment of immortal souls by angry gods. Thus, to relieve men of their fear of death is to correct their false opinion, to demonstrate to them first that souls are mortal and gods do not exist, or at any rate are not angry, and then that the mortality of mortals is not an injury to them.

Although men commonly claim not to fear death, in adversity this claim is shown to be idle boasting; in fact, fear of death is the root of men's unhappy delusions as expressed in the excesses of their passions. Avarice and the blind desire for honors, which compel miserable human beings to transgress the bounds of right (*iuris*) and sometimes to strive night and day with extreme effort, as partners and helpers in crimes, to rise up to the highest power— these wounds of life are fed not least by the fear of death (59–65). For wealth and honor seem to be the conditions of a sweet and secure life, and a sweet and secure life seems to be the only kind of life that is vibrant enough and robust enough to really feel like life, whereas being contemptible and poor is like being already, so to speak, at the gates of death (65–67). Thus it is that human beings, driven by their false terror, want to flee as far as possible from what they take to be the "gates of death," by amassing wealth and getting honor. In the pursuit of wealth, since they mistake this for the preservation of their own life, they will not hesitate to shed civil blood, rejoice cruelly at a brother's death, and hate and fear the table of their close kin; and as a result of that same fear they become racked with envy, seeing others powerful and respected and themselves in the dark slime; they perish for statues and a name (68–78). And often it reaches the point, from fear of death, where hatred of life itself so takes hold of human beings that they inflict death upon themselves, having forgotten that it is fear of this very thing that is the source of their troubles (79–82). Thus men violate shame, friendship, piety, fatherland and parents in their attempts to avoid the realms of Acheron (83–86).

The fear of death then is the source of men's avarice, political ambition, hatred, envy, and fear of other men. Just as men commit suicide because they have forgotten that fear of death is the source of their misery in life, so society sets about suppressing men's criminality by threatening them with death because it has forgotten that fear of death was the source of men's criminality. This threat would be unnecessary if it were possible to dispel men's fear of death in the first place, and Lucretius seems to claim that this is possible, since he in fact claims that it is necessary:

> hunc igitur terrorem animi tenebrasque necessest
> non radii solis neque lucida tela diei
> discutiant, sed naturae species ratioque.

> Therefore it is necessary that this terror of the mind be dispelled, not by the rays of the sun and the bright shafts of day, but by the aspect and rational account of nature.
>
> (3.91–93)

The rational account of nature shows that the passions have a natural basis that, although ineradicable, is nonetheless extremely limited and not dangerous; while the destructiveness and unlimitedness of men's passions as we know them is the unnecessary result of false opinions. The control of the passions requires then correcting men's false opinions, rather than terrorizing them by appealing to those same false opinions.[22]

The fundamental passions are anger and fear, and their natural basis lies in the elements of heat and wind (*calor, ventus*) that are two of the four fundamental components of the soul (of the other two, one is the nameless "soul of the soul," which has no visible manifestation, and the other is air, whose visible manifestation is tranquillity or placidity) (3.288–293). All souls are commingled of all four elements, but with some variations in the proportions. Souls with a lot of heat in them are visibly inclined to anger, and souls with a lot of wind are visibly inclined to fear; indeed, strictly speaking, anger *is* the visible manifestation of heat in the soul, and fear *is* the visible manifestation of wind in the soul. Thus men do not differ from beasts with respect to the manifestation in their visible passions of the components of their souls; and indeed Lucretius begins by giving as examples the lion for heat or anger, the deer for wind or fear, and the ox for air or placidity (294–306). The key difference between men and beasts is that in beasts a particular mix of soul-elements is a species characteristic, whereas in men this mix varies within the species: some men have a preponderance of heat, some of wind, some of air. This variability within the human species is the atomic substratum of men's need for and their difficulty in living together. Their need for living together seems to arise from the incompleteness of each man as a man: every lion is a complete instantiation of the lion kind, but the complete character of the human kind is not instantiated by any human being but only by mixed groups including the full range of human soul-types. On the other hand, while their natural differences make human beings dependent on each other for the realization of their humanity as such, these same differences make it peculiarly difficult for them to recognize each other as fellows. Thus, while the political life of men is both necessitated and made problematic by the varied composition of their souls, the happiness of each man is also complicated in a particular way by the degree to which a given soul-element preponderates in him: very angry or very fearful men have difficulty in achieving divine (philosophic) pleasure, and there is even such a thing as an excess of placidity.

> sic hominum genus est: quamvis doctrina politos
> constituat pariter quosdam, tamen illa relinquit
> naturae cuiusque animi vestigia prima.
> nec radicitus evelli mala posse putandumst,
> quin proclivius hic iras decurrat ad acris,
> ille metu citius paulo temptetur, at ille
> tertius accipiat quaedam clementius aequo.
> inde aliis rebus multis differre necessest
> naturas hominum varias moresque sequaces.

So [as of the beasts] is the race of human beings: to whatever extent *doctrina* may form certain ones equally polished, still it leaves those primary traces of the nature of each *animus*. Nor is it to be thought possible that the evils be torn out by the roots, so that it would not be the case that one would run more readily to harsh angers, another be assailed a little more quickly by fear, and a third accept certain things more mildly than is commensurate. And in many things it is necessary that the various natures of human beings and their consequent habits differ.

(3.307–315)

Lucretius cannot now explain all the hidden causes of these things, but he sees that in these matters there is one thing that he is able to affirm:

> usque adeo naturarum vestigia linqui
> parvola, quae nequeat ratio depellere nobis,
> ut nihil inpediat dignam dis degere vitam.

that only such tiny traces of the natures are left which *ratio* cannot drive out
of us, that nothing prevents us from living a life worthy of gods.

(3.320–322)

The differences among men relevant to their ability to lead lives worthy
of gods lie in the atomic substrata of their passions, not in their intellectual
abilities. Lucretius contrasts here the effect of *doctrina* with that of *ratio* in
moderating the different soul mixtures. Neither can eradicate the traces of
the natures—that is, the preponderances of one element over the others in
different men. What *doctrina* can do is to give equal polish to "certain ones";
what *ratio* can do is to make a life worthy of gods accessible to "us." The distinction therefore seems to be, as Bailey argues *ad loc.*, between *paideia* and
natural philosophy[23]: *paideia* affects certain ones, the rulers or the wealthy,
with a homogenizing polish, while *ratio* is able to make "us" like gods. "Us"
here, in concluding the section on the soul-mixtures of the human race
(307–322), apparently means "us human beings."[24] Lucretius does not explain the atomic basis of men's ability to reason. He does suggest that, while
the human race is varied in its soul mixtures, it has as a species characteristic the ability through reason to prevent its various soul mixtures from preventing any of its members from living a life worthy of gods. Lucretius does
not say whether certain other animals whose soul mixtures are not too extreme can also lead a life worthy of gods. However this may be, and whatever
the physiology of the rational faculty may be, we need to ask how, if anger is
heat and fear is wind, either of these passions could be moderated by reason
any more than the heat of the lion or the lightning bolt, or the wind of the
ox or the storm, can be moderated by reason.

The ability of men to moderate their fear and anger appears to have two
parts. One is the power of habituation:

> consuetudo concinnat amorem.
> nam leviter quamvis quod crebro tunditur ictu,
> vincitur in longo spatio tamen atque labascit.
> nonne vides etiam guttas in saxa cadentis
> umoris longo in spatio pertundere saxa?

> Habituation produces love. For no matter how lightly something is struck by con-
> stant blows, still over the long run it is overcome and crumbles. Don't you see that
> even drops of water falling onto rocks in the long run strike through the rocks?

(4.1284–1287)

This is presumably the mechanism used by *doctrina* in "polishing" some men,
and usable by anyone as a practice of reason: by a constant raining of light

blows, men are able to polish away most of their superfluous heat or wind. It is not entirely clear what matter men would use to wear away their heat or wind; perhaps they can direct the atoms of the images of divine pleasure that are motivating them in a gentle but unremitting stream so as to dislodge some of the atoms of their heat or wind over time.

Beyond this, though, is the massive fact that the excessive and destructive passions in men as we know them are not natural at all: the behaviors we call "fear" and "anger" in men are not, as in beasts, simply the visible manifestation of limited preponderances of wind and heat, but have accreted to them certain opinions, which give them their extravagant and indeed unlimited human form. Fear in men is actually wind plus the opinion that angry gods punish men's souls after death, and anger in men is actually heat plus the opinion that death is an indignity to men. Expectation of divine punishment and indignation at death, not natural elements but false opinions, are the causes why men's passions prevent them from living lives worthy of gods. The naturally limited and rationally refinable heat and wind themselves cannot prevent men living well, but the infinite imaginative constructions that human beings erect on these tiny foundations are the bane of their lives individually and in their communities. The whole vast array of men's avarice, ambition, envy, anger, fear, and love is constructed by men in their delusory and self-defeating efforts to escape *the* opinionated fear, fear of death as Acheron, *funditus humanam qui vitam turbat ab imo,* "which disorders human life from the foundations up" (3.38), and *the* opinionated anger, indignation at death (*indignatur se mortalem esse creatum,* "he is indignant that he has been created mortal," 3.884).[25] All of Book 3 in particular, and of the *De Rerum Natura* as a whole, may be said to be aimed at providing the *ratio* by which "we" may tear down the towering structure of our false opinions about death, the soul, and the gods, thus disarming our naturally limited passions and expelling all but such miniscule traces of the actual heat and wind in our souls as will not prevent us from living a life worthy of gods. Once the infinite imaginative excesses of passion have been expelled from "us" by reason, "we" will no longer be in need of religion or for that matter of government; as reason will replace the fear of divine punishment in our souls, so friendship will replace justice in our cities.

That Cicero was correct in characterizing Epicureanism as a doctrine addressed to the multitude with practical designs against the Roman order is borne out by the aspects of Lucretius' poem that have been traced here. The sweet poetic images of heroism and divinity with which Lucretius honeys the cup of his teaching are avowedly aimed at motivating the *vulgus* to seek the bitter truth about heroism and divinity. The popular accessibility of the

Lucretian honey is aimed at counteracting in practice the practical causes of religion among the vulgar. And Lucretius' theoretical account of the relationship between reason and the passions in human beings indicates that there is no natural obstacle to the enlightenment of the many—that the human passions as we know them have been constructed from false opinions, that the falseness of these opinions is demonstrable in popular poetry, and that this demonstration is sufficient to disarm those passions in human beings as such.

On the other hand, the whole conception of Lucretius' poem acknowledges at least that there is now an *actual* difference between the few and the many, in that the few are pleasurably healthy and the many are painfully sick, and one has to ask finally whether Lucretius' philanthropic enterprise of curing the many does not, after all, accept and perpetuate the fundamental difference of the many in the following way. The pleasurably healthy Epicurean philosopher is in the first place a philosopher, and as a philosopher he does not base his thought on any authority. While he may, perhaps must, be drawn to or inspired by a teacher, as Lucretius himself has been drawn to and inspired by Epicurus, in the end he will not accept any of the teaching of his teacher unless he has acquired it for himself through his own reasoning from the first principles of things, as Lucretius himself has done. The non-philosophers, on the other hand, take their bearings by authority, and especially by the authority of poets. Lucretius in his poem offers to the multitude the results or conclusions of his own philosophizing, avowedly in a form ("honey"), which should, on the one hand, be immediately accessible as a comfort and relief to wretched mortals and which should, on the other hand, ultimately motivate them to philosophize for themselves, as is made possible by the sufficiency of reason in human beings as such. Lucretius' intention that his pupils outgrow his authority is clearly stated in the honeyed-cup simile itself ("until you fully perceive the whole nature of things") and is promoted by the direction of the poem as a whole, from the most prominent friendly presence of Lucretius' own voice in the earliest and sweetest parts of the poem to his finally complete removal of himself and his own voice from the bitter ending of the poem.[26] The poem is so constructed that its philosophic reader, looking about himself at the end for the author's familiar support and finding himself utterly alone, thereby also finds that he is standing, if shakily, on his own feet, and from here on will begin to traverse the boundless All in mind and spirit for himself. But while Lucretius' poem is so constructed as to promote this outcome, it is also so constructed as to allow another: the pupil may find he is unwilling to be left on his own, and instead of stepping out of the book on his own feet will return to the honeyed part of it (perhaps with the argument that this is what Lucretius would have recommended if he had been able to put the finishing touches to the poem), thus becoming not a philosopher but a Lucretian. So finally, since his poem allows for either outcome, we must ask whether in Lucretius' opinion the universal acceptance of the results of his philosophizing on the authority of his poem, as opposed to universal philosophizing, would be a clear benefit for men and societies. If, according to his argument, it would be, then Lucretius' instruction of Memmius could be seen as the founding of a universal order emanating from a poet-philosopher and propagated by a converted non-philosopher, like the founding of Carthage in Vergil's *Aeneid*.

Since the twofold cause of religion is false interpretation of images and ignorance of the causes of celestial phenomena, the complete cure of men's false opinions would require a complete understanding of nature from its first principles, so as to replace the false interpretation of images with the true one and ignorance of the causes of celestial phenomena with knowledge of their causes; this would be "fully perceiving the whole nature of things." But the therapeutic benefit of philosophy to human beings need not wait for men's full understanding. A man who has hitherto believed that gods are the providential causes and rulers of the phenomena of the world is already benefitted by the doctrine that the world is too defective to be thought controlled by superior beings, even if he is still completely unaware of what *does* cause these phenomena (2.177–182). A man who has hitherto believed that angry gods will punish him for his offenses, or require sacrifices from him, is already benefitted by the doctrine that the gods' self-sufficiency makes them inaccessible either to being won over by our services to them or touched by anger at us, even if he has not yet learned that there are no gods (1.44–49). A man who has hitherto believed that the Homeric heroes are the supreme exemplars of human greatness is already benefitted by the doctrine that Epicurus' contemplative life far surpassed their active lives in immortal glory, even if he has not yet learned that glory cannot be immortal because the world itself is mortal (3.13, 6.8). A man who has hitherto believed that the venerable ancient poets taught that the earth is a great goddess and that the dead are wretched forever in the house of Hades is already benefitted by believing that those poets were symbolically teaching that the earth is the inert source of living things and that the unenlightened are wretched now in this life, even if he has not yet learned that the ancient poets were simply ignorant of the nature of things and in error about the earth and the afterlife (2.598–645, 3.978–1023).

The benefits that accrue to men from what we may call these provisional or partial doctrines are of two kinds. First, every step in this provisional education makes it more likely that the pupil will ultimately be prepared for philosophizing: every weakening of traditional, superstitious, Homeric beliefs helps to clear the way for the possibility of replacing them with true knowledge of causes, and helps to produce desire and emulation of the philosophic life. This is a benefit whose existence cannot be demonstrated until its end has been reached: only in the case of one who has actually become a philosopher can one say that his provisional opinions were tending toward this end; until the end is reached, he is simply replacing one authoritative opinion (say, Homer's) with another (Lucretius'). Second, however, there is a real benefit in happiness to men at any intermediate stage between the most benighted superstition and philosophy itself, and this is the psychological benefit of increasing freedom from the fear of divine punishment and thus from the fear of death, *the* illness of the human soul. The relief gained by a soul that is freed to some extent from the fear of eternal torment is a substantial benefit in happiness even to a man who has otherwise the most childish or mistaken notions of the whole nature of things.

The apparently absurd suggestion of the honeyed-cup simile that men could be tricked by art into philosophic enlightenment points to the second kind of benefit that does in fact arise from the provisional, authoritative doctrines: men *can* be tricked by art into psychologically useful opinions, opinions that free them from some of the obsessive terror in their souls and thus to some extent cure them and make happiness possible to them. Such healing is a trick of art in that the provisional opinions are artificially introduced into and the authoritative opinions artificially maintained in men's souls without having there any true foundation in first principles. It may be that Lucretius' cure is complete or perfect only for those who finally leave everything else aside and devote themselves to coming to know the nature of things (3.1071–1072), so that in them the provisional or authoritative opinions are replaced by knowledge of causes; but the benefit of even a partial cure is very great and universally accessible, and the honey of Lucretius' poem promotes the realization of that universality by making available to human beings the benefit of the provisional teaching along with the benefit of guidance towards actual philosophizing. The greatest benefit to the human race, which Lucretius poetically ascribes to the god he calls Venus at the opening of the *De Rerum Natura*, turns out to be *the* work of Lucretius, who on this account must surely be called a god (5.8):

nam tu sola potes tranquilla pace iuvare
mortalis.

for you alone are able to benefit mortals with tranquil peace.

(1.31–32)

CHAPTER SIX

Furor

Like Lucretius in the *De Rerum Natura*, Vergil proposes in the *Aeneid* to re-place Homer as the poetic teacher of the best life for men. Whereas Lucretius presents Epicurus as a hero whose intellectual exploits far surpass the com-bined warring and voyaging exploits of Achilles and Odysseus, Vergil pre-sents Aeneas as a hero whose deeds include and transcend those of the two Homeric heroes. In this way Vergil's Aeneas becomes the rival of Lucretius' Epicurus: Lucretius was correct in rejecting the Homeric heroes as models for men's emulation, but incorrect in replacing them with the philosopher; not the philosopher but the pious founder is the proper model of the praisewor-thy man. Lucretius is correct in rejecting the Homeric heroes because he is correct in rejecting Homer's account of the nature of things: there are no powerful gods who help or harm men, there is no afterlife in the house of Hades, there is no deathless world in which a man's glory could be immortal, and there is no love that is not founded on a delusion; thus the aspirations and achievements of both Achilles and Odysseus stand condemned as false models of the best life.

However, it does not follow from the truth of Lucretius' physics that men's happiness lies in the direction of emulating the physiologist[1]; for Lucretius did not adequately reckon with *human* nature. In particular, Lucretius was fundamentally mistaken in believing that the true teachings of Epicurus are universally or even widely beneficial to men, that Epicurus' victory makes "us" the "equals of heaven." His error is twofold: first, "we" do not have the indispensable qualification—sufficiently warm blood around our hearts[2]—to philosophize for ourselves, so the path from traditional belief to science is one "we" can follow only to some intermediate point where we still depend on the authority of another; second, "we" are harmed rather than helped by such an incomplete or provisional journey that removes us from traditional religion without bringing us all the way to the goal of science. Our traditional Homeric beliefs are both untrue and injurious to us; but what benefits us is not enchantment with science, which we cannot attain, but enchantment with true rather than Homeric piety. The philosophic life is best in itself, but emulation of what is best in itself is harmful to beings whose nature is inadequate to that goal—it could lead only to deformity, self-loathing, and madness. According to Vergil it is not true, as Lucretius taught, that men are benefitted by losing their fear of angry gods and eternal torment without understanding for themselves from first principles the causes why such fear is unjustified, or the whole nature of things. The reason they are not benefitted is that their fear of gods and punishment is the only thing that enables them to govern themselves, to govern the irruptions of anger, cruelty, and hatred that seem to spring up spontaneously in their souls. The infernal passions needing government are real; while the gods and punishments feared by the unenlightened are illusory, the fear of them is itself real and efficacious. A true understanding of the whole nature of things could tame the infernal passions by rationally disarming all illusory desires; but a mere debunking of the gods and the afterlife must remove the only check on the infernal passions that men have, short of true science. Lucretius underestimated both the extent of the natural basis of the passions and the imperviousness of the passions to the reasonings of men who are not philosophers themselves. According to Vergil's myth, men who are not philosophers and are not governed by fear of gods are not governed by anything; what reveals the defect of such men, and is itself revealed by that defect, is an unquenchable demonic fury that leaps out wherever there is a breach in piety.

The centrality to the *Aeneid* of the problem of fury[3]—its source and its government, and especially its connection to the gods—is announced in the proem together with the piety of its hero: "Is there such anger in celestial spirits?" (1.11). The first action of the *Aeneid*, Juno's visit to Aeolia, begins to unfold the thematic problem of the source and government of anger while presenting the ruling symbol of the *Aeneid*, the cave of Furor.

i. Juno's Visit to Aeolia (1.34–86)

The first direct speech in the *Aeneid* is Juno's speech to herself, a speech arising from an irritation of the eternal wound she keeps deep beneath her heart:

Vix e conspectu Siculae telluris in altum
vela dabant laeti et spumas salis aere ruebant,
cum Iuno aeternum servans sub pectore vulnus
haec secum: . . .

Barely out of sight of Sicily and onto the high seas, the Trojans were joyfully giving sail and bearing down on the spume of the salt sea with the bronze, when
Juno, keeping the eternal wound deep beneath her heart, said to herself: . . .

(1.34–37)

The passion alluded to in this "wound" is the anger whose causes are the
theme of the Aeneid. Like the wound of love to which Lucretius refers in his
invocation to Venus, praying that Mars may succumb to it (aeterno devictus
vulnere amoris, DRN 1.34), Juno's wound is "eternal," but although it is related to love (18, 24), it is first and foremost the wound of anger.[4] Like Lucretius' assertion of the eternity of the wound of love, Vergil's assertion of the
eternity of the wound of anger forces us to wonder about "eternity," for Juno
herself was born, as she reminds us in this first speech (46–47); either she suffers from a "wound" that somehow eternally preexisted her, to which she became subject by virtue of being born, or "eternal" here means only "deathless." Thus at the outset we do not know whether the causes of Juno's anger
indicated at 1.12–19 are first or second causes: either the Trojan War and the
fates of Troy wounded Juno with an undying wound, or Juno was born with
an eternal wound deep beneath her heart, and the Trojan War and the fates
of Troy became irritations of that wound or occasions of her anger. However
this may be, if Juno's wound is in any case deathless, Jupiter's prophecy that
Juno will ultimately "turn her counsels towards the better" (1.279–282) cannot mean that her wound will be healed; and indeed when Juno does turn
her counsels towards the better at the end of the poem (12.841), she does so
while showing her kinship to Saturn and Jupiter by the floods of anger she
still revolves deep in her heart (12.830–831).

According to Vergil's account in the proem, Juno's anger seems to arise
from fear (23) and envy or resentment at dishonor (27–28). In her own first
speech, Juno emphasizes the elements of envy: in comparing her own power
with that of Pallas she sees that she is not omnipotent and therefore feels impotent and subject to dishonor:

'mene incepto desistere victam
nec posse Italia Teucrorum avertere regem?
quippe vetor fatis. Pallasne exurere classem
Argivum atque ipsos potuit summergere ponto

unius ob noxam et furias Aiacis Oilei?
ipsa Iovis rapidum iaculata e nubibus ignem
disiecitque rates evertitque aequora ventis,
illum exspirantem transfixo pectore flammas
turbine corripuit scopuloque infixit acuto;
ast ego, quae divum incedo regina Iovisque
et soror et coniunx, una cum gente tot annos
bella gero. et quisquam numen Iunonis adorat
praeterea aut supplex aris imponet honorem?'

Am I to give up my undertaking in defeat, and be unable to turn the king of
the Teucrians away from Italy? To be sure, I am prohibited by the fates. Was
Pallas able to burn down the fleet and submerge the men themselves in the sea,
all for the crime and furies of Oilean Ajax? She herself hurled from the clouds
the swift fire of Jupiter, dashed apart the ships and turned up the sea with
winds; as he breathed flames from his transfixed heart she seized him up in a
whirlwind and impaled him on a sharp cliff—but I, I who walk as queen of the
gods and both sister and wife of Jupiter, I wage war so many years with one nation. Does anyone any longer pray to the divinity of Juno, or will anyone give
honor to her altars as a suppliant?

(1.37–49)

According to Lucretius, the spirited or angry desire for honors is one of the
"wounds of life" that are kept alive by the fundamental fear of death or
Acheron (3.59–64; cf. above, pp. 69–70). But according to Vergil's myth as
it begins to unfold here, the desire for honors cannot be dependent on the
fear of death but must be itself something fundamental, since it is revealed
in the eternal wound of the deathless goddess. If the immortal gods suffer
the passion of desire for victory, vengeance, adoration and honor, it is not
likely that human ambition and anger depend on a false fear of death, but
rather that they depend on the same eternal wound from which the goddess suffers.

As the instrument of her anger against the Trojans, Juno would best like
to send down the Jovian thunderbolt from the clouds as Pallas did, but
failing that, she will settle for sending up the savage winds from the cave
of Aeolus; as she puts it in the close parallel to this scene in Book 7,
flectere si nequeo superos, Acheronta movebo, "If I cannot bend the heavenly
ones, I shall stir up the infernal things" (7.312).

Talia flammato secum dea corde volutans
nimborum in patriam, loca feta furentibus Austris,
Aeoliam venit.

Turning over such things with herself in her inflamed heart, the goddess came to the fatherland of storms, the places pregnant with raging winds, Aeolia.

(1.50–52)

Jupiter has confined the angry winds in caves and made Aeolus their king to suppress or unleash them at Jupiter's command, in accordance with his celestial intentions; if not for this arrangement, the winds would sweep away the seas, the lands, and the deep heaven. In fact it was for fear of this event that Jupiter, the omnipotent father, suppressed the winds and subjected them to rule (52–63). As Vergil's introduction of Juno had emphasized the connection of her immortality to her envy or ambition, so this introduction of Jupiter emphasizes the connection of his omnipotence to his fear of the utter dissolution of the cosmos: the ground of the passions is not, or not only, human mortality and weakness.

In this first action of the *Aeneid*, Juno strives for omnipotence by attempting to emancipate the raging winds from their celestial government, to make them infernal extensions of the eternal fury that she nourishes in her own heart and by which she in turn is ruled. Thus begins the unfolding of Vergil's thematic question: is there such anger in celestial spirits? (1.11). Is the rule of the celestial subverted by the rule of the infernal? Are the gods anarchically angry? Juno, who wishes to be adored by suppliants in acknowledgment of her power, pursues this end by herself adoring Aeolus as a suppliant (1.64), acknowledging in speech his powers and their source in the omnipotent Jupiter while simultaneously subverting in deed the very line of command she acknowledges:

'Aeole, namque tibi divum pater atque hominum rex
et mulcere dedit fluctus et tollere vento,
gens inimica mihi Tyrrhenum navigat aequor
Ilium in Italiam portans victosque penatis:
incute vim ventis summersasque obrue puppis,
aut age diversos et disice corpora ponto.
sunt mihi bis septem praestanti corpore Nymphae,
quarum quae forma pucherrima, Deiopea,
conubio iungam stabili propriamque dicabo,
omnis ut tecum meritis pro talibus annos
exigat et pulchra faciat te prole parentem.'

Aeolus—for to you the father of gods and king of men has granted both to soothe the floods and to raise them with wind—a people hostile to me is sailing the Tyrrhenian Sea, bringing Troy and its conquered *penates* to Italy: strike up violence with winds and sink and drown the ships, or drive the men apart and scatter their bodies on the sea. I have twice seven Nymphs of excellent body; of these the one most beautiful in form, Deiopea, I shall join in lasting marriage and declare your own, so that, in recompense for your deserts, she may spend all her years with you and make you the parent of beautiful offspring.

(1.65–75)

Juno considers the Trojan people her enemy because she was injured by the judgment of Paris, the spurning of her beautiful form (1.27–28); here she herself has the beautiful forms of goddesses at her disposal, bribing Aeolus with the most beautiful Nymph as Paris had been bribed with the most beautiful woman. Aeolus grants Juno's request while being entirely silent about her bribe and appearing to correct her view of her own powers:

> 'tuus, o regina, quid optes
> explorare labor; mihi iussa capessere fas est.
> tu mihi quodcumque hoc regni, tu sceptra Iovemque
> concilias, tu das epulis accumbere divum
> nimborumque facis tempestatumque potentem.'

> Your task, o queen, is to ascertain what it is that you wish; for me the right thing (*fas*) is to execute your commands. You are the one who wins over for me this kingship, such as it is, you win over the sceptre and Jupiter, you allow me to recline at the meals of the gods, and you give me power over storms and tempests.

(1.76–80)

He does not refer to Deiopea but claims that he will do Juno's bidding because he is subject to her commands and because he is grateful to her for his own powers; he speaks as if Juno has at her disposal the favors not of Nymphs but of Jupiter himself. Thus it is that in the first action of the *Aeneid* Aeolus releases the winds that shipwreck Aeneas on the North African shore (81–123), and that are finally restored to order not by Jupiter, who indeed appears oblivious to the near-realization of the fear that had caused him to put the winds under rule in the first place, but by Neptune, who restores the winds to their cave and the sea to its calm, just as a man grave with piety restores order when sedition has arisen in a great people (124–156).

As the proem to the *Aeneid* has indicated that Vergil will rival Homer by including or unifying the *Iliad* and the *Odyssey* in one, so this first action of the *Aeneid*, Juno's visit to Aeolia, is so constructed as to include or unify Hera's beguiling of Zeus in the *Iliad* (14.153–351) and Odysseus' visit to Aeolia in the *Odyssey* (10.1–79). But as the scene begins from Vergil's rivalry with Homer, so it leads to his rivalry with Lucretius:[5] Vergil corrects Homer in the light of the nature of things as found out by Lucretius, and corrects Lucretius in the light of human nature as found out by Vergil.

In *Iliad* 14.153 ff. Hera, in order to distract Zeus from Poseidon's activities in favor of the Achaeans, persuades Hypnos to put Zeus to sleep by bribing him with the promise of the nymph Pasithea. Hera acts with the explicit intention of undermining the government of Zeus, who has decreed that the gods not intervene in the war so long as he is fulfilling his promise to Thetis, his promise to give Achilles glory by allowing the Trojans to prevail during Achilles' absence from the fighting. Hypnos is reluctant to grant Hera's request; although she addresses him flatteringly as "king of all gods and men" (233), he knows he does not rule Zeus but is subject to Zeus' commands and, in particular, to Zeus' punishments (247f.). Hypnos explains his reluctance by reminding Hera of his experience of Zeus' anger the last time Hypnos had beguiled Zeus at Hera's request, the time when Hera used Zeus' sleep to shipwreck Heracles' crew and send Heracles himself off course to Cos, after Heracles' sack of Troy (249–258). Zeus had refrained from punishing Hypnos that time because Hypnos had taken refuge with Night, who has power over "gods and men" (258–261); but that experience of Zeus' anger, even Zeus' frustrated anger, has made Hypnos wary of acting against, or without, Zeus' direct orders (248). Thus Hypnos is not accessible to Hera's flattering suggestion that he is "king of all gods and men" in the sense of being superior to Zeus; but he is accessible to the bribe with which Hera then attempts to persuade him:

> Come now, do it, and I will give you one of the younger
> Graces for you to marry, and she shall be called your lady;
> Pasithea, since all your days you have loved her forever.
>
> (14.267–269, trans. Lattimore)

It is the promise of Pasithea that makes Hypnos willing to brave Zeus' anger; after insisting that Hera swear to this promise, he carries out her request (270–280, 352–360).

From this *Iliad* scene Vergil has borrowed Juno's idea of bribing Aeolus with the nymph Deiopea to shipwreck the Trojans by unleashing the winds against them. Aeolus himself, however, is borrowed from *Odyssey* 10.1–79, where he is a mortal king, beloved by the immortal gods, whom Zeus has set "in charge over / the winds, to hold them still or start them up at his pleasure" (10.21–22, Lattimore). Zeus' reason for giving Aeolus charge of the winds is not mentioned; presumably it is because he is "dear to the immortal gods" (10.2). Aeolus' power to still and rouse the winds is a power over fair and foul navigation: he gives Odysseus fair sailing by letting the West Wind free and tying up the other winds in a bag.

In unifying the Iliadic beguiling of Zeus and the Odyssean visit to Aeolia, Vergil follows an internal connection between the two scenes that is already present in Homer: the storm winds that throw both Heracles' and Odysseus' navigation off course, and that Vergil's Juno raises for the specific purpose of ruining Aeneas' navigation. Vergil, however, has further unified the two scenes by extending from the Hypnos narrative to the Aeolus narrative the problematic character of the divine government, or the question who really rules the gods and the world. Vergil's Aeolus is not, like Homer's Aeolus, a lucky mortal given free rule over the winds, but, like Homer's Hypnos, a subordinate god governing a subordinate portion of the world under a higher authority presumed to be Jupiter's. As Homer's entire conception of the beguiling of Zeus calls Zeus's authority into question, the fickleness of Vergil's Aeolus expresses disobedience to the rule of Jupiter, and the question whether it is not Juno rather than Jupiter who has the greatest authority.[6] Vergil's Aeolus owed allegiance, according to the poet's account of things, to Jupiter, who gave him conditional authority over the winds (1.62–63); but he accedes with striking eagerness to Juno's request, and not for gain like Hypnos but apparently from a preference for obeying Juno's commands over obeying Jupiter's commands. Thus Vergil, in unifying the scenes from Homer's two poems, radically changes the meaning of the Homeric Aeolus' fickleness from lucky freedom to a sinister question about the government of the world: how can Jupiter be the "omnipotent father" if he fears, apparently with reason, the dissolution of the world, and has appointed as viceroy, to prevent the realization of his fear, a god who is not loyal to him? What is the status of Jupiter's celestial government of the world if his commands are prevented with ease by the machinations of Juno in her infernal anger? The celestial Jupiter is said to rule the cave of the winds, but the infernal anger that rules Juno appears to have the greater force or authority.

Vergil's account of Juno's visit to Aeolia is constructed then in such a way as to unify Homer's Iliadic and Odyssean scenes while bringing to the fore the question how the world is ruled. Beyond this, though, Vergil has constructed this scene so as to correct the unified Homeric myth in two chief ways. First, Vergil has revised Homer's mythical account of the source of the winds; and second, he has corrected Homer's mythical account of the specific power of the winds so as to take into account Lucretius' doctrine of the mortality of the world.

In the *Odyssey*, the home of the winds is the floating island of Aeolia, and Aeolus' method of stilling the winds is to stuff them into ox-hide bags (10.19–20). In the *Aeneid*, the home of the winds is the cave of Aeolia, and Aeolus' method of stilling the winds is to lord it over them in their imprisonment there:

> . . . nimborum in patriam, loca feta furentibus Austris,
> Aeoliam venit. hic vasto rex Aeolus antro
> luctantis ventos tempestatesque sonoras
> imperio premit ac vinclis et carcere frenat.
> illi indignantes magno cum murmure montis
> circum claustra fremunt; celsa sedet Aeolus arce
> sceptra tenens mollitque animos et temperat iras.

> . . . the fatherland of storms, the places pregnant with raging winds, Aeolia. Here in a vast cave King Aeolus restrains the struggling winds and sounding storms with *imperium*, and reins them in with chains and prison. They roar indignantly with a great growl around the bolts of the mountain; Aeolus sits on the lofty citadel holding the sceptre, and calms their spirits and tempers their angers.

> (1.51–57)

Vergil has thus corrected Homer's island myth by replacing it with a myth based on Lucretius' account of the natural history of storms in Book 6 of the *De Rerum Natura*.[7] According to Lucretius, the storm winds are air heated under the pressure of containment in clouds. In his explanation, Lucretius poetically compares the wind-containing clouds to caves in which wild beasts are confined:

> Contemplator enim, cum montibus adsimulata
> nubila portabunt venti transversa per auras,
> aut ubi per magnos montis cumulata videbis
> insuper esse aliis alia atque urgere superne
> in statione locata sepultis undique ventis:
> tum poteris magnas moles cognoscere eorum
> speluncasque velut saxis pendentibus structas
> cernere, quas venti cum tempestate coorta
> conplerunt, magno indignantur murmure clausi
> nubibus, in caveisque ferarum more minantur.
> nunc hinc nunc illinc fremitus per nubila mittunt,
> quaerentesque viam circum versantur, et ignis
> semina convolvunt e nubibus atque ita cogunt
> multa, rotantque cavis flammam fornacibus intus,
> donec divolsa fulserunt nube corusci.

Contemplate, when the winds carry mountainlike clouds through the breezes, or when you see the clouds heaped up one above another along great mountains, pushing down from above and fixed in place, when the winds are buried all around; then you will be able to come to know their great masses, and to discern their caves built up, as it were, from hanging rocks; when a storm has arisen, the winds fill these caves and, shut up within the clouds, show their indignation with a great growl and threaten like wild beasts within the caverns. First from one side, then from another, they emit roars through the clouds and turn round and round, seeking an exit; and they roll together the seeds of fire from the clouds and thus force many of them out, and they whirl up flame within the hollow furnaces until the cloud is rent apart and they flash out blazing.

(6.189–203)

Vergil refers us to Lucretius here not only through the general conception of the natural source of storm winds and the imagery of caves and caged wild beasts, but also and emphatically through his Lucretian language.[8] Lucretius' account of the winds here forms part of his discussion of the causes of lightning (6.160–218); his argument is that winds in clouds become heated under great pressure until they ignite and force their way out of the clouds. His immediate purpose in poetically comparing (*adsimulata* 189, *velut* 195, *more* 198) the clouds to caves and the winds to wild beasts seems to be to make present to the imagination both the unapparent solidity of clouds as chambers or containers and the unapparent heatedness of the winds (6.127, 176–179). But the ultimate purpose of this entire account of the celestial phenomena is to demonstrate reliably, in a way that will be deeply and not just superficially persuasive to men, that these phenomena are not caused by gods. Men's belief in powerful and angry gods having been traced to faulty interpretation of images on the one hand and ignorance of the causes of celestial phenomena on the other (5.1161–1193), and the correct interpretation of images having been set forth in Book 4, it remains for Lucretius to replace men's ignorance with knowledge of the causes of celestial phenomena, a task he has begun in Book 5 (509–771) and completes in Book 6. The supreme importance of this account of the causes of these phenomena in Lucretius' therapy of souls is indicated by Lucretius' statement that even men who have learned well the true interpretation of the images of gods are still liable to be "brought back into the ancient religions" if they wonder how things happen, especially things in the heavens (6.58–67): "Ignorance of causes compels them to attribute things to the *imperium* of gods and to concede kingship to them" (6.54–55). Thus the account of the causes of celestial phenomena is the most true reasoning, *ratio verissima* (6.80), since it is the ultimate defense against men's danger of losing the benefit of all the rest of the *vera ratio*. Since thunderstorms are the celestial phenomena most likely to suggest imaginatively the existence of angry punishing gods, it is most important that precisely these thunderstorms be explained with sufficient liveliness, vividness, concreteness, sharpness, to displace the very old and powerful imaginations of gods. Thus in the imagery of his explanation of the storm winds, Lucretius appeals to his readers' experience of the hot fury of caged living beings while keeping as far as possible from any suggestion of divine purpose toward men or towards the world.

Lucretius' comparison of the winds to angry wild beasts is based upon his earlier analysis of the anger of living beings as the natural effect of a preponderance of heat in their souls (3.288 ff.). Anger itself *is* atomic heat; the anger of lions and of men is a kind of explosion or boiling out of a hot fluid from within their breasts. The physiology of anger in living beings—men and beasts—is thus analogous to the physiology of lightning.[9] Men's imagination that the lightning is the expression of a god's anger has all too compelling a foundation: the lightning *is* the same thing that we call anger when we experience it in ourselves or sympathize with it in the brutes. But the correct interpretation of this sameness is not that the heavens are angry as we are, but that we are hot as the heavens are.

Anger in beasts and storm clouds is irremediable; but in men, though anger cannot be eradicated, it can be so moderated that nothing prevents us from living a life worthy of gods (3.319–322). In lions and storm clouds the building up and release of the natural pressure of *ira* follows a natural cycle, but in men this pressure has become attached to indignant opinions that prevent it from being naturally discharged, and especially to the opinion that death is an injury to a human being. Men's vain desires for wealth, power, and love, which they get not from their own senses but from listening to what other people say (5.1132–1134), arise from their indignation at death and become exacerbated by increasing indignation at other men who are in competition with them for the scarce objects of these desires—which they, too, mistakenly believe to be defenses against death or at least against the awareness of mortality; thus men's anger becomes directed at other men whom they wish to overcome, and on whom they wish to take vengeance for their attempts to overcome in turn. The moderation of human anger by reason would seem, then, to be attainable through men's separating out their indignation from their internal heat or anger, and dissipating their indignation by learning that death is not an indignity to them: this is the reasoning that, while it cannot eradicate those traces of anger that arise from the heat in the soul, can nevertheless so moderate men's anger, by removing indignation from it, that nothing prevents them from living a life worthy of gods.

It is therefore very striking that in Lucretius' comparison of the storm winds to wild beasts he describes them as "indignant" (6.197). He seems to begin here from the false opinion of the unenlightened reader that the loud noises heard in the heavens express the indignation of gods against men. This indignation of gods is the core of the thoughts unworthy of gods (*dis indigna*, 6.69) that Lucretius, in Book 6, aims to remove by reason, in order that his reader may not continue to be harmed by the supposition that great waves of anger set the peaceful gods to storming (6.73–74). The image of the storm winds imprisoned in the cloud caves moves from the appearance of indignation to the reality of atomic motion or heat, as the reader's understanding of the heavenly disturbances is to move in Book 6 as a whole from the opinion unworthy of the gods, that the indignant-sounding noises of the heavens signal the anger of the gods, to the true account—indeed the truest account, *ratio verissima* (6.80)—of storms and thunderbolts.

Vergil's Aeolia refers not to Homer's account of the winds, in which they are tame enough to be controlled by being stuffed into an ox-hide bag, but to Lucretius' account of the winds. From the caves to which Lucretius compares the wind-containing clouds, Vergil has constructed his mythical cave-home of the clouds;[10] from the wild beasts to which Lucretius compares the roaring winds, Vergil has constructed his mythical winds as violently angry living beings (struggling, indignant, growling, having spirits and anger). Vergil's reference to Lucretius appears at first to borrow the strictly poetic elements of Lucretius' argument—the caves and wild beasts to which Lucretius compares the clouds and winds—while ignoring or even rejecting the truest meaning of that truest argument. For Lucretius' analysis of storms is meant to free men from the abject fears that arise from their ignorance by showing that no gods have kingship or *imperium* over these things (6.48–55); but according to Vergil's myth, the winds are ruled by Aeolus as their king (*regem*, 1.62), controlling them with *imperium* (1.54) under the higher authority of omnipotent Jupiter (60). Lucretius promptly analyzes the apparent indignation of the wind beasts into its real physiologic elements; but in Vergil's imitation their indignation is real enough: their imprisonment in caves is not natural but is imposed on them by their ruler, without apparent care for their own good, by a combination of forcible constraint and scepter-wielding softening of their spirits (1.54, 57). When Lucretius' winds sometimes become trapped in clouds it is by a natural necessity; there is no trapping agent who has thereby injured or wronged them. But Aeolus' government of the winds does violence to the nature of the winds: they are truly like caged animals whose captor has deprived them of their natural liberty. The indignation of Vergil's winds is in protest against

their oppression under the regime of Aeolus and Jupiter. What is the omnipotent father's reason for this oppression?

In the *Odyssey*, the power to still and arouse the winds, which Zeus has
given to Aeolus, is a power over fair and foul navigation. But in Vergil, Aeolus' power over the winds is the power to preserve or destroy the world. In
Vergil's myth, the reason why Jupiter has put Aeolus in charge of the winds
is that Jupiter fears the sweeping away of the world of ocean, earth, and
heaven that would occur if the winds' fury were not forcibly pent up:

> ni faciat, maria ac terras caelumque profundum
> quippe ferant rapidi secum verrantque per auras.
> sed pater omnipotens speluncis abdidit atris
> hoc metuens molemque et montis insuper altos
> imposuit, regemque dedit qui foedere certo
> et premere et laxas sciret dare iussus habenas.

> Should he not do so, they would certainly in their rushing carry off with them
> seas and lands and lofty heaven, and sweep them away through the breezes. But
> the omnipotent father, fearing just this, hid them away in black caves, and put
> on top of them a great mass and high mountains, and gave them a king who
> should know how, by fixed rule, to check them and give them free rein when
> so ordered.

> (1.58–63)

According to Vergil's myth, then, the oppression of the winds under Jupiter's
regime is for the sake of the continued existence of the world. Without Aeolus' government, the world would be swept into oblivion: sea, land, and sky
would vanish. The winds' indignation is therefore unjustified, if the existence
of the world is necessary or even desirable to the activity of the winds; like
men's indignation at their mortality, so the winds' indignation at their government is based on a false notion of their own good. The world is the ordered
world of sea, land, and sky; the nature of the winds is to disorder the world;
but if the winds' nature were not restrained, they would destroy the world
once for all and have no world to disorder in accordance with their nature.

Just as Vergil's mythical "cave" of the winds is drawn not from Homer but
from Lucretius, so this account of the power of the winds—the power to undo
the world—is drawn not from Homer but from Lucretius. The first impression that Vergil, in his account of the winds, adopts the poetic trappings of
Lucretius' account while ignoring the truest meaning of that account must
therefore be reconsidered. For the truest meaning of Lucretius' account may
be said to be that the world—this ordered world of sea, land, and sky—is
mortal; Lucretius' teaching that no gods govern the world with kingship and

imperium means that nothing has both the will and the power to prevent the natural death of the world:

> principio maria ac terras caelumque tuere;
> quorum naturam triplicem, tria corpora, Memmi,
> tris species tam dissimilis, tria talia texta,
> una dies dabit exitio, multosque per annos
> sustentata ruet moles et machina mundi.

First, observe the seas and the lands and the heaven, whose threefold nature—three bodies, Memmius, three so dissimilar forms, three textures each of its own kind—one single day will give over to destruction, and the mass and mechanism of the world, sustained through so many years, will fall to ruin.

(5.92–96)

Earlier, in persuading Memmius of the existence of invisible bodies, Lucretius had appealed to the example of the winds in a passage that alludes to, though it does not yet state explicitly, the eventual collapse of the tripartite world:

> sunt igitur venti nimirum corpora caeca
> quae mare, quae terras, quae denique nubila caeli
> verrunt ac subito vexantia turbine raptant.

Thus there are undoubtedly invisible corpuscles of wind, which sweep the sea, and the lands, and finally the clouds of heaven, and tear them away, harrying them with sudden whirlwind.

(1.277–279)

Here indeed it is only the clouds that are swept *away* by the winds, which sweep *over* the sea, earth, and heaven. Vergil has taken Lucretius' example of the invisible winds' sweeping action and turned it into the sweeping-away action, the destruction of the three parts of the world, which Lucretius only hints at here. It is not until the passage from Book 5 cited above that Lucretius presents his teaching on the mortality of the tripartite world baldly and without the poetic image of the winds, which, after all, are part of what will be swept away rather than the agent of their sweeping away.

Vergil's Aeolia, then, reminds us, in accordance with Lucretius' teaching, that the tripartite world is subject to dissolution; but it suggests, in opposition to Lucretius' teaching, that this dissolution is prevented by the providential care of omnipotent Jupiter. Jupiter's paternal omnipotence guarantees the eternity of the natural world by forcibly suppressing the furious power of the winds, which would otherwise undo the natural world. Nevertheless, the first action of the *Aeneid* emphasizes not the security but the precariousness of Jupiter's arrangements.[11]

In Lucretius' account, what will ultimately dissolve the tripartite fabric of this world is the instability of the atomic bondings that have composed this world; this world's three parts—heaven, earth, and ocean—will be undone not by any fourth thing external to them, but from within. This world has only three parts; in particular, the fourth part alleged to exist by Homer, the Underworld (*Il.* 15.187–195), does not exist.

In Vergil's myth, the danger of dissolution to the tripartite world of heaven, earth, and ocean comes from the fourth part, symbolized in the first action of the *Aeneid* by the cave of the furious winds. The winds that must be suppressed for the protection of the world's existence represent the infernal furies that oppose the peaceful realization of Jupiter's providential plan for an eternally secure regime in heaven and on earth. That the cave of the winds represents the Underworld is shown in the first place by its being the home of the infernal *irae* (57) whose presence in celestial spirits Vergil has raised thematically in the invocation (1.11). This symbolic identification of the cave of the winds with the Underworld, contained in germ in the opening scene, unfolds throughout the *Aeneid* in a series of poetic images: first the prison of enchained Furor in Jupiter's prophecy later in Book 1, then the belly cavity of the Trojan horse in Book 2, the cave of love from which springs the cause of death in Book 4, Tartarus itself in Book 6, the Underworld home of Allecto in Book 7, and the cave of Cacus[12] in Book 8. In all of these images the Underworld is represented as a dark cave containing furious beings pent up by force and straining to emerge destructively into the upper or outer world. Cumulatively, these images develop the notion of a hidden source of destruction—ultimately, destruction of the world—which is at the same time the foundation of the world, and on whose secure government the stability of the world depends.

Vergil's account of the cave of the winds is then framed so as to point toward agreement with Lucretius about the mortality of the world but disagreement about whether this mortal world has three or four parts: Lucretius explicitly denies, and Vergil poetically asserts, that the Underworld is the fourth quarter of the world. The meaning of this disagreement is explained in the central passage of the *Georgics*, where Vergil contrasts Lucretian felicity with Vergilian fortunateness (2.490–492). Vergil in that passage links scientific knowledge of the causes of things, dismissal of fear of the Underworld, and the highest happiness (*felicitas*); but in the myth of the *Aeneid* he embraces the Underworld as the justifiably feared fourth quarter of the world. The crux of the disagreement between Vergil and Lucretius concerns the effect on men of belief in the Underworld: Lucretius teaches that this belief is not only untrue but causes men the greatest unhappiness, whereas Vergil teaches that this belief causes not unhappiness but fortunateness—a condition admittedly inferior to the perfect felicity of the philosopher, but nonetheless so far from unhappiness that in fact it is the greatest good that most men can hope for.

ii. Aeolia and the Theme of the *Aeneid*

The Aeolian cave of the winds is the ruling symbol of the *Aeneid*: it symbolizes the problem of the rule of Furor in the cosmos, in political communities, and in men's souls. The action of the *Aeneid* opens with a rent in the security of the cosmos through which ungoverned Furor spews forth under all the pressure of its constraint, and threatens to undo the world. That the furious winds symbolize a kind of furor that arises in political communities[13] is already shown in the denouement of the Aeolia scene itself. The cosmos is luckily saved in this opening scene by the ability of Neptune to persuade the escaped winds to return to their cave. Vergil compares Neptune's restraint of the storm winds to a pious statesman's restraint of sedition in a great people:

> ac veluti magno in populo cum saepe coorta est
> seditio saevitque animis ignobile vulgus;
> iamque faces et saxa volant, furor arma ministrat;
> tum, pietate gravem ac meritis si forte virum quem
> conspexere, silent arrectisque auribus astant;
> ille regit dictis animos et pectora mulcet:
> sic cunctus pelagi cecidit fragor, aequora postquam
> prospiciens genitor caeloque invectus aperto
> flectit equos curruque volans dat lora secundo.

> And just as when sedition has often arisen in a great people, and the ignoble multitude becomes savage in its spirits—already torches and rocks are flying, furor supplies arms—then, if perchance they have got sight of some man grave with piety and merits, they fall silent and stand by with attentive ears; he rules their spirits with his words and soothes their hearts: so the whole smashing of the sea subsides when the father, looking out over the waters and borne along the cleared heaven, guides his horses and gives rein to his speeding chariot as he flies.

> (1.148–156)

Vergil's simile, remarkable for its reversal of the usual direction of comparison from the political to the natural order,[14] thereby emphatically asserts the identity of the principle that orders both: the natural order, like the political, is composed of heterogeneous parts precariously ordered. A storm in the natural world, like sedition in a great people, threatens to undo the ordering. "*Seditio*"—going apart, breaking up—is the political analogue of the sweeping away of the parts of the cosmos: the furor that wells up savagely in the spirits of the ignoble multitude is a force that can sweep away all the parts of the political world. Neptune calming the storm is compared to a pious man ruling the spirits of the multitude with words. What kind of words would these be? The words that Neptune has just spoken to the winds (1.132–141) are based on a vague threat of future punishment: "Another time you will pay me for your misdeeds with another sort of penalty" (136); the words with which Neptune disarms the rebels are words reminding of power to punish, like the words of the pious man that disarm the furious multitude. But even this provision for the rule of furor by words backed up with punishments is insecure, as Vergil brings out by the chancy conditional *si forte* (1.151): if perchance the seditious people notice some man grave with piety, then by falling silent they enable him to rule them with his words; but if perchance they fail to notice such a one and thus fail to fall silent, then the arms provided by their furor are not to be put down by any words however pious.

In Book 7, where everything in Book 1 recurs to show the birth of a greater order of things (7.43), the sedition of the simile recurs in the action, at the beginning of the Italian wars, and is compared in its turn to a storm. The parts of the "great people" whose coherence is here threatened by furor are on the one hand the newly allied Trojans and Italians, who together are to compose the Roman people, and on the other hand the parts that compose the Italian people itself—Latinus' royal household, Turnus' noble household, and the households of the country folk. As the angry Juno in Book 1 opens the way for the suppressed winds to emerge ungoverned into the world of heaven, earth, and ocean, so in Book 7 she opens the way for Allecto to emerge ungoverned into the community of king, nobles, and farmers, or of Italians and Trojans. As in the Neptune simile "furor supplies arms" (1.150), so here the furious multitude's "anger makes weapons" for them (7.508), and their rising in arms is likened to a storm at sea, indeed to the very storm at sea whose rising in Book 1 was compared to the sedition in a great people:

> fluctus uti primo coepit cum albescere vento,
> paulatim sese tollit mare et altius undas
> erigit, inde imo consurgit ad aethera fundo.

As when the wave has begun to whiten at the first wind, gradually the sea raises itself up and lifts its billows higher, and finally surges from its lowest depths up to the ether.

(7.528–530)

As this "storm" is arising among the people, one of the first to fall is the elder Galaesus, the single justest man that was, in the very act of "throwing himself between the combatants to moderate" (7.536). The furious combatants do not happen to notice him, and his words thus do not happen to rule their spirits. The furor released by Juno (7.286–340) splits apart the nascent compact of Trojans and Italians ("Now try telling them to unite in friendship and make compacts!" 546); in order to do this it also splits apart the existing coherence of the Italians among themselves: King Latinus cannot hold together the mixture of women (341–405, 580–582), nobles (406–474, 577–579), and countrymen (475–539, 573–576) storming around him:

> certatim regis circumstant tecta Latini;
> ille velut pelagi rupes immota resistit,
> ut pelagi rupes magno veniente fragore,
> quae sese multis circum latrantibus undis
> mole tenet; scopuli nequiquam et spumea circum
> saxa fremunt laterique inlisa refunditur alga.
> verum ubi nulla datur caecum exsuperare potestas
> concilium, et saevae nutu Iunonis eunt res,
> multa deos aurasque pater testatus inanis:
> 'frangimur heu fatis' inquit 'ferimurque procella!'

Contesting with each other, they surround the house of King Latinus; he, like an unmoved rock of the sea, stands firm—like a rock of the sea when a great crash comes, which maintains itself by its massiveness while many waves roar all about it; to no avail the cliffs and spuming rocks around it roar, and the seaweed crashes against its side. But, since he was given no power to overmaster their blind resolve, and affairs were going according to the will of savage Juno, father Latinus called to witness the gods and the empty winds: "Alas, we are broken by the fates," he said, "we are being carried away by the storm!"

(7.585–594)

Like Neptune restoring the winds to order, Latinus threatens the seditious Latins with future punishments:

> 'ipsi has sacrilego pendetis sanguine poenas,
> o miseri. te, Turne, nefas, te triste manebit
> supplicium, votisque deos venerabere seris.'

"You yourselves will pay the penalty for this with your sacrilegious blood, poor men! Unspeakably harsh punishment awaits you, Turnus, and then you will worship the gods with prayers that come too late."

(7.595–597)

But since they do not happen to notice him, his words do not rule them:

> nec plura locutus
> saepsit se tectis rerumque reliquit habenas.

> He said no more, but fenced himself off in his palace and dropped the reins of affairs.

(7.599–600)

So begin the Italian wars that are to end in the foundation of eternal Rome. Vergil thus symbolizes the meaning of Rome as the solution to the problem of governing Furor: Rome is to be that community that is no longer subject to the unforeseen irruptions of Furor into the world, in whose foundation there is better provision for rule over the arms of Furor than the chance that armed multitudes will notice a pious man and be ruled by his threatening or conciliatory words.

Ungoverned furor irrupting unforeseen into the outer world, as symbolized in the Aeolia passage, is then presented in the *Aeneid* as the cause of the breaking apart of human communities. The community of the Phoenicians is split apart by the furor that breaks out between Pygmalion and Sychaeus (1.348), and that leads to the fatal separation of Phoenician gold from Phoenician arms (1.338–368), and thus to the foundation of Carthage. So also, in Book 5, it is the irruption of furor that splits apart the heterogeneous group of Trojans seeking Italy (2.796–798) into one group of old men and weary matrons (5.715)—spirits desiring no great praise (5.751)—and another group of warriors, small in number but having a lively virtue in war (5.754). The furor that dissolves the community of Trojans into these heterogeneous elements arises from Juno's insatiable "ancient resentment" (*antiquum dolorem*, 5.608; cf. 1.25), that is, from the divine anger that is the theme of the *Aeneid*. The composition and maintenance of political communities, and ultimately of Rome, depends on the government of furor.

iii. Furor and Government

The first action of the *Aeneid*, Juno's visit to Aeolia, lays out the content of the thematic problem of the *Aeneid* established in the proem, the problem of anger or furor. Where the proem has indicated that knowledge of the causes of divine anger is the key to the contest between Rome and Carthage for sovereignty over the nations, Juno's visit to Aeolia has begun to show mythically what the problematic character of the divine anger is. Anger is eternal or undying, while the natural world is a weak compound of heterogeneous parts—heaven, earth, and ocean—inadequately protected from the dissolving capacity of furor: Jupiter's regime is insecure. Jupiter is right to fear the sweeping away into oblivion of heaven, earth and ocean, but his provision for averting this outcome is insecure against the subversion of Juno's eternal anger. As the natural world is an insecure compound, so the human world or the political communities are insecure compounds: sedition arises "often," but its restraint by the multitude's awe of a pious man comes about only "by chance;" there is no secure provision for the preservation of political communities.

Juno's visit to Aeolia, which brings to light the problem of the government of furor, is answered in Book 1 by Jupiter's prophecy concerning his providential plan for the ultimate achievement of a secure government of furor. In this prophecy (1.257–296), Jupiter assures Venus that her son Aeneas will become, in spite of Juno's angry attempts to prevent it, the founder of an empire whose full development will lead to the parallel security of Jupiter's regime in heaven and Augustus' regime on earth. The contest between Carthage and Rome for sovereignty over the nations, from which the *Aeneid* begins, rests on the presupposition that the nations will not remain divided into many sovereign cities but will be united under the sovereignty of one city. The meaning of this presupposition comes to light in Jupiter's prophecy that the end of human history will be the establishment of universal and permanent peace:

> his ego nec metas rerum nec tempora pono:
> imperium sine fine dedi.

> For them I set neither boundaries nor time limits: empire without end I grant them.
>
> (1.278–279)

Jupiter's "empire without end" will be inaugurated by the closing of the gates of war, so that

> . . . Furor impius intus
> saeva sedens super arma et centum vinctus aënis
> post tergum nodis fremet horridus ore cruento.

> . . . impious Furor, sitting within upon fierce arms and bound from behind with a hundred brazen knots, will roar horribly with bloody mouth.
>
> (1.294–296)

The meaning and end of history, according to Jupiter's prophecy, is the collection of sufficient force to confine furor forever, end war, and put on a permanent footing the fraternity and softness of a peaceable world. The hardness of the Iron Age is for the sake of securing the softness of the Golden Age.

According to Jupiter's prophecy, the permanence of all cities depends on their being united with all other cities into a world ruled by divine legislation. It is in accordance with this providential plan of the divine sovereign of the universe that the contest between Carthage and Rome for sovereignty over the nations develops, not as the enmity of two cities among other cities but as a contest between *the* two cities, that is, the two cities representing the two contesting principles for the unification of all cities. These contesting principles, science/gold versus piety/arms (iron), emerge sharply from the commissioning dreams that Vergil attributes to the two founders.

Before Aeneas' first sight of Carthage, he learns the story of Dido's commission from his mother Venus disguised as a Punic maiden (1.335–368). Later that same night, in Dido's court, Aeneas narrates to her his own commissioning dream (2.268–297). Venus' account of the commissioning of Dido is so framed as to prepare Aeneas to see in Dido a kindred soul. The account Aeneas subsequently gives Dido of his own commissioning dream is so framed as to bring home to Dido the full force of that kindredness, which she was in any case inclined to notice, having spoken to Aeneas and the Trojans of the "similar fortune" (1.628) that made her sympathetic to their plight.[15] At the same time, precisely because Aeneas' account emphasizes the parallel between his own dream and that of Dido, it also brings into striking prominence the characteristic difference between the two commissions.

Venus narrates to Aeneas the Phoenician palace intrigue that Dido entered as a virginal bride and from which she emerged as the founder of Rome's rival. Dido's marriage to Sychaeus was a love match (1.344), but it also put her into the delicate position of being the link between Tyrian power and Tyrian wealth: sister of Pygmalion the king, wife of Sychaeus, the richest man of Phoenicia. Sychaeus' manifest wealth was in land (343); his gold was buried. But furor arose between Dido's brother and her husband (348). King Pygmalion, knowing or suspecting the existence of Sychaeus' gold, and blinded by desire for it, killed Sychaeus impiously, at the altar; stealthily, with Sychaeus off his guard; and heedless of Dido's love for her husband (348–351). Pygmalion kept the murder secret for a long time, putting Dido off with false stories in the misery of her cheated love. He had done the murder for the sake of Sychaeus' gold, but he still did not have that gold; his only link to the gold was Dido, who, however, herself did not know where the gold was buried. And thus an impasse was reached at Tyre, which could be broken either by Dido's learning of the murder or by Pygmalion's finding the gold.

Dido at this time was a woman helplessly given up to love, and at the mercy of her impious and deceitful brother (1.351–352). The experience that transformed her from a weak victim of love and a gullible victim of her brother's schemes into the founder of a great city was the appearance to her in sleep of her unburied husband's image:

> ipsa sed in somnis inhumati venit imago
> coniugis ora modis attollens pallida miris[16];
> crudelis aras traiectaque pectora ferro
> nudavit, caecumque domus scelus omne retexit.
> tum celerare fugam[17] patrique excedere suadet
> auxiliumque viae veteres tellure recludit
> thesauros, ignotum argenti pondus et auri.

> But in her sleep the very image of her unburied husband came, lifting up his pale face in wondrous ways: he exposed the bloody altar and his heart pierced through by iron, and revealed the whole hidden crime of the household. Then he urged her to hasten her flight and leave her fatherland, and as aid for the way he uncovered from the earth the ancient treasures, the unknown weight of silver and gold.

(1.353–359)

The effect of this apparition on Dido was utterly transforming: not only did she prepare to flee, not only did she excavate the buried gold, but she collected a company of disaffected Tyrians, those who hated or feared her brother, the tyrant (1.360–363). They seized a fleet of sea-ready ships, loaded them with the excavated gold, and thus set out to sea with "the wealth of greedy Pygmalion" (362–364), cheating him of the profit of his crime; Dido, though a woman, was no longer weak, deceived, lovesick, or dependent on her menfolk: *dux femina facti* (364), she, a woman, was the leader of the deed.

Sychaeus' commission to Dido required no more than that she take the gold and seek refuge abroad; it did not require that she found the new city that Juno would favor for kingship over the nations (1.17–18). Venus does not explain to Aeneas why Dido so far exceeded Sychaeus' instructions in the direction of Juno's desires. But later in Book 1, Dido herself narrates to Aeneas the experience that shows what her model was for the course she took (1.619 ff.). When Dido was still a girl in her father Belus' house, Teucer had come to Tyre, expelled from his fatherland and seeking therefore a new kingdom; Belus had helped him in founding a new kingdom in Cyprus. Dido imitated the proud regality of this hero: as exiled Teucer came not abjectly to seek refuge but proudly to seek a new kingdom, so did self-exiled Dido. Teucer, however, relied on arms to take his new kingdom; arms were the *aux-*

ilium he sought from Belus (1.621). Dido, to whom Sychaeus had revealed his buried treasure as *auxilium viae* (358), took the site of Carthage not in war but in trade: *mercati solum* (367). The great commercial nation of Carthage was founded on the gold revealed to Dido in her commissioning dream. Carthage is destined to be not only wealthy but also great in war (1.14, 444–445); at its founding, though, Carthage has the ancestral gold of Phoenicia without the ancestral iron or arms or martial virtue of Phoenicia, and it remains uncertain, until Dido's curse near the end of Book 4 (622 ff.), how this lack is to be supplied.

When Aeneas tells Dido his own story, he is addressing a woman whose soul-transforming experience of her husband's image he already knows, and who has addressed him already as sharing a "similar fortune." Aeneas frames his account of the appearance to him of Hector's shade in such a way as to indicate to Dido how close indeed their two fortunes have been, and especially how a vision of the dead was for him, as for her, the turning point of his life, the event that led to his exile from his homeland and his quest for a new kingdom. Aeneas' account recalls, in conception and vocabulary, Dido's experience as recounted by Venus. Aeneas and the Trojans were at the time the dupes of Sinon's impious lies, as Dido was of Pygmalion's. At the time when first sleep comes to wretched mortals (*mortalibus aegris*, 2.268, as Dido had been *aegra*, 1.351, at the time of her vision), Hector appeared to him in sleep (*in somnis*, 2.270, cf. *in somnis*, 1.353). Hector appeared as he had been when dragged by Achilles' chariot, pierced with the thong through his swollen feet (*perque pedes traiectus lora tumentis*, 2.273, as Sychaeus had shown his *traiecta pectora ferro*, 1.355). In particular, the emphasis Aeneas places on his mysterious dream-ignorance of Hector's death, as if he had been expecting Hector to return alive, recalls Dido's genuine ignorance of Sychaeus' death (2.282–285). Like Sychaeus, Hector counsels flight from the fatherland (*fuge . . . patriae*, 2.289, 291; cf. *fugam, patriaque*, 1.357), and uncovers a hidden (*adytis . . . penetralibus*, 2.297, cf. *tellure recludit, ignotum*, 1.358, 359) help for the flight he counsels. To Dido is uncovered the buried gold; to Aeneas are brought forth the Penates of Troy, mighty Vesta, and the eternal hearthfire. Dido is instructed to flee with the help of the gold; Aeneas is instructed not only to flee, not only to raise a great city, but to rescue the Trojan Penates and to raise a great city *for them*:

> sacra suosque tibi commendat Troia penatis;
> hos cape fatorum comites, his moenia quaere
> magna, pererrato statues quae denique ponto.

Troy commends to you her sacred things and her penates: take these as companions of your fates, seek for them the great city-walls which you will establish at last when you have sojourned across the sea.

(2.293–295)

Aeneas' account of his commissioning dream shows us the principle of the
Roman founding[18] with special emphasis by way of contrast with Dido's
dream: Tyrian gold, Trojan gods. This is the germ of the decisive difference
between the two rivals for world empire, the "city of science" and the "city
of piety." And herein lies a central puzzle of the *Aeneid*: if a providential
Jupiter aims to unite the communities of the world into one universal empire, *imperium sine fine*, is not Juno's intention of making Carthage sovereign
over the nations more suitable to the fulfillment of Jupiter's plan than
Jupiter's own intention of making Rome sovereign over the nations? The
foundation of Carthage on Phoenician gold makes Carthage freely open to
the inclusion of all peoples "without distinction" (1.574), while the foundation of Rome on the penates of Troy makes its inclusion of all nations depend
on some alliance or accommodation of their own gods with the Trojan or Roman gods; but the gods of other nations (like Juno) are hostile to the Trojan
penates, while it does not appear that any gods are hostile to gold. The operation of the "gold principle" is illustrated by Dido's first speech in the
Aeneid (cf. pp. 28–33, above), where, by being silent about the gods, she is
able to offer equal citizenship to the Trojans without further ado.

Through the tragedy of Dido and Aeneas, Vergil forces us to wonder why
Aeneas could not have remained in Carthage after all and founded Rome
there. Is not Jupiter's insistence on Aeneas' departure for Italy more willful
and arbitrary than Juno's scheme of absorbing Aeneas and the Trojans into
Carthage, precisely in view of Jupiter's providential purpose of unifying the
world of nations in perpetual peace? What is the special virtue of Italy that
is so essential to the project of universal empire? Or, if the virtue of Italy is
not the determining factor, what is the special vice of Carthage that makes
it an impossible setting for that project in spite of its apparent plausibility?
To be sure, Rome was destined to arise in Italy and not in Libya. But is this
destiny entirely arbitrary? Is the tragedy of Dido, and the suffering of the
Punic Wars, just a senseless product of a random whim of fate? Vergil's portrayal of the loveableness of Dido and Carthage in Books 1–4 forces us to
seek a reason for the fate Aeneas so painfully executes.

The love affair of Dido and Aeneas shows the attractiveness, the greatness, and the defect of Dido and of Carthage as the attractiveness, greatness,
and defect of Epicureanism in the foundation of souls and cities. The at-

tractiveness of Epicureanism lies in its promotion of pleasure and friendship over punishment and justice; its greatness lies in its courageous reliance on the human capacity for seeking the truth about nature and the true good for human beings; its defect lies in its insufficient attention to the vigor of the passions in human beings who are not Epicurean philosophers, and consequently in its failure to provide sufficient protection against the irruptions of furor in the soul and in the city. The defect of Carthage may be said to be the defect of gold, its softness: the "golden," that is, Golden-Age quality of peaceableness requires the suppression of furor, but the suppression of furor requires iron, that is, the Iron-Age quality of harshness or warlikeness. Gold would be able to hold the political world together if furor could be extirpated or disarmed by reason; but furor cannot ever be extirpated from the cosmos, from cities, or from men's hearts. The apparent optimism of Jupiter's plan for mankind is radically qualified by the limit it sets on what can be hoped for: not the annihilation or the rationalization but the forcible suppression of the passions; the achievement of Jupiter's plan for eternal peace will require the application of eternal force against eternal furor.

CHAPTER SEVEN

⁓

Dido in Love

Dido's purpose in founding Carthage was to avenge the murder of Sychaeus and to punish her brother Pygmalion:

> urbem praeclaram statui, mea moenia vidi,
> ulta virum poenas inimico a fratre recepi.

> I have established an illustrious city, I have seen my own walls; in avenging my husband I have exacted punishment from my enemy-brother.

(4.655–656)

The character and depth of the injury done to Dido at Tyre—the murder of the husband she passionately loved, the cruel playing on her sisterly credulity, the leaving her childless—gave her a thirst for vengeance powerful enough to animate her founding a new city. On the one hand, her forming and caring for this city replaces her conceiving and raising Sychaeus' child; on the other hand, it punishes Pygmalion by removing from him the gold for which he killed Sychaeus, and perhaps by threatening commercial competition from the well-appointed site of her own new port. Thus her capacity to found Carthage is the heroic measure of the capacity of both her love and her anger.

The totality of Dido's transformation of her private passions into the public or political passions of founding a city is accompanied by an almost total break with her Phoenician past. Unlike Aeneas' conception of his founding mission as a refounding of Troy, a preservation of Troy's ancestral customs and especially its ancestral gods, Dido's founding mission is conceived as a radical break with Phoenicia. This difference is brought out sharply by the contrast between Aeneas' sailing from Troy with "the penates and the great gods" (3.12) and Dido's sailing from Tyre with the treasure of Sychaeus but under the auspices of no gods: "the woman was leader of the deed" (1.360–365). Dido takes with her from Tyre a group of tyrant-haters who are not very attached to their fatherland, preferring exile to tyrannicide, and a store of Phoenician gold which, however, is as efficacious abroad as in Phoenicia, which, that is, is entirely removable from its specifically Phoenician context. Upon their arrival in Africa, their gold enabled them to buy territory instead of fighting for it, so that they did not need to appeal for the help of any god against their enemies; "the woman was leader of the deed." The break of Dido and her band with their Phoenician past is expressed in the self-sufficiency or godlessness of their flight from their fatherland and their establishment of a new city in Africa.

The central role of both Juno and Iopas in Carthaginian affairs seems to be intimately connected to the moment of Dido's arrival in Libya with gold and without gods.[1] There is no suggestion anywhere in the *Aeneid* of any connection between Juno and Dido or Juno and the Phoenicians before Dido's flight from her fatherland: Juno's election of the Carthaginians to be her people and to promote her project of averting the rise of Rome seems to have taken place only when they had just reached Africa with Sychaeus' gold, Dido's thwarted love and anger, and no patron god. Only then did Juno elect them as a people suited to carry out her own ambitions, leading them to the sign of the horse's head (1.441–445); Dido's ambition of avenging her husband and punishing her brother was adaptable to Juno's ambition of founding the anti-Roman seat of a world empire. Iopas too, the poetic pupil of African Atlas, appears to have connected himself to the Carthaginians as a result of their break with Phoenicia. Iopas could never have become the accepted court poet and philosophic teacher in a traditional society attached to its ancestral gods and customs; for Iopas too the moment of the exiled Phoenicians' arrival as a self-sufficient, godless band was the moment when he elected them to promote his project of founding an enlightened city. The ambitions of Juno and of Iopas become attached to Dido's project without ever becoming central to Dido herself. Juno's ambition to found the anti-Roman regime and Iopas' ambition to educate the founder of the enlightened regime are intimately connected within Vergil's whole narrative: as the Roman regime is the regime of piety, so the anti-Roman (Junonian) regime is the enlightened (Lucretian) regime. Juno opposes the regime that suppresses the passions by force; Iopas/Lucretius opposes the regime that suppresses the passions by fear of gods. But these differently motivated oppositions are at least temporarily in harmony: Dido's impious temple to Juno and Dido's un-philosophic tuition under Iopas do not come into conflict with each other, while Dido's own founding purpose always remains neither world empire nor enlightenment, but vengeance and punishment.

i. Love and Astronomy

Iopas' singing at Dido's royal feast for the Trojans may be understood to mean that Dido and her court are the audience for the Lucretian teaching as a whole. The particular part of the De Rerum Natura that Iopas sings at this feast may be said to be the fifth book, whose subject matter is the birth and death of our world and the causes of the motions of heavenly bodies (DRN 5.64–90). According to Lucretius these two subject matters have the follow-ing relationship: knowledge of the origin of our world in general leads to knowledge of the origin of belief in gods in particular, and thus to freedom from belief in gods. However, this knowledge of origins is not a sufficient bul-wark against men's backsliding into fear of gods, for when men wonder how things happen, especially with regard to those things that are seen above our heads in the celestial regions, then they are brought back into their ancient religions (5.83–86) because of their ignorance of the natural explanation of these things. Knowledge of the causes of the motions of heavenly bodies is then the crown and seal of freedom from fear of gods, perfecting and pro-tecting knowledge of the origin of our world.

The unfolding of the story of Dido, however, shows her being brought back into the ancient religion with a vengeance and not because of her ig-norance of astronomy but because of her unprotected vulnerability to the furor of love. Vergil's account of Dido is then a critique of Lucretius in the following sense. Lucretius supposed that the furor of love and anger is easily disarmed by rational knowledge of the nature of things, and that the greater danger to men is the fear arising from their wonder at celestial phenomena. However, the passions of love and anger—the two chief divisions of furor—can become disarmed by reason only in men who follow the way of life of Lucretius, i.e., who leave aside everything else to seek knowledge of the na-ture of things; these passions cannot be disarmed in men who, while learn-ing from poetry Lucretius' account of the nature of things, themselves fol-low the way of life of the founders or rulers or citizens of cities. The salutary effect of Epicurean physics on men's passions does not take place among men who absorb Epicurean physics from poetry, men who are deceived by art into knowledge of the nature of things, men for whom the nature of

things is known on the authority of the poet. Such men may enjoy a temporary mastering of the terrors that arise from ignorance of nature; but they
are always in danger of being overmastered by those terrors again, not
through ignorance of astronomy but through the irruption in their souls of
immortal furor.

That the disarming of furor is more problematic than the mastery of astronomy in freeing men from religious terror is indicated in *Aeneid* 1 by the
relationship between Cupid and Jupiter, or love and the thunderbolt.
Jupiter is thought to rule the affairs of men and gods by terrifying them with
the thunderbolt, and Venus addresses him in this character (1.229–230).
But Venus addresses her son Cupid as not subject to Jupiter's rule of men
and gods:

> nate, meae vires, mea magna potentia, solus,
> nate, patris summi qui tela Typhoea temnis.

> My son, my strength, my great power, you alone, my son, who contemn the Ty-
> phoean weapons of the supreme father.

> (1.664–665)

The contempt of the Jovian weapons here attributed by Venus to Cupid is related to the contempt of god-supported human weapons attributed by
Ilioneus to the Carthaginians (1.542–543): the emancipation of the passions
from fear of divine punishment is at the heart of the Carthaginian narrative.
How easy it is to come to think that thunder is not caused by divine anger is
illustrated by the barbarian king Iarbas who, though reputed to be a son of
Jupiter Ammon himself and though worshiping Jupiter at a hundred shrines,
is readily persuaded by the frustration of his own passions to regard Jupiter as
an empty rumor and his alleged angry thunderbolts as blind fires in the
clouds (4.208–210, 218). But how difficult it is to disarm the passions, to separate out the real atomic substratum of satisfiable erotic desire from the imaginary amorous desires, is illustrated in the story of Dido by the natural unsatisfiability of the imaginary longings that spring from her love. The first effect
of Cupid on Dido is that she "cannot be satisfied mentally, and is inflamed
by looking" (1.713). Starting here, Vergil's myth of the undoing of Dido by
the furor of love closely follows Lucretius' analysis of love in Book 4 of the
De Rerum Natura:

> unaque res haec est, cuius quam plurima habemus,
> tam magis ardescit dira cuppedine pectus.
> nam cibus atque umor membris adsumitur intus.

quae quoniam certas possunt obsidere partis,
hoc facile expletur laticum frugumque cupido.
ex hominis vero facie pulchroque colore
nil datur in corpus praeter simulacra fruendum
tenuia, quae vento spes raptat saepe misella. . . .
sic in amore Venus simulacris ludit amantis,
nec satiare queunt spectando corpora coram. . . .

This is the only thing of which the more we have, the more our breast is inflamed with fierce desire. For food and drink are absorbed within the limbs; so,
since these things can occupy definite parts, the desire for wine and grain is
easily satisfied. But from a human being's face and beautiful complexion, nothing is given to the body to enjoy but fine *simulacra*. . . . Thus, in love, Venus
deceives lovers with *simulacra*, and they cannot get satisfaction by looking at
the bodies. . . .

(DRN 4.1089–1096, 1101–1102)

These imaginary desires of love lead to *rabies* and *furor* (1117), which embit-
ter the lives of lovers even in the best case; while in the case of adverse love
the evils arising from this unsatisfiable delusory desire are innumerable
(1141–1144). When Aeneas arrives at Carthage, Dido's spirit has long been
settled and her heart disaccustomed (1.722); having devoted her passion to
the cares of founding a new city, she appears to be as invulnerable to the furor
of love as a veritable physicist. But this appearance is false. She has in fact
no resources at all for resisting the full-blown delusionary furor of love; so far
from protecting her against the irruption of furor within herself, her Epicurean education itself helps to emancipate that furor; it makes her helpless
to govern herself in the only way open to her, through fear of the thunderbolt as divine punishment.

ii. The Two Songs

On the night of her royal feast, Dido listens to two songs: the song of Iopas
on the nature of things and the song of Aeneas on obedience to the gods.
These two songs make two utterly opposed claims on Dido: Iopas' song
about the origins and causes of things reminds her of the non-existence of
the gods, her own break with ancestral religion, and the need to resist
falling back upon the ancient religions; Aeneas' song about heroic piety argues that reverence for and obedience to the ancestral gods is the highest
task of human life. By the end of Aeneas' song, Dido is in love with a man
who she knows regards himself as bound by divine commands to leave her

and her city. Both Iopas' song and Aeneas' song tell Dido that her love for Aeneas can have no fulfillment. According to Iopas, Dido's love for Aeneas is a delusion that requires reflection on the nature of things, since its cure lies in full understanding of the natural unsatisfiability of vain desires; according to Aeneas, her love is hopeless because Aeneas is divinely commanded to take his gods to Italy where a kingdom and a royal consort have been appointed for him by divine providence.

The tragedy of Dido in Book 4 may be described as the tragedy of a woman who is helpless to restrain what she knows from the start to be the irruption of an unsatisfiable passion. In someone else, in a Iopas or an Aeneas, this passion might be either disarmed by science or restrained by piety; but Dido's science has softened the restraints of piety in her without, however, having succeeded in disarming her passion. Until Aeneas' arrival, Dido's situation has been obscured by fortune: her founding activities have not been threatened by passions opposed to those activities; her suitors have not pleased her, so it appeared as if she was inaccessible to the delusions of love. The result of Aeneas' pleasing her is that her old religion returns upon her in the form of vulgar superstition, while her Epicurean science returns upon her in the form of vulgar hedonism. She lacks the theoretical part of Epicureanism and the obedient part of piety: she rejects the false images of the Underworld without rejecting the false images of amorous passion, and she tries to bend the gods to her passionate will without trying to know what the gods require of her.

After hearing the song of Iopas and the song of Aeneas, Dido makes a desperate attempt to govern herself by a return to the old religion of her pre-Carthaginian education, while her sister Anna shows her the desperation of her attempt by reminding her of nature and pleasure.

> At regina gravi iamdudum saucia cura
> vulnus alit venis et caeco carpitur igni.

> But the queen, now long wounded by grave care, feeds the wound with her veins and is consumed by hidden (blind) fire.

$$(4.1-2)$$

The *caecus ignis* of *Aeneid* 4 is twofold: it is the "invisible" fire of love, and the "blind" fire of the thunderbolt understood *naturaliter*: "blind fires in the clouds/ terrify the spirits" (4.209–210).[2] The relation between the two is expressed by Dido's opening speech, in which she seeks to master the *caeci ignes* of love by rejecting the *caeci ignes* of the heavens in favor of Jupiter's punishment of perjury.

iii. Dido's Speech to Anna (4.9–30)

During the night, Dido says, dreams have terrified her in her suspense or uncertainty. Her suspense is between "the impulses of her passion on the one
hand and the terrific warning of her dreams on the other."[3] Her dreams are
likely to have been dreams of the dead (Sychaeus) on the one hand and of
the object of her waking thoughts, Aeneas, on the other (*DRN* 1.132–135,
4.962 ff.). The dreams have terrified her by representing the clash between
her impulse of love towards Aeneas and her impulse of self-reservation in favor of Sychaeus' memory. Dido's loyalty to the memory of Sychaeus is connected with her founding of Carthage in the sense that this founding is her
way of avenging Sychaeus' death; her suspense between Aeneas and Sychaeus is thus suspense between Aeneas and Carthage, or between the most
private and the most public passions.

Dido's dreams and suspense are caused by "this new stranger" (4.10) whose
strength and courage so impress her that she protests to Anna that she really
does believe that he is of the race of the gods, *genus deorum* (4.12)—a view
to which formerly she agreed without therefore crediting it (1.615–618). The
fates by which he has been tossed according to his narrative,[4] the wars he has
sung of (4.14), have shown her his courage and thereby persuaded her of his
divinity. According to Lucretius' teaching, the essential delusion of love is
that one attributes to the beloved more than is right to concede to any mortal (*DRN* 4.1183–1184). Before Dido was in love with Aeneas, she could call
him *nate dea*, "goddess-born," without thereby infecting her mind with vile
religion, but now her love makes her consider that this attribution is not a
vain belief, *vana fides*; though she knows of course that her likeminded sister
Anna, educated like herself in Lucretian science, will certainly regard this
belief as vain, and thus protests (*equidem*) her difference from her likeminded
sister: "I for my part believe—nor is this a vain belief—that he *is* of the race
of the gods" (4.12).

Dido's first love had cheated her, catching her unawares with death
(4.17): thus she had learned in the most harsh manner how much more she
had attributed to Sychaeus than is due to any mortal. Her longing for more
than human permanence and significance, cheated by the death of her husband who turned out to be all too human, has been invested now in her
founding the illustrious city of Carthage; looking back on this time after having fallen in love with Aeneas, she says that her *pudor*, her chaste loyalty to
the memory of Sychaeus, was to have been her *fama* (4.322–323): she was going to make a lasting reputation, an enduring monument, from her love.
Dido's discovery of the terrible groundlessness of her hopes of Sychaeus' love

itself had caused it to become fixed in her mind that she would not desire to join herself to anyone else by the marriage bond (4.16); marriage itself, she says, had become repulsive to her (18).[5] If not for these results of being cheated by the death of Sychaeus, she tells Anna, she might have been able to succumb to this one *culpa* (19). The *culpa* Dido thinks of is ambiguous. It may be this one instance of desiring to bind herself to someone by the marriage bond; this would be a *culpa* by the standard of her fixed intention not to desire this, which she calls her *pudor*. But it may also be her love for Aeneas itself, conceived as a *culpa* by the standard of marriage itself: for Dido knows from Aeneas' narrative that she cannot hope for marriage to him and that her love for him, if she succumbs to it, will necessarily remain outside the bonds of marriage altogether. In this second sense, *pudor* and its rights are the restriction of erotic love within the bonds of marriage, and what Dido is trying to avoid is not a second marriage but an erotic attachment outside of marriage. Since she learned of Pygmalion's murder of Sychaeus her feelings have been inflexible and her spirit unwavering; but now she recognizes the traces of the old flame (20–23). Dido does not wish to yield to her desire for Aeneas, as being both a violation of her loyalty to the memory of Sychaeus and a violation of the sanctions of marriage itself, not to say an attribution of too much to the mortal Aeneas. In order to rule herself so as not to yield, she appeals to the old religion for the strongest remedy and self-protection; she renounces her desire under a terrible oath:

> sed mihi vel tellus optem prius ima dehiscat
> vel pater omnipotens abigat me fulmine ad umbras,
> pallentis umbras Erebo noctemque profundam,
> ante, pudor, quam te violo aut tua iura resolvo.

> But I hope that either the earth will gape open from its depths for me or the omnipotent father will drive me with his thunderbolt to the shades, the pale shades and the profound night in Erebus, before I violate you, *pudor*, or undo your rights.

(4.24–27)

In order for Dido's oath to serve the purpose for which she makes it—the purpose of her self-restraint—it cannot be taken with a view to what "people say" but must be taken in simple belief in Jupiter's omnipotence and in his punishment of perjury with the thunderbolt; it cannot be taken with doubts about the other world but must be taken in simple belief in both the possibility of eternal punishment for her own soul and the continuing existence of Sychaeus' soul after death:

ille meos, primus qui me sibi iunxit, amores
abstulit; ille habeat secum servetque sepulcro.

He who first joined me to himself has taken away my love; let him have it with
him and keep it in the grave.

(4.28–29)

Dido doubtless has been helped to retrieve these beliefs, these *antiquae religiones*, by the very love for Aeneas against which she invokes them—both
because of the claims Aeneas himself makes on behalf of the gods and because the passion of love itself, like all the passions, disorders sober thought
or makes men open to longings for and attributions of divinity.

The insight and boldness of Dido's attempt to rule herself by embracing
fear of angry gods shows her greatness of character, but the impossibility and
ultimate failure of what she attempts is suggested already by her action upon
completing her oath:

sic effata sinum lacrimis implevit obortis.

After saying this, she flooded her bosom with welling tears.

(4.30)

The welling up of Dido's tears shows the implausibility of what she has just
sworn: rather than being collected to strength by the force of her extraordinary effort, she weeps under the pressure "to bring about what she had just
condemned with a rejecting spirit."[6]

iv. Anna's Speech to Dido (4.31–53)

Dido's tears show the weakness of her attempt at resolve; but what actually
undoes that weak resolve is Anna's speech, in which she lays out the arguments against Dido's resisting her love for Aeneas. Anna speaks first of the
happiness of love in companionship, children, and erotic pleasure, and
the connection of love to Dido's youthful time of life; she does not think
that the rewards of founding and ruling a great city could compensate Dido
for these lacks (31–33). Having represented Dido as lacking love above all
things, Anna proceeds to speak as if the oath Dido has just taken were an
argument rather than an oath: she produces the counterargument, as if Dido
were deliberating with her rather than making her the witness to an awful
oath. Dido has sworn not to violate *pudor* or undo its rights, which she has
said consist of leaving in the dead Sychaeus' possession the love he has

received from her. Anna reminds Dido that the dead do not care about this (34). She thereby reminds Dido that the dead do not care about anything, including the romances of their widows—any more than the gods care about anything, including the sanctity of oaths; she reminds Dido of the harmlessness not only of the love Dido has just sworn to suppress, but also of the breaking of the oath by which she swore it. There is no Jupiter blasting perjurers into Erebus with the thunderbolt; there is only *ignis caecus*, the invisible fire of love and the blind blaze of the thunderbolt. Anna's encouragement of Dido to remember that she does not believe that the dead care about the living is also encouragement to remember that she does not believe that her own soul will be subject to care after her own death: her yielding to her desire for Aeneas will bring her comfort now, and no punishment later; whereas her resisting that desire will bring her sorrow now, and no reward later. There are no shades of the dead. In Dido's nightmares that so terrified her, Sychaeus doubtless appeared as a shade claiming Dido's loyalty; but Anna and Dido know that these appearances of the dead in sleep have a natural explanation as mere appearances. In the old days at Tyre, the appearance of Sychaeus to Dido in his "commissioning dream" (1.353–359) seemed to show that the spirits of the dead do care for their widows; but that was before Anna and Dido learned from Iopas how to interpret these things naturally.[7] With her question, "Do you believe that ashes and buried shades care about this?" Anna reproaches Dido for backsliding into the *antiquae religiones*. In Anna's opinion it would be good for Dido to enjoy the love of Aeneas and best for her to enjoy it with the good conscience of a Lucretian who does not fear punishment for innocent enjoyments; Anna tries to shore up this good conscience for Dido in the early part of her speech.

Anna then takes up Dido's claim that her feelings had been inflexible and her spirit unwavering until Aeneas appeared in her life. Although Dido meant this partly as proof of the extraordinariness of the impression made on her by Aeneas, she also meant it as a reminder of her own strength of character: she had been firm against other kindlings of the old flame; she had demonstrated the very toughness she is in need of now. Anna takes up her point in order to urge that no strength of character had been involved in this at all; it was simply that all Dido's former suitors had failed to please her, while Aeneas, or the love of Aeneas, does please her (35–38). Dido cannot then look to any strength in resisting former suitors as a pledge of her ability to resist Aeneas. *Placitone etiam pugnabis amori?*, "Will you fight against a pleasing love as well?" (38). Anna's question suggests that in her opinion it is both undesirable to fight against the pleasing and impossible to succeed in such a fight.

From these personal considerations Anna moves to the interests of Carthage, which she recognizes as a concern of Dido's; and these interests she links with a second method of giving Dido a good conscience, the method of appealing to the *antiquae religiones*. Anna itemizes the military threats to Carthage: the warlike Gaetulian, Numidian, and Barcaean tribes surrounding Carthaginian territory, the wars of reprisal threatening from their brother at Tyre (4.39–44). Anna does not at once draw the conclusion from these circumstances; she leaves Dido to reflect first herself on the great virtue of Aeneas and the honor of his race that had been coursing through her mind in any case (4.3–4), which go all the way back to her admiration of Trojan valor in the days when Teucer visited Belus, and which are illustrated on the walls of her temple to Juno. Before speaking explicitly of the utility of Trojan arms to Carthage, Anna declares that she, for her part, thinks that it was under auspicious gods and with the favor of Juno that the Trojan ships came to Carthage. In saying this, she suggests that the gods, and Juno in particular, brought the Trojans to Carthage providentially for the sake of both Dido and Carthage, to provide Dido with love or marriage and Carthage with an army. Seeing Dido turning to religion in her trouble, Anna is prepared to assure her that her desires are nothing but what the gods themselves desire and approve.[8] Of course, the arrival of the Trojan ships *was* caused by Juno's being favorable to Dido and Carthage, but also by her being unfavorable to Aeneas and Troy; Anna's words completely discount Aeneas' narrative in Books 2–3, which had shown that for the Trojans, everything preventing them from reaching Italy is inauspicious. Anna in any case does not believe Aeneas' claims that he has been divinely commanded to refound Troy in Italy, so she is as free to call his shipwreck a sign of the gods' favor as to call it an accident; and she is willing to do so if this will help Dido see her way to yielding to her love for Aeneas. After suggesting this thought of divine approval, Anna completes her argument about the military exigencies of Carthage:

> quam tu urbem, soror, hanc cernes, quae surgere regna
> coniugio tali! Teucrum comitantibus armis
> Punica se quantis attollet gloria rebus!

> What a city, sister, you will see here, what a kingdom you will see arise, with such a husband! With the arms of the Trojans accompanying us, in what great affairs will Punic glory raise itself up!

(4.47–49)

Anna's speech has been an appeal to Dido to break the oath she has just taken. It began with an attempt to stiffen Dido's Epicurean views so as to make her oath meaningless in her own eyes; but as a second position, in the face of Dido's manifest backsliding, it continued with an attempt to assure Dido of the gods' approval of her desires. And on this note it ends, with the advice to seek the indulgence of the gods with sacrifices while seeking to detain Aeneas with pretexts of delay from continuing on the way he says he must go (4.50–53).

Anna's speech undoes Dido's *pudor* (55) and leads to the greatest evils for Dido. Her intention is to promote the happiness of the sister she loves; she has no doubt what this happiness is; and she does not recognize any considerations—such as Aeneas' alleged duty to find in Italy his kingdom and his queen, or Dido's perhaps over-hasty oath forswearing this love—that might tell against the prudence of snatching that happiness. Her speech illustrates the union of imperfect Epicureanism and imperfect religion that is the product of the Carthaginian enlightenment, and whose unfolding in Dido herself will become central to the narrative of Book 4. Her Epicureanism is defective because, while holding that the soul cannot suffer apart from the body, she holds that love is a true standard of the pleasing; she has not understood the illusoriness of love. Her Epicurean opinions about gods, oaths, and the soul, so far from disarming the passion of love or lowering her opinion of its pleasures, have simply emancipated her from the restraints she would otherwise have felt—ominous dreams, *pudor*, fear of oaths. Anna's is an Epicureanism in the service of the passions, a vulgar hedonism; not knowing what the true pleasure is, she uses the bits of Epicurean doctrine she has picked up from Iopas' poetry as rhetorical resources in pursuit of false pleasures. Epicureanism has removed from her the restraints on pleasure-seeking without correcting her understanding of pleasure. At the same time, the version of religion she suggests as a fallback position is itself a vulgarized religion: a religion of bending the gods to men's desires and interpreting events as divine confirmation of men's own wishes. The effect of the Carthaginian enlightenment is a mixture of vulgar hedonism and vulgar superstition whose outcome is the emancipation of furor.

Dido acts on Anna's advice.[9] As the newness of her kingdom had compelled her to break Jupiter's alleged law of *hospitium*, so the pleasingness of her love now leads her to undo the rights of *pudor*, to break her oath sanctioned by Jupiter's thunderbolt, and to employ Jupiter's *hospitium* (4.51) as a snare by which to divert the pious Aeneas from his intention to obey what he regards as divine commands.

v. Dido and Iarbas

It is against Dido's will that she has fallen in love with Aeneas: first because it is her will to devote her energies to the founding of Carthage as vengeance for her husband and punishment of her brother; second because she knows from Aeneas' narrative (Books 2–3), that he cannot remain with her in Carthage since he is under divine command to go on to Italy. The grandeur, pride, and self-possession that she shows as queen and founder before falling in love with Aeneas are rooted in her Epicurean enlightenment. Dido's inability to restrain her erotic furor in accordance with her own will is the core of Vergil's portrayal of the inadequacy of partial Epicureanism as the foundation of a human soul—Epicureanism being necessarily partial in the soul of someone who is not herself a philosopher. In the course of Book 4, after the conversation with Anna in which Dido tries and fails to replace her proud atheism with god-fearing piety as a brake on her unwanted passion, Vergil portrays Dido gradually breaking up on the shoals of her inadequate Epicureanism and her inadequate religion. In the unfolding of Book 4, Dido, under the pressure of her passion, at first swings back and forth between the two poles of her partial belief, until, in the crisis of her soul, she gradually reinvents Olympian religion. Vergil thus presents in the tragedy of Dido a correction of Lucretius' account of the cause of religion: not misinterpretation of images and awe of the heavens, but the inability of unaided human beings to govern love and hate without gods.

Dido's first action after her conversation with Anna is a desperate attempt, in accordance with Anna's advice, to "ask the gods' indulgence" (4.50) for the breaking of her oath by earth and Jupiter:

> principio delubra adeunt pacemque per aras
> exquirunt; mactant lectas de more bidentis
> legiferae Cereri Phoeboque patrique Lyaeo,
> Iunoni ante omnis, cui vincla iugalia curae.
> ipsa tenens dextra pateram pulcherrima Dido
> candentis vaccae media inter cornua fundit,
> aut ante ora deum pinguis spatiatur ad aras,
> instauratque diem donis, pecudumque reclusis
> pectoribus inhians spirantia consulit exta.

First off, they (Dido and Anna) approach the shrines and ask for peace at all the altars; they offer sacrificial animals, according to custom, to lawgiving Ceres and Phoebus and father Lyaeus, to Juno above all, whose concern is for the marriage bonds. Most beautiful Dido herself, holding a libation-bowl in her right hand, pours it between the horns of a shining white cow, or strides to the rich altars before the faces of the gods, renews the day with offerings and, gaping over the opened breasts of cattle, inspects the still-breathing entrails.

(4.56–64)

Thus Dido, who before her passion for Aeneas had conducted herself with the utmost independence of gods, conceding at most the outward forms of temple and libation in fastidious allowance for what "people say," is here thrust by the vicissitudes of her passion into the most needy, obsessive, ritualistic attempts to win the divine favor. Dido's activities here recall Lucretius' description of false, superstitious, or self-serving piety in his discussion of the origins of religion in Book 5:

nec pietas ullast velatum saepe videri
vertier ad lapidem atque omnis accedere ad aras,
nec procumbere humi prostratum et pandere palmas
ante deum delubra, nec aras sanguine multo
spargere quadrupedum, nec votis nectere vota,
sed mage pacata posse omnia mente tueri.

It is no piety to be seen often turning veiled towards a stone and approaching every altar, or to lie prostrate on the ground and stretch forth one's hands before the shrines of the gods, or to moisten the altars with much blood of four-footed beasts, or to bind vows with vows—but rather to be able to contemplate all things with a mind at peace.

(5.1198–1203)

Unlike all other performances of religious rites in the *Aeneid*,[10] Dido's here are marked precisely by the promiscuity, excess, compulsiveness, and cumulative bloodiness that mark Lucretius' type of the superstitious man, the type furthest removed from the philosopher's pacific contemplation. Dido has been transformed from her earlier human autonomy, in which she disdained the support of gods, into the utter dependency of the guilty perjurer trying to "take back" her oath by propitiating all the gods with offerings. Dido's offerings to Juno in particular are conditioned by Juno's connection with the marriage bonds, not by her connection with Carthage and the interests of Carthage. Evidently the entrails as interpreted by the priests are not favorable; thus she repeats the sacrifices ("renews the day with offerings"), and increasingly takes over the rites from the priests: pouring the libation "herself," anxiously inspecting the uncooperative entrails herself. Dido's gradual elbowing in on the role of the priests suggests that she has the peculiarly insistent magical intentions of the superstitious, rather than the obedient intentions of the pious;[11] until finally, in an extraordinary (and ambiguous) rhetorical outburst, Vergil expresses (among other things)[12] Dido's impatient dismissal of the priests and their rites: the omens won't come right, so what use are vows and sacrifices to Dido in her erotic furor!

heu, vatum ignarae mentes! quid vota furentem,
quid delubra iuvant? est mollis flamma medullas
interea et tacitum vivit sub pectore vulnus.

Ah, the ignorant minds of seers! What good are vows, what good are shrines
to one raving? The thin flame is eating all the while into her marrow, and the
silent wound is alive beneath her breast.

(4.65–67)

Later, after Aeneas' break with Dido, "many predictions of the former seers
horrify her with their terrible warning" (4.464–465). These "former seers" are
in the first place the ones whose warning she here ignores as she gapes over
the entrails herself, seeking to compel from them the message she desires. But
Dido's dismissal of the extispicy of the Carthaginian seers is itself a reflection
of her dismissal of still earlier seers, the seers credited in Aeneas' narrative
with announcements of Aeneas' obligation to the gods to found a new city
in Italy.[13]

After the failure of her efforts to secure signs of divine support or approval
through sacrifice, Dido becomes abandoned to furor and madness (65, 69, 78,
91, 101), having no more thought of the gods than a wounded doe ranging
the forests in unconscious efforts to escape the intolerable pain of her wound
(69–73). The proud and independent queen has become utterly dependent,
no longer on divine signs but on the human object of her love. She shows Aeneas the wealth of her city, seeing it no longer as her own to dispose of as she
will but as "readied" for Aeneas, dependent on completion in Aeneas' acceptance of it. As she had repeated the sacrifices when they did not come out
right, so she seeks to repeat the feast at which she first fell in love with Aeneas (4.77), and to hear yet again about the fall of Troy, "hanging from his
mouth"[14] as he repeats it (78–79). Dido's "hanging" on Aeneas' words and
deeds expresses her attribution to him of the source of her own vitality; she
has given over to him the power to animate her own life. When she is apart
from him she still hears and sees him in his absence,[15] and, captivated by the
image of the father, tries to cheat her unspeakable love by holding the son on
her lap (83–85). Not only does Dido "hang from" Aeneas' mouth, but
Carthage itself "hangs interrupted" (88), since the energies she had directed
to building it have been diverted to Aeneas: Dido and her city have become
enchanted, as it were, depending on Aeneas to bring them back to life. In
these lines Vergil delicately constructs a portrayal of Dido's love based on Lucretius' analysis of the essential error of love, its false attribution to another
human being of "more than is right to concede to a mortal" (4.1184). Because
love is stimulated by images of the beloved that in reality have no way to be

incorporated into the body as food and drink are, it has the effect of making the lover falsely imagine that his life depends on acquiring something, the images of the beloved, which the body has no equipment for acquiring.

The scheming of Juno and Venus to bring the love of Dido and Aeneas to consummation is understood by them as scheming on behalf of Carthage and Rome respectively. Juno's plan for bringing the two together, to unite them in a cave during a thunderstorm, is a repetition of her attempt in Book 1 to wreck Aeneas through the emancipation of the storm winds from their cave; but now the thunderstorm has also become connected to the terms of Dido's fatal oath: "But I hope that either the earth will gape open from its depths for me or the omnipotent father will drive me with his thunderbolt to the shades" (4.24–25). Juno's plan is to use the natural elements of the storm both expediently as a means of getting Dido and Aeneas alone together in a private place and symbolically as cosmic or divine participants in or guarantors of an unearthly marriage ceremony (4.120–127). When the storm comes,[16] it presents Dido with a conundrum to amaze her mind and heart: is this storm the fulfillment of her awful oath—the opening of the earth, the punishing thunderbolt of Jupiter; or is it a divine fulfillment of her sacrificial prayers for safe breaking of her oath and union with Aeneas; or is it just a storm, a naturally cyclical release of excessive wind and heat from clouds, which does not refer to her at all, or indicate any divine intentions to punish or to gratify her? In fact, Vergil indicates, the storm is in some sense the beginning of the fulfillment of her oath: "that day was the first cause of death and the first cause of evils" (4.169–170); but Dido decides disingenuously to interpret it as a cosmic justification of the very *culpa* (19) she had forsworn in that oath: "she calls it marriage, with this name veils her *culpa*" (172).

The storm of Book 4 brings to a crisis, in a way prepared by the storm of Book 1, the fundamental question about furor in cosmos, city, and soul: Is the fire blind, or does the lightning have a purpose related to human beings? Are the heavenly phenomena indications of the obscure workings of divine providence, or are they manifestations of the blind clashings of the atoms? Vergil links in Dido's psychology the two extreme views: the thunderbolt as atomic nature, as in Iopas' song (*unde imber et ignes*, 1.743), and the thunderbolt as divine response to human will, as in her pretense of a higher-than-human marriage (4.172). The delicacy and restraint with which Vergil expresses the conflict of science and religion in Dido's soul has its counterpart in the grossness and directness with which he represents it in the soul of the barbarian king Iarbas; Iarbas is somehow a comic foil to tragic Dido.[17]

Iarbas, the African chieftain who had sold Dido the site of Carthage and whom she had rejected in marriage, is crucial to the action of Book 4—it is his appeal to Jupiter that is the cause of Aeneas' departure from Carthage and thus of Dido's fall and suicide. The strangeness of Iarbas' role is striking.[18] Of all the possible ways in which Vergil might have motivated Jupiter's message to Aeneas, he has chosen to present a challenge by Jupiter's reputed son to Jupiter's reputed godhead. The question about Jupiter's power and justice, not to say his existence, which was raised implicitly in Book 1 by the Aeolus incident, is raised explicitly in Book 4 by the barbarian king's prayer. Reputedly the son of Jupiter Ammon by the African nymph Garamantis, Iarbas is a comic doublet of Dido in her period of superstitious fervor after the conversation with Anna, with the exception that his excesses of ritual devotion are directed not at all or many gods but only at Jupiter:

> templa Iovi centum latis immania regnis,
> centum aras posuit vigilemque sacraverat ignem,
> excubias divum aeternas, pecudumque cruore
> pingue solum et variis florentia limina sertis.

> He had established in his broad kingdom a hundred huge temples to Jupiter, a hundred altars, and had consecrated an unsleeping fire, eternal sentries of the gods, earth fat with the gore of cattle and thresholds blooming with varied wreaths.

(4.199–202)

When Fama brings it to Iarbas' ears that Dido, who had rejected him, has accepted Aeneas, Iarbas is outraged and has the idea that Jupiter, if he were aware of this situation, would confirm his outrage, as at an injustice, by punishing the guilty ones. He apparently reasons as follows: "By introducing the worship of Jupiter into my nation, and that in a really large-scale way, I have established a claim on Jupiter's favor and protection. Dido is guilty of rejecting my suit and accepting Aeneas; Aeneas is guilty of ravishing Dido. My prior claim on Dido makes me like Menelaus to Dido's Helen and Aeneas' Paris; Aeneas, true to the national type, is starting another Trojan War. Menelaus appealed to Zeus to protect his claim on Helen and to punish Paris for the violation of his hospitality. I in turn call on Jupiter to vindicate my right—and my claim is all the greater in that Jupiter is my father, not just my father-in-law." Iarbas prays:

> Iuppiter omnipotens, cui nunc Maurusia pictis
> gens epulata toris Lenaeum libat honorem,
> aspicis haec? an te, genitor, cum fulmina torques
> nequiquam horremus, caecique in nubibus ignes
> terrificant animos et inania murmura miscent?

femina, quae nostris errans in finibus urbem
exiguam pretio posuit, cui litus arandum
cuique loci leges dedimus, conubia nostra
reppulit ac dominum Aenean in regna recepit.
et nunc ille Paris cum semiviro comitatu,
Maeonia mentum mitra crinemque madentem
subnexus, rapto potitur: nos munera templis
quippe tuis ferimus famamque fovemus inanem.

Omnipotent Jupiter, to whom now the Maurusian nation, feasting on embroidered couches, makes libation offerings, do you see this? Or is it without reason that we fear you when you wield the thunderbolts, while it's really blind fires in the clouds that terrify our spirits by mingling empty growl-sounds? A woman who, as a wanderer in our territory, established a tiny city for a price, to whom we gave some seashore for plowing and the laws of the place, has rejected marriage with us and received Aeneas into her kingdom as master. And now that Paris with his half-male crew, with a Maeonian cap tied about his beard and his perfumed hair, takes possession of what he has ravished: while we, forsooth, bring offerings to your temples and cherish an empty rumor.

(4.206–218)

It belongs to Vergil's poetic tact not to put Epicurean doctrine too fully or crassly in the mouth of Dido herself. What he is representing in Dido and the Carthaginians is not Epicureanism proper but Epicureanism vulgarized, Epicureanism as it becomes diffused "in the air" in a society that looks up to an Epicurean poet as its first teacher. Tact does not permit Dido's own characterization to go beyond the most discreet indications, viz. her being the audience of Iopas' teaching and of Anna's argument; her silence about the gods and about the status of Aeneas' divine mission; her decision to "succumb" to her guilty love of Aeneas, and her deeds following upon this decision. But in order to maintain this delicacy regarding Dido herself, it was necessary to put the positive Epicurean doctrine, in both its pure and its vulgarized form, into the mouths of other characters. In Book 1, Iopas is the spokesman of the pure doctrine.[19] This is the key to Iarbas' strange role in the tragedy, and explains what is otherwise obscure and superfluous in his appearance.

For Iarbas' role is, at first glance, obscure. His dramatic function is to call Jupiter's attention to Aeneas' lapse from cleaving to his divine mission; but his speech, his prayer to Jupiter, is quite disproportionate to that dramatic function. Iarbas' self-understanding in his speech is entirely unrelated to Aeneas' mission, or to Jupiter's true interest in Aeneas. Iarbas' speech is, dramatically, the spring of Jupiter's renewal of Aeneas' mission; but his speech is framed in terms only of the theological question as to Jupiter's reality, power, and justice. Iarbas has no idea of the considerations that lead Jupiter to act on his prayer, to appear to be fulfilling his prayer.[20] To Iarbas, the events of Book 4 appear to vindicate the assumptions underlying his prayer; but that appearance is almost entirely deceptive.

Iarbas' prayer challenges Jupiter to prove his existence by fulfilling Iarbas' designs and protecting Iarbas' honor. In Iarbas Vergil writes large what in Dido is written faintly: the intimate connection in non-philosophers between superstition and atheism—the opinion that the gods are either humanly manipulable or mere empty rumors. Iarbas' prayer intervenes between Dido's attempt to bend the gods to her own will (4.56 ff.) and her scornful discounting (4.376–380) of divine providence; his prayer is indeed the link between these two poles of Dido's opinion. Vulgar Epicureanism is a doctrine that makes men not pacific contemplators of all things but contemptuous challengers of the gods. Like Mezentius, the untaught "scorner of gods" in *Aeneid* 8–10,[21] Iarbas' best approximation to true Epicureanism is to taunt Jupiter with being an empty rumor, and in particular, to allege against Jupiter the blindness of the lightning bolt.

The role of Iarbas then is not merely to put in motion the events leading to Aeneas' departure from Carthage, but also to present with comic grossness the controversy of science against religion that in Dido is developed with tragic delicacy.[22] In the argument of his prayer, Iarbas indicates that the root of his belief is the hope that his impotent indignation may be supported by an omnipotent god, *Iuppiter omnipotens*, and the root of his unbelief is the suspicion that his impotent indignation is supported by nothing at all; indignation underlies both sides of the argument. But indignation at what? The injustice that smarts in Iarbas is that of unrequited love: he offered himself to Dido and she rejected him, indeed not only rejected him but then accepted Aeneas. The impotence of Iarbas' indignation is not impotence to harm Dido (cf. 4.326) but impotence to get his own back, to make the punishment fit the crime, to make her in turn suffer the smart of rejected love. This is the notorious impotence of rejected lovers in general to get their own back: if you injure me by bloodying my nose I can get my own back by bloodying yours; but if you injure me by rejecting my love or my offer of marriage I cannot get my own back by rejecting yours. In cases where I cannot return your aggression against my property because you are stronger, richer, or more powerful than I am, I may reflect that my impotence is an accident that may in principle be reversed; but when I cannot return your rejection of my love in such a way as to hurt you back and thus punish you, I may feel, like Iarbas, that I am up against a humanly incorrigible injustice;[23] and precisely here, like Iarbas, I may come to feel that human affairs require fulfillment in divine punishment if the universe is a moral cosmos and not a moral chaos. Then I come to formulate the matter as Iarbas does: "either Jupiter punishes human injustice or the thunderbolt is blind" (206–210); "if injustice prevails then Jupiter is an empty rumor" (211–218).

The relevance of Iarbas' ideas to the tragedy of Dido unfolds from these considerations on the connection between unrequited love and reliance on divine punishment and thus belief in gods. When Dido was so profoundly hurt as a young bride by her brother's murder of her husband, she found herself able to avenge her husband and punish her brother, to get her own back, by her own unaided actions. In this condition, experiencing herself as deeply wronged but also as completely autonomous and potent in punishing adequately the wrong against her (*dux femina facti*, 1.364), she became at Carthage, while in the process of founding it as vengeance and punishment, the pupil of Iopas. From Iopas she learned a doctrine that seemed to be in accordance with her own experience: there is no divine punishment, indeed there are no gods at all; human beings are on their own; the thunderbolt is a blind fire in the clouds; we are unprotected. Her Epicurean education was, however, defective, for while learning how to understand naturally the images of gods and underworld, and thus to free herself from reliance on but also from fear of gods and underworld, she did not learn how to understand naturally the images of love and thus to free herself from attributing to human beings more than is right, or from being dependent on the reciprocation of human love more than is right. The defect of her education was revealed by the change in her circumstances brought about by the arrival of the Trojans. As she puts it:

> urbem praeclaram statui, mea moenia vidi,
> ulta virum poenas inimico a fratre recepi,
> felix, heu nimium felix, si[24] litora tantum
> numquam Dardaniae tetigissent nostra carinae.

> I established an illustrious city, I saw my walls, I avenged my husband and exacted punishment from my brother-enemy—happy, ah, all too happy, if only the Dardanian ships had never touched our shores.

> (4.655–658)

But then, with this change of circumstances, her experience of her own autonomy was shattered by her falling in love with Aeneas against her own will; and her experience of her own power was shattered by the impotence of rejected lovers to get their own back. At this point, in the position of dependence and impotence belonging essentially to the experience of rejected love, Dido finds herself returned to a form of the conflict between science and religion that had not been alive for her at the time of her conversion to science: for a human being whose experience is not that of autonomy and power, but rather that of dependence and impotence, is life bearable without divine support, divine justice, and divine reward and punishment? As Dido enters into this experience and elaborates her response to it, her inclination now to religion and now to atheism leads her by degrees to the crisis of her ambiguous suicide.

vi. Dido Furiosa

That same impious Fama that had brought to Iarbas the news of Dido's union with Aeneas (4.173–197) now brings to Dido the news that the Trojan fleet is preparing to sail (4.298–299). In Dido's next speech to Aeneas (4.305–330) she accuses him of intending to wrong her by abandoning her; she lays out to him just where the wrong lies; and she appeals to him to change his plan out of considerations of justice towards her. The wrong that she accuses him of is "perfidy" (305): she considers that "our love" and the "right hand given" (307) constitute a mutual promise by which she has given over the sustaining of her very life to Aeneas:

> nec te noster amor nec te data dextera quondam
> nec moritura tenet crudeli funere Dido?

> Does neither our love hold you, nor the right hand given, nor [the prospect that] Dido will die a cruel death?

> (4.307–308)

The smart of Dido's position is the thought that Aeneas is leaving her for no other reason than that he has become repelled by her (*mene fugis?*, 314), a conclusion she reaches from the unreasonableness of his departing in the middle of winter: such a sailing, she rightly thinks, is not an act of sober prudence, and so, she wrongly concludes, it must be an act of repugnance (4.309–313). When she reaches the conclusion of these thoughts, the formulation of the idea that Aeneas rejects her, she wishes to follow it with the strongest possible appeal to him to change his intention. The strongest appeal she can make to him is "by these tears and your right hand, by our marriage, by the wedding rites undertaken" (314, 316), but, though it is her strongest appeal, she qualifies it: "since I myself have left nothing else to my wretched self" (315). What "else" does she find she has not left to her wretched self? She proudly stands by her disdaining to appeal to any god: the "wedding rites undertaken" were undertaken by her without divine sanction, in proud reliance on the human confidence that love promises continued love. Dido at the time of these hymeneals "called it marriage, with this name veiled her *culpa*" (172); she knew it was not marriage in the usual sense, and even if at the time she was half-confused by her emotional struggles into imagining that nature itself divinely attended her nuptials, she is certainly too proud now to appeal to gods to whom she did not appeal then as guarantors of Aeneas' fidelity; she acknowledges that "guest," *hospes*, is now the only name remaining from what was once "husband," *coniunx* (323–324). Dido has left herself "nothing else" to appeal to but the human fidelity she felt was implied in the great love scene in the cave; she banked on Aeneas putting aside the foolishness of his fidelity to divine dreams and oracles in favor of the wisdom of fidelity to their mutual human love. Now too she has the pride and self-recollection to disdain anything "else" and appeals to Aeneas only by their human connection and by the totality of her consequent dependence on him:

> si bene quid de te merui, fuit aut tibi quicquam
> dulce meum, miserere domus labentis et istam,
> oro, si quis adhuc precibus locus, exue mentem.

> If I have merited anything good from you, or if anything of mine has been sweet to you, take pity on my falling house and, I beg, if there is any room still for prayers, change that intention of yours. . . .

> (4.317–319)

In all of this speech Dido mentions no gods. She sees the issue as a life-and-death matter for herself, and in the face of this she is grand enough, self-possessed enough, to present herself still as she first did to the amazed Trojans when they had washed up on her shore, relying altogether on human calculation and human generosity, and disdaining to bind herself or others by divine sanctions of any kind.[25]

As in the first exchange between Dido and Aeneas in Book 1 (see above, pp. 33–34), so in this one: Dido is altogether silent about the gods while Aeneas appeals to them as the ultimate authorities. With the recent admonitions from Jupiter firming his spirit, Aeneas acknowledges Dido's merits (*merui*, 317; *te . . . promeritam*, 333–335), while correctly denying that he ever married her, and attributing his decision to leave Carthage to the fates (340), to Apollo (345), to the Lycian lots (346), to the image of Anchises (351–353), to a messenger of the gods sent by Jupiter himself and seen and heard by Aeneas himself (356–359): "Cease to inflame both me and yourself with your plaints: it is not of my own will that I make for Italy" (361).

Aeneas in this speech is as sincere and as true to himself as Dido had been in her preceding speech. In his very first words to Dido he had expressed out-right his human dependence on the gods (1.601–605) and indicated that other lands than Carthage were summoning him; and in his long narrative at Dido's feast that night he had described in vivid detail the interlocking dreams, oracles, prophecies, and visions by which his life was being deter-mined. Aeneas indeed had been inspired by his love for Dido and Carthage to forget, or stray from, or tentatively try out an alternative to the founding responsibilities he had taken on himself; Mercury had discovered him to all appearances quite Punicized[26] as well as uxorious (4.260–267). Aeneas' self-forgetful love for Dido and Carthage is profoundly important to an under-standing of his development. But Dido, in imagining that Aeneas' longings, experiments, and self-forgettings meant that he had been converted to her view of the nature of things, somehow missed the essential core of the man she loved.[27] At last as at first, Aeneas and Dido are divided as the founder of the pious city and the founder of the enlightened city. Here in response to Dido's proud appeal to her first principles, Aeneas just as proudly affirms and abides by his own, as he had presented them from the beginning.

Aeneas' speech evokes from Dido first a denunciation of his claims about the gods and then a hope or conviction or determination that Aeneas will be punished for wronging her. No goddess, she says, was Aeneas' mother (365)—"for why should I dissimulate, or for what greater occasions am I holding myself back?" (368). From the first moment when she addressed Ae-neas as *nate dea* (1.615), Dido has been dissimulating,[28] that is, tactfully hold-ing herself back from openly denying or questioning his delusions; she was holding herself back for greater occasions, occasions perhaps when Aeneas under her tutelage would have abandoned those delusions of his own accord; but now there is no greater occasion to hold back for, no reason not to speak all her thought. Her thought is that no goddess is his mother; his hard and pitiless character suggests that he was born of a rock and nursed by tigers (cf. 4.11–13); for why dissimulate any longer? After disdaining to dissimulate any longer, Dido begins to speak of Aeneas in the third person (369) and does not resume explicit second-person forms until line 380. It is as if for Aeneas' benefit she presents her case before an imaginary just judge,[29] as if in this way she might make more objectively clear to Aeneas exactly what her case is:

num fletu ingemuit nostro? num lumina flexit?
num lacrimas victus dedit aut miseratus amantem est?
quae quibus anteferam? iam iam nec maxima Iuno
nec Saturnius haec oculis pater aspicit aequis.

nusquam tuta fides. eiectum litore, egentem
excepi et regni demens in parte locavi.
amissam classem, socios a morte reduxi
(heu furiis incensa feror!): nunc augur Apollo,
nunc Lyciae sortes, nunc et Iove missus ab ipso
interpres divum fert horrida iussa per auras.
scilicet is superis labor est, ea cura quietos
sollicitat.

Has he groaned at my weeping? Has he turned his eyes? Has he been so over-come as to shed tears, or has he taken pity on his lover? What shall I adduce first, what next? Now, now [it is clear that] neither great Juno nor the Saturn-ian father regards these things with just eyes. Nowhere is good faith safe. I took him in when he was thrown up on the shore and in need, I gave him a place, though I was mad to do so, in my kingdom. I restored his lost fleet, I restored his companions from death (oh, I am inflamed and carried away by furies!): now Apollo as augur, now the Lycian lots, now a messenger of the gods sent ac-tually by Jupiter himself brings dread commands through the breezes. This, for-sooth, is a labor for the gods, this concern worries them in their tranquillity.

(4.369–380)

Her case is that Aeneas is without human pity for the woman he has made to depend on him through love; that it is demonstratively clear now, from the manifest unprotectedness of good faith, that the allegedly great gods do not look at human things with a care for justice; that Dido independently, and not any gods at all, rescued Aeneas and his men when they were really in danger of death and thus most in need of divine aid if there were such a thing; that it is only now[30] (when he wishes for his own reasons to abandon Dido) that Aeneas claims that gods are looking out for him and ordering him around; that it is ridiculous to imagine that Aeneas' travels could be the con-cern of any gods.[31] The just judge before whom Dido dramatically argues her case is one who agrees with her that the failure of any Juno or Jupiter to look at these things with just eyes shows that good faith is everywhere unpro-tected; who sympathizes with her being inflamed by furies when she recalls all her unrequited generosity to Aeneas and the Trojans; who appreciates the scorn in her report that Aeneas claims divine instruction and imagines the gods concerned with his affairs. Before this imagined judge she indicts the be-lief in the justice of the Olympians, the ingratitude of Aeneas, the belief in divine providence.[32] This judge is perhaps the Epicurean sage of her imagi-nation,[33] who like her denies divine reward and punishment while promot-ing the life of erotic passion; it is perhaps this imagined Epicurean sage whom she has regarded as the ideal she was holding up to Aeneas and herself all along in their life together. Having made her case before this judge for Aeneas' benefit, she turns back to Aeneas himself in direct address:

> neque te teneo neque dicta refello:
> i, sequere Italiam ventis, pete regna per undas.

I do not hold you nor do I refute your words—go, make for Italy with the winds, seek your kingdom through the waves.

(4.380–381)

And now, having made the case that there is no divine intervention on behalf of human justice, Dido is turned in the manifest unprotectedness of her position to hope nevertheless to get her own back:

> spero equidem mediis, si quid pia numina possunt,
> supplicia hausurum scopulis et nomine Dido
> saepe vocaturum. sequar atris ignibus absens
> et, cum frigida mors anima seduxerit artus,
> omnibus umbra locis adero. dabis, improbe, poenas.
> audiam et haec manis veniet mihi fama sub imos.

I for my part hope, if pious gods can do anything, that you will drink down torments among the rocks and often call on Dido by name. Separated from you, I shall pursue you with black fires and, when frigid death has separated my limbs from my soul, I shall be present in all places as a shade. You shall pay the penalty, wicked one. I shall hear of it, and this report will come down to me among the deepest shades.

(4.382–387)

In these closing words Dido first hopes for and then predicts the punishment of Aeneas for his wrong to her. The hope that she expresses conditionally is that gods will punish Aeneas; the prediction she makes affirmatively is that she herself will punish him. Dido's hope for divine punishment is expressed as a scornful parody of the hope he had expressed, in his first speech to her, for divine reward:

> di tibi, si qua pios respectant numina, si quid
> usquam iustitia est et mens sibi conscia recti,
> praemia digna ferant.

May the gods, if any deities respect pious men, if justice is anything anywhere, and mind conscious within itself of the right—may the gods bring you worthy rewards.

(1.603–605)

May the gods, Dido counters, if pious gods can do anything at all, bring you condign punishment. The punishment that she envisions is condign in the sense that it is calculated to bring home to Aeneas his ingratitude to Dido: Dido rescued him from shipwreck (4.373–375); she imagines him calling her name in vain in shipwreck, which is to say, being compelled to repent his wrongdoing. But since there are no pious gods who can do anything, Dido turns from this bitter mockery of Aeneas' prayer to an assertion that not gods but she herself will punish Aeneas, just as not gods but she herself had punished Pygmalion. She punished Pygmalion by founding Carthage; but how is she to punish Aeneas for leaving her? "Though absent, I shall pursue you with black fires." The appropriateness of this punishment is that she fell in love with him in the first place through the operation upon her of visual and auditory images of him in his absence: "Though absent, she hears and sees absent him" (4.83). As he had that power over her, to affect her through mental images of himself, so she claims that power over him. But from what act of hers will the image of "black fires" arise to torment Aeneas with remorse? Dido, in the impotence of the rejected lover, thinks of her own death as the event potentially able to fill Aeneas with guilty remorse and thus darken his life.[34] As in her earlier speech to Aeneas she referred to her own impending death as something that ought to hold him in Carthage (4.308, cf. 323),[35] so here she begins to imagine her impending death as something that will *punish* him by striking him with intolerable consciousness of his guilt; her own death will be the instrument of Aeneas' torment. But in that case, since she will die in the process of punishing him, how will she get the satisfaction of it? "Do you believe that ashes and buried shades feel concern?" (4.34). Under the pressure of her passion for punishment, Dido is so far impelled out of herself as to imagine herself surviving her own death: her disembodied soul will be "in all places," she will hear among the shades of Aeneas' punishment: in this way only does Dido imagine getting satisfaction, getting her own back.

Dido's leap from intolerable anger into belief in the afterlife, from impotence to punish Aeneas into belief in other-worldly powers, leads from her imagination of punishing Aeneas by her death to her resolve to die: *mortem orat* (4.451). As her imagination of her death began as her imagination of knowing after death that she has thereby punished Aeneas, so her resolve to die swings her back again into the full panoply of the *antiquae religiones*. If Dido's first return to religious practices (4.56 ff.) was characterized by excess and obsession, this, her second return, is characterized by private and hallucinatory horror arising from her fear and guilt before the divine powers. She sees her libations turn black and wine turn to blood (4.453–455);[36] the voice of Sychaeus "appears" (4.461) to call to her from the marble temple to him that is within the palace (457–461) (and which she "used to serve with amazing worship," though this has not been mentioned before and sorts ill with her assent to Anna's view that the dead do not care for the living and with her own dismissal of Aeneas' claim to be visited by the image of his dead father [353, 365]); an owl appears to cry from the roof (462–463); the predictions of the former seers horrify her (464–465); in nightmares she is hounded by Aeneas and deserted by her people, like mad Pentheus seeing the troops of Eumenides or like Orestes fleeing his mother while the Dirae sit on the threshold (465–473). This combination of Dido's suicidal intention with her sudden liability to other-worldly horrors introduces her lying (4.477) speech to Anna, 478–498, in which she successfully disguises her preparations for suicide as a plan to use magical arts either to restore Aeneas to herself or to sever her own affections from Aeneas (479). In this speech she reminds us of the chasm now separating her from her enlightened self: at her feast for the Trojans she had entertained them with the song of Iopas, the pupil of "maximus Atlas" (1.741); now she claims to have a priestess from the land where "maximus Atlas" (4.481) turns on his shoulder the pole fitted out with gleaming stars. Where Iopas had sung of the nature of things, the reasons for the motions of the heavenly bodies and the terrestrial phenomena, the priestess promises through her songs to stop the water in the rivers and turn the stars back the other way, to stir up the nocturnal ghosts, to make the earth moo and the ash-trees come down from the mountains. With the recurrence of "maximus Atlas" here, Vergil forces us to reflect on the common source of atheistic science and superstitious magic:[37] Superstitious magic is the form of religion resorted to by people who wish to be atheists but lack the strength for it; it is the form of religion most frightening with malevolent and capricious deities, but it is also the form most holding out the prospect of human control over divine beings. A more sober religion presents gods less malevolent and less in need of conciliation, but also less manipulable by human practices. Dido's speech is not sincere, but a pretext; nevertheless, however Dido inwardly disowns its magical content, her choice of precisely this pretext is fully in accord with the horrified derangement of her. It is in this speech that, for the first time since her abortive oath, she solemnly invokes the gods (*testor . . . deos*, 4.492), and though she does so here in a specious context, she follows these words with deeds more genuine, if only in a tentative way:

ipsa . . .
testatur moritura deos et conscia fati
sidera; tum, si quod non aequo foedere amantis
curae numen habet iustumque memorque, precatur.

> She herself . . . on the verge of death, calls to witness the gods and the stars conscious of fate; then, if any just and mindful divinity has as its concern those who love unrequitedly, to it she prays.
>
> (4.517–521)

And for the first time now, on this wave of prayer and rage, Dido begins to regard her suicide not only as a means of punishing Aeneas but as a means of her own punishment for her perjury (*quin morere ut merita es*, 547; *non servata fides cineri promissa Sychaei*, 552).

In the great soliloquy that culminates in her imprecation of undying war between Carthage and Rome, Dido, seeing that the Trojan fleet has sailed once for all, begins with an incredulous juxtaposition of "Jupiter" and "Aeneas' impunity": "By Jupiter! is this fellow to go then, and thus to have cheated our kingdom, the foreigner?!" (4.590–591). The solemn invoking of the gods that Dido had begun in order to disguise the preparations for her suicide shows here its true source in the springing desire for punishment: Dido's "angry oath"[38] recalls the angry prayer of Iarbas in which he had challenged Jupiter to prove his existence by punishing injustice: "Omnipotent Jupiter! . . . a woman who, when she was astray within our borders, established here a little city for a price . . . ." (4.206 ff.). But the comic outline of Iarbas' argument is transmuted in Dido's speech into a heightened summary of Dido's tragic predicament. She cannot approve the way in which punitive anger impels resort to gods; she turns from her outburst *pro Iuppiter!* to a consideration of the possibilities for human punishment. Will not the Carthaginians fall upon the fleeing Trojans with fire and arms? (4.592–594). But in overhearing herself uttering this battle cry, Dido is brought up short by the "insanity" of it: "What am I saying? or Where am I? What insanity is altering my mind?" (4.595). This insanity that Dido hears in her own words is the insanity of imagining that the Carthaginians could attack the Trojans now. When the Trojans were helplessly shipwrecked the Carthaginian coast guard was able to threaten them (1.525, 539–541); but now that Dido herself has helped them to restore their fleet, now that they are re-armed, all the wealth of Carthage is helpless against them. Dido's idea, seconded by Anna, had been to unite Carthaginian gold with Trojan arms; failing that, it is "insane" now to think of Carthaginian sailors taking on the Trojan navy. "Unhappy Dido, now the impious deeds come home to you? It would have suited then, when you were handing over the scepter" (4.596–597). Dido repents of having shared her kingdom with Aeneas. The impious deeds she thinks of are the infidelities of Aeneas, all the more shocking because he had presented himself as the very exemplar of piety:

"Behold, the right hand and the faithfulness of him who, they say, carries with him his ancestral penates, who carried on his shoulders his age-worn father!" (4.597–599). But, through Dido's reference to the impious deeds connected with her handing over the scepter, Vergil reminds us how Dido's offer of fellow citizenship to the Trojans was itself without regard for the ancestral penates or, for that matter, any gods at all; it is as a result of Dido's attempt at an enlightened and humanly autonomous union of the peoples and sovereigns that Aeneas and the Trojans are now bound to Dido and the Carthaginians by "nothing else" than human purposes and agreements, and thus that Carthage can neither punish the Trojans militarily nor threaten the Trojans with divine punishment. Dido regrets, therefore, the punishments she might have been able to execute herself: tearing Aeneas' body apart or serving to him the flesh of his son Ascanius. Her success would not have been assured; but since she was prepared to die in any case, why need she have feared? (600–606). These lost opportunities are irrecoverable, though, now that Aeneas' fleet has sailed. Neither the Carthaginians nor Dido herself have the means to punish Aeneas in any way.

Dido's review of the obstacles to human punishment of Aeneas reaches two successive crests of intensity, first in her "insane" war cry and then in her imagination of killing Aeneas herself. The tragic cruelty of Dido's wishes is here the measure of the depth of her impotent fury, and leads to a great rhetorical break at this moment of her speech: between these frenzied lines and lines 607 ff. we must surely hear a pause, a silence in which Dido moves internally from the transports of her rage to her full realization of her impotence. At this point the wild appeal to Jupiter that had opened her speech and then vanished from it finds its completion: Dido prays for the just punishment of Aeneas to Sol, to Juno, to Hecate, to the avenging Dirae and the "gods of the dying Elissa" (4.607–612). What she prays is that Aeneas may be personally injured and grieved, even if it is "necessary" that he achieve his mission in Italy (4.612–621). Vergil reminds us of the extremity of this prayer in the mouth of the enlightened Dido by making her gloss "necessary" in two ways: necessary in that the "fates of Jupiter" require it, and necessary in that "this boundary is inherent" (614): necessity in terms of divine providence, and necessity in terms of the nature of things as expressed in "one of Lucretius' great signature-phrases,"[39] *hic terminus haeret.*

This prayer, the final version of her hope of punishing Aeneas himself, is Dido's first and last unequivocal prayer to the gods. From this she turns to her imprecation of unending war between Carthage and Rome, where she speaks of purely human military vengeance to take place some time in the future when Carthage's military defect will have been supplied:

> tum vos, o Tyrii, stirpem et genus omne futurum
> exercete odiis, cinerique haec mittite nostro
> munera. nullus amor populis nec foedera sunto.
> exoriare aliquis nostris ex ossibus ultor
> qui face Dardanios ferroque sequare colonos,
> nunc, olim, quocumque dabunt se tempore vires.
> litora litoribus contraria, fluctibus undas
> imprecor, arma armis: pugnent ipsique nepotesque.

Then you, o Tyrians, harry with hatred his offspring and all his future race, and send these death offerings to my ashes. Let there be no love and no compacts between the peoples. May you arise, some avenger, from my bones, to pursue the Dardanian colonists with torch and iron—now, later, at whatever time the force will be available. Shores against shores, waves against floods, I pray, arms against arms: let them themselves and their descendants fight.

(4.622–629)

How Carthage is to become a great military power without union with the Trojans is finally suggested here: the "exercise of hatred" as a death-offering to Dido's ashes is to work over time as the cultivation of the Carthaginians' martial virtue. Their valor in war is to arise not from their wealth but from the consecration of their hatred to the memory of their founder, whom they are to conceive as a spirit living on in the next world: through becoming pious toward their founder the Carthaginians are finally to become warriors. In her great imprecation Vergil makes Dido express what she has learned, so to speak, from her great enemy: men do not become warriors without piety, without devotion to the dead, without a divinized founder.[40]

In the final, quieter words of her death scene, Dido recapitulates the great and ultimately decisive division between Aeneas and herself: Aeneas was ruled by "fates and god" (4.351), while her own life was a course given by "fortune" (4.353).[41] She closes on the question of vengeance, accepting, after all her furious attempts to conceive of either the gods or her own ghost as her avengers, that there will be no vengeance, no punishment of Aeneas, beyond his present sight of her blazing pyre and whatever ominous suggestion it may carry for him:

> 'moriemur inultae,
> sed moriamur' ait. 'sic, sic iuvat ire sub umbras.

hauriat hunc oculis ignem crudelis ab alto
Dardanus, et nostrae secum ferat omina mortis.'

"We shall die unavenged; but let us die," she said. "Thus, thus, I gladly go down to the shades. May the cruel Dardanian drink in this fire with his eyes from the high seas, and carry with him the omens of our death."

(4.659–662)

PART TWO

THE GREATER
ORDER OF THINGS

~

CHAPTER EIGHT

The Theme of the *Aeneid* Again

The *Aeneid* begins anew at Book 7; it has a new proem, and a new invocation that claims for this second beginning a higher status than for the first: *maius opus moveo*, "I am setting in motion my greater work" (7.45).

In the new proem, 7.1–45, the three elements of the first proem, Rome-anger-Carthage, are answered by Rome-anger-Italy. In the proem to Book 1, Vergil had set in motion the contesting claims of the two types of city, the Roman and the Carthaginian, to be the well-founded city—the city that has the key to the rule of anger in the souls and cities of men. "Rome" is represented in the second proem by Caieta's eternal fame, and "anger" by Circe's beasts. "Carthage," whose claim to be the political rival or alternative to Rome has been defeated in the first half, is now replaced by "Italy," whose relationship to Rome is to be taken up in the second half: the meaning of Rome's becoming the "kingdom over the nations" (*regnum gentibus*, 1.17), and the Roman people's becoming "king far and wide" (*late regem*, 1.21), will be shown by Rome's becoming in the first place king over the Italian nations. Like Carthage, Italy is championed by Juno, nursing her eternal wound.

i. Rome

Tu quoque litoribus nostris, Aeneia nutrix,
aeternam moriens famam, Caieta, dedisti;
et nunc servat honos sedem tuus, ossaque nomen
Hesperia in magna, si qua est ea gloria, signat.

> You also, Caieta, nurse of Aeneas, in your death gave eternal fame to our
> shores; and now your honor preserves your resting place, and a name identifies
> your bones in great Hesperia—if this is any glory.
>
> (7.1–4)

With *tu quoque* the poet calls for our taking stock: at the beginning of the
second half of the *Aeneid*, Caieta "also" is apostrophized as having given eternal glory to "our shores" by her death. "Also" means in addition to Misenus
and Palinurus,[1] whose names are eternal through the names of places on "our
shores." The mountain that is now called Misenus, after the one buried there,
keeps his name eternal throughout the ages (6.234–235); as, according to the
Sybil, the place where Palinurus will be buried "will keep the name of Palinurus eternal" (6.381). Is it the place that gives eternal fame to the person, or
the person to the place?[2] The statements about Palinurus and Misenus are
ambiguous. Our shores are given eternal glory by Caieta having died there;
but the fame, honor, name, glory ("if this *is* any glory") of Caieta are preserved eternal only by Rome being preserved eternal. The places named for
Palinurus, Misenus, and Caieta may formerly have been nameless, or have
had non-Roman names;[3] it is the eternity of Rome through the generations
of mortal individuals, not the eternity of the individuals, that has given eternal fame to the people who are commemorated through the naming of Roman places.

In addition to the clear reference to Misenus and Palinurus, "*Tu quoque,
Aeneia nutrix*" recalls two other ideas. The Aenean nurse[4] who gives eternal
fame recalls the opening invocation of Lucretius' *De Rerum Natura*: *Ae-
neadum genetrix . . . alma Venus . . . aeternum da dictis, diva, leporem* (1.1–2,
28). The words to which Lucretius asks the nurturant mother of the descendants of Aeneas to give eternal charm are Latin words and, especially, new
Latin words to the invention of which Lucretius is compelled by the poverty
of the Latin language and the newness of the things (1.136–139)[5]. The eternal charm of Latin words, like the eternal fame of the names of "our shores,"
identifies eternity with the lifetime of Rome.

That the lifetime of Rome will be "eternal" is dependent, in turn, on the
second idea recalled by "*Aeneia nutrix*": Italy's transformation into eternal
Rome is to take place, as Jupiter has indicated in his prophecy in Book 1,
through the preservation of Aeneas' descendant Romulus by the most celebrated nurse of all:

> regina sacerdos
> Marte gravis geminam partu dabit Ilia prolem.

inde lupae fulvo nutricis tegmine laetus
Romulus excipiet gentem et Mavortia condet
moenia Romanosque suo de nomine dicet.
his ego nec metas rerum nec tempora pono:
imperium sine fine dedi.

The priestess-queen Ilia, pregnant by Mars, will give birth to twin offspring.
Then Romulus, rejoicing in the tawny hide of his wolf-nurse, will continue the
race and found the Mavortian walls and call the Romans after his own name.
For them I set no boundaries or times of their affairs: empire without end I
grant.

(1.273–279)

Romulus' wolf-nurse made it possible for there to be Romans to whom Jupiter
might give the empire without end in which alone the Roman name could
be preserved eternal; Aeneas' nurse "too" gave eternal fame to our shores.

The phrase "our shores" refers us back to the opening of the first proem of
the *Aeneid:* the poet will sing of arms and of the man who was the first to
have come from Troy to the Lavinian shores (1.1–3), the man from whose
founding deed have sprung the walls of lofty Rome (1.5–7). At the opening
of Book 7, however, the three whose names are eternally intertwined with
the eternity of the Roman places or place-names are remembered for deaths
that did not take place under arms: Palinurus the navigator died after falling
from the helm of Aeneas' ship; Misenus the trumpeter died while challenging the gods at song; and Caieta the nurse died while sailing with Aeneas'
company from Cumae to the mouth of the Tiber. The eternal glory of the Roman places is in the first place the glory not of armed heroes but of the pilot,
the musician, the nurse. The pilot and the musician had met death each by
pressing beyond its human limits his special calling: Palinurus while attempting to resist divine Sleep in his knowledge of the treacherousness of the
sea, Misenus ("if it is worthy of credence," 6.173) while challenging the gods
to contest in trumpeting. Caieta's death too, though not stemming from a direct challenge to any god, takes place while she is pressing her devotion to
her calling beyond its moderate exercise, following Aeneas to Italy rather
than joining the matrons and "souls not desiring great praise" who had remained with Acestes in Sicily (5.751).[6] Although each of the three died
while in some sense seeking glory, none of them died as a warrior or armed;
they achieved glory through their exercise of the arts, and, at least in the
cases of Palinurus and Misenus, through their defying the gods in that exercise. One might have thought that the defeat of the Carthaginian principle
in the first half of the *Aeneid* subordinated arts to arms, but the opening of

the second half reminds us that Rome too founds human glory on the arts; only in the second half will the glory of arms be added "also" to that of arts. "*Tu quoque*" sums up the first half of the *Aeneid*,[7] while reminding us that the account of the glory of Roman arms is yet to come.

Although in dying, Caieta gave "eternal fame" to our shores, the poet brings us up short at the opening of the Iliadic *Aeneid* by calling into question whether that *is* any glory. Aeneas has come to the place that is now called Caieta, the place where the nurse Caieta dies, from the Underworld through the gate of false dreams; his father Anchises' last direct words to him had been, with reference to his funeral offerings to Marcellus, *fungar inani munere*, "let me perform the empty rite" (6.885–886), on which Servius comments, "unavailing, according to the Epicureans" (*secundum Epicureos, non profuturo*). It is not Anchises of course who speaks *secundum Epicureos*— Anchises means that the funeral rites for Marcellus will be of no avail in averting his fated early death—but Vergil, by putting these words in his mouth, prepares us for the Epicurean conclusion of the catabasis in the episode of the gates of dreams. The entire catabasis, insofar as it may be said to provide a justification for funeral rites by showing that souls survive and are sensible after death, has been thrown into doubt by its conclusion. The poet's throwing the glory of Caieta into doubt, though startling, is in fact a resumption in small of his having just concluded the catabasis as a whole by throwing the immortality and judgment of souls into doubt.

"It is well," says Servius, "that he takes part in a funeral after he has returned from the Underworld, just as he took part in one before he descended, in order to frame the action in between."[8] When the Sybil prophesies, during the catabasis, Palinurus' burial by neighboring natives at the instigation of the gods, Vergil emphasizes by Palinurus' response the efficacy of the funeral rites both in giving welcome rest to the dead (6.371, "so that at least I may come to rest in death in the tranquil resting places") and in giving them joy in the preservation of their name (6.383, "he rejoices in the land named after him"). This is in harmony with the overall teaching of the catabasis, the reward and punishment of immortal—that is, immortally sensible—souls. Before the catabasis, in the burial of Misenus, it was the insensibility of the dead that had been emphasized:

> Nec minus interea Misenum in litore Teucri
> flebant et cineri ingrato suprema ferebant.

> Meanwhile the Teucrians were bewailing Misenus on the shore and bringing the last offerings to his thankless ashes.

(6.212–213)

After the catabasis one might have expected that the efficacy of the funeral rites for the dead, as demonstrated to Aeneas in the episode of Palinurus, would have come at last to be known; but what is emphasized in Caieta's burial is the doubtfulness of glory, *si qua est ea gloria*—on which Servius remarks again, *secundum Epicureos.*[9] The opening lines of the second half of the *Aeneid* sum up the first half by framing the catabasis and thus completing the context for judging its falsity: the efficacy of Caieta's rites is still, after the catabasis, as doubtful as was the efficacy of Misenus' rites before the catabasis. The first half of the *Aeneid* has ended with a climactic false teaching, which goes to form the soul of the hero while being repudiated by the poet: it is because he is formed by this false teaching that the pious hero[10] is precisely a hero:

> At pius exsequiis Aeneas rite solutis,
> aggere composito tumuli, postquam alta quierunt
> aequora, tendit iter velis portumque relinquit.

> But pious Aeneas, after performing the exsequies according to rite and erecting the mound of her tomb, when the deep waters are stilled, proceeds on his way under sail and leaves the port.[11]

> (7.5–7)

ii. Anger

After sailing from Caieta with a good wind and a bright moon, Aeneas' fleet passes the nearby shore of Circe, where she, the wealthy daughter of Sol, makes her remote grove resound continually to her singing, and burns fragrant cedar to light her weaving (7.8–14).

> hinc exaudiri gemitus iraeque leonum
> vincla recusantum et sera sub nocte rudentum,
> saetigerique sues atque in praesepibus ursi
> saevire ac formae magnorum ululare luporum,
> quos hominum ex facie dea saeva potentibus herbis
> induerat Circe in vultus ac terga ferarum.

> From here were heard the groans of raging[12] lions protesting against their chains and roaring late into the night; bristling boars and bears in pens, raging; and the forms of great wolves howling, which the savage goddess Circe had changed with potent herbs from the appearance of human beings into the faces and bodies of wild beasts.

> (7.15–20)

The groans heard coming from the groves of Circe recall those heard by Aeneas from Tartarus:

> hinc exaudiri gemitus et saeva sonare
> verbera, tum stridor ferri tractaeque catenae.
> constitit Aeneas strepitumque exterritus hausit.[13]

> From here were heard groans and savage lashes resounded, then too the screech of iron and chains being dragged. Aeneas halted and in terror drank in the din.
>
> (6.557–559)

The groans heard from Tartarus are those of human souls being punished; those heard from Circe's groves are those of human beings whom she has changed into the form of wild beasts: they groan with anger at their restraints. They are like the caged winds of Aeolus' cave that are likened to wild beasts (1.55–57), or Furor chained like a wild beast within the gates of War (1.294–296).

Like the proem to the first half, so the proem to the second half has at its center unintelligible anger, divine and bestial: *tantaene animis caelestibus irae?* Circe, the savage goddess (*dea saeva*, 7.19) who turns men into beasts, corresponds to the savage goddess Juno (*saevae . . . Iunonis*, 1.4). In the first proem it is the causes of Juno's anger that Vergil asks the Muse to bring to his mind: *Musa, mihi causas memora.* In the second proem the savage goddess Circe is not herself said to be angry; it is the anger of the men she has turned into beasts that is described; she herself alone by herself sings as she weaves her web. But why has she turned the men into angry beasts? Later in Book 7 we learn that she turned Picus, breaker of horses, into a bird because she was captivated by love for him, *capta cupidine* (7.189). Servius explains, "*Circe, cum [Picum] amaret et sperneretur, irata eum in avem, picum Martium, convertit,*" "Because she loved Picus and was spurned by him, she got angry and turned him into a bird, the Picus Martius" (*ad* 7.190). Servius' explanation suggests the connection between Circe's spurned love and one of the causes of Juno's anger:

> necdum etiam causae irarum saevique dolores
> exciderant animo; manet alta mente repostum
> iudicium Paridis spretaeque iniuria formae. . . .

> Not yet had the causes of her angers, her savage griefs, subsided from her spirit; deep in her mind remains fixed the judgment of Paris and the injury of her beauty spurned. . . .
>
> (1.25–27)

Circe is angry at men because she loves them; she turns them into beasts because she is *capta cupidine*,[14] and wishes to punish them for their power over her by exercising the like power over them: "*haec libidine sua et blandimentis homines in ferinam vitam ab humana deducebat, ut libidini et voluptatibus operam darent*" (Servius *ad* 7.19). The mystery of divine anger is its connection with the "eternal wound" of unrequited love: indignation at not being loved compels human beings to look to gods as punishers, as Vergil has shown in his portrayal of Dido; not being loved is also an important cause of divine anger, but the indignant gods punish their injurers themselves. Here on the shores of Italy, the destined center of the universal empire of the returned Golden Age, the howlings of the night recall the chains by which immortal Furor is forcibly restrained. The scene points ahead to the story of the conquest of the half-beast Cacus by Hercules: Hercules' suppression of that monster has not extirpated the immortal forces of Furor from Italy. The wars in Italy too will have at their core the relationship between the wound of love and the wound of anger: Turnus' love for his own, for Lavinia and for his local kingship, will be the cause of Turnus' ungovernable anger, and Aeneas' love for his own (*meorum*, 12.947), for Pallas, will be the cause of Aeneas' performing his last action of the poem "inflamed by furies and rage" (*furiis accensus et ira*, 12.946).

Circe, like Aeolus and like Rhadamanthus, is in charge of the restraint of furor. Her changing human beings into wild beasts makes their furor more furious by emancipating it from the rule, however feeble, of their own reason; but it also enables her, by the same token, to rule them simply by chaining them and penning them in. In Homer, the striking and pitiable thing about the men transformed by Circe is that they keep the minds of men in the bodies of beasts, as they show by their mildness and fawning on Odysseus' crew (*Od.* 10.214–219, 239–40). In the *Odyssey* there can be beast-men, mixing of kinds, but this is because Homer is ignorant of the connection of spirit with physical constitution according to the *foedera naturae*. In reality, though, "there never have been Centaurs, nor can there at any time be creatures of double nature and twofold body compounded from the limbs of differing animals. . . ." (*DRN* 5.878 ff.). Lucretius has shown that the similarity of anger in winds, beasts, and human beings is an identity: anger is heat, the motion of heat. The rational mind of a human being is a certain arrangement of the human being's atoms; that arrangement cannot be maintained in a wild beast. The anger of winds is like that of wild beasts; the anger of wild beasts is like that of human beings; but the peculiarity of human (as of divine) anger is that it adds to the motion of heat the pressure of indignant thoughts and thus the impulse to punishment. The second half of the *Aeneid* opens with a reminder, remote and sinister, of the underlying furor whose government is the unique purpose of Aeneas' imperial mission.

iii. Italy

Italy presents an appearance of unspoiled placidity: at the Trojans' approach the winds drop, the swell subsides, the Tiber appears flowing into the sea from a grove full of birds that sweeten the air with their song (7.25–36). The scene recalls Lucretius' account of the sweetening effect of Venus' presence on the countryside in the invocation to the *De Rerum Natura* (1.6–20), except that Vergil's scene lacks the marks of the underlying venereal violence that runs through Lucretius' scene, and which has been replaced or displaced by Vergil in the preceding account of Circe. Vergil's collocation of the threatening roars from Circe's cave with the sweetness, the peaceableness of Italy in this opening movement of the Iliadic *Aeneid* raises the same question raised by the invocation to the *De Rerum Natura*: love brings peace, as Lucretius prays to Venus to pacify Mars; but love also brings violence, anger, indignation, punishment: how is Italian peace protected from the angry love of Circe? The Trojans have been protected from Circe's monsters by Neptune because of their piety, *quae ne monstra pii paterentur talia Troes* (21); what protection have the Italians against that sinister underside of Italian peace?

Vergil invokes the Muse Erato to help him remember the first beginnings of the wars he is about to set forth:

> Nunc age, qui reges, Erato, quae tempora rerum,
> quis Latio antiquo fuerit status, advena classem
> cum primum Ausoniis exercitus appulit oris,
> expediam, et primae revocabo exordia pugnae.
> tu vatem, tu, diva, mone. dicam horrida bella,
> dicam acies, actosque animis in funera reges,
> Tyrrhenamque manum, totamque sub arma coactam
> Hesperiam.

> Come now, Erato—who were the kings, what the times of things, what was the situation in ancient Latium, when first the foreign army brought its fleet to the Ausonian shores, I shall set forth, and recall the beginnings of the first fight. You, goddess, you instruct your bard. I shall tell of dreadful wars, I shall tell of battle lines and kings driven to their deaths by their courage, the Tyrrhenian band, and all Hesperia compelled to arms.

(7.41–44)

The invocation is full of verbal reminiscences of Lucretius: *Nunc age . . . expediam; tempora rerum; primae exordia pugnae.*[15] Vergil's insistent reminiscence of Lucretius here compels us to give special attention to the greatest peculiarity of his invocation: the Muse he calls upon to sponsor his setting forth the first beginnings of the war and the unfolding of the war itself is Erato. The oddity of the poet's invoking Erato, the goddess of love poetry, in this connection[16] recalls the oddity of Lucretius' invocation to Venus, the goddess of love, to sponsor his setting forth the first beginnings of all things and their unfolding. The first beginnings of all things are the blind interactions of the atoms, which have the character of erotic mingling or bellicose clashing: "you will see throughout the void many minute bodies commingling in many ways . . . and giving rise to battles and fights as if in eternal contest" (2.116–119). The connection between love and anger will be thematic to the second half of the *Aeneid* as it was to the first; the ambiguity of peace and war that resides in the nature of things will be expressed in the ambiguity of peace and war in Italy (see pp. 167–178).

The beginnings of the first fight are traced back from King Latinus. He, already old, was ruling tranquil cities in longstanding peace (45–6); his father, "we learn from tradition" (*accipimus*), was Faunus; Faunus' father was Picus (the man whom Circe in her angry love changed into a bird); Picus' father was Saturn. The first beginnings of the wars go back to the peaceful ages of Saturn, to the Golden Age—as the first beginnings of peace, the *longa pax* in which Latinus has been ruling, also go back to the ages of Saturn.[17] How did the beginnings of the first fight arise out of the pacific lineage of Saturn? Why did Saturn's pacific Golden Age come to an end? What is the meaning of the claim, made by Anchises to Aeneas near the end of the preceding book, that Rome is finally to restore that Golden Age under Caesar?:

> aurea condet
> saecula qui rursus Latio regnata per arva
> Saturno quondam.

> who will re-found the Golden Ages once ruled by Saturn throughout the Latin lands.

> (6.792–794)

The second proem of the *Aeneid* resumes the complex triadic theme of the first: Rome-anger-Carthage becomes Rome-anger-Italy. Where the Odyssean *Aeneid* proposed to present the defect of "Carthage's" claim to have the key to the rule of anger in the souls and cities of men, and thus to become king of the nations, the Iliadic *Aeneid* proposes to unfold the virtue of "Rome's" claim by showing "Rome" becoming king of the Italian nations. As Juno's eternal wound is the root of her championing "Carthage" in the first part of the *Aeneid*, so it is the root in the second half of her championing "Italy," the remnant of the Golden Age, with which she is identified as "Saturnia Juno."[18] What Carthage and Italy have in common is "gold" (Carthaginian commerce and science; the Italian Golden Age) as opposed to "iron" (Roman arms and piety), and therewith the favor of Juno, the angry goddess who favors the regime that allows for the ungoverned incursion of infernal anger into the world above. As the Odyssean *Aeneid* was a critique of the Carthaginian regime, of the flaw in its understanding of anger that made it inadequate to secure peace, so the Iliadic *Aeneid* will be a critique of the Italian or Saturnian regime; it will be a critique of the traditional myth of the Golden Age.

CHAPTER NINE

~

The Golden Age

i. The Ruling Prophecy of the *Aeneid*

Maior rerum mihi nascitur ordo,
maius opus moveo.

A greater order of things is coming to birth, I am putting in motion my greater
work.

(7.44–45)

The second half of the *Aeneid* is to be the greater part, *maius opus*. It is
"greater" because it is the Iliadic half, the half that deals with arms and
dreadful wars;[1] but not only because of that. In it a greater order of things,
maior rerum ordo, comes to birth.

Whatever this greater order of things is, it cannot be simply the dreadful
wars; for the dreadful wars, *horrida bella*, are of the same order of things as the
things of the first half.[2] These wars have been foretold to Aeneas by the Sibyl
at 6.83–97 (*bella, horrida bella*, 6.86), where the most dreadful thing about
them is precisely that they are to be a *repetition* of the Trojan War:

non Simois tibi nec Xanthus nec Dorica castra
defuerint; alius Latio iam partus Achilles,
natus et ipse dea; nec Teucris addita Iuno
usquam aberit, cum tu supplex in rebus egenis
quas gentis Italum aut quas non oraveris urbes!
causa mali tanti coniunx iterum hospita Teucris
externique iterum thalami.

147

Neither Simois nor Xanthus nor the Doric camps will be lacking; another Achilles is in store for you in Latium, he too born of a goddess; and Juno, scourge of the Teucrians, will nowhere be absent, while you, in needy circumstances— what Italian peoples and what cities will you not beseech as suppliant! The cause of such great evil for the Teucrians will be again a foreign bride, again marriages with foreigners.

(6.88–94)

The Odyssean first half of the *Aeneid* has itself been full of "repetitions" of Troy and the Trojan War.[3] To the extent that the Italian wars of Books 7–12 are, in accordance with the Sibyl's words, yet another repetition of the story of Troy, this time in deed and not just in word, the second half of the *Aeneid* could not be said to show the birth of a greater order of things. Even the difference prophesied by the Sibyl between the defeat of the Trojans in the first Trojan War and their victory in the new one (6.95–97) shows only a new thing, not a new order of things.

But the very relationship between the Sibyl's prophecy in Book 6 of the renewed Trojan War and the occurrence of that war in Books 7–12 is itself a first clue to what Vergil means by the lesser and greater parts of the *Aeneid*. The first half contains prophecy, the second half contains fulfillment. Jupiter has prophesied in Book 1 that Aeneas will wage a huge war in Italy and beat down savage peoples (1.263–264). Creusa has prophesied in Book 2 that after long travels Aeneas will reach the Hesperian land where a kingdom and royal consort await him (2.780–784). In Book 3 Apollo has prophesied that the Trojans will be received back in the land from which their race first originated (3.94–96); the Trojan Penates have prophesied that Italy will turn out to be their own proper home (3.167); Celaeno has prophesied that before the Trojans can fortify a city in Italy, grim starvation will force them to eat their tables (3.255–257); Helenus has prophesied that a white sow surrounded by her thirty sucklings will mark the spot of the Trojans' proper settlement in Italy (3.389–393) and that the fates and Apollo will work out a resolution of Celaeno's curse (3.394–395). In Book 4 Dido has solemnly cursed Aeneas with the imprecation that he be harried by the arms of an audacious people, torn from the embrace of Iulus, forced to see the unmerited deaths of his men and to submit to the terms of an unequal peace (4.612–620). In Book 5 Anchises has prophesied that a race hard and harsh in its customs must be warred down by Aeneas in Latium (5.730–731). In Book 6 the Sibyl has prophesied the repetition of the Trojan War in Italy and the aid of a Greek city in the Trojans' future victory (6.83–97). All these prophecies, great and small, are fulfilled in the narrative of Books 7–12. We may say that the second half of the *Aeneid* is greater than the first as the fulfillment is greater than the prophecy.

But when prophecy prophesies the repetition of former things, the fulfillment can be said to belong to a "greater order of things" only if the first things, the things to be repeated, belonged to a greater order of things. What first things of the Odyssean *Aeneid* are of such a character, though? Certainly not the Trojan War itself, nor, before that, the first founding of Troy, nor yet, before that, the Italian origin of the Trojans. But all these former things whose repetition is prophesied in the Odyssean *Aeneid* are in fact organized or ruled by one supreme first thing that *was* a greater order of things, and whose repetition is therefore to be the return of the "greater order of things" that begins to come to birth in the second half of the *Aeneid*. This is the Golden Age.

The ruling prophecy of the whole first half of the *Aeneid* is that of the return of the Golden Age. The wanderings of Aeneas, the renewal of the Trojan War, the re-founding of Troy, the return of the Trojans to their Italian origin—all these are but preliminaries to the return of the Golden Age. The Golden Age is the reign of Saturn, *Saturnia regna,* an order of things that antedates the heroic age altogether and is altogether of a different character from the heroic age; its return is the return of a greater order of things. The second half of the *Aeneid* is related then to the first as the Saturnian fulfillment to the Jovian prophecy; it shows the coming to birth of a greater order of things.[4]

That the ruling prophecy of the *Aeneid* is the return of the Golden Age is shown by the two great prophecies that frame the Odyssean *Aeneid*: Jupiter's prophecy to Venus in Book 1 (257–296) and Anchises' prophecy to Aeneas in Book 6 (722 ff.). Anchises prophesies to Aeneas in the Underworld that Aeneas' Italian mission will initiate a series of events whose completion will be the re-establishment by Augustus Caesar of the Golden Age:

hic vir, hic est, tibi quem promitti saepius audis,[5]
Augustus Caesar, divi genus, aurea condet
saecula qui rursus Latio regnata per arva
Saturno quondam, super et Garamantas et Indos
proferet imperium; iacet extra sidera tellus,
extra anni solisque vias, ubi caelifer Atlas
axem umero torquet stellis ardentibus aptum.

This is the man, this is he whom you often hear promised to you, Augustus Caesar, the offspring of a god, who will found the Golden Ages once more in Latium, in the territories once ruled by Saturn, and extend the empire yet further beyond the Garamantians and Indians; the land [to which he will extend it] lies beyond the constellations, beyond the paths of the year and of the sun, where heaven-bearing Atlas turns on his shoulder the pole fitted out with its shining stars.

(6.791–797)

The reestablishment of the Golden Age, which is to begin in the territories "once ruled by Saturn," reminds us of Saturn's expulsion from the throne of heaven, and thus of the manifest obstacle to the reestablishment of the Golden Age: for was not the first Golden Age brought to an end by Jupiter? The two orders of things are the Golden Age and the Iron Age, ruled respectively by Saturn and by Jupiter. Anchises' reference to the fact that Saturn ruled during the first Golden Age raises the question whether the returned Golden Age will again by ruled by Saturn or will be ruled this time by Jupiter. Either possibility is problematic, to say the least. Anchises surely does suggest that the returned Golden Age will extend not only beyond the boundaries of the Latin territories once ruled by Saturn, but also beyond the scope of Jupiter's present regime, or beyond the cosmic settlement Jupiter has now made with Atlas, the one-time Titanic opponent of Jupiter's regime.

The man here prophesied to Aeneas by Anchises as the refounder of the Saturnian Golden Age recalls the man earlier prophesied to Venus by Jupiter as the one under whom the harsh ages will soften:

nascetur pulchra Troianus origine Caesar,
imperium Oceano, famam qui terminet astris,
Iulius, a magno demissum nomen Iulo. . . .
aspera tum positis mitescent saecula bellis.

A Trojan Caesar will be born of noble stock, who will bound his empire by Ocean and his glory by the stars—Julius, a name derived from great Iulus. . . . Then the harsh ages will soften, wars laid aside.

(1.286–288, 291)

Vergil has tactfully refrained here from making Jupiter refer to the identity of the softening of the harsh ages with the return of the Golden Age, since the Golden Age is the Saturnian Age. Nonetheless, he forces us to wonder how Jupiter, whose regime is the Iron Age, understands his own prophecy of the softening of the ages in the end of days. For would not the soft ages be the Golden Age?[6] And would not the return of the Golden Age mean the elimination of Jupiter himself, and the reinstatement of Saturn on the throne of heaven?

ii. Latinus vs. Evander

The myth of the Golden Age is a traditional and familiar one, but the meaning of the Golden Age in the *Aeneid*, and thus the meaning of Vergil's "greater order of things," can be understood only by carefully noting its altogether surprising divergences from the traditional myth. The most important elements of the traditional myth, as recounted by Hesiod and Ovid, are that the golden race of men were the first men and lived the best life;[7] that the Golden Age took place when Saturn (or Cronos) was king in heaven;[8] and that the Golden race of men did not know labor, war, or law.[9] The myth of the *Aeneid*, however, while assigning the very greatest importance to the Golden Age, rejects every one of these essential elements of its traditional meaning; under cover, as it were, of the most familiar and traditional myth, it proposes an altogether new, strange, and revolutionary myth.

The traditional understanding of the golden life under Saturn is represented in the *Aeneid* by King Latinus, who introduces his people, the Latins, to an embassy of the Trojans with the explanation:

> neve ignorate Latinos
> Saturni gentem haud vinclo nec legibus aequam,
> sponte sua veterisque dei se more tenentem.

> Be not unaware that we Latins are the race of Saturn, righteous not by bond or laws, but self-restraining of our own accord and by the custom of the ancient god.
>
> (7.202–204)

Latinus' understanding of the reign of Saturn as a condition of righteousness without law,[10] or spontaneous (*sponte sua*) self-restraint, is in accord with the traditional myth of the Golden Age[11] as elaborated by Hesiod in the *Works and Days* and as reflected by Ovid in the *Metamorphoses*. According to this myth, the golden race were the first men, made by the gods when Saturn was king, living in abundance and peace without labor or war:

> First of all the deathless gods who dwell on Olympus made a golden race of mortal men who lived in the time of Cronos when he was reigning in heaven. And they lived like gods without sorrow of heart, remote and free from toil and grief; miserable age rested not on them; but with legs and arms never failing they made merry with feasting beyond the reach of all evils. When they died,

it was as though they were overcome with sleep, and they had all good things; for the fruitful earth unforced bare them fruit abundantly and without stint. They dwelt in ease and peace upon their lands with many good things, rich in flocks and loved by the blessed gods.

(*Works and Days* 109–120)[12]

Hesiod explicitly emphasizes the leisure and ease of the golden race rather than their righteousness, which however emerges implicitly by contrast with the degenerate ages of which unjust violence is a marked characteristic. The men of the silver race could not keep from doing violence to each other (ὕβριν γὰρ ἀτάσθαλον οὐκ ἐδύναντο / ἀλλήλων ἀπέχειν, 134–135); the men of the iron race are χειροδίκαι, ones whose right is might (189, 192). Zeus, who has been king in heaven since the time of the silver race, has provided for the injustice that came in after Cronos' time by giving men δίκη, right, as their νόμος, law:

For the son of Cronos has ordained this law for men, that fishes and beasts and winged fowls should devour one another, for right is not in them; but to mankind he gave right which proves far the best.

(*Works and Days* 276–280)

The spontaneous righteousness of the golden race, implied in Hesiod's myth, is drawn out explicitly and emphatically in Ovid's version:

Aurea prima sata est aetas, quae vindice nullo,
sponte sua, sine lege fidem rectumque colebat.
poena metusque aberant, nec verba minantia fixo
aere legebantur, nec supplex turba timebat
iudicis ora sui, sed erant sine vindice tuti.

The Golden Age grew up first; it cherished good faith and the right with no avenger, spontaneously, without law. Punishment and fear were absent, and no threatening words were to be read inscribed in bronze; no suppliant crowd dreaded the face of its judge; but all were secure without any avenger.

(*Metamorphoses*, 1.89–93)

But the traditional view of the Saturnian life that Latinus expresses at 7.202–4, a life of spontaneous righteousness without need of bond or laws, is shown by the narrative of the *Aeneid* to be mistaken:[13] the Golden Age was *not* an age of righteousness without laws. The consequence of Latinus' mistake about the reign of Saturn, and therefore about the character of his own "Saturnian" people, is that when the Latins show themselves most unrighteous, most unrestrained and most in need of government, he is unable to govern them:

> nec plura locutus
> saepsit se tectis rerumque reliquit habenas.

He said no more, but hid himself in his house and dropped the reins of affairs.
(7.599–600)

The "beginnings of the first fight," *primae exordia pugnae*, arise among the descendants of the pacific Saturn because these descendants mistake the characteristic mark of the regime of the ancient god for spontaneous righteousness rather than obedience to divinely given law.

It has often been suggested that in Evander's account of the history of Latium, Vergil not only has contradicted Latinus' account but also has conflated two opposed theories of human history, an evolutionary/progressive view associated with Aeschylus and Lucretius and a regressive/Golden-Age view associated with Hesiod.[14] While it will be argued here that neither carelessness nor syncretism can account for the surprising features of the story Vergil puts in Evander's mouth, it is worth taking note of those surprising features at the outset so as to make clear what it is that needs to be explained.

"The ages that people call golden took place under him [Saturn] as king" (*aurea quae perhibent illo sub rege fuere / saecula*, 8.324–325). Evander formulates his explanation in the manner of a correction, calling attention to the distinction between what people call something and what it really is;[15] in his speech he tells what the ages that people call golden actually were.[16] That they took place when Saturn was king is what people who speak of the Golden Age say themselves; but they say Saturn was king in heaven,[17] while Evander says Saturn had been expelled from heaven by Jupiter and was king in Latium.[18] People say, in fact, that the Golden Age, which took place when Saturn was king in heaven, was the first age[19] of human beings, who had been made by the gods in their original golden condition;[20] but Evander says that human beings had already been in existence when Saturn instituted the Golden Age among them, and that the first human beings had not been made by the gods at all but had been born from trees. People say that the Golden Age under Saturn was a time before war had come into existence;[21] but Evander says that Saturn, when he instituted the Golden Age, had himself been expelled from his own kingdom by the arms of Jupiter. People say that in the Golden Age there was no agriculture and the eating of meat was unknown,[22] as men lived on what the earth spontaneously brought forth; but Evander says that Saturn instituted the Golden Age by teaching the arts of agriculture, and that men had been meat-eaters from the beginning. People say that in the Golden Age there was no acquisitiveness or wealth, because of the sufficiency of the earth's spontaneous production; but Evander says that Saturn instituted the Golden Age by teaching human beings how to store up their resources and be sparing of their use. People say that in the Golden Age there was justice without law;[23] but Evander says that Saturn instituted the Golden Age by giving laws. Finally, people say that the Golden Age was the best age and that the human race degenerated afterwards. With this Evander agrees.

According to Evander's account, then, people are correct in saying that the Golden Age was the best age or the best life for men, but incorrect in everything else they say about it. People are incorrect, in other words, in what they imagine was or is best. Evander agrees with what people say to the extent that the best took place in the past; as to what the best was, and when and how it came about, here he corrects what they say.

iii. Vergil's Golden Age

Evander's unorthodox account of the Golden Age[24] does not seem to be the result of careless conflation or loose syncretism on Vergil's part, however; it appears rather to be the clearest and fullest direct statement in the *Aeneid* of a new myth carefully elaborated by Vergil for this poem.[25] This new myth has been made in such a way as to reflect both the substance of the Lucretian truth about the origin of the human race, *unde hominum genus et pecudes* (*Aen.* 1.743), and the form of Lucretius' own method of myth-making. Evander's Golden Age appears to have the same function in Vergil's *Aeneid* that the gods have in Lucretius' *De Rerum Natura*. As Lucretius offers the impelling image of a god or hero as a ready-made object of emulation while revising from the ground up the traditional notion of what a god or hero is, so Vergil offers the impelling image of the Golden Age as a ready-made object of hope or striving for the future of mankind, while revising from the ground up the traditional notion of what the Golden Age is. Just as men can continue to say "Bacchus" while coming to understand by it nothing other than "wine," just as they can continue to say "god" while coming to understand by it nothing other than "philosopher," so they can continue to say "Golden Age," "Saturnian Kingdom," while gradually coming to understand by it something utterly different from what the old poets who first invented these names meant by them. As Lucretius can agree with the many that "god" means "happiest living being" while rejecting everything else they mean by it, so Vergil, through Evander, agrees with them that "Golden Age" means "best life for men" while rejecting or replacing everything else they mean by it.

The most powerful reason why Evander's history of Latium cannot be dismissed as "conflating" or "syncretizing" is that the surprising or unorthodox features of it appear everywhere in the *Aeneid* where the Golden Age is at issue, with the single exception of Latinus' speech at 7.202–204. It turns out to be Latinus' orthodox version, not Evander's unorthodox one, that stands in need of special explanation.[26]

For the *Aeneid* as a whole radically revises the traditional myth of the Golden Age, most strikingly by prophesying its imminent return[27] as the providential plan of Jupiter for the human race. But this very notion of the return of the Golden Age, which as even Evander agrees is the age of Saturn, raises the question what is to become of Jupiter when his Iron-Age regime is confronted by the returned Golden-Age regime of his father. Anchises' account of the Golden Age identifies it with the time when Saturn ruled the Latin lands: *aurea . . . saecula . . . Latio regnata per arva Saturno quondam* (6.792–794); but he does not say when that time was—certainly he does not say it was when Saturn was ruling in heaven, or when the human race was first made. The localization of Saturn's rule in Latium is at odds with the Golden Age tradition, and in Evander's account we learn that the tradition is mistaken not only about the place of the Golden Age but also about its time: the Golden Age was *not* the first age, either in heaven or on earth. Instead of a general decline from the golden first to the worse later ages,[28] human history has been an ascent from brutal origins to a Golden Age, then a decline from the Golden to another debased age (this time iron rather than brutal); in the future it will ascend again to another Golden Age, which will then finally become permanent.[29]

The meaning of this version of the Golden Age myth is essential to an understanding of the ruling prophecy of the *Aeneid*. It means, most generally, that the Golden Age was not man's original condition, and therefore that the prospects for a returned Golden Age do not depend on a return to the human beginnings; more particularly, that the Golden Age was brought about in the first place by *divine legislation*, rather than arising spontaneously or naturally in the absence of law; and finally, that the first Golden Age took place during the reign of Jupiter in heaven, and therefore that the prospects for a returned Golden Age are not necessarily incompatible with the continuation of Jupiter's regime—the returned Golden Age on earth does not depend on a return *in heaven* back before the reign of Jupiter.

Vergil's revision of the Golden Age myth in the *Aeneid* appears to be guided by Lucretian doctrine in the same way that Lucretius' revision of the myth of the gods is guided by Epicurean doctrine. Lucretius' true account of the origins of human and civil life is incompatible with the traditional Golden Age myth. Whereas the traditional myth presents man as having been made by the gods, Lucretian doctrine presents him as having been born from the earth like the brutes:[30]

> quare etiam atque etiam maternum nomen adepta
> terra tenet merito, quoniam genus ipsa creavit
> humanum atque animal prope certo tempore fudit
> omne, quod in magnis bacchatur montibus passim,
> aeriasque simul volucres variantibus formis.

> And thus indeed the earth rightly got and still keeps the name of "mother," since she herself created the human race and poured forth at a more or less fixed time both every animal that haunts the great mountains as well as the birds of the air with their various forms.
>
> (5.821–825; cf. 925–926)

Whereas the traditional myth presents man as having been made in a perfect felicity from which he has gradually declined, Lucretian doctrine presents him as rising gradually to an ambiguous humanity that, through the development of arts, eventuates simultaneously in the greatest human misery and degradation and in the possibility of philosophic felicity.[31] Misery and degradation arise from the discovery and improvement of weapons, navigation, agriculture and medicine:

> denique eos vita privarent vermina saeva
> expertis opis, ignaros quid volnera vellent.
> at non multa virum sub signis milia ducta
> una dies dabat exitio, nec turbida ponti
> aequora lidebant navis ad saxa virosque. . . .
> tum peniuria deinde cibi languentia leto
> membra dabat, contra nunc rerum copia mersat.
> illi imprudentes ipsi sibi saepe venenum
> vergebant, nunc dant aliis sollertius ipsi.

> Finally fierce pains robbed them [early men] of life, since they were without any resource, ignorant of what wounds require. But many thousands of men were not drawn up under standards and given over to death on a single day, nor did the turbid expanses of the sea smash ships and men against the rocks. . . . In those days lack of food used to give over their wasting limbs to death, whereas now it is the abundance of things that overwhelms them. Early men in their imprudence would often themselves serve poison to themselves; now with their greater knowledge they give it to others.
>
> (5.997–1001, 1007–1010)

The possibility of philosophic felicity, or the "sweet solaces of life," also springs from the development of the arts:

> sic unum quicquid paulatim protrahit aetas
> in medium ratioque in luminis erigit oras:
> namque alid ex alio clarescere corde videbant,
> artibus ad summum donec venere cacumen. . . .
> et primae dederunt solacia dulcia vitae,
> cum genuere virum tali cum corde repertum,
> omnia veridico qui quondam ex ore profudit.

Thus time gradually brings forth each thing into the open, and reason raises it into the shores of light: for they saw one thing being illuminated by another in their heart, until they came by means of the arts to the highest summit. . . . And [Athens] was the first to give the sweet solaces of life, when she bore a man who has been found to have such a heart, who once poured forth all things from his truth-speaking mouth.

(5.1454–1457, 6.4–6)

Vergil, following the principle of assimilating the traditional myth as closely as possible to the Lucretian truth, affirms that human origins were brutish, but also that a Golden Age occurred in the past under divine guidance and legislation. The significance of Vergil's modification is that, while retaining the notion of a past Golden Age and thus justifying the greatest ancestral piety, Vergil identifies that Golden Age not with the artless and lawless but with the cultivated and ordered era of mankind. Thus, the posture of looking forward to a returned Golden Age no longer means longing for man's first origins (which are seen to be brutish or subhuman), but longing for and striving towards the previous heights of man's civilized achievement under divine rule.[32]

Evander's account of Latin history is the fullest single statement in the *Aeneid* of the new myth in question. According to Evander's account, the native population of Latium was composed of Fauns, Nymphs,[33] and a race of men sprung from hard oaks. This race of men, although consorting with divine beings, was completely brutish. They had no *mos* or *cultus;* they did not know how to yoke oxen, store resources, or manage produce; their nourishment came from the branches of (uncultivated) trees (as they themselves came from trees) and from hunting (8.314–318). Here we must note the significant divergences from the traditional myth. The acorn diet of the first men was not a diet of fat abundance or at least simple comfort, as in Ovid's account,[34] but was like the grim *victus infelix* described to the Trojans by Achaemenides, the man left behind by Odysseus, as his last resort among the savage Cyclopes:

victum infelicem, bacas lapidosaque corna,
dant rami, et vulsis pascunt radicibus herbae.

A miserable living, berries and stony cornels, is furnished by the branches and
grasses pulled up by their roots.

(3.649–650)

So Evander: *rami atque asper victu venatus alebat,* "the branches and the hunt,
with its harsh food, nourished them" (8.318). The first men were then not
pacific vegetarians, but hunters: the killing of animals for food was in man's
original nature, and was not a degenerate development as in the traditional
myth.[35] But although they had the aggressive nature of hunters, according to
Evander's account, the first men in fact, so far from being actively aggressive
towards one another, suffered a sort of atomic repulsion from one another
and thus lived dispersed in the mountaintops like the Cyclopes in Homer:

the lawless outrageous Cyclopes. . . .
These people have no institutions, no meetings for counsels;
rather they make their habitations in caverns hollowed
among peaks of the high mountains, and each one is the law
for his own wives and children, and cares nothing about the others.
(*Od.* 9.106–7, 112–115)[36]

Still, the original carnivorousness of men in Evander's account is the sign of
their potential greed, anger, aggressiveness and cruelty towards their own
species as well, as in the traditional Golden Age myth the herbivorousness of
the first men was connected with their mildness, contentedness, and peaceableness towards their fellows.[37] As the meat-eating of Homer's lawless and
unsociable Cyclopes becomes cannibalism when confronted with a sociable
human being, so the meat-eating of Evander's first men indicates the reason
why Saturn's bringing them out of isolation into community had to be accompanied by his giving them divine laws to restrain them:[38] *sic placida populos in pace regebat,* "in this way it was that he ruled the peoples in tranquil
peace" (8.325).

The prospects for the recovery of the Saturnian peaceableness among human beings, therefore, depend not on recovering but on rightly governing
man's original nature. This idea has of course been developed from the outset of the *Aeneid;* it has appeared in Jupiter's prophecy in Book 1 (especially
291–296), according to which peace will be achieved not by the extinction
but by the forcible suppression of the forces of war, and before that in the Aeolus incident (especially 58–63), where the stability of the cosmos is secured
not by the extinction but by the government of the winds.

According to Evander, the Golden Age occurred not when Saturn was ruling in heaven but when Saturn was expelled from heaven, *arma Iovis fugiens et regnis exsul ademptis* (8.320). The Golden Age was thus brought about somehow by Jupiter, or at least under Jupiter's regime in heaven; if Saturn had never been dethroned, human brutishness would never have been ended. Saturn appears here as the original type of the exiled king, a type that takes many forms in the *Aeneid*.[39] In the present context, Saturn is most significantly the type of Evander himself, the founder of the Roman *arx* (*me pulsum patria . . .*, 8.333 ff.), as also of Aeneas, to whom Evander is telling this tale.[40] Like Saturn himself, Evander and Aeneas in turn come to Latium at first in dire need of asylum, but ultimately so as to bring the land back to its Saturnian or Golden Age condition by preparing for the rule of Augustus Caesar.

The exiled Saturn found the Latins in man's original, and in this sense "natural," condition: living in scarcity without arts, custom, or cultivation (316–318), indocile and isolated, scattered throughout the mountaintops like the Cyclopes; he drew them from isolation into community but also gave them the laws that enabled them to live in this community. According to Evander's account, the best life for human beings is this life in peaceful community, but this life is not "natural" or innate in human beings, nor can it be developed by human beings on their own; its founding and preservation depend upon divine legislation. Because Saturn found the Latins dispersed, he brought them together; because he found them unteachable, he gave them laws. Laws, divine laws, are necessary because men are unteachable. If they were teachable, Latinus' account of Saturn's regime would have been possible: *sponte sua veterisque dei se more tenentem*. As Servius observes, Latinus' statement suggests that the men under Saturn's regime are philosophers: "This is a saying of Xenocrates, who . . . when asked what benefit philosophy could give his students, replied that they would do of their own free will (*voluntate*) what others are forced to do by law (*iure*)."[41] Latinus was mistaken: the first men, so far from being philosophers, were unteachable; they needed laws. Under the laws he therefore gave them, Saturn ruled the Latin peoples in tranquil peace (325),

> deterior donec paulatim ac decolor aetas
> et belli rabies et amor successit habendi.
> tum manus Ausonia et gentes venere Sicanae,
> saepius et nomen posuit Saturnia tellus;
> tum reges asperque immani corpore Thybris,
> a quo post Itali fluvium cognomine Thybrim
> diximus; amisit verum vetus Albula nomen.

until a degenerate and discolored age, and war-madness and love of having, gradually came in. Then the Ausonian band and the Sicanian nations came, and the Saturnian land too often put off its name; then came kings and harsh Thybris with his huge body, after whose name we Italians later called the river "Thybris;" ancient Albula lost its true name.

(8.326–332)

The Golden Age of Saturn was defective; it lacked whatever is needed for *permanence*, and thus could not prevent a baser age from following and the true names of places from being replaced with others. According to the ruling prophecy of the *Aeneid*, the restoration of the Golden Age will not have this defect: it will be "empire without end," and thus in particular it will keep the names of places eternally: Caieta, Palinurus, and Misenus. What was the defect of that first divine legislation?

In human beings, *amor habendi* is not innate; it arose as a result of the development of the arts that Saturn instituted among them.[42] Vergil's myth follows the doctrine of Lucretius here: the earthborn men (*terrigenae*) were satisfied with acorns, but after the human race began to reproduce sexually and practice the arts, it got a hatred of acorns (*DRN* 5.1416) and began to wear itself out in the quest for luxuries:

nimirum quia non cognovit quae sit habendi
finis et omnino quoad crescat vera voluptas.
idque minutatim vitam provexit in altum
et belli magnos commovit funditus aestus.

and no wonder, since it did not know what is the limit of having and, altogether, how far true pleasure can grow. This ignorance gradually led life out to sea and stirred up from the depths great waves of war.

(*DRN* 5.1432–1435)

So, according to Evander, at first men did not know how to accumulate wealth (8.317); Saturn's institution of agriculture among the Latins began by leading them themselves to both *amor habendi* and prosperity, and then as a result provoked invasion by other peoples and a state of war. Saturn's legislation emancipated the passions of acquisitiveness without providing adequately for their control. Being unteachable, the Latin race did not learn what is the limit of having; nor did Saturn provide for this limit in his legislation. And because Saturn's regime was limited in extent to the territory of Latium, his institution of wealth in this territory led to the envy of other peoples who were not subject to the laws that he had given the Latins and who therefore "stirred up from the depths great waves of war" and overmastered the pacific native population. Saturn had not shown the Latins either how to moderate their own acquisitiveness or how to defend their wealth against the incursions of others. Nor were the Latins able to work this out for themselves; they had Saturn's laws because they were not teachable; but because they were not teachable, they were at a loss when the law turned out not to have provided for the problems of envy and war.

The inability of the Latins to defend themselves against the invaders might have been foreseen from the circumstance that brought about the Golden Age of Saturn in the first place: Saturn was unarmed. Arms had been introduced in heaven by Jupiter, who had used them to expel his father from the kingship. The defect at the heart of the pacific Saturnian regime would seem to have been the combination of its spatial limitation with its softness or lack of arms: this combination made it vulnerable to overthrow by invasion. If it had been unarmed and universal, there would have been no one to invade it and it would not have needed arms. If it had been armed and local it could have protected itself from invasion, provided the other peoples were and could be kept unarmed.

To supply the defect of Saturn's regime it would seem then at first that one might either make it universal or make it uniquely or preeminently armed. In fact, however, it is necessary to do both at once. Arms without universality are insufficient because the necessity of their regular use against the others would change fundamentally the pacific character of the regime: it would become permanent at the cost of becoming a different regime. Universality without arms is insufficient because *amor habendi* leads not only to the envy and invasion of foreigners but also to the strife and civil war of the citizens. In order to make the Golden Age permanent while keeping its fundamentally pacific character it is necessary to make it both universal and armed. This is the providential plan of Jupiter in the myth of the *Aeneid*: strong universal government, universal to obviate foreign war and strong to keep the peace by putting down internal war.

The ages that people call golden lacked not only gold but also iron. Moreover they were, although occurring under Jupiter, at odds with the then principle of Jupiter's regime: they were pacific, while Jupiter's regime was polemic. The Saturnian legislation was unable to be perduring as long as it was out of harmony with the new universal regime of Jupiter. But it was precisely the newness of Jupiter's regime that gave it its emphatically polemic character (much as it was the newness of Dido's regime that caused her to ignore Jupiter's law); that character was temporary and contingent; with the consolidation of his regime emerged its essentially pacific, or at any rate stable, character. Jupiter's own prophecy in Book 1 connects the pacification of the world with the legislation of the reconciled Romulus and Remus; Anchises' prophecy and Evander's history suggest a further connection between the returned Golden Age and the reconciliation of Saturn and Jupiter. If the impermanence of the first Golden Age was a result of the discord, indeed the war, between Saturn and Jupiter, their reconciliation in the returned Golden Age will guarantee that that return is not merely repetition but perfection: it will not degenerate again. The Saturnian legislation lacked the Jovian sanctions of force, the force to suppress or imprison war and *furor*; thus it was undone by *belli rabies* (327). The legislation of Fides, Vesta, and the reconciled Romulus and Remus will have the sanction of Jovian force and Jovian punishment (especially the thunderbolt). The reconciliation of Jupiter and Saturn is represented potentially by the reconciliation of Jovian Aeneas (7.219–221) with Saturnian Latinus (7.45–49).

Latinus was mistaken in believing that the Latins were righteous without bond or law. By the end of Book 7, the incursion of underworld forces into Latium at the behest of Juno has led the Latins into impious (583) war. Wild furor has sprung up out of the underworld into the upperworld (323 ff.), out of the ruled part of the Latin souls into the ruling part (460 ff.). The opening book of the Iliadic *Aeneid* repeats the thematic material and the thematic questions of the opening book of the Odyssean *Aeneid*: the government of the underworld forces of *furor, ira, bellum*. The cave of the insurgent storm winds, the prison of *furor*, and the gates of war are developed in Book 7 in the prison of Circe's insurgent beasts, the Underworld of the insurgent Allecto, the "storm of war" (222–230), and Juno's opening of the Gates of War (607–622). *Tantaene animis caelestibus irae?* Is there such (infernal) fury in the celestial gods? Is fury not confined to the infernal gods? Is the infernal *ungovernable* by the celestial?

iv. Vergil's Myth and the Truth

Vergil's revision of the myth of the Golden Age is calculated to present his novel conception of Rome as the perfected restoration of the ancient condition of human beings. The differences between Vergil's Golden Age and the traditional myth point to two converging observations about Vergil's intention. First, Vergil brings the myth as closely into harmony with the truth about human origins taught by Lucretius as the truth about human nature overlooked by Lucretius allows; and second, he makes the myth not only an account of man's past but also explicitly a model for his future.

The truth about human origins, as alluded to by Iopas in his song at the Carthaginian court, is not, as in the traditional myth, that human beings were first made in a perfect condition by the gods, but that they arose like the brutes spontaneously from the earth, *unde hominum genus et pecudes* (1.743). In the beginning, the mutually repellent human individuals did not differ essentially from the brutes; what first began to make them human, or to indicate what humanity is, was divine law. By nature, human beings neither could nor would associate with one another; they were both useless and dangerous to each other. Law, by enabling them to associate, enabled them to develop the arts, and the arts led on the one hand to acquisitiveness and war (as in Italy) and on the other hand to philosophy (as at Carthage).[43] War furnished the setting for heroism, and philosophy for happiness; in both cases the arts, whose practice institutes the fear of death since they are aimed at providing for the protection of life, also culminate in a way of life that overcomes the fear of death. Both the heroic life and the philosophic life had the human meaning of overcoming the fear of death brought in by the cultivation of the arts: the heroic life by subordinating self-preservation to immortal glory, the philosophic life by bringing to light the pleasure of rational thought, which is the greatest pleasure and which sees a natural end to pain.

"Divine law" is a redundant expression, though: law *is* divine. The humanization of man *is* the confrontation of brute man with legislating and punishing gods, or the putting before man's eyes his intermediate position between the brutes and the gods. As Lucretius suggests in his account of the origins of human social life, the rise of religion is inextricably connected with the rise of law. The earliest men began to see images of the gods only after they had first seen rulers, and simultaneously with their receiving laws: life under law brings along with it fear of discovery and punishment by angry gods (5.1143–1157).[44] The meaning of the common origin of laws and gods may then be said to be that the greatest men, the law-givers, are gods compared with the meanest men, or, the meanest men are brutes compared with the greatest. In Vergil as in Lucretius, the imagination of gods arises naturally from the natural difference between the greatest and the meanest men; it is this natural difference, in fact, that accounts for the ability of men to become human, to understand themselves as intermediate between brutes and gods. If, as suggested by Lucretius' project in the *De Rerum Natura*, the generality of men are not ultimately prevented by nature from enjoying the pleasures of philosophizing, it follows that the difference between the greatest and the meanest men, while great, is in principle a remediable difference in degree: men are mistaken in concluding from the existence of legislation that the legislator is divine; only the philosopher is divine (5.8), but the men addressed by Lucretius are invited to become philosophers themselves. In Vergil's view though, as we have seen, it is on precisely this point that Lucretius is radically in error. The original coincidence of law and gods implies that the difference between the meanest and the greatest men is so great and so irremediable as to be for all practical purposes a difference in kind; and since it is irremediable, the overcoming of men's dangerousness to one another can never be achieved by the extirpation but only by the promotion of religion. Universal atheism, the denial of the divine origin of law, could only lead back to the pre-civilized, certainly to the pre-philosophic, age of mankind; it could not be the basis of an enduring order that would protect the general cultivation of the arts and the particular cultivation of the philosophic life. Once the fear of death has been institutionalized through the establishment of the arts, its destructive effects could be controlled only through the increase, not the lessening and certainly not the extirpation, of religion. At first religion was merely fear of the manifest (i.e., this-worldly) superiority of the local legislator, as the first men feared Saturn and therefore obeyed his laws until acquisitiveness and war undermined their community. The perfection of the Golden Age, the ability to secure it from a speedy overthrow, must arise from the perfection of Saturn's regime: the legislator-god must become universal, and the rewards and punishments that support his laws must become eternal. The weakness of the first legislator-god, and thus of the first Golden Age, lay in his failure to institute universal rewards and punishments in the afterlife, and this failure in turn was the inevitable consequence of his being in flight from the arms of a greater god. The strength of the restored Golden Age would have to lie in its unification or universalization of the gods: if there is to be certain reward and punishment of men's immortal souls, there must be perfect harmony among the gods who impose these rewards and punishments.

With these remarks on the defect of the original Golden Age we have moved from our first observation about Vergil's intention in this myth, his bringing it as closely into harmony with the Lucretian truth about human origins as the un-Lucretian truth about human nature allows, into our second observation, his making the myth not only an account of mankind's past but also explicitly a model for its future. Here the crucial element is the universalization of the originally local divine legislation that first humanized men. For the original situation of men as isolated and hostile individuals, from which Saturn rescued the human race by instituting the first human community, is repeated in the original situation of the human communities, from which no one has yet rescued them. What enabled Saturn to begin the humanization of men was his appearing among them in his manifest divinity, on the strength of which they accepted his laws that enabled them to live together safely. But the humanization he began cannot be secured except by universalizing it. This is the meaning of Anchises' prophecy to Aeneas that

Augustus Caesar, the offspring of a god, will not only re-found the Golden Age in Latium where Saturn first founded it, but will this time extend it to the ends of the earth (6.791–797); and of Jupiter's prophecy to Venus that the future Caesar, who will "measure empire by Ocean" and himself ultimately be deified, will usher in the peaceable age that has neither borders nor times (1.286–296).

The permanence of the future Roman Empire depends upon its universality: it is because the Roman Empire will have no borders that it will have no times. The hitherto unending succession of the rise and fall of the separate cities, represented preeminently by Troy and Carthage, is to be resolved finally into a regime that, by including all the cities, will itself be deathless. Vergil's empire is to be literally universal, but of course it cannot be literally eternal; nothing is eternal but the atoms, the void, and the all, the *summa summarum*. The universal Roman Empire could last only as long as this world lasts; it can be thought of as eternal only so long as one forgets that this world itself must necessarily die.

Cicero, in a passage from his *Republic* cited by Augustine as illustrating its author's Platonic opinion that the world is imperishable, compares the constitution of regimes with that of the world:

> debet enim constituta sic esse civitas, ut aeterna sit. itaque nullus interitus est rei publicae naturalis ut hominis, in quo mors non modo necessaria est, verum etiam optanda persaepe. civitas autem cum tollitur, deletur, extinguitur, simile est quodam modo, ut parva magnis conferamus, ac si omnis hic mundus intereat et concidat.

> For a state ought to be so constituted as to be eternal. Thus there is no death that is natural for a republic as for a human being, in whom death is not only necessary but very often actually desirable. But when a state is overthrown, destroyed, extinguished, it is in a certain way—to compare small things with great—as if this whole world should perish and collapse.

> (*De Re Publica* III 34; cited in Augustine, *De Civitate Dei* XXII 6)

In Cicero's account, the imperishable world is presented as the proper model, but an unrealizable model, of the perishable regimes: the regimes "ought" to be eternal like the world, but in fact to compare them with the world is to compare small things with great and thus to see the necessary difference between the eternal world and the mortal regimes.[45] The death of a political community is only "in a certain way" like what the death of this whole world would be, for the death of this whole world is not possible.

According to Lucretius' teaching, on the other hand, the truth about eternity is that not this world but only the atoms, the void, and the sum of sums are eternal.[46] Vergil constructs his poetic empire without end by assimilating the mythical eternity of Rome to the eternity of that which is eternal in truth, the *summa summarum*. The sum of sums is eternal because, since it is all-inclusive, "there is neither any space outside it where things could fly away to, nor any bodies outside it that could invade it and break it up with a strong blow" (*DRN* 5.816–818). Rome as the sum of sums is represented poetically in the *Aeneid* in two complementary ways: first, by its geographical extension to the limits of the world; and second, by its inclusion of oppositions hitherto thought to be necessarily "outside" one another: Troy and Greece; tameness and savagery; the celestial and the infernal.

For the most part, Vergil's myth of the eternity of Rome abstracts from the true eternity by proceeding as if this ordered world were the sum of sums, whereas in truth this world is only a local and temporary concatenation of atoms and void within the unordered sum of sums.[47] But precisely on this point Vergil provides an opening to the truth in the form of his thematic allusions to the precariousness of the foundations not only of the Roman but also of the cosmic order: a strong invisible chaos underlies and compromises the visible order of all things. This theme appears at the beginning of the *Aeneid* in the form of the cave of Aeolus. The stability of Rome requires the stability of the world; but the stability of the world depends on Aeolus' rule of the cave of the winds. Without that rule, the winds would sweep away the three parts of nature— ocean, earth, and heaven—into chaos (1.58).[48] But what the opening of the *Aeneid* shows is emphatically the questionableness or fragility of Aeolus' rule: he is charged by Jupiter with ruling the winds by a *certum foedus* (1.62),[49] but he is readily bribed by Jupiter's opponent into overstepping the condition of this *foedus*. It is on the rule of this king, to whose easy corruption is owed the world-shaking collision of Rome and Carthage, that the continued existence of this world depends. The cave of the winds is the emblem of foundation in the *Aeneid*: as the foundation of this natural world, it is the model of the foundation of the human world on the cave of the Underworld, and of the restored Golden Age on the cave of Furor. The myth of the *Aeneid* recurs again and again to the ambiguity of the foundations as not only supporting the visible order but also threatening to bring down the visible order.

The myth of the *Aeneid* is that Rome, like the sum of sums, is eternal because it is universal or all-comprehensive. The truth is that by uniting the world under one central strong government of divine laws backed up by inexpugnable military force and the threat of eternal punishments in the next life, Rome may be able to rule the peoples in tranquil peace for a long time— until one single day gives over the triple nature of seas, lands, and sky to destruction, and the massive machine of this world, sustained through so many years, comes crashing down (*DRN* 5.93–96).

~

CHAPTER TEN

Aeneas' Founding of Rome

Aeneas' Italian peace settlement in Book 12 of the *Aeneid* represents in small the universal peace settlement to be concluded by Vergil's contemporaries. This settlement, indeed, *is* Aeneas' founding of "Rome." Aeneas does not choose the site of Rome, does not erect any walls or buildings there, and does not institute any laws or political regime in any usual sense. He founds Rome by making a peace settlement in Italy. It is therefore of the first importance, for an understanding of the "greater order of things" that Vergil is recommending in the *Aeneid*, to study both the character of the war in Italy to which Aeneas' treaty puts an end, and the terms of the treaty by which the peace is concluded. To the extent that Italy in the *Aeneid* represents the world, Vergil's portrayal of the ambiguous situation of pre-Aenean Italy as between war and peace implies an analysis of the situation of the world as between war and peace, and his portrayal of Aeneas' peace settlement as consisting emphatically in a religious innovation implies an analysis of the principal desideratum for Rome's pacification of the world.

i. Peace or War?

The "situation in Latium" (*Latio status*) at the arrival of Aeneas is characterized by the poet in Book 7 as long-standing peace:

> Rex arva Latinus et urbes
> iam senior longa placidas in pace regebat.

King Latinus in his old age was ruling rural territories and tranquil cities in long-standing peace.

(7.45–46)

and by the god Tiber in Book 8 as continual war:

hi bellum adsidue ducunt cum gente Latina.

[The Pallanteans] are continually waging war with the Latin nation.

(8.55)

The effect of Aeneas' arrival on the situation in Latium is hard to make out as long as we cannot say what the situation was when he arrived. The events following his arrival are a peace treaty, then a war, and then another peace treaty. Are we to understand that Aeneas' arrival brought war to a previously peaceful country (in order, to be sure, to achieve a final peace), or that it brought peace to a previously war-torn country? Or in other words: did Aeneas' arrival first *cause* the Italian wars, and only then end them? Or were the Italian wars first caused by something else, so that Aeneas' arrival merely coincided with them and, so far from causing them, only ended them? The mission of Rome, in the phrase of Anchises in the underworld, is to "impose the custom of peace" (*pacisque imponere morem*, 6.852) on a world from which the causes of war can, however, never be extirpated. Peace, in other words, must somehow be established on a foundation of ineradicable war: the peace of the cosmos on the war of the winds, the peace of cities on the war of Furor, the peace of souls on the war of the atoms. Insofar as Aeneas' imperial mission in Italy prefigures Rome's imperial mission in the world, are we to understand that the imposition of the habit of peace is itself essentially a bellicose or a pacific activity?

The poet's assertion that Latinus at the time of Aeneas' arrival was ruling the placid cities of Latium in long-standing peace refers to a sort of confederation of these Latin cities, each with its own prince, under the leadership of Latinus. According to Latinus' own account of things, these Latin cities would appear to be easy enough for him to keep tranquil and rule peaceably: for in his view the Latins are just and self-restrained not by bond or laws but spontaneously, by the custom of the ancient god (7.203–204). Presumably, then, both the citizens of each Latin city and the Latin cities among themselves either have no disputes or settle their own disputes equably without much or any need of Latinus' intervention. Nor does Latinus himself, apparently, have either any foreign enemies threatening his city or any designs on foreign cities himself.

In accordance with this general character of tranquillity and long-standing peace, the narrative of Book 7 emphasizes the unarmed condition in which the armed Trojans initially find the Latins. Vergil's account of the *primae exordia pugnae* (7.40), the first hostilities between Trojans and Latins, emphasizes above all else the incongruity between the warlike hunting of Ascanius' squadron and the extreme vegetarian gentleness of Silvia and her family (7.475–510). Ascanius' hunting at Carthage (4.151–159), and later his leadership of the boys in the war game called "Troy" (5.545–603), had, in their contexts, appeared to reflect as of course the nobility of war and of hunting as adult pursuits; but now the way of life of Silvia's family seems to be a reproach to or at least a questioning of these or any aggressive activities. When Ascanius' wounding of Silvia's stag[1] enrages the local countryfolk, it emerges that these friends of the animals are not only without the habit of hunting but also without the habit of fighting:[2] they have no proper weapons of any kind. To be sure, they are *duri* (504), not soft or weak; they are valiant enough in their indignation at the injury done by Ascanius to Silvia's stag, in their rising to defend both Silvia and themselves against what clearly seems to be a threat to their whole way of life; but in order to act on their rage they must improvise weapons from various domestic and agricultural tools:

> hic torre armatus obusto,
> stipitis hic gravidi nodis; quod cuique repertum
> rimanti telum ira facit.[3] vocat agmina Tyrrhus,
> quadrifidam quercum cuneis ut forte coactis
> scindebat rapta spirans immane securi.

> One armed with a scorched stake, one with a knot-laden log; their anger makes a weapon of whatever each finds as he gropes for something. Tyrrhus calls them into ranks, panting deeply and grabbing the axe with which he happened to be splitting an oak by driving wedges into it.

> (7.506–510)

The emphasis on the pacific and unarmed condition of the Latins in this first local skirmish appears again when this band of countryfolk, after suffering their first casualties at the hands of what is beginning to look like an invader, approach King Latinus, with the support of Turnus and Amata, to ask for a solemn declaration of war (573 ff.). For a declaration of war requires that the Gates of War be open, but they are shut (601 ff.); that is, Latium has been at peace until now; which indeed is what Latinus seems to mean a few lines earlier when he regrets that his life will not end in the *quies* he would have expected (598–599). Latinus himself refuses to authorize the change from long-standing peace to war by opening the Gates; when Juno therefore performs that office herself, the poet emphatically characterizes "Ausonia" as having been "undisturbed" and "at rest" until now: *ardet inexcita*[4] *Ausonia atque immobilis ante* (623).[5] And now that Ausonia *is* stirred up, the call to arms is followed first by a general polishing and sharpening of apparently long unused shields, darts, and axes (625–627); then by the devotion of five cities to an emergency manufacture (or possibly reconditioning) of helmets, breastplates, and swords (629–636). The arms manufacture displaces the love and honor formerly given to agricultural tools; perhaps it is suggested that these tools are actually being reforged into arms.

> vomeris huc et falcis honos, huc omnis aratri
> cessit amor; recoquunt patrios fornacibus ensis.

> The honor of ploughshare and pruning-hook, their love of the plough, yields to this; they reforge their ancestral swords in furnaces.

> (7.635–636)

Only after this extensive arms manufacture, this widespread turning from peaceful to warlike things, are the kings, roused for war at last (*bello exciti*, 642), ready to muster their troops. In the great catalogue of the Latin forces that concludes Book 7, the previous peacefulness of the Latins is again noted in the account of Messapus:[6]

> iam pridem resides populos desuetaque bello
> agmina in arma vocat subito ferrumque retractat.

> Suddenly he calls to arms peoples long at rest and ranks disaccustomed to war; he takes up iron again.

> (7.693–694)

As against this portrait of a Latium long at peace, unarmed, and unaccustomed to the usages of war until suddenly disturbed by the arrival of the Trojans, there emerges also a very different portrait summarized by Tiber's information to Aeneas that the Pallanteans "are continually waging war against the Latin people" (8.55). Tiber's purpose in telling Aeneas about this continual warring between Pallanteans and Latins is to encourage Aeneas about the prospect of gaining ready allies in his own war against the Latins.[7] We may well wonder, therefore, whether in his encouraging intention he is not exaggerating[8] somewhat when he claims that there is such a "continual war" going on. Certainly Tiber exaggerated quite a bit at the beginning of his speech in urging Aeneas to take heart on the grounds that "all the swelling and anger of the gods has subsided" (*tumor omnis et irae / concessere deum*, 40–41); near the end of his speech he modifies this claim considerably by urging Aeneas himself to overcome Juno's anger and threats with suppliant offerings (*Iunoni fer rite preces, iramque minasque / supplicibus supera votis*, 60–61). In his account of the Pallanteans' "continual war" his expression "*cum gente Latina*" is indeed equivocal: it is natural to take it as referring to the Latins collectively, "*the* Latin nation," but conceivably it might refer only to some particular Latin nation, "*a* Latin nation." In that case Tiber's statement would be consistent, loosely speaking, with the statement that Latium as a whole was in a condition of long-standing peace. As we learn with the development of the narrative in Book 8, the Pallanteans are in fact allied with the Tuscan league, which is at war or at least in some sort of hostilities with the Rutulans, who are a Latin nation.

On the face of it, there appear to be several directions in which to seek a resolution of the apparent contradiction between the "long-standing peace" and the "continual war" of the Latins. It may be that (a) the long peace in which Latinus has been ruling the Latins is a long peace among the Latins themselves, as opposed to the continual war between the Latins, or some Latins, and the Tuscans; perhaps the situation in Latium is one of long-standing *domestic* peace and continual *foreign* war. Or perhaps it is that (b) what Tiber refers to is not so much actual or open hostilities as the intention to open hostilities: the Tuscans haven't actually marched on Latium yet, since in accordance with the oracle they are waiting for a foreign commander; the situation in Latium then would be one of continually postponed war, which is a kind of long-standing peace. Or perhaps (c) the claim that Latinus was ruling in long-standing peace describes only the first or superficial appearance of things, the appearance presented to outsiders such as Aeneas and the Trojans, whereas the development of the narrative gradually complicates this initial impression, revealing the tensions, quarrels, and outright wars brewing under the pacific surface. In this case the situation in Latium would be one of long-standing apparent peace and continual real war.

(a) Domestic (Latin) Peace vs. Foreign (Italian) War

The Latin cities, as shown above, have in some sense been at peace—undisturbed, at rest, unarmed—until Aeneas' arrival. But in fact the characterization "tranquil cities in long-standing peace" does not quite hold true, upon reflection, even of the internal relations of the Latin cities among themselves. The closest relationship among the Latins is that between Latinus and Turnus, who had been the heir apparent until the oracles enjoined Latinus to await a foreign son-in-law. Latinus is not apparently confidential with Turnus. Although he himself has been persuaded by the oracles that he must not marry

Lavinia to Turnus after all, he does not tell Turnus this; he contracts a peace treaty with Aeneas which includes a grant of lands to the Trojans and the marriage of Aeneas with Lavinia (7.259–273)—all without consulting Turnus himself. Latinus' failure to tell Turnus about the oracles, and thus about his own decision to exclude Turnus from the succession in favor of Aeneas, appears to spring from weakness—certainly the weakness of being reluctant to break bad news (like Aeneas' reluctance to tell Dido about the divine vision that persuaded him he must leave her); but also the weakness of a weak ruler: Latinus, although said to be ruling the Latin cities in peace, cannot in fact count on Turnus' obedience. Turnus is a much more active ruler than Latinus is. His territories include not only the kingdom of his father Daunus but also many towns that he has captured in war (12.22–23). When Turnus ultimately learns from Allecto that Latinus has given away to Aeneas the wife and kingdom that should have been his, Allecto's bitter taunt to him suggests that it has been in fact Turnus himself, not Latinus, who has secured "peace" for Latium, by defeating the Latins' Tyrrhenian enemies in dangerous campaigns: *i nunc . . . tege pace Latinos* (7.425–426).[9] In connection with these campaigns against the Tyrrhenians, Turnus has given refuge to the ousted Tuscan tyrant Mezentius and his son Lausus, both of whom have brought with them large numbers of troops from their home city (647–654). In Aeneas' view, Turnus' intention is nothing less than to become master of all Italy:

> gens eadem, quae te, crudeli Daunia bello[10]
> insequitur; nos si pellant nihil afore credunt
> quin omnem Hesperiam penitus sua sub iuga mittant,
> et mare quod supra teneant quodque adluit infra.

> The same Daunian nation [Turnus' Rutulans] that is harrassing you with cruel war is doing the same to us; they believe that if they drive us out nothing will prevent them from putting all Hesperia completely under their yoke and occupying the territories washed by both the upper and the lower sea.
>
> (8.146–149)

Even allowing for the rhetorical color of Aeneas' speech to Evander as a potential ally against Turnus,[11] still one would have to say that Aeneas' imputation of large imperial motives to Turnus seems to be not entirely unfounded. A man who already possesses so many conquered towns, who has campaigns afoot against the neighboring cities of Tuscany, who is acknowledged to be militarily the backbone of Latium, who is at present harboring a foreign army, who is ambitious for the kingship of Latium and in love with Lavinia—King Latinus does not seem to be in a position to renege on his promise to Turnus with impunity. There is, after all, a good deal of truth in Amata's otherwise tendentious characterization of Turnus' land as *sceptris terram quae libera nostris / dissidet*, a land that is separate from ours, independent of our sovereignty (7.369–370). Thus the situation between Turnus and Latinus, though undoubtedly in a sense "peace," is a most precarious peace fraught with possibilities of explosion, as the event shows.[12]

Nor is Turnus the only empire builder among the Latins; there is also Oebalus. Like Turnus, Oebalus too was not content with his father's kingdom (737); by the time of Aeneas' arrival he had conquered the Serrastian peoples, the lands around the river Sarnus, the inhabitants of Rufrae, Batulum, Celemna, and Abella (7.733–743). Even if Oebalus was finally content with these additions to his kingdom (the poet does not say so), his acquisition of them sorts ill with the alleged long-standing peace among the Latins; and though his conquests have so far kept well to the south of Turnus, he seems to be on a collision course with that conqueror as well.

In the light of these empire-building activities of Turnus and Oebalus before the arrival of Aeneas, perhaps we must reinterpret the "tranquillity" of the Latin cities as blame of these cities' spiritlessness rather than praise of their security: perhaps, that is, most of the Latin cities, being unarmed and disaccustomed to war, fall so easily to armed conquerors like Turnus and Oebalus that one could say that their "peace" has never been disturbed at all. It was in this sense that Anchises in the Show of Heroes had followed his account of Numa's legislation with praise of Tullus for breaking the peace or spiritlessness (*otia*) of Numa's regime, and *thus* beginning to carry out Numa's mission of "great empire" (*missus in imperium magnum*, 6.812) by arming the previously peace-softened Romans:[13]

> otia qui rumpet patriae residesque movebit
> Tullus in arma viros et iam desueta triumphis
> agmina.

> Tullus, who will break the peace of the fatherland and move to arms indolent men and ranks disaccustomed to triumphs.

> (6.813–815)

Although at first it makes some sense, then, to think that the long-standing peace in which Latinus is said to have been ruling the tranquil Latin cities is domestic rather than foreign peace, nevertheless this view cannot be pressed very far. For if peace is understood in a positive sense of harmony, cooperation, devotion to agriculture, satisfaction with one's own, then some Latins enjoy domestic peace while others practice domestic war and threaten more war; while if one insists on characterizing *all* the Latins as at peace, then peace must be understood not as happy security but as spiritless capitulation (and war, by the same token, not as glorious conquest but as businesslike incorporation of one's unresisting neighbors).

(b) Intended War vs. Open or Actual War

At the time of the Trojans' arrival in Italy, the hostilities between Pallanteans and/or Tuscans on the one hand and Latins or Rutulans on the other have not yet decisively taken the form of open war. The Rutulans have made raids into Tuscan territory, or at any rate into Pallanteum (8.474); and "all Etruria" (494) has organized an army and a fleet for a war against the Latins, or at least against the Rutulans; but the war has not yet actually broken out. If not for Aeneas' arrival, moreover, the war may never have broken out, since the Tuscans may never have found the foreign commander demanded by their haruspex; the result may have been, like Turnus' and Oebalus' operations within Latium, the conquest of Etruria without a fight, the Tuscans being in effect disarmed by their fear of the gods.

The cause of the enmity between the Rutulans and "all Etruria" is Mezentius, the spurner of the gods, "*contemptor divum.*" According to the account of Italian affairs given to Aeneas by Evander in Book 8 (470 ff.), this tyrant of Agylla, after wearing down his subjects with atrocious cruelties, was ultimately overthrown by them; but he managed to escape during the coup, together with his son Lausus and an army of their loyal followers, and has been given asylum with Turnus. Turnus' motive in receiving Mezentius is not specified by Evander; perhaps Turnus owes Mezentius gratitude for some past benefit, or hopes for some future benefit if he can help to reinstate Mezentius in his tyranny; perhaps he sympathizes with Mezentius' contempt of the gods (certainly he is contemptuous of the priestess, *vatem inridens*, impersonated by Allecto, 7.435–444, and unwilling to accept the divine oracles barring him from the succession to the Latin throne); perhaps he has his own designs on the extra army that Mezentius brings with him. As for Mezentius, doubtless he hopes to regain Agylla with Turnus' help; or perhaps at least he hopes that Turnus can help him win some other city. The Tuscans, however, are not satisfied with the expulsion of Mezentius from Agylla: they wish to punish him, as Evander explains to Aeneas:

> ergo omnis furiis surrexit Etruria iustis,
> regem ad supplicium praesenti Marte reposcunt.

> Therefore all Etruria has arisen in just fury, demanding by threat of war the return of the king for punishment.

(8.494–495)

Thus it is that the old haruspex who restrains them in expectation of the "foreign commander" addresses them as "those whom just resentment moves against the enemy and whom Mezentius inflames with righteous anger" (*quos iustus in hostem / fert dolor et merita accendit Mezentius ira*, 8.500–501); as after the war has actually begun the poet too refers to the Tuscans as *iustae quibus est Mezentius irae*, "those for whom Mezentius is the object of just anger" (10.714). Mezentius is the *casus belli* here in the sense that his revolted subjects are not content with having rid themselves of his rule but are resolved to *punish* him.

But as for Evander and the Pallanteans—and according to Tiber it was the Pallanteans in particular who were engaged in continual war with the (or a) Latin nation—what was the cause of their alliance with the indignant Tuscans, and what was the cause of their being at war with Latins? Did the Tuscans seek alliance with Evander because he was already Turnus' enemy for other reasons; or did the Tuscans win his alliance by appealing to his sense of justice against their deposed tyrant, so that Turnus then became Evander's enemy because Evander supported the enemies of Turnus' ally Mezentius? The importance of the question lies in Vergil's understanding of the causes of war (and thus of the means of imposing peace). In the first case, nothing but alliance against a common enemy would be involved, whereas in the second case, justice itself—an interest in the punishment of someone else's enemy as a wrongdoer, rather than defense against one's own enemy—would be the cause of enmity. Although the sequence of events is not spelled out explicitly, there does not appear to be any root of enmity between Turnus and the Pallanteans other than the Pallanteans' alliance with Mezentius' angry former subjects.[14] Evander's account of the history of Mezentius is so framed as to express Evander's indignation at Mezentius' conduct not toward Pallanteum but toward Mezentius' subjects, and Evander's own wish that Mezentius be *punished* for that conduct—by the gods in the first place, to be sure, but also by the angry armies:

hanc multos florentem annos rex deinde superbo
imperio et saevis tenuit Mezentius armis.
quid memorem infandas caedes, quid facta tyranni
effera? di capiti ipsius generique reservent!

When this city [Agylla, Caere] had been flourishing for many years, finally King Mezentius took it over with haughty *imperium* and savage arms. Why should I rehearse the unspeakable slaughters, the bestial deeds of the tyrant?! May the gods keep such things in store for his own head and his family!

(8.481–484)

Later, in his parting speech to his son Pallas, Evander mentions that he himself had been outraged by Mezentius:

> . . . neque finitimo Mezentius umquam
> huic capiti insultans tot ferro saeva dedisset
> funera, tam multis viduasset civibus urbem.

[If I had had the strength of my lost youth] . . . Mezentius never would have heaped outrage on my head—me, his neighbor—by causing so many savage deaths by the sword and bereaving the city of so many citizens.

(8.569–571)

It is not clear from Evander's formulation whether the city he refers to is Agylla or Pallanteum: did Mezentius, in addition to torturing his own subjects, also make raids on Evander's neighboring city? Or was Evander outraged by the conduct of his neighbor-king Mezentius against Mezentius' own subjects, as if feeling that Mezentius ought to have been swayed in his domestic conduct by the remonstrances of a neighbor? Does Evander mean that if he had been younger and stronger he would have intervened in Agylla's domestic affairs because of the unjust conduct of Agylla's king—that he would have instigated civil war in Agylla perhaps sooner than the unaided Agyllans were able to stage their coup, or perhaps more successfully than the Agyllans in preventing the escape of Mezentius? The latter seems more likely,[15] since 1) Evander has in his previous speech expressed his own indignation against Mezentius' Agyllan atrocities, and 2) there is nowhere else any mention of any incursions of Mezentius during his tyranny against Pallanteum (though the Rutulans are *now* making raids on Pallanteum, 8.474; but this is presumably to punish Evander for making common cause with the Tuscans against Mezentius, or possibly as part of Turnus' general policy of harrassing weak kingdoms where he may be able to extend his territories without much of a fight). Thus it appears that Evander's posture, bearing out his name, is that of the "good man" rather than of the good king: or as Servius has it, Evander calls Mezentius' domestic policy an outrage against his own (Evander's) head "because it is the concern of a strong man and a good man that no injury be done to any human being; therefore he considers it a cause for (self-) reproach that he did not protect his neighbors from injury by the tyrant" (*ad* 8.570).

At the time of Aeneas' arrival, then, Italy was at peace in the sense that there was not general open war between the Tuscans and the Latins; the Rutulans, without the support of any other Latins, were confining themselves to bringing the pressure of arms to bear on Pallanteum, and the Tuscans, for all

their indignation and intention to punish Mezentius, were confining themselves to waiting for the foreign commander prophesied by their haruspex. So
in a sense there was "still" long-standing peace, since war had not definitely
broken out; though in another sense there was continual war, since Rutulans,
Pallanteans and Tuscans were carrying on a variety of piecemeal warlike hostilities.

(c) Superficial Peace vs. Deep War

This third explanation of the situation in Latium includes aspects of the first
two, but viewed from a somewhat different, more comprehensive point of
view. The narrative of Book 7 reveals that Latinus' belief in or claim of the
Latins' spontaneous justice is false. But not only are the Latins not spontaneously just; they do not justly obey any outside authority either. There is
nothing in fact to arm them against Junonian furor—neither their own free
will, nor their obedience to law, nor their loyalty to their king. Latinus only
appeared to be ruling them, so long as they happened to be calm;[16] when the
need for actual rule arose—when it was a matter of commanding and for-
bidding, of demanding obedience to the terms of the treaty he had rightfully
made with the Trojans—Latinus turned out not to be ruling the Latins at
all. As his ruling the Latins at all was only apparent, so his ruling them in
long-standing peace was only apparent. With the development of affairs the
true underlying situation became visible: strong Latin rulers were taking advantage of the weakness of their neighbors to increase their territories; Turnus' active empire building was becoming an implicit threat to the authority of the more passive or pacific Latinus; hostilities were brewing between
the Tuscans and the Rutulans, which might at any moment erupt into a war
in which the Rutulans would claim the support of the rest of the Latins,
while Latinus was not in control of this situation; and Latinus had become
convinced that he could not fulfill his undertaking to make Turnus his heir
without defying the will of the gods, but had not made this fact known to
Turnus; this piece of news was a civil war waiting to happen, and one in
which Turnus held all the human advantages. By the end of Book 7 Junonian furor has erupted in Latium: a hunting incident has incensed the countryfolk, Turnus has found out what Latinus has done to him, Amata has
taken a group of angry women bacchanizing into the mountains in support
of Turnus' claim to marry Lavinia and succeed Latinus; Latinus, unable to
rule the countryfolk, Turnus, or his own wife, has secreted himself in his
palace and dropped the reins of affairs, *saepsit se tectis rerumque reliquit
habenas* (7.599–600). But meanwhile it has become evident that Latinus
had never really held the reins of affairs; he dropped the pretension to rule

when it was in any case evaporated by a situation demanding actual rule rather than benevolent acquiescence or benign neglect.

The "lesser half" of the *Aeneid* had portrayed the impotence of Carthage to impose the custom of peace. This impotence had sprung from its underestimation of the ineradicable force of anger, or rather its mistaken judgment that the force of anger is eradicable or even eradicated, and its consequent failure to provide such arms and gods as might govern that force. The "greater half" proceeds to portray the superiority of Rome over Carthage by showing the roots of Rome's ability to impose the custom of peace. Italy in the *Aeneid* represents the world, and Aeneas' first founding of Rome in Italy represents the founding of the Roman world empire in Vergil's time. The Iliadic *Aeneid* begins to portray the Roman world empire by portraying as "the situation in Latium" the problematic world situation: the world before or without Roman rule is in an ambiguous condition as between war and peace. Aeneas' arrival in Italy ends the ambiguity by bringing the hidden condition of war to the surface and ending it, six books later, with a conclusive peace. Aeneas' Italian peace settlement is his founding of Rome.

The ambiguity of the situation in Italy rests on the uncertain status of the gods in Italy. Some Italians—Latinus, the Tuscan army—are restrained by their respect for gods; others—Turnus, Mezentius—are not. Respect for gods is represented here preeminently by subjection to the restraint of the oracles' command to await the coming of foreigners. The imminent war between Tuscans and Latins revolves around the Tuscans' need to punish Mezentius adequately for the atrocities to which his scorn of the gods has led him; meanwhile, though, his would-be punishers seem to be disarmed by their very respect for the gods, which inhibits them from taking punitive action on their own. Pending Aeneas' foundation of Rome, the situation in Italy would seem to call for resolution through the equalization of men either in their fear of or in their scorn for the gods: either men like Turnus and Mezentius must be made to fear the gods, or men like Latinus and the Tuscan army must be made not to fear them. The latter possibility has been considered and rejected in the lesser half of the *Aeneid*, where it is the heart of the Carthaginian project. The former possibility, the universalization of fear of the gods, is the heart of Aeneas' founding of Rome.

ii. Foreign Rulers

The regime of the first Golden Age was the direct rule of formerly godless men by a god who had had nothing to do with them until he sought asylum among them. His regime radically improved their lives by bringing them out of their brutish isolation into a community using arts and laws, but this regime was not able to be perduring. The ruler-god had not provided his laws with "teeth"—perhaps because he was not sufficiently prudent, perhaps because he was not sufficiently familiar with the constitution of human souls, surely because he lacked sufficiently biting teeth to provide, as indicated by his being at that time in hiding himself from the superior arms of a yet greater god. Since the decline of the Golden Age, the gods have not directly ruled any human communities. According to the myth of the *Aeneid*, the future Golden Age will be superior to all regimes since the decline of the first Golden Age in that it will again be ruled directly by gods; it will also be superior to the first Golden Age in that it will be ruled by gods not in hiding but openly, in the manifest superiority of inexpugnable arms.

"The situation in ancient Latium" at the arrival of Aeneas and the Trojans turns out to be marked most significantly by two situations in which priests have persuaded peoples that they cannot provide for their own affairs—succession to the throne in Latium, military command in Tuscany—but must await the appearance of foreigners, *externi*, to supply their need. In Latium, Turnus' courtship of Lavinia, though promoted by Amata, has been checked by omens:

> continuo vates 'externum cernimus' inquit
> 'adventare virum et partis petere agmen easdem
> partibus ex isdem[17] et summa dominarier arce.'

> At once the seer said, "We perceive that a foreign hero is coming, and a battle line is attacking from the same direction and in the same direction, and holding dominion over the summit of the citadel."

> (7.68–70)

And Latinus' inquiry into the meaning of the omens has been answered by the oracle of Faunus:

> 'ne pete conubiis natam sociare Latinis,
> o mea progenies, thalamis neu crede paratis;
> externi venient generi, qui sanguine nostrum
> nomen in astra ferant, quorumque a stirpe nepotes
> omnia sub pedibus, qua Sol utrumque recurrens
> aspicit Oceanum, vertique regique videbunt.'

> "Do not seek to unite your daughter with a Latin husband, o offspring of mine, and do not rely on the marriage that is in preparation: foreign sons-in-law will come, who will bear our name to the stars in their bloodline, and the offspring

of whose stock will see all things revolving and being ruled beneath their feet,
everywhere that Sol in his regular course looks upon either Ocean."

(7.96–101)

In Tuscany, meanwhile, a seer prevents the departure of the fleet that is ready
to set sail against the Latins:

toto namque fremunt condensae litore puppes
signaque ferre iubent, retinet longaevus haruspex
fata canens:. . . .
'nulli fas Italo tantam subiungere gentem:
externos optate duces.'

For the ships, collected all along the shore, roar and command that the standards be taken up; but an aged haruspex holds them back, singing the fates:
". . . . To no Italian's command is it permitted to submit this so great nation:
choose foreign commanders."

(8.497–499, 502–503)

What is striking is that in neither case does the seers' demand for foreigners
spring from any visible defect in the native resources of the peoples in question to provide for their own affairs. The succession to Latinus' throne appears in every way provided for by the long alliance of the Latins with the
Rutulans, the close ties between Latinus' household and Turnus', and the
love of Turnus and Lavinia. The campaign of the Tuscan armies appears in
every way provided for by the battle-readiness of the fleet and troops and the
leadership of King Tarchon. The priestly inhibition in each case expresses
not a defect in the resources at hand but the inadequacy of the otherwise
most perfect native resources simply because they are native.

The question of what is native and what is foreign is elaborated in each
case. In Latium, Amata argues in the first place that by a son-in-law from a
"foreign" nation (*gener externa . . . de gente*, 7.367) the oracle means one from
a land that is "independent of our scepter" (*sceptris . . . libera nostris*, 7.369),
a definition under which Turnus' Ardea would qualify as foreign; and in the
second place that Turnus' Greek ancestry actually makes him "foreign" to
Italy, even apart from the foreignness of Ardea with respect to Laurentum
(7.367–372). Meanwhile, in Tuscany, Evander would qualify as a foreign
commander for the Tuscans and has in fact been asked by Tarchon to serve,
but is too old; he in turn would put his son Pallas in command of the Tuscan
armies if it were not that Pallas is of Sabine blood on his mother's side and
thus does not qualify as "foreign" (8.496–513).

The requirements of the oracles in both cases, then, turn out to be requirements for almost absolute foreignness that have prepared Latinus and Tarchon respectively to accept the Trojan Aeneas as meeting the gods' standards. The necessary foreignness is only *almost* absolute, though; for Aeneas is deemed to meet the standard in spite of being descended from the native Italian Dardanus,[18] a lineage that is perfectly well known to both Latins and Tuscans (7.195, 219, 240; 8.134) without being deemed to compromise Aeneas' fitness to marry Lavinia and command Tarchon's troops in accordance with the divine strictures. All human beings are natives, if their ancestry is traced back far enough; but natives are able, with time and distance, to become "foreigners" and, as such, to become entitled to command and to rule.[19]

The divine provision for human affairs represented by the oracles to the Latins and Tuscans seems to indicate what is ultimately meant by the need of natives for foreigners to provide for their affairs: the gods, like Saturn, are the foreigners par excellence. The idea that the foreigners are gods—that Aeneas' foreignness is divinity—is hinted at most clearly by the Faunus-oracle's description of the *externi* as those who will see everything turning and being ruled beneath their feet (7.100–101). This understanding of "*externi*" has been rather strongly prepared in Book 6 by the passage in Anchises' prophecy to Aeneas where he describes the oracles to the nations,[20] oracles that are "already now" preparing the nations for the advent, centuries hence, of Augustus Caesar, *divi genus*, restorer of the Golden Age once ruled by Saturn (6.791 ff.): there is an intimation to all the nations that they are all to be ruled directly by a god as the aboriginal Latins were once ruled directly by Saturn. The oracles to the various Italians, preparing them severally to submit their dynastic and military affairs to divinely appointed foreigners, are the first manifestation in small of the oracles to all the nations, preparing them to submit their political affairs altogether to a divine ruler. Vergil's expressions for the fearful divinity of these intimations reverberate from one passage to the next: the far-flung representatives of the nations shudder at the oracles of the gods (*responsis horrent divum*, 6.799); in Latium, when Turnus presses his suit for Lavinia, portents of the gods stand in the way with varied terrors (*variis portenta deum terroribus obstant*, 7.58, and cf. 7.102); the Tuscan army hangs back from its campaign in terror of the oracles of the gods (*monitis exterrita divum*, 8.504).

In the power of the Latin and Tuscan priests to inhibit the self-provision of royal households and battle-ready armies, Vergil portrays the openness of human beings to rule by gods. Such rule as men provide for themselves is felt by men themselves to be incomplete or defective; the nations have arisen

from the convergence of men's openness to divine rule with divine inclination to rule men. As the Latin nation was originally open to Saturn's rule, the
nations have always been open to the rule of their own gods, who make them
foreign to one another; each nation's gods are its "own" foreigners. Rome is
to exploit men's natural openness to their "own" foreigners by introducing
among them the universal foreigner. The heart of Aeneas' foundation of
Rome is his introducing his gods into Latium (1.6), as Rome is to introduce
her gods into the whole world. Rome's unification of the world is adumbrated
in the Iliadic *Aeneid* by Aeneas' unification of Italy.

iii. Aeneas' Italian Settlement

excudent alii spirantia mollius aera
(credo equidem), vivos ducent de marmore vultus,
orabunt causas melius, caelique meatus
describent radio et surgentia sidera dicent:
tu regere imperio populos, Romane, memento
(hae tibi erunt artes), pacisque imponere morem,
parcere subiectis et debellare superbos.

Others will forge more delicately the breathing bronze—well can I believe it—
and draw out living faces from marble, plead cases better, mark out with their
measure the motions of the heaven, and tell the rising stars: you, Roman, remember to rule the peoples with empire (these will be your arts), to impose the
custom of peace, to spare the subject and war down the defiant.

(6.847–853)

At first glance, Anchises' prophecy appears to dismiss the "others'" arts as inferior and raise the Roman arts of empire above them in dignity.[21] But after
all the Roman arts are for the sake of peace,[22] which in turn is for the sake of
the "others'" arts. The Roman arts are more necessary, since the others' arts
depend upon the peace secured by the Roman arts. But the others' arts, while
less necessary, not to say unnecessary, are for that very reason of higher dignity: they are the pursuits that are for their own sake. The others' arts are preeminently the arts of Greeks as opposed to Romans; within the myth of the
Aeneid, they are the arts of the Carthaginians. The culminating art, astronomy, stands for philosophy, as shown by Iopas' song and by his being the pupil
of Atlas. The defect of Carthage is a defect not in the dignity of the
Carthaginian arts, but in the ability of Carthage to provide the peace necessary to the cultivation of those arts. The arts of Rome are for the sake of the
arts of Carthage, and thus ultimately for the sake of philosophy: men cannot

safely be Carthaginians unless some men are Romans.[23] The Roman mission is to protect the arts of Carthage. Life is quite possible without sculpture, rhetoric, and astronomy; certainly the first human men, the men of the Golden Age, lived without these arts. But as soon as one compares the life of the Golden Age as described by Evander with the life of the Carthaginians, one sees that in the absence of the Carthaginian arts the men of the Golden Age were not fully human; and these arts are not possible without peace. Anchises recommends the Roman arts not for their own sake but for the sake of the others' arts; in reading his words we cannot help reflecting that Vergil's own art, the art of poetry, would seem to belong not to the Romans but to "the others." No doubt in directing his poem to the formation of such Romans as would devote themselves to the arts of ruling the peoples with empire, Vergil brings the art of poetry as close as possible to the arts of ruling; nevertheless, it is hardly possible to avoid the thought that Vergil himself belongs among the Greeks or Carthaginians.

The peace treaty that Aeneas concludes in Italy is his realization of Anchises' exhortation to impose the custom of peace. It is this treaty that constitutes Aeneas' founding of Rome; or to put it the other way around, the foundation of Rome is a peace treaty. In order, therefore, to understand Vergil's conception of Rome as the principle of the greater order of things, it is first necessary to understand the terms of Aeneas' peace treaty. As it turns out, the terms of this treaty recur to and finally explain the opening statement of the *Aeneid* that the sufferings of its hero continued until he could "found the city and introduce gods into Latium" (1.5–6). The peace treaty in virtue of which Aeneas founded Rome was emphatically the means of Aeneas' introducing gods into Italy.

The terms Aeneas offers immediately before his final duel with Turnus are that if he loses, he will withdraw peaceably to Pallanteum; but if he wins,

> non ego nec Teucris Italos parere iubebo
> nec mihi regna peto: paribus se legibus ambae
> invictae gentes aeterna in foedera mittant.
> sacra deosque dabo; socer arma Latinus habeto,
> imperium sollemne socer; mihi moenia Teucri
> constituent urbique dabit Lavinia nomen.

> I for my part shall not command the Italians to obey the Trojans, nor do I seek the kingdom for myself: let both nations unconquered submit themselves under equal laws to an eternal compact. I shall give rites and gods. Let Latinus as my father-in-law keep his arms, his established *imperium*; the Trojans will build walls for me, and Lavinia give her name to the city.

> (12.189–194)

Aeneas' statement of his terms notes at greater length what he does not claim than what he does. He does not claim as the prize of victory what the victor would be expected to claim—the obedience of the vanquished, kingship over them, legal superiority over them, their arms or their *imperium*. He does claim the right to build a settlement in Latium and wed Lavinia (and thus, as he does not mention, to succeed Latinus); but this is only to reclaim what had already been granted him by Latinus in Book 7 (7.259–273). By contrast to all this, the one demand that Aeneas does make, placed as it is in the midst of the things he foregoes and expressed rather as a gift than as a claim, stands out: "I shall give rites and gods." According to Aeneas' statement, the chief or only change that his victory will bring about for the vanquished is that they will receive rites and gods from him.[24] This is a considerable difference from the original terms offered by Latinus in Book 7. There, with respect to gods, Ilioneus had requested and been granted only "a small seat for our ancestral gods," *dis sedem exiguam patriis* (7.229). At that point it had seemed that Aeneas' mission to seek great walls for Troy's Penates and sacred things (2.293–294) would be fulfilled by securing this small Trojan seat for them; but now, it turns out, it is not by settling the gods within Trojan walls but by giving them to the Italians that Aeneas' mission is truly to be accomplished.[25]

These astonishing terms that Aeneas offers on the battlefield are confirmed and elaborated later in Book 12 in a conversation in heaven between Jupiter and Juno. Juno pronounces herself willing to concede the victory to Aeneas on the one condition, which she says is prevented by no law of fate, that this victory make no change in the life of the vanquished:

> ne vetus indigenas nomen mutare Latinos
> neu Troas fieri iubeas Teucrosque vocari
> aut vocem mutare viros aut vertere vestem.
> sit Latium, sint Albani per saecula reges,
> sit Romana potens Itala virtute propago:
> occidit, occideritque sinas cum nomine Troia.

> Do not command the native Latins to change their ancient name, nor to become Trojans and be called Teucrians, nor command these men to change their speech or their dress. Let Latium be forever, forever Alban kings; let Rome's posterity be mighty with Italian virtue. Troy is dead; let it die together with its name.

> (12.823–828)

To this condition Jupiter assents, but with the reservation that he will change—"add"—one thing only for the Latins, a thing moreover that will assimilate their nation as a whole to its pious conqueror in his piety, while in every other respect the nation of the conqueror will be assimilated to theirs:

> sermonem Ausonii patrium moresque tenebunt,
> utque est nomen erit; commixti corpore tantum
> subsident Teucri. morem ritusque sacrorum
> adiciam faciamque omnis uno ore Latinos.
> hinc genus Ausonio mixtum quod sanguine surget,
> supra homines, supra ire deos pietate videbis,
> nec gens ulla tuos aeque celebrabit honores.

The Ausonians will keep the speech and customs of their fathers, their name will be what it is now; except through being bodily commingled, Trojans will sink away. I shall add the customs and rites of sacred things, and I shall make them all, with one tongue, Latins. The race that shall arise from this, with mixed Ausonian blood, you will see surpassing human beings, surpassing gods, in piety; nor will any nation celebrate your honors so much as they.

(12.834–840)

Whereas Aeneas had spoken of giving *sacra* and gods, Jupiter speaks only of adding *sacra*, without mention of gods. While this might suggest that he is envisioning only new rites for the old gods, it is more plausible to think, especially as his words are calculated to recall Aeneas' own statement, that Jupiter is envisioning new gods as well but is restrained by a certain tact from mentioning them. For while the new gods to be added certainly include the Trojan Penates,[26] perhaps the principal new god in question is Jupiter himself. The pre-Aenean Latins are not Jupiter-worshipers; they are the men whose king regards them as the Saturnian people and keeps among the divine images in his royal hall an image of Saturn but not of Jupiter (7.170 ff.). Except for his echoing Aeneas' words in the oath-taking before the final duel,[27] Latinus never refers to Jupiter. Jupiter's speech explicitly promises Juno that the new rites he is going to add will increase the honors done to her;[28] implicitly his speech suggests that it is he himself whose worship is to be extended by the new rites to the previously "Saturnian" people. In accordance with this, Jupiter introduces this speech with his only explicit reference to Saturn in the *Aeneid* (12.830), calling attention to the kinship between himself, Saturn, and Juno with respect to anger. In his prophecy to Venus in Book 1, Jupiter had foretold this moment of Juno's reconciliation (1.279–282), and the eventual surcease of wars to follow upon the deification of the Trojan Caesar (1.286–296). Because his prophecy of the future peaceable age had suggested the return of the Golden Age, his silence there about Saturn had raised the troubling question whether the return of the Golden

Age must not mean the return of Saturn's kingship in heaven, and thus the end of Jupiter's regime. Vergil's radical revision of the Golden Age myth in the course of the *Aeneid* has meanwhile answered this question by showing that Jupiter was already king in heaven when the original Golden Age took place. But he was not yet king on earth; and the Latins, who did not know him then, still regard themselves, at the time of Aeneas' arrival in Italy, as the men of Saturn rather than of Jupiter. Jupiter's providential plan for empire without end requires that the peoples come to acknowledge Jupiter, with his laws, his arms, and his eternal reward and punishment of souls, as the sovereign god who has decisively replaced Saturn, with his custom of spontaneous justice.

The gods whom Aeneas will give to Italy include then Jupiter as well as the Trojan Penates. But in addition to these, Aeneas himself, by showing himself to be the "foreigner" for whom both Latinus and the Tuscans have been waiting at the behest of their seers, will give himself to them as a new god. Although the divinity of Aeneas is not explicitly present to his own thoughts or the Italians', it is certainly present to Jupiter's and to ours: Jupiter's very first words in the *Aeneid* had been his promise to Venus that Aeneas' deification was assured by the fates and by Jupiter's own will (1.257–260). To be sure, Aeneas will not be deified until his death. Nonetheless, the foreigner who appears among the Italians in fulfilment of divine oracles, and who is within three years of becoming a god (1.265–266), is surely one of the gods whom Aeneas "will give" to the newly united Trojan-Italian people.

In the light of these observations about the Italian situation before Aeneas' arrival and the peace ultimately imposed upon Italy at the close of the poem, it is now possible to collect some reflections on the question of what Vergil intends us to understand by the greater order of things, the empire without end, or Rome's imposing the custom of peace on the world. The world in itself, before or without Rome, is in an uncertain state as between war and peace. As the natural world is on its surface in a state of temporary, unprotected, accidental peace that must ultimately be undone by the wars of the atoms that make up its substructure, so the peace of the human world is superficial, unprotected, accidental, and necessarily temporary. If there were a god who cared for this world, he would make it his business to secure and deepen its temporary and superficial stability, as the Jupiter of the *Aeneid* makes it his business to secure the coherence of this world against being swept away by the winds.[29] Jupiter's providential care for the world cannot prevent its necessary ultimate dissolution, but can only ward off that dissolution for a longer time than if he had imposed no divine government over the winds. A providential god is one who regards this world not from the standpoint of eternity, from which the longer or shorter holding out of one world against its necessary dissolution must be indifferent, but from the standpoint of that mortal world itself, from which alone the reprieve of a year or a millennium could be worth strenuous efforts.

So too in the human world. If there were a god who cared for it, he would make it his business to protect and strengthen its precarious, accidental stability through such divine government as might hold off its day of doom. Vergil's "greater order of things" is this divine government, which may now be summarily described as follows: it is to be *world* government under *laws* enforced by *gods* with inexpugnable *arms* in this world, and eternal *rewards and punishments* in the next.

As Aeneas' founding of Rome was his imposing a peace treaty to unite the Trojan and Italian peoples through an innovation in their common rites and gods, so the perfected founding of Rome will be the peace treaty unifying the Romans with all the peoples of the world through this same innovation. The customs and costumes, the governments and languages of the nations need not be changed in order to unite them by equal laws under an eternal compact of peace, so long as Rome "adds" her gods. The unification and pacification of the world had proved to be out of reach of Carthage because Carthage's lack of gods and arms had made it incapable of governing the incursions of immortal furor into men's souls and cities. The pre-Aenean Saturnian religion of the Latins had in common with Carthaginian atheism its reliance on men's spontaneous right-doing, and thus its absence of effective laws and effective arms. The Jovian religion through which Aeneas unified Italy points to the universal religion through which Vergil means to unify the world.

As in Aeneas' first founding, so in the inauguration of the greater order of things the Olympian gods are to conquer the local gods of all the nations, since it is these local gods, rather than local languages, regimes, and customs, that make the nations, nations. Dido was right in identifying the gods as the obstacle to the unification of the nations, but not in her method of trying to overcome this obstacle. The Shield of Aeneas prophetically represents the Battle of Actium as the climactic battle by representing it as pitting the monstrous Egyptian brute-gods against the Olympian man-gods:

> omnigenumque deum monstra et latrator Anubis
> contra Neptunum et Venerem contraque Minervam
> tela tenent.

> Monstrous gods of every species, including the barking Anubis, draw their
> bows against Neptune and Venus and against Minerva.

> (8.698–700)

The Egyptian gods are subhuman not only because they are brutes but because it is brutish for men to have gods who are the gods of their nomes. As Saturn began to humanize the originally brutish nature of men by bringing them out of hostile isolation into regulated intercourse, so Rome is to perfect his work, raising the nations out of their still brutish dispersedness under the universal aegis of the human or humanizing gods. The humanizing gods supply the defect of Saturn's dispensation by furnishing the harshest punishments, but also the greatest rewards, which were lacking to it: as the preparation and ground of the triumph of the Olympians at the Battle of Actium, Vulcan prophetically portrays on the Shield the torments of Tartarus and the bliss of Elysium:

> hinc procul addit
> Tartareas etiam sedes, alta ostia Ditis,
> et scelerum poenas, et te, Catilina, minaci
> pendentem scopulo Furiarumque ora trementem,
> secretosque pios, his dantem iura Catonem.

> Far from this he adds also the habitations of Tartarus, the tall gates of Dis, and the punishments of crimes: you, Catiline, hanging from a menacing cliff in dread of the faces of the Furies; and the pious separately apart, with Cato giving laws to them.
>
> (8.666–670)

But the "great" Olympian gods are to be accompanied by the "small" gods, the Trojan Penates, by whom in turn they are linked to the Roman rulers themselves:

> hinc Augustus agens Italos in proelia Caesar
> cum patribus populoque, penatibus et magnis dis,
> stans celsa in puppi, geminas cui tempora flammas
> laeta vomunt patriumque aperitur vertice sidus.

> Augustus Caesar, leading into battle the Italians with the senate and people, the Penates and the great gods, stands high on the stern, pouring forth twin flames from his glad brow, with his father's star showing above.
>
> (8.678–681)

As Aeneas was to be deified at his death (1.259–260, 12.794–795), so Augustus, the son of the deified Julius, is to be deified at his (1.286–290, 6.789–805). But rulers of whom it is known that they are destined to become gods at death are already gods, as Vergil shows in his address to Augustus in the invocation to the Georgics: *votis iam nunc adsuesce vocari*, "get accustomed already now to being invoked with prayers" (*Geo.* 1.42). As only a god ruling them directly

was able to begin to civilize the first men, so Rome is finally to secure the
peaceable order of the world by supplying it with a line of gods to rule it:

> ipse sedens niveo candentis limine Phoebi
> dona recognoscit populorum aptatque superbis
> postibus; incedunt victae longo ordine gentes,
> quam variae linguis, habitu tam vestis et armis.
> hic Nomadum genus et discinctos Mulciber Afros,
> hic Lelegas Carasque sagittiferosque Gelonos
> finxerat; Euphrates ibat iam mollior undis,
> extremique hominum Morini, Rhenusque bicornis,
> indomitique Dahae, et pontem indignatus Araxes.

He himself, sitting at the snow-white threshold of Phoebus, acknowledges the
gifts of the nations and fixes them on the proud doorposts; the conquered peoples march past in a long line, as various in their languages as in their costumes
and arms. Here Mulciber had represented the Nomad tribes and loose-robed
Africans, there the Lelegans, the Carians, and the arrow-bearing Geloni; the
waves of the Euphrates were moving more gently already, and the Morini, most
remote of men, and the two-horned Rhine, the untamed Dahans, and the
Araxes resenting its bridge.

(8.720–728)

Under the dispensation of the universal Roman ruler-gods, the imposition
of the habit of peace takes on a peculiar character because war itself can no
longer be conceived as the contest of nation against nation, but only as civil
war or, from another point of view, as guilty violation of divine law. The narrative of the *Aeneid* shows what is meant by the transformation of foreign
into civil war by showing the transformation of Italians and Trojans, in the
very war between them, from foreigners into fellows—fellow Romans. Vergil
refers to the unity of the Roman people in his own day by perplexing us during the battle scenes with repeated uncertainties about the nationality of the
warriors: the names of the combatants, so far from automatically indicating
to us which are the Trojans and which the Latins, make us rather notice that
we are sometimes in uncertainty about this. The meaning of the uncertainty
induced in us by this aspect of the narrative is brought to expression in one
of the rare passages where the poet makes an observation in his own name
through an apostrophe. In introducing the last general engagement before
the single combat between Aeneas and Turnus, Vergil exclaims:

> tanton placuit concurrere motu,
> Juppiter, aeterna gentis in pace futuras?

Was it your will, Jupiter, that peoples who were going to be in eternal peace
should clash in so great a war?

(12.503–504)

As one may look back at the original Cyclopean individuals in wonder at the
mutual repulsion among men soon to be united into a community under Saturn's dispensation, so Vergil induces us to look back at the mutual hostility
of Trojans and Italians in wonder that nations soon to be mixed into one
originally regarded themselves as two; and this prepares us to conceive a future day when what are now the nations, understanding themselves to be at
war and peace with foreign nations, will understand themselves rather as one
mixed nation (commixti corpore, 12.835), among whose parts war could only
be understood as civil war. Since the decisive element in this transformed
self-understanding of the nations is to be the "addition" of the Roman gods,
it emerges that what made them nations (i.e. foreign nations) in the first
place was not the various languages and costumes, which have not changed,
but their various gods. Given the conquest of the particular local gods by the
universal Roman gods, even the Morini, "most distant of human beings," are
discovered to be Romans. After this discovery, war between Morini and Romans can only be civil war, a temporary disruption or delay of the eternal
peace in which they are to live.

This transformation of the nations' self-understanding from multiple foreignness to single citizenship converges with the transformation of the old-
style glory of national warriors into the new-style guilt of transgressors of the
divine order. This transformation is powerfully illustrated in the episode of
the Latins' appeal to Diomedes for an alliance against his old enemy the Trojans. Diomedes' reply shows his considered rejection of the heroic interpretation of the Trojan War in favor of a pious interpretation. Second only to
Achilles, Diomedes in the Iliad had been the exponent of the view that war
is the arena of the quest for immortal glory, of men's approach to the condition of the gods. In his aristeia in Iliad 5, Athene had removed from his eyes
the mist that prevents men from distinguishing, as gods can distinguish, between men and gods. Then, having achieved the divine condition of this
god's-eye insight, he had gone on to perfect his godlikeness in doing battle
against the very gods of his enemies, wounding Aphrodite herself. But in his
reply to the embassy of Latinus in Aeneid 11, Diomedes shows that he has
since rejected as mistaken his earlier heroic understanding of the Trojan War.
The Greeks at Troy were not waging a glorious war against worthy enemies
but so "violating" the Trojan fields as to have owed unspeakable recompense
and penalties for their crimes (11.255–268); Diomedes himself in wounding

Venus was displaying not his almost superhuman excellence but a fit of madness in which he so "violated" her as to have brought down upon himself and his men condign punishment from the gods (11.269–277). Diomedes concludes that in the light of Aeneas' piety (292) the Latins would be better advised to make terms with him than to take up arms against him: to fight against the pious Aeneas is to invite not the chances of human victory and defeat but the certainty of divine punishment. The divisions among the Olympians in the *Iliad* had given the appearance that enmities between nation and nation only reflected and emulated enmities between the gods themselves. But in accordance with the settlement of Olympian affairs in the *Aeneid*—the reconciliations between Jupiter and Juno and between Jupiter and Saturn, and the defeat of the barbarian gods by these now-unified Roman Olympians—Diomedes has come to reinterpret both the Greeks' war against the Trojans and war itself not as glorious emulation of the gods but as impious and punishable defiance of the divine order.

Vergil's greater order of things as sketched here, while conceived with a view to securing universal peace for the sake of the fortunateness of the many and the philosophic felicity of the few, raises at the same time the specter of universal tyranny. What is to prevent the rulers of the world empire not only from oppressing the many and suppressing the philosophers, as various rulers have done at all times, but from doing so with such an inexpugnable concentration of armed force and universal opinion as would for the first time put the recovery of both political and philosophic freedom beyond human hope? Vergil invites reflection on this question at the conclusion of the *Aeneid* by connecting the episode of Jupiter's providential oversight of the Italian peace settlement with the episode of Jupiter's rape of Juturna. Vergil's treatment of this grave question of the relationship between world empire and world tyranny will be taken up at the conclusion of the following chapter, where a consideration of Dante's *Monarchy* will have sharpened the issues involved.

CHAPTER ELEVEN

～

World Empire

The *Aeneid* opens with the contest between Carthage and Rome to have kingship over the nations (*regnum gentibus*, 1.17; *late regem*, 1.21). It is presupposed that some city will be ruler over the nations, though at the outset the reason for this rather surprising presupposition, and the exact sense of "the nations," are obscure. As the poem unfolds it becomes clear both why there must be a single ruler over the nations and why it is Rome rather than Carthage that is by rights that ruler; and simultaneously it becomes clear that "the nations" means *all* the nations—the entire human race and the whole inhabited world. The reason why the rule of one nation over all the others is presupposed lies in the object of government. Human happiness in both its forms, the felicity of the few and the fortunateness of the many, requires peace. But the secure maintenance of peace against the ineradicable incursions of immortal furor or divine anger into souls and cities can be achieved only as universal peace; and universal peace can be achieved only through the unification of all the nations under a single regime.

Vergil's understanding of the contest between "Rome" and "Carthage" has been analyzed in Part I as a representation of the conflicting claims of "golden" scientific enlightenment and "iron" armed piety to be the key to the rule of anger and thus to the rule of the nations. The victory of "Rome" in this contest emerges at first negatively in the defeat of "Carthage": Vergil shows that the defect of "Carthage" in its claim to rule the nations is its fatal underestimation of the immortal vitality of Furor, and its consequent failure to deploy "iron"—arms and gods—in the government of that Furor. The gold of Carthage recalls the defective first Golden Age of Saturn, which could not secure itself against the incursions of acquisitiveness and war: it lacked the iron arms of Jupiter, from which Saturn was in hiding. The world of the Golden Age requires defense by the world of the Iron Age; the virtues of Carthage require defense by the virtues of Rome. Vergil's positive account of the victory of "Rome" unfolds in the second half of the poem; in Aeneas' arrival in Italy and in the wars that ensue there, Vergil represents the character of "Rome," the regime of iron and gods, as the one suited to unify the world and keep the peace.

In the myth of the *Aeneid*, Rome's conquest, unification, and rule of the world is represented in small by Aeneas' conquest, unification, and rule of Italy. The present chapter will explore both Vergil's poetic representation of "the world" as a single empire and the theoretical doctrine of world empire that underlies this poetic representation.

i. The Lands and the Nations

That "the nations" whose rule is in question in the *Aeneid* are *all* the nations is developed throughout the poem in both geographic and ethnographic terms. Geographically, it has been promised by Jupiter that the Romans are to hold "the sea and all lands" in their dominion: *qui mare, qui terras omnis dicione tenerent* (1.236).[1] In Book 1, Jupiter not only confirms this promise to Venus but doubly extends it,[2] first to Ocean and heaven and then to the Underworld. Explicitly he says that their "empire without end" will come to pass when Caesar "bounds his empire by Ocean and his glory by the stars" (*imperium Oceano, famam qui terminet astris*, 1.287); implicitly he extends their empire to the Underworld by indicating that they will forcibly govern impious Furor. The link between earth, ocean, heaven, and underworld is the stars. In natural terms, the stars are the visible measure of the sea and all lands: they correspond to or mark the places on the earth.[3] In mythical terms, the region of the stars is the region of the gods: to measure one's glory by the stars means to be as glorious as a god. In natural terms, then, Jupiter says that Roman rule will extend to the ends of the inhabited earth;[4] in mythical terms, that it will, like the rule of the gods themselves, extend to all the four quarters of the world: earth, ocean, heaven, underworld.[5]

The extension of Roman rule to "the stars"[6] is expressed also by its being made equal to "Olympus" or "heaven." Anchises prophesies to Aeneas in the Underworld:

. . . illa incluta Roma
imperium terris, animos aequabit Olympo.

. . . Glorious Rome will make its empire equal to the lands, its spirits to
Olympus.

(6.781–782)

And Anchises' words are recalled by the poet's phrase, at the Trojans' first
sight of Pallanteum, *tecta vident quae nunc Romana potentia caelo / aequavit*,
"they see the buildings that Roman power in our times has made equal to
heaven" (8.99–100). "Equal to Olympus" or "equal to heaven," like "measured by the stars," means 1) embracing the entirety of earth, all the lands of
earth in their correspondence to the regions of heaven; and 2) having divine
rule over men, ruling over the human natives of earth with the manifest superiority of gods.[7] But in addition, these expressions—*aequabit Olympo, caelo
aequavit*—emphatically recall and contest Lucretius' expression of the
achievement of Epicurus:

quare Religio pedibus subiecta vicissim
opteritur: nos exaequat victoria caelo.

Thus Religion in its turn is conquered and trodden beneath the feet: his victory makes us equal to heaven.

(1.78–79)

According to the myth of the *Aeneid*, as against the science of Lucretius, the
victory that "makes us equal to heaven" is not comprehensive philosophic
insight but comprehensive world empire.[8] The oracle of Faunus prophesies to
Latinus that the offspring of his future foreign son-in-law

omnia sub pedibus, qua Sol utrumque recurrens
aspicit Oceanum, vertique regique videbunt.

will see everything turning and being ruled beneath their feet, in the whole orbit where Sol in his circuit looks upon either Ocean.

(7.100–101)

The Roman rulers are to be as only the all-seeing god Sol is now, having a
comprehensive view of the whole of earth spread out beneath them. To see
everything beneath one's feet is to be a god or godlike,[9] to inhabit the
heavens. The "everything" these rulers are to see is everything on earth,
everything subject to rule (*vertique regique*).[10] It is quite distinct from the

"everything" that Lucretius describes himself seeing beneath his feet when the reasoning of Epicurus dispels the terrors of the soul:

> moenia mundi
> discedunt, totum video per inane geri res. . . .
> nec tellus obstat, quin omnia dispiciantur,
> sub pedibus quaecumque infra per inane geruntur.

> The walls of the world draw aside, I see the things taking place throughout all space. . . . No land stands in the way of everything being seen, everything that takes place beneath the feet down throughout space.
>
> (DRN 3.16–17, 26–27)

The philosophic "view" of the world is an understanding of its causes and is quite distinct from, indeed opposed to, rule; the Lucretian philosopher is like the gods themselves who see everything but do not rule anything.[11] According to Lucretius, one of the two causes of the rise of religion is that men saw the annual motion of the heavens turning *above their heads* but could not find out its causes (5.1184–1185); to find out the causes is to see the heavens turning *beneath one's feet*. Vergil's Iopas, the philosophic poet of the Carthaginians, already "sees" what the future Roman rulers will see from ocean to ocean of the sun's course: he knows the causes *why* the winter sun so hastens to dip itself into Ocean. Vergil makes the oracle say of the future Romans not that they will know the causes of the motions of the heavens, but that they will rule the lands whose disposition in the earth is marked out by those motions in the heavens.

Although Rome's "empire without end" is to embrace the whole world, the narrative of the *Aeneid* itself shows not the Roman conquest of the whole world but the Trojan beginning of the conquest of all Italy. But Italy represents the whole world; the project of conquering and ruling Italy represents the project of conquering and ruling the whole world. Jupiter's commission to Mercury in Book 4 indicates that rule over Italy is the prelude to rule over the world. Aeneas is to be

> qui gravidam imperiis belloque frementem
> Italiam regeret, genus alto a sanguine Teucri
> proderet, ac totum sub leges mitteret orbem.

> the one who will bring under rule an Italy pregnant with empire and roaring with war, who will bring forth a race from the high blood of Teucer, and put the whole world under laws.
>
> (4.229–231)

As Italy is pregnant with empire, bringing Italy under rule is pregnant with bringing the whole world under rule: Aeneas' pacification of war-roaring Italy will represent in small the pacification of the whole world by the descendants of Teucer.[12] Similarly, Anchises in his speech to Aeneas in the Underworld, after describing the ultimate extension of Roman virtue to the whole world—beyond the lands visited by Hercules and Bacchus and indeed "beyond the stars"—exhorts him *therefore* to initiate this universal extension by occupying Ausonia:

> et dubitamus adhuc virtutem extendere factis
> aut metus Ausonia prohibet consistere terra?

> and [in the light of the ultimate universality of the empire] do we still hesitate to extend our virtue by our deeds, does fear hold us back from occupying the Ausonian land?

$$(6.806–807)$$

This deed of occupying[13] the Ausonian land, which is the subject matter of the Iliadic *Aeneid*, is the germ, the model in small, of occupying the whole world by force and putting it under law.

The destined universality of Rome is expressed in the *Aeneid* not only by the geographic notion of "all lands" but also by the ethnographic notion of "all nations." Anchises' account of the extent of Roman rule, for example, mingles the names of places with the names of peoples, describing how Roman rule will extend out of Latium all the way to the Garamantes, the Indi, and the Caspian kingdoms (6.794–805). The most elaborate picture of Rome's rule over all the nations, though, is that represented on the shield of Aeneas, where the triumph of Augustus brings to Rome a procession of the subject peoples of the world (8.720–728; see above, p. 189). Besides dwelling in widely separated places, the nations have differing languages, dress, weapons, climates, customs, arts, resources, regimes; above all, they have different gods. Even what appear to be the most superficial differences, like those of dress, are grave obstacles to the union of peoples, as we are reminded when Juno finally demands, as part of the terms of federation between Trojans and Latins, that the Latins not be required to change their dress (*vertere vestem*, 12.825).[14] The most profound difference, that of their gods (represented most explicitly on the shield in the face-to-face combat between the Olympians and the monstrous gods of the Egyptians, 8.698–700), would appear by comparison to be an insuperable obstacle: for the same reasons that the nations are open to the rule of their own gods, they and their gods are closed to the rule of others' gods, foreign gods: the nations are nations by virtue of their own gods.

But the nations are represented on the shield of Aeneas precisely in the act of making obeisance to the gods of Rome—to Apollo and to the divine Augustus. And indeed this scene shows something of what is meant by the very opening lines of the *Aeneid*. Because of the unforgetting anger of fierce Juno, Aeneas suffered many things in war until he could found the city and introduce his gods into Latium (*inferretque deos Latio*, 1.6); his achievement was the model for the future founding by Augustus, which is to introduce the Roman gods and the divine Roman rulers themselves into the whole world. Saturn's introduction of himself into Latium brought scattered Cyclopean in- dividuals together into a single community by teaching them arts and law. Aeneas' introduction of the Trojan penates into Italy is to begin bringing to- gether the diverse Trojans and Italians into a single Roman community. The work of the returned Golden Age will be, by introducing Roman gods and Roman piety into the world, to bring together the dispersed human nations into a single community ruled permanently, or stably, by imperial Rome, *im- perium sine fine*.

The principle by which nations can become united under any rule at all has been made a pressing question by the very first book of the *Aeneid*, where Dido had proposed to unite the Trojans and Carthaginians into one people under a godless rule, or, as the narrative represents it, without taking any ac- count of the two nations' gods. This Carthaginian hope of overcoming the resistance of the nations and their gods to union by excluding the gods alto- gether had proved illusory. The narrative had left an obscure suggestion that Rome would provide a principle of union opposed to and superior to Carthage's; and the elaboration of this principle is one of the great subjects of the Iliadic *Aeneid*. The climactic scene of this development occurs near the end of the last book, where the conditions of the future peace and union are negotiated by Juno and Jupiter (12.791–842).

Like the whole world, so the whole of Italy and for that matter the whole of Latium is, to begin with, articulated into different nations, separated in space, differing in many ways, and on this account roaring with war, *bello fre- mentem* (4.229). The narrative of the Italian wars lays out in small the causes of wars among the nations at large, and the way of securing peace among them that is to be followed by the Rome of Vergil's teaching. Perhaps the most celebrated lines in the *Aeneid* are Anchises' exhortation to Roman rule of the nations:

tu regere imperio populos, Romane, memento,
—hae tibi erunt artes—pacisque imponere morem,
parcere subiectis et debellare superbos.

You, Roman, remember to rule the peoples with *imperium*—these will be your arts—and to impose the custom of peace, to spare those who surrender and to war down the defiant.

(6.851–853)

The manner of carrying out this charge is elaborated in Aeneas' conduct of the Italian wars in the Iliadic *Aeneid* in a way that points towards the extension of the charge from the lands and nations of Italy to the lands and nations of the whole world.

ii. The Doctrine of World Empire

It is one thing to have been moved as a patriot-poet to glorify the aspirations of one's nation to world empire; to have concluded from first principles that the world empire of one's nation is desirable or possible is another. Vergil's myth of Rome's imperial destiny in the *Aeneid* might on the face of it reflect his patriotic enthusiasm as an advocate of contemporary Roman imperialism, or his poetic enthusiasm as a wielder of the potent images offered by that imperialism for the representation of human life; or it might reflect a theoretical doctrine of universal empire that he had reached from his reflection on the whole nature of things. The purpose of the present section is to consider this latter possibility.

In the preceding pages the narrative of the *Aeneid* has been treated as expressing the political fruits of Vergil's theoretical reflection on the nature of things. This means that Vergil's myth *is* a myth precisely in that it represents most accessibly not what Vergil found to be the truth about the nature of things, but rather what he found to be, in the light of that truth, the most salutary beliefs for the formation of men's characters through heroic poetry. At the same time, though, as has been argued in our interpretation of the Carthaginian narrative, Vergil's myth is so formed as to give access indirectly—through allusions in language, subject matter, and dramatic action—to his understanding of the true nature of things. Thus in interpreting Vergil's underlying account of the truth about physics and psychology in the Carthaginian narrative, we were helped by the familiarity of the doctrines, authors, and traditions of argument that he recognizably alludes to, and most notably by his references to Lucretius' *De Rerum Natura*. Our situation is somewhat more difficult in interpreting Vergil's underlying account of the truth about world empire in the Italian narrative. If there was a speculative "question of world empire" as vividly controversial for Vergil's contemporaries as the "question of universal enlightenment" discussed previously in Part I, it would be a matter of course to assume that Vergil takes some position on this question in a poem in which the subject of world empire is manifestly thematic. But, although some notion of world empire undoubtedly animated the ambitions and deeds of a line of conquering emperors in antiquity, and although some theoretical reflections on world empire appear in ancient authors, world empire itself was not a leading theme of classical political philosophy. Over a millennium after Vergil, Dante was able to claim with justice, in the introduction to his *De Monarchia*, to be the first to set forth fully the argument for world empire. Thus at the outset, however insistently certain aspects of Vergil's poem suggest to us that its myth may be pointing toward a doctrine of world empire, we face some uncertainty about how far it is reasonable to pursue the suggestions of such a doctrine in the poem.

The suggestion that emerges from the following study may be briefly described as follows. The known lines of thought leading to a doctrine of world empire both in Vergil's time and in Dante's appear to have been two: a "theoretical" claim on behalf of the rule of reason and a "practical" claim on behalf of securing peace. The "theoretical" claim is that philosophy's discovery of man as an object of thought (the idea of man, the nature of man, the human species) requires the extirpation of politics as an unnatural, unreasonable way of life. The "practical" claim is that peace is the necessary condition for philosophizing and world-empire the necessary means of securing peace. Both versions take the requirements of philosophy as properly determinative of human arrangements; but the "theoretical" version is guided by the view that life should be so organized as to display the truth of philosophy, the "practical" version by the view that life should be so organized as to protect the activity of philosophers.[15] (The terms "theoretical" and "practical" have been used in quotation marks here in order to emphasize the peculiar circumstance that it is actually the "theoretical" version that aims to put philosophy into *practice* directly and universally, while it is the "practical" version that aims to insulate philosophy and practical life from one another for the benefit of both.)

Universal empire is evidently not a leading theme of classical political philosophy. While a complete explanation of this fact would require lengthy considerations, it is perhaps enough for our present purposes to make two observations: 1) the end of the best regime, the character of which is *the* leading theme of classical political philosophy, is understood by Plato and Aristotle to necessitate a definite limitation in size;[16] and 2) although peace is, according to the classical political philosophers, a desideratum for the best regime, even a condition of all blessings, it is not the end of the best regime; and as for universal or perpetual peace, it is not clear that this is either possible or desirable.[17]

Unlike the idea of universal empire or perpetual peace, however, the idea of "the human being" or "the human race" *is* a leading theme of classical political philosophy, insofar as classical political philosophy takes its bearings in the question of the best regime by the question of the best life for a human being. While "the human race" per se was prevented by the requirements of the best regime from becoming an object of more than passing political interest for the Platonic and Aristotelian traditions, its existence as an object of philosophic thought immediately provides for the possibility of its being thought by *someone* to have a potential political expression, i.e., to suggest some form of universal government corresponding to the universal class of men. And indeed it has been suggested by both ancient and modern thinkers that this someone was Alexander—that Alexander's career, that is, was based on a philosophic doctrine of world empire. The case of Alexander is therefore of central interest in reflecting on the possible background for Vergil of a theory of world empire. The fullest and clearest extant account of Alexander's career as the expression of a doctrine is Plutarch's, which draws upon an important strand of Stoic thought in this matter.

It would be a mistake, according to Plutarch in *On the Fortune or the Virtue of Alexander*, to judge that world empire is not a leading theme of classical political philosophy; for such a judgment does not take sufficiently into account the philosophy of Alexander. To the objection that Alexander is not a philosopher, that he conquered many cities but wrote not one word on philosophic subjects, Plutarch retorts that by this standard Socrates is not a philosopher. Only let Alexander be judged by the standard by which Socrates is judged, and "it will be seen from what he said, what he did, what he taught, that he is a philosopher" (*Fortune or Virtue*, 328B). In fact, Alexander's philosophic career is not just one among others, but is the decisive one that corrects the defect of all previous philosophers, their inability to make philosophy effective in the world. Socrates failed to introduce new gods in his own home town, but Alexander introduced new gods all over the once-barbarian world (328D). Plato's *Laws* are hardly read even by us Greeks, but myriads of human beings have used and are still using Alexander's laws (328E). Aristotle taught Alexander and a few other Greeks; but Alexander both corrected Aristotle's view of the true relationship between Greeks and barbarians (329B) and, having entered Persia "with the resources rather of his teacher Aristotle than of his father Philip" (327E–F), taught lawless and ignorant tribes throughout the world the principles of law and peace (328B).

"Moreover," Plutarch continues, "the much-admired *Republic* of Zeno, who founded the sect of Stoics, is devoted to this one chief point: that we should not live separately by cities and peoples, each within the horizon of its private version of justice, but we should consider all human beings to be members of the same people and city, and that there should be one life and order, just as a herd that pastures together and is grazed upon a common pasturage.[18] This is what Zeno wrote, imaging forth a sort of dream or phantom of a philosophic well-legislated state[19] and polity; but it was Alexander who supplied the deed for the word" (329A–B).[20]

According to Plutarch's account, then, the supreme achievement of the pre-Alexandrian philosophers is their discovery of the human being, or of the universal human nature, and from this discovery flows not only the Stoic Zeno's theory of the human race as a world-herd but the immediate practical task of arranging the human world to display its truth. The pre-Alexandrian philosophers were too impressed by the long-standing familiarity of political life to see the true, revolutionary meaning of their own discovery of man. The philosophy of Alexander shows the decisive truth of the philosophy of Aristotle, which Aristotle himself had missed: man, by virtue of having a knowable existence as a species, is by nature not a political but a species-animal. To live differentiated into distinct πόλεις with separate laws is to submit to the continued distortion of what philosophy has revealed to be our one universal nature; to live in accordance with nature is to obliterate the arbitrary, conventional boundaries among cities and put into practice the theoretically known universality of humanity. Only Alexander showed the truth of the philosophic teaching; for his career can be understood only in the light of his intention "to show forth the things on earth as subject to one *logos* and one *politeia*, and all the human beings as one people" (330D). The only *politeia* is the *cosmopoliteia*. The famous or infamous "longing," πόθος, of Alexander was not a vulgar lust for conquest or dominion but the purest philosophic longing to effectuate the supreme philosophic truth;[21] "and if the daimon that sent Alexander's soul down here had not recalled it so quickly, one law would now be governing all human beings and they would all be looking to one justice as to a common light" (330D).

The ancient interpretation of Alexander's career as the practical expression of a philosophic doctrine of the world-state has found its modern proponent in Alexandre Kojève.[22] "What characterizes the political action of Alexander," Kojève claims, "distinguishing it from that of all his Greek predecessors and contemporaries, is the fact that it was directed by the idea of *empire*, that is, a *universal* state."[23] To answer the question how Alexander came to conceive this distinctive and novel idea, Kojève proposes that, that same Socratic tradition that had caused classical political philosophy to take its bearings by the limited *polis* also enabled Alexander to conceive of universal empire: "It is the student of Aristotle who could believe it necessary to create (by mixed marriages) a biological foundation for the unity of the empire. But it is only the disciple of Socrates-Plato who could conceive of this unity, taking as his point of departure the 'idea' or the 'general notion' of Man brought forward by Greek philosophy."[24] From "Socrates-Plato," according to Kojève's analysis, Alexander could get the idea that the unitary *essence* of "all men," of "the human race," is the ground of the possibility of the *political expression* of the human race in a universal civilization. This unitary essence that grounds the idea of empire is "'*Logos*' (language-science)." Thus, Kojève concludes, the widespread view that "all political men, 'tyrants' in the first rank, have always despised the 'general ideas' of the philosophers"[25] is false: the lesson to be drawn from history is rather that "Alexander, a Greek philosopher"[26] was the inaugurator of a radically new political idea, "which even today has nowhere been actualized in all its purity" and is "still a subject for 'discussion.'"[27] This radically new political idea, that it is desirable for universal humanity to have a universal political expression in the form of a universal state, is dependent on the old philosophical idea of the existence of the human being or the human race as such and, in Kojève's formulation, is derived directly from it as by a rule that what exists in thought should be realized in practice: "The empire planned by Alexander is not the political expression of a people or a caste . . . it is the material actualization of a 'logical' entity, universal and one, just as *Logos* itself is universal and one."[28]

Like Plutarch, then, Kojève suggests that Alexander's imperial ambitions were animated by the intention to complete the achievement of the classical political philosophers by drawing the furthest inference from their discovery of the human race. Plato and Aristotle, having achieved knowledge of the universality of mankind, unphilosophically continued to assert in the face of this knowledge not only the necessity but the desirability of political life, life in separate cities with their private laws; while only the philosopher Alexander dared to draw the conclusion that the human race can and should live in one single world-empire. Now the existence of a unitary human race is certainly the necessary condition for the political expression of the human race in a universal empire; and knowledge of the idea of the human race is certainly owed to philosophy; so in this sense the idea at the root of Alexander's enterprise may be said to be a philosophic idea. But, as Plutarch's account suggests, the existence of the idea of the human race is not a sufficient cause for concluding the desirability of a universal empire. The analogy of the herd animals that Plutarch cites from Zeno indicates as much: the existence of the race of cattle is a necessary condition of the possibility of all cattle living in a single world-herd, but it does not suffice to show that this would be desirable; and indeed if Zeno ever argued that cattle, merely because they have a knowable existence as a class,

ought therefore to live in one single universal herd rather than in many separate herds, Plutarch does not mention it. The question remains, then, regarding the alleged philosophic foundations of Alexander's career, what the link
was by which he moved from the theoretical knowledge of the unity of the
human race to the practical conclusion of the desirability of world empire.
Going beyond the "material actualization of a 'logical' entity," which does not
explain to what end it is desirable that logical entities should be materially
actualized, Plutarch suggests that Alexander's aim was to furnish "unanimity
and peace and partnership with one another for all human beings" (πᾶσιν
ἀνθρώποις ὁμόνοιαν καὶ εἰρήνην καὶ κοινωνίαν πρὸς ἀλλήλους, 330E). But
Plutarch does not explain on what grounds Alexander, using the "resources" of
his teacher Aristotle, nonetheless rejected Aristotle's teaching that the human
being is by nature a political animal and that the end of the political association is living well (Politics I.8–9), in favor of the teaching that the human being is by nature a universal animal and that the end of the universal association is peace.

On behalf of the pre-Alexandrian political philosophers, or in criticism of
Plutarch's suggestion that Alexander's world-empire was an inference just
waiting to be drawn from their premises, Cicero in his treatment of the "universal commonwealth" in the Laws (I.21–32) draws out the inconsequence
of the existence of the human race as an object of thought for the desirability of the organization of the human race into a universal empire as an object of political action. As indicated by, among other things, their titles, Cicero in his Republic and Laws aims to recover the true Academic teaching as
against the teachings of the later schools.[29] As he had introduced his Republic with a passage criticizing the political teaching derived by the Epicureans
from their account of nature, so in the introduction to his Laws he implicitly
criticizes the political teaching derived by the Stoics, or by Zeno, from their
account of nature.

Cicero argues here from the sharing of correct reasoning (recta ratio) and
thus of right (ius) in common between men and gods not that this whole
world ought to be united into one universal commonwealth of gods and men
but that "this whole world is to be thought one single commonwealth of gods
and men," universus hic mundus sit una civitas communis deorum atque hominum
existimanda (Laws I.23). Whatever beings share a commonality of right (com-
munio iuris) are thereby to be considered (habendi sunt) as belonging to one
and the same commonwealth; and indeed if they also obey the same commands and powers in common, then how much the more so!—but in any
case, whether or not they obey the same political authorities, they do as a matter of fact, insofar as they share in correct reasoning, obey "this celestial sys-

tem, divine mind, and supremely powerful god" (*ibid.*). Where Kojève (p. 182) and Plutarch (330D) formulate the idea of the essential unity of man as residing in λόγος, Cicero formulates it as residing in man's "participation" in reason (*solum est enim ex tot animantium generibus atque naturis particeps rationis et cogitationis*, I.22), with the reservation that the consequent unity of the human race in theory is quite independent of its division into communities ruled by different governments, "*imperia et potestates*," in practice (I.23). Cicero concludes from the commonality of right resting on reason that right is established by nature and not by opinion (I.28–29), and thus that the legislation of the various political communities ought to be based on natural right; but not that all human beings ought to obey the same *imperia et potestates*. If human weakness did not expose reason to distortion by customs and opinions, all human beings would already be as identical to one another as each is to himself (I.29); in that case the unity of the human race would not need to be expressed by obedience to "commands and powers" at all, since it would already be expressed by the unanimity of hearts and minds ruled by right reason. But human weakness *is* open to the distortion of that essential *ratio* by virtue of participation in which human beings are human; and Cicero does *not* recommend the use of "commands and powers" to bring about in practice the unity of the human race whose existence in thought is already actual.

Cicero's account of the "universal commonwealth" thus raises against the argument of Plutarch and Kojève, as it were, the following objection. Alexander's alleged intention to bring about human unanimity (ὁμόνοια) through universal government is implicitly a claim to have discovered the way of overcoming the condition of human weakness, or deviation from right reason, that causes human multanimity in the first place. But this amounts to a claim to have discovered the way to make human beings into gods; for the species-characteristic of human beings as such is precisely not "wisdom," which is the divine perfection of reason, but only "participation"—partial sharing—in reason (I.22). If human beings were not exposed to the distortion of reason through weakness, they would not *be* human beings; they would be gods. The project of "unifying" the human race in practice, as opposed to recognizing in thought the divine reason through *partial sharing* in which human beings are constituted a single class, reflects not the idea of expressing "the human race" politically but the idea of abolishing the human race by transforming it into the race of gods.

If anything in the *Aeneid* corresponds to the interpretation of Alexander's career as an attempt to realize in practice the theoretical unity of the human race, it would appear to be the Carthaginian project of uniting the nations directly in common citizenship without regard to their particular gods, i.e., with regard only to universal reason or science. Vergil's own view of such a project has emerged from the Carthaginian narrative as a demonstration of its misguidedness: the human race, like the race of cattle, is a leading theme of Iopas' theoretical teaching (*unde hominum genus et pecudes*, 1.743), but Dido's direct translation into political practice of the theoretical insights of Iopas is doomed to political failure because it does not take account of the essential "weakness" of human beings, the intractable reason why almost all human beings are not philosophers (to say nothing of wise men). Vergil, in other words, takes the part of Cicero in indicating that it was not from laziness or cowardice but from their understanding of man's not perfectly rational nature that the classical political philosophers failed to infer from their own discovery of man the desirability of universal empire. On the other hand, Plutarch's suggestion that universal peace was *also* a goal of Alexander's imperial project (330E), insofar as it may imply some difference between unanimity and peace, i.e., some possibility of peace without unanimity, may be answered in Vergil's *Aeneid* by the idea of Rome's mission as that of "imposing the custom of peace," *pacis imponere morem*, and thus by the Italian narrative that dramatizes this idea. But if Alexander's career had this goal, nothing in Plutarch's interpretation of it explains on what grounds universal peace could have held this weightiest or most comprehensive and decisive place in Alexander's theory of world empire.

The argument that universal peace is the desideratum requiring world empire for its realization is first made thematic by Dante in his *Monarchy*. By "temporal monarchy" or, simply, "monarchy," Dante means world empire, the rule of the entire human race by one emperor.[30] Dante's claim to be the first to bring the knowledge of it to light from its "hiding-places" (*latibula*, I.1.) does not mean that he is the first to think of it or to discover its principles, but that he is the first to connect, elaborate, synthesize these principles into a coherent doctrine showing how the necessity and desirability of world empire is consequent upon them. The chief "hiding-places" of the principles themselves are the texts of Aristotle, Vergil, and the Scriptures; Dante will appeal to evidence drawn from each of them (as well as from other poets and philosophers) in his presentation of his argument.

Dante's demonstration of the necessity of universal empire to the welfare of the human race proceeds as follows.[31] The human race is the multitudinous collectivity of human individuals,[32] and human civilization is the potential political expression of the human race. God and nature brings everything into being for some end; there is then an end for which God has brought the human race as a whole into being. This end is the actualization of the potential intellect, which necessitates the human race since it cannot be attained in full by any human individual, family, district, city, or kingdom. The actualization of the potential intellect is thus the proper activity of the human race (I.3). Now, it is in conditions of quiet and tranquility that the human race can most freely and easily carry out its proper activity. From this "it is manifest that universal peace is the best of those things that are ordained as means towards our beatitude," "for clearly the most direct means by which one proceeds towards that towards which, as to the ultimate end, all our activities are ordered, is universal peace, which will be presupposed as the first principle of the following reasonings" (I.4).

In the following reasonings, then, Dante proceeds to argue that just as universal peace is the most direct or in fact the only sure means to the actualization of the potential intellect, so universal empire is the surest or in fact the only sure means to the attainment of universal peace. Since the human race is a multitudinous collectivity ordered towards one end, it must have one regulator or ruler, the Monarch or Emperor (I.5).[33] Although Dante implies that the parts of the human race are the individual human beings, he explains in the next section that we are to think not just of many human beings ruled by one human being or "monarch," but also of many kingdoms ruled by one kingdom or "monarchy" (I.6). But in any case, whatever the proper parts of the human race may be, it is not only a whole with respect to those parts, but also a part with respect to the whole universe; and as each part is ordered with respect to its whole in virtue of some one single principle, so the human race must be ordered with respect to the whole universe in virtue of one single principle, namely, one single prince (per unum principium tantum, scilicet unicum principem) (I.7).

After two further arguments for the unity of the human race drawn from Scripture and Aristotle (I.8–9), Dante returns to the presupposition of the necessity of peace that he has said would underlie all this reasoning. As long as the human race is organized politically into coequal sovereignties, disputes between its sovereigns, in the absence of a competent adjudicator, must issue in war. But "wherever there can be contention, there must be judicial authority: otherwise there would be an imperfection without a perfection proper to it, which is impossible since God and nature does not lack what is necessary" (I.10). Thus, if peace is to be preserved, disputed claims between princes must ultimately come before a first and highest judge to whom they are all equally subordinate, and this will be the Monarch (I.10).

The foregoing argument shows that the Monarchy is necessary in order to secure universal peace in the negative sense of preventing disputed claims from issuing in war. But universal peace in Dante's understanding has also a

positive content, which is the prevalence of justice in the world; for the identification of the best times with the prevalence of justice, Dante cites Vergil's
Fourth Eclogue (I.11). What opposes the prevalence of justice in the world
is the limitless cupidity of human beings. So long as human beings are organized into a multiplicity of coequal sovereignties, their sovereigns, as human beings whose possessions are manifestly limited by the possessions of
others, must be moved by their unbounded cupidity towards acquiring the
possessions of the other sovereigns; their care for justice must be compromised by the pressure upon them of their cupidity.

There is, then, according to Dante's argument, only one way to insure the
rule of human beings by a sovereign who will not be diverted from justice by
cupidity, and that is to institute a world empire whose ruler will already have
everything at his disposal. For the Monarch there is nothing to covet, since
his jurisdiction is bounded only by Ocean (*terminatur occeano solum*, like the
dominion promised to Caesar by Jupiter at *Aeneid* 1.287). So it follows that,
since the Monarch is the only human being who already has everything at
his disposal, he alone is not subject to cupidity, and is therefore the human
being most sincerely subject to justice, who has therefore the greatest will as
well as the greatest power to secure the prevalence of justice in the world.
This is the heart of Dante's argument that universal empire, so far from even-
tuating in universal despotism, would rather secure the human race from
despotic rule: despotism is the tendency of sovereigns whose limited sovereignties irritate their unlimited cupidity, but not of the Monarch, whose unlimited sovereignty cures him of human cupidity once and for all. It follows
that the Monarch is the only one who can be completely or at any rate to the
greatest degree well disposed for governing, because he can secure judgment
and justice to the highest degree of all mortals (I.13). Thus the necessity of
universal peace, both in its negative aspect as the avoidance of war through
competent judicial authority and in its positive aspect as the prevalence of
justice in the world, necessitates in turn the institution of universal empire
or Monarchy.

Dante's account of the parts or members of the world-empire is resumed
from chapter 6 in chapter 14. Although the parts of the human race are the
multitudinous human individuals who only in their totality are able to actualize fully the potential intellect, these members of the human race are articulated into nations in their relationship to the Monarch.[34] The nations
differ from one another in their properties, and therefore require regulation
by means of differing laws. For example, the Scythians who inhabit the extremely cold climates require different regulation from the Garamantes who
go naked because of the extreme heat of their climate. The multiplicity of

the human race resides not only in its multiple individuals but also in its multiple nations. The world empire is not to supercede the nations as the direct ruler of the human individuals, but it is to preserve the individuality of the nations, with their differing properties and laws, as the particular manifestations of universal principles received from the supreme ruler of all the nations.

"But if all the above deductions are true—as they are—then it is necessary to the highest welfare of the human race that there be in the world a Monarch, and consequently it is necessary for the well-being of the world that there be a Monarchy" (I.15). Dante has now demonstrated from first principles that universal empire is necessary to the welfare of the human race. The actualization of the potential intellect is the end of the human race; universal peace is necessary to the actualization of the potential intellect; Monarchy is necessary to universal peace.

Dante turns in Book II to the demonstration that the Roman people are naturally fitted and providentially appointed to exercise this Monarchy. He appeals to Vergil's authority most directly in connection with two of his arguments for the natural fitness of Rome for universal rule (II.3, 6), and to the authority of Scripture for his arguments for Rome's providential appointment (II.7–10). Then, having demonstrated the necessity of universal empire to the welfare of the human race, and the natural and divine ordination of Rome to exercise universal empire, in Book III Dante proceeds to demonstrate that the authority of the empire is derived immediately from God and is not dependent upon the authority of the church. For the clinching of this argument in the last chapter of the last book of the treatise (III.16), Dante has a surprise in store: man is a being who has not one single end but *two* ends—the happiness of this life, to which philosophic teachings are the means, and the happiness of eternal life, to which spiritual teachings are the means. These ends and these means have been clearly demonstrated to us—the former by human reason, which has become wholly known to us through the philosophers, and the latter by the Holy Spirit, which has revealed to us such supernatural truth as is necessary to us. But in spite of these demonstrations, human beings are still, because of cupidity, in need of a twofold directive power: a supreme Pontiff to guide the human race to eternal life in accordance with revealed things, and a Monarch to direct the human race to temporal felicity in accordance with philosophic teachings. Without entering into a discussion of the Averroism imputed to Dante on the basis of this passage,[35] it will be sufficient for our present purposes to indicate the following. Whatever Dante's view of the revealed teaching on the next life, he is at pains in the *Monarchy* to emancipate the argument for world empire completely from any revealed teaching at all.

The claim in III.16 that "man" (*homo*) has a twofold end does not after all modify in the least the carefully elaborated argument of Book I that the human race or the human collectivity (*genus humanum*) has one single end, the actualization of the potential intellect; for as Dante argued there, the existence of the human race is necessitated by the incapacity of any single human individual to actualize the whole of the potential intellect at once; but there is no corresponding incapacity of the human individual to attain the whole of eternal salvation at once. The necessity of the Monarchy for the welfare of the human race arises from the single end of the human race, not from the twofold end of the human being: it is for the sake of philosophizing, not for the sake of salvation, that universal peace is necessary; it is for the sake of universal peace, not for the sake of the next life, that Monarchy is necessary.[36] Thus the doctrine of world empire that Dante professes to be the first to bring out of its hiding-places in Aristotle, Vergil, and Scripture is ultimately in no way dependent on any revealed teaching; however abundantly he illustrates the argument of the *Monarchy* with the evidence of Scripture, that evidence is finally as unnecessary to Dante's argument as it is unknown to Vergil's.

iii. World Empire and World Tyranny

Dante's claim to be the first to present the argument for world empire might mean that in his view Vergil presented no such argument, or it might mean that Vergil presented an argument that is, however, in Dante's view, defective, incomplete, or erroneous. And indeed the first of the first principles of Dante's argument, that every thing has been created by God and nature for a certain end,[37] is the opposite of the first of the first principles of Lucretius' argument, that nothing ever comes into being from nothing by divine agency.[38] Intimately connected with this fundamental disagreement between Vergil and Dante about the first principles of the argument for world empire is their disagreement about the foundations of justice, or about the distinction between universal empire and universal tyranny. As shown above, Dante argues that world empire, so far from posing the danger of world tyranny, is rather the only regime in which justice could be incorruptible; for the emperor of the world, being the only human being who already has everything at his disposal, is therefore the only human being who is immune to cupidity and can devote himself wholly to securing the prevalence of justice in the world.

Vergil's *Aeneid* raises against Dante, as it were, the following objection. In the *Aeneid* the ruler of men and gods promises to the future emperor of the world that his empire will be bounded only by Ocean (*imperium Oceano . . .*

terminet, Aen. 1.287; cf. the empire of Dante's Monarch, *sua namque iurisdic-
tio terminatur occeano solum*, I.11). Now the everything that the ruler of men
and gods already has at his disposal is surely at least as great as the everything
that the emperor of the world will have at his disposal, and yet even the ruler
of men and gods is driven to injustice, because he does not have at his disposal the requital of his love. The "eternal wound," the unassuageable grief
and furor arising from the frustration of the insatiable desire of even the immortal gods to be limitlessly loved, first comes to sight in the *Aeneid* in Juno,
aeternum servans sub pectore vulnus (1.36).[39] The causes of Juno's world-
destructive anger are injuries to her self-esteem consisting in others' failure
to adore and honor her: "is there anyone, after all this, who adores the divinity of Juno or brings a suppliant's honor to her altars?" (1.48–49). Juno's
raging at the eternal wound of these injuries is reenacted in the story of Dido,
where Vergil represents dramatically the reduction of this enlightened ("celestial") queen by unrequited love to the depths of infernal furor. Within the
myth of the *Aeneid* both the goddess's and the queen's erotic rages appear at
first, or at one level, to represent infernal aberrations from or rebellions
against the celestial dispensation of Jupiter. But in Book 12 it emerges finally
that Jupiter himself is subject to the furor of the same eternal wound.

When Juno seeks support for Turnus in his final battle, she appeals to Turnus' sister Juturna as goddess to goddess; and the poet explains how it has
come about that the mortal Turnus' sister is an immortal goddess:

> hunc illi rex aetheris altus honorem
> Iuppiter erepta pro virginitate sacravit.

> Jupiter, the lofty king of the aether, consecrated this honor to her in compen-
> sation for having raped her virginity.

> (12.140–141)

Later when Jupiter, after his final speech to Juno, sends the Dira to remove
Juturna from the battlefield, Juturna expresses her own estimate of the honor
with which Jupiter has recompensed her:

> ne me terrete timentem,
> obscenae volucres: alarum verbera nosco
> letalemque sonum, nec fallunt iussa superba
> magnanimi Iovis.[40] haec pro virginitate reponit?
> quo vitam dedit aeternam? cur mortis adempta est
> condicio? possem tantos finire dolores
> nunc certe, et misero fratri comes ire per umbras!
> immortalis ego? aut quicquam mihi dulce meorum

te sine, frater, erit? o quae satis ima dehiscat
terra mihi, manisque deam demittat ad imos?

Do not terrorize me in my fear, obscene birds: I recognize the beating of your
wings, their deadly noise; I am not deceived by the haughty commands of mag-
nanimous Jupiter. This is his recompense for my virginity!? Why has he given
me eternal life? Why has the condition of mortality been stolen from me? Now
at least I would have been able to end these great griefs and pass through the
shades in company with my poor brother. I, immortal? Will anything of mine
be sweet for me without you, my brother? O, what land could gape open deep
enough for me, and send me down, goddess that I am, to the deepest shades?!
(12.875–884)

The meaning of Jupiter's rape of Juturna is that with all his possessions he desired her but could not make her desire him. The possession of "everything,"
everything that can be possessed, does not destroy the object of the passions;
for the preeminent object of the passions is the free and limitless return of
one's love or desire, but this is something that in the nature of the case cannot be at one's disposal (since in that case it would not be free). The meaning of Jupiter's futile attempt to recompense Juturna for his injustice by turning her into a goddess is that he is not only driven to injury or injustice but
also incapable, from lack of wisdom, of righting wrong: he mistakenly judges
that his own condition of immortality, which is good for him, would be good
for a human being, and therefore gives it as a "reward" to one for whom it is
an injury. Jupiter's love of his own—his immortality—prevents him from seeing the centrality to human beings of their own love of their own. Human
beings love the mortal beings they are attached to; immortality compels
them to live with the permanent loss of the object of their love. The king of
gods and men, the guarantor of the ultimately just reward and punishment of
human souls, is himself both driven to injustice by erotic furor and unable to
distinguish correctly between reward and punishment.

The core of the disagreement between Dante and Vergil on the relationship
between universal empire and universal tyranny lies then in their disagreement
about the status of desire or love. For Dante, there is a term to men's desire or
love in a fully adequate object.[41] For Vergil, in accordance with Lucretius'
analysis, there is no adequate object of love; it is an illusion that arises from the
false attribution to its object of "more than is right to attribute to a mortal"
(DRN 4.1184): the extravagant furor of love can be terminated only by the rational understanding of the error in attributing to any being the divine power
to animate the lover or make him more fully alive. Lucretius shows how the
enlightened human being, perceiving that the desires for wealth, power, and

love are fundamentally mistaken ways of mastering the groundless fear of death, and that the only real protection against this fear is a full knowledge of its groundlessness, is thereby able to be liberated from those desires. Vergil's poem, while following Lucretius' analysis of the illusory foundation of love, also shows in the drama of Dido that philosophic enlightenment cannot be, and fear of angry gods therefore must be, the cure of this illusion for almost all human beings. It would be folly to hope for the disarming of the erotic passions by reason in any but the rarest philosopher, and certainly in any ruler: Dido in spite of her philosophic tutor, certainly pious Aeneas, and ultimately even Jupiter himself are subject to the furor of these passions.[42]

As in the myth of the Aeneid Jupiter cares for the well-being of the human race and promotes it in some respects while being ultimately impotent either to avert the necessary dissolution of the world or to restrain the furor of his own passions, so it is on his model that one may envision a human world-emperor whose inclination to rape human women would be accompanied or counterbalanced by his inclination to provide for the well-being of the human race; but one may not envision a world-emperor who would not be inclined to rape human women. The emperor of the world must necessarily be, like Jupiter, a tyrant. As Vergil had presented grossly in Iarbas the Epicurean doctrines that he indicated only delicately in Dido, so at the end of the poem he presents grossly in Jupiter's rape of Juturna what he indicates only delicately in Aeneas' seizure of Lavinia: the ravishing of women is the mark of tyranny.[43] Aeneas, as the model in small of the world emperor to come, is a tyrant. On both occasions in the Aeneid when Aeneas is actually referred to as tyrannus, the speaker is in fact thinking of him as the usurper of Lavinia. Latinus says to the embassy from Aeneas, agreeing to terms of peace:

pars mihi pacis erit dextram tetigisse tyranni.
vos contra regi mea nunc mandata referte.
est mihi nata. . .

My part in the peace-making will be to have touched the tyrant's hand. You in turn report to your king as I enjoin: I have a daughter . . .

(7.266–268)

And Turnus says to Idmon, when he sends him to challenge Aeneas to single combat:

nuntius haec, Idmon, Phrygio mea dicta tyranno
haud placitura refer: . . .
illo quaeratur coniunx Lavinia campo.

Report to the Phrygian tyrant these my words that will not please him: . . . on
that field [of battle] let him fight for marriage to Lavinia.

(12.75–76, 79)

If Aeneas is a more restrained or milder tyrant than Jupiter is, that is because
he has been formed to fear the (avoidable) anger of Jupiter; while what
Jupiter fears is not anger or punishment but the necessary dissolution of the
world (1.58–63).

Reflection on the crucial differences between Dante's argument for world
empire and Vergil's brings into focus as well the core of agreement between
them: for both of them it is philosophy that necessitates world empire, in the
sense that philosophy is the end for which world empire is the necessary
means.[44] It is philosophy that requires universal peace, and universal peace
that requires world empire.

> effice ut interea fera moenera militiai
> per maria ac terras omnis sopita quiescant.
> . . . suavis ex ore loquellas
> funde petens placidam Romanis, incluta, pacem.
> nam neque nos agere hoc patriai tempore iniquo
> possumus aequo animo nec Memmi clara propago
> talibus in rebus communi desse saluti. . . .

> Bring it to pass that the savage works of war may be stilled to rest throughout all
> lands and seas. . . . Pour forth sweet plaints from your mouth, beseeching for the
> Romans, glorious goddess, tranquil peace. For neither can I perform my work
> with a calm mind in the uncalm emergency of the fatherland, nor can the bril-
> liant offspring of Memmius fail the common safety in such circumstances. . . .

(DRN 1.29–30, 39–43)

Lucretius prays for universal peace in order that he himself may philosophize
with equanimity and in order that the Roman Memmius may have leisure to
open himself to the claims of philosophy and thus to the possibility of human
happiness. Given the underlying microcosmic war of the atoms and the necessary dissolution of the cosmos, the macrocosmic peace for which Lucretius
prays has no stable foundation in nature and could at best be temporary; but
this would not diminish its worth for Lucretius or for any philosopher or potential philosopher who had the good fortune to live during a time of peace
and thus to be enabled to pursue philosophy with equanimity. Lucretius offers no political program for the achievement of this much-desired peace
other than his philosophical program of making philosophic enlightenment
as widely accessible as possible through his beautiful poetry. The carrying out

of Lucretius' philosophical program, if it were possible, would ensure universal peace by demonstrating to men the unreasonable character of the desires that spring from the fear of death and lead to war. Lucretius' provision for peace is to demonstrate the unreasonableness of war.

Vergil in the *Aeneid* proposes to provide for peace through the political means of universal empire rather than the philosophic means of demonstrating the truth about the whole nature of things. Vergil's political program is not simply an alternative means to peace, however; it is the means required by that aspect of the nature of human beings that Lucretius did not grasp, the impermeability of the angry passions of almost all human beings to the dictates of reason. According to Lucretius, peace is the precondition of philosophy and universal enlightenment is the precondition of universal peace. According to Vergil too, peace is the precondition of philosophy; but universal empire secured by laws, arms, and gods is the precondition of peace.

While Vergil and Dante agree with each other and with the tradition of ancient political philosophy in deriving the best political arrangement for men from the primacy of the philosophic life, they differ from the classical tradition in their common insistence on the necessity of universal peace for the protection of philosophy, and thus in the importance they attach to "international" as against "domestic" politics. But while united on the necessity of universal peace to philosophy and thus to human welfare, Vergil and Dante differ profoundly on the foundations of this very primacy of philosophy, and therefore on the character of the universal empires they envision. Dante, finding the foundations of the philosophic life in "God and nature," envisions a world empire protected from tyranny on the one hand and from dissolution on the other by its harmony with the ends of all things; Vergil, finding the foundations of the philosophic life in men's provision for themselves as over against uncaring and accidental nature, envisions a world empire only precariously protected against tyranny and necessarily subject to the ultimate dissolution of the cosmos itself.

The myth of the *Aeneid*, then, reflects Vergil's doctrine of world empire in the following way. The rule of one city over "the nations" is required for universal peace, which in turn is required for the welfare of the human race. "Carthage," the city of gold and science, is not able to provide world empire; as philosophic gods and philosophers are neither able nor willing to rule anything, so Carthage lacks the (tyrannical) force required for the imposition of universal peace. "Rome", the city of iron and gods, is able to provide rule and thus peace; but Rome provides it *for the sake of* "Carthage": Rome is for the sake of Carthage. Anchises' expression of the relationship between the Romans'

arts and the arts of the "others" means that Roman government, the imposition of the habit of peace, is the *means* to promote the others' pursuit of the
arts, and thus ultimately of philosophy.[45] Vergil brought Aeneas to Carthage in
order that the founder of the world empire might know, as the pupil of Iopas
and Dido, what the object of that empire is: it is to provide for the existence of
"Carthaginians" by providing for universal peace.

PART THREE

PIETATIS IMAGO

CHAPTER TWELVE

~

Piety and Heroic Virtue

i. The Problem of Pius Aeneas

The design of "a heroic poem, truly such," as Dryden remarks in the dedication to his translation of the *Aeneid*, is "to form the mind to heroic virtue by
example;" but "Virgil is arraigned for placing piety before valour, and making
that piety the chief character of his hero."[1] The arraignment implies that
piety, though admittedly some kind of a virtue, is not heroic virtue; and thus
that the *Aeneid* is not a heroic poem truly such. The trouble is that *pius
Aeneas* seems unmanly; as Fustel de Coulanges puts it, "Men often complain
at not finding in Aeneas bravery, dash, passion. They tire of that epithet of
pious, which is continually repeated. They are astonished to see this warrior
consulting his Penates with a care so scrupulous, invoking some divinity at
every new turn of affairs, raising his arms to heaven when he ought to be
fighting, allowing himself to be tossed over all seas by the oracles, and shedding tears at the sight of danger. Nor do they fail to reproach him with coldness towards Dido."[2] Indeed not only in valor but also in understanding
Aeneas is criticized as a weakling: "Aeneas is altogether wanting in energy,
spontaneity, intellectual resource, and insight. . . . The only exercise of
thought required of him is the right interpretation of an omen, or the recol-
lection of some dubious prediction at some critical moment."[3] Defenders of
the propriety of Vergil's poem must then begin by dealing with the imputation against the manliness of its hero.

Dryden's own explanation is that Vergil made Aeneas pious because he "designed to form a perfect prince" and therefore "found himself obliged to make

him without blemish, thoroughly virtuous,"[4] that is, to add piety in among Aeneas' other virtues. But Vergil does not thereby place piety *before* valor; indeed he has put in the poem "so many instances of the hero's valour" that "more could not be expected from an Amadis, a Sir Lancelot, or the whole Round Table, than he performs;" and if men complain that "he wept more often . . . than well becomes a man of courage," and trembled, too—still, it was "not for himself, but for his people. And what can give a sovereign a better commendation, or recommend a hero more to the affection of the reader? They were threatened with a tempest, and he wept."[5] Contemporary critics, much more impressed by Aeneas' frequent tears than by the many instances of his valor, rejoice to find in him an amazingly contemporary new type of heroism. Aeneas is "an ordinary man . . . bewildered, frightened of the elements,"[6] a hero of "human frailty,"[7] precisely not a manly but a humane hero. He is a man of "sensitivity to tragedy," "tragically compassionate sorrow," a "sensitive heart;" he "suffers for the sake of others. A new humanity announcing the Christian philosophy bursts forth from him. He prefigures the Christian hero, whose heart remains gentle through struggle and sorrow and beats in secret sympathy with all suffering creatures."[8] Aeneas' *pietas*, on this view, veers from the sphere of piety toward that of pity;[9] and Aeneas, so far from needing to be defended from charges of unmanliness, is rather exonerated from any suspicion of being such a brute as the barbaric Achilles. It is true that he has accesses of anger and even kills his enemies on the field of battle, but these are his tragic flaws, his failures to live up to the ideal of the ordinary man's human frailty and the pity arising from it. On the other hand, Fustel de Coulanges, who has formulated so vividly the modern accusations against Aeneas, avers that "we must not judge the *Aeneid* after our modern ideas," for under the character of piety "the poet wishes to represent a priest." Therefore it is right that he not be manly: he is "not a man, but an instrument of the gods."[10]

But is it really a "modern idea" that a hero ought to be a man? The earliest observer of the need to defend Aeneas against the imputation of unmanliness is Vergil, who puts the charges in the mouths of Aeneas' enemies in far more provocative terms than ever essayed by the hero's latter-day critics. Vergil makes the African king Iarbas in his prayer to Jupiter describe Aeneas as

> ille Paris cum semiviro comitatu,
> Maeonia mentum mitra crinemque madentem
> subnexus

> that Paris with his half-male entourage, his chin and pomaded hair tied in a
> Maeonian bonnet.

(4.215-7)

Vergil makes the Italian warrior Numanus taunt the Trojans:

vobis picta croco et fulgenti murice vestis,
desidiae cordi, iuvat indulgere choreis,
et tunicae manicas et habent redimicula mitrae.
o vere Phrygiae, neque enim Phryges, ite per alta
Dindyma, ubi adsuetis biforem dat tibia cantum.
tympana vos buxusque vocat Berecynthia Matris
Idaeae, sinite arma viris et cedite ferro.

What you like is clothing embroidered in colors of saffron and glowing murex—tenderness of heart—indulgence in dances; your tunics have sleeves, your caps have ribbons—O you Phrygianesses—for you're not even Phrygians—go to the peaks of Dindymus, where the flute offers its two-holed song to the habitués. The Berecynthian cymbals and boxwood of the Idaean Mother are calling you—leave arms to men, and yield to iron.

(9.614–20)

Vergil makes Turnus say, when preparing to meet Aeneas in single combat:

da sternere corpus
loricamque manu valida lacerare revulsam
semiviri Phrygis et foedare in pulvere crinis
vibratos calido ferro murraque madentis.

"Let me lay low his body, let me rip away the breastplate from the half-male Phrygian and tear it with my strong hand, and befoul in the dust that hair all curled on hot irons and pomaded with myrrh."

(12.97–100)

If, then, it occurs to the reader of the Aeneid to worry that its hero is rather weak-spirited and weak-minded, not to say effeminate, this can hardly be taken as a sign of Vergil's thoughtlessness. The Aeneas whom Vergil so insistently exposes to these taunts of his enemies is the very man whom he also so insistently holds up to Achilles and Odysseus on the one hand, and to Epicurus/Lucretius on the other, as outmatching them all in heroism. Vergil's project in the Aeneid is to win the hearts and minds of men to Aeneas' brand of heroism as the object of the fullest or loftiest human aspiration.[11] This means winning men away from the charms and claims of the heroism of Homer and Lucretius, spoiling the Homeric and Lucretian heroes forever as fundamentally small, incomplete, misguided. Aeneas is so conceived as to show men a heroism that is as grand as that of the ancients, while being at the same time far more harmonious with a sober understanding of the nature of things. It is Aeneas' piety that is somehow at the root of his superiority to the Homeric and Lucretian heroes.

ii. True or False?

A. It is asked about many things in your *Marius* whether they are false or true; and some insist on having the truth from you on the grounds that you are dealing with events in recent memory and with a man from Arpinum.

M. By Hercules, I certainly don't wish to be thought a liar; but those "some," Titus, are acting naively by demanding in such a case the truth not as from a poet but as from an eyewitness. Doubtless those same people think that Numa conversed with Egeria and that the eagle put Tarquin's cap on his head.

Q. I take you to mean, brother, that different laws are to be observed in a history than in a poem.

M. Yes indeed, since in a history things are mostly related to truth; in a poem, to pleasure.

(Cicero, *Laws* I.4–5)

Aeneas' catabasis is the centerpiece of the *Aeneid* and the central event in the formation of Aeneas as the pious founding hero of Rome. It is the school in which he learns the most important things about the gods, the soul, and the world: that men's souls are immortal, that they are justly rewarded and punished in the afterlife for their conduct in this life, that the souls of the dead care for the living, that the nature of things is ruled by providential mind, and that the mission of Rome is to bring about the returned and perfected Golden Age on earth. In his cautious conditional prayer for Dido, 1.603–605, Aeneas had prayed that the gods would give her worthy rewards "if there are any divinities that have regard for pious men, if justice is anything anywhere, and mind conscious within itself of the right." It is in his visit to Hades that Aeneas learns everything about the questions raised by these "ifs." All the support there is for Aeneas' heroic founding mission, for the renunciations this mission requires of him, for his piety in carrying out this mission, resides in what he learns during his visit to the Underworld. Vergil concludes his account of the supreme education of Aeneas with the famous words:

Sunt geminae Somni portae, quarum altera fertur
cornea, qua veris facilis datur exitus umbris,
altera candenti perfecta nitens elephanto,
sed falsa ad caelum mittunt insomnia manes.

his ibi tum natum Anchises unaque Sibyllam
prosequitur dictis portaeque emittit eburna,
ille viam secat ad navis sociosque revisit.

There are twin gates of sleep, one of which is said to be of horn, by which easy exit is given to true shades; the other is said to be made of bright shining ivory, but by it the ghosts send false dreams toward the heaven. There, then, with these words, Anchises accompanies his son and the Sibyl, and sends them forth through the ivory gate; Aeneas speeds back to the ships and sees his men again.

(6.893–899)

One way of expressing the difficulty of the Twin Gates passage is suggested by the passage from Cicero's *Laws* quoted above. Vergil seems to confuse the jurisdiction of poetry with that of history, and to ask us in the midst of our pleasure in what he has said to judge what he has said by the standard of truth, rather than the standard of pleasure. According to Servius, the meaning of the Twin Gates passage is that Vergil "wishes it to be understood that all the things he has said are false" (*ad loc.*). The explanations of this passage offered by modern students of the *Aeneid* testify to the revulsion of Vergil's modern readers from the thought that Vergil's only full-scale account in the *Aeneid* of the ultimate truth about things is intended by Vergil to be simply false: perhaps this thought can be warded off, or at least softened, by symbolic interpretation. The present discussion will stay close to Servius' more straightforward account of the matter, while being open to the thought that Vergil's wish to make it clear that what he has said is false may include the wish to encourage readers to elaborate many different accounts of the way in which the false things he has said can be interpreted to symbolize or refer to true things.

A poet whose whole purpose is to symbolize psychological or moral truths mythically does not rudely trip up his reader by challenging him to say whether the narrative is "true or false." However impressed that reader is with the symbolism of Aeneas' catabasis as psychological rebirth, moral purification, or religious edification, and however he may approve the psychology, morality, or religion of Aeneas to which the catabasis may seem to point, Vergil requires him to ask finally, "But is it *true?*"

Sometimes critics speak as if the gates of ivory and horn had been in the Underworld, or in the *Aeneid*, before Vergil, so that Vergil had been compelled to choose which of them would serve as the exit of Aeneas from the Underworld;[12] then the question becomes, why did Vergil choose the ivory one, and some of the reasons that have been suggested are quite arcane. But the proper starting point must be the reflection that nothing compelled

Vergil to put the Twin Gates into the Underworld in the first place. By putting them there at all, Vergil chooses to compel his readers to think the alternative "true or false?" Undoubtedly his formulation impels most readers to choose "true," or to long for Vergil to affirm "true," and to feel offended at the intimation that Vergil has raised the question only to answer "false." But the offense here precedes Vergil's choice of "false," and lies in the very posing of the alternative: Is the Underworld teaching true or false? That is, even if Vergil had sent Aeneas out by the gate of horn, his very raising of the question "true or false?" already offends the reader whose pleasure in the poetic or mythical narrative is rudely interrupted by the question whether that narrative is "true or false." By allowing this question to infiltrate his narrative at all—not to say raising it overtly and sharply as he does—the poet is being unpoetic: he indicates that the question of the truth of things is pertinent to his poetic narrative. The Twin Gates passage may be said to show Vergil's boldness as a poet in submitting his poetry to the judgment not only of pleasure but also of truth: he puts us on notice that we have not finished interpreting his poem until we have understood not only the pleasure it affords but also its connection to the truth of things. Vergil compels us to think about the possibility that Aeneas' exemplary piety is founded on false beliefs; or in other words that the *Aeneid* itself proposes for praise and imitation an ideal type of character that Vergil himself regards as formed by false beliefs. The Twin Gates passage compels the thought that what is good for the formation of Aeneas' character is not necessarily true.

But the relationship of the catabasis of Aeneas to the truth is that it is false. No more did Aeneas see the gods' providential rule over immortal souls in the Underworld than Numa held conversations with Egeria. The purpose of Numa's pretending to converse with Egeria was, according to Livy's account, through a pleasing fiction to replace the Romans' fear of enemies with fear of gods as a restraint on the extravagance of their spirits.[13] Is this also the purpose of Vergil's pretending that Aeneas conversed with the Sibyl in the Underworld? The problem presented to Numa by the security of the early Romans with regard to Italian enemies is as nothing beside the problem to be presented by the security of the future Romans with regard to all human enemies. According to the proem to *Georgics* 3, the conquest of the nations by Augustus will have to be secured by a fear of the Underworld terrible enough to suppress Invidia, which will otherwise undo the effects of that conquest. This need to replace fear of the enemy with fear of the Underworld is to be supplied by Vergil in his poem about Caesar.

Vergil's analysis of the connection between Invidia and fear of the Underworld has its foundation in Lucretius' discussion of Invidia at *De Rerum*

Natura 5.1117–1135. After the invention of property and gold, men came to admire wealth more than courage and beauty. In the hope of being able to secure their wealth and live peacefully, they wanted to be famous and powerful; but their hope was futile, since in vying with one another for the highest honors they made the path to honors dangerous; and in any case whoever did come out on top was thrust down to Tartarus by Invidia. For it is generally the highest things, whatever things are raised up above others, that are vaporized by Invidia, just as is the case with lightning. For this reason it is much more satisfactory to obey quietly than to wish to rule affairs with *imperium* (*regere imperio, DRN* 5.1130) and hold kingdoms. Is Anchises' recommendation of ruling with *imperium* as the specifically Roman art (*Aen.* 6.851) based upon some flaw in or exception to Lucretius' argument?

Lucretius' analysis of Invidia as the destructive by-product of men's misguided competition for eminence[14] prompts the thought that if Invidia could be controlled, the desire to rule might turn out to be more satisfactory than quiet obedience. As it is, the desire to rule is based on a fundamental mistake—being wise from someone else's mouth and desiring things on the basis of hearsay rather than on the basis of the senses themselves (5.1131–1135). So the self-defeating desire to rule would be dismantled if people could be taught to rely on their own senses rather than on hearsay. But what if they can't be taught this? Then the self-defeating character of the desire to rule could be corrected if Invidia could be tamed, taught not to strike down the highest things. Lucretius doesn't think this is possible; but Vergil, in the proem to *Georgics* 3, promises to do it.

At the center of the *Georgics* Vergil had catalogued the political ills of the late Republic, ills of which the fortunate ruralist, as well as the happy physiologist, is free (2.495–512). There Vergil had adumbrated three ways of curing these ills: Epicurean natural science, with its trampling out of the fear of angry gods; a return to a pre-political, rural and familial, way of life; and the suppression of Invidia by fear of punishing gods. The first is the way of Lucretius' *De Rerum Natura*, the second is the way of Vergil's *Georgics*, and the third is the way of Vergil's *Aeneid*. The first two cure the ills of political life by abandoning political life, the third by supplying political life with sufficient fear of Underworld punishment to be an effective restraint on Invidia. The *Georgics* are subordinate and preparatory to the *Aeneid*; the *Georgics* prepare the question whether Lucretian science or Vergilian religion, the extinction or the revival of the din of greedy Acheron, is the cure of Rome's ills. The *Aeneid* is Vergil's triumph on behalf of Caesar. As the center of the *De Rerum Natura* had been Lucretius' denial of Acheron, the center of the *Aeneid* is Vergil's assertion of Acheron. The *Aeneid* is Vergil's battle against

Lucretius on behalf of men's belief in divine anger and punishment. But while Vergil's Underworld is the summit of the education of Aeneas, it is not the summit of Vergil's thought.

In part I of this study, Vergil's judgment of the superiority of the *Aeneid* to the *De Rerum Natura* was considered with respect to the practical effects of the two poems: the *Aeneid* has the effect of insuring peace by suppressing Invidia, while the *De Rerum Natura* has the effect of emancipating the angry and lawless passions so as to lead to the greatest unhappiness. The suppression of Invidia is brought about by fear of divine punishment in the Underworld, and the *Aeneid* indeed presents at its center a vivid account of divine justice in the next life. The Underworld is experienced by the hero Aeneas as the scene of his perfected education; it confirms the propriety of piety as his leading virtue by showing how this piety reflects the truth about the nature of things. By ending this central passage with the Gates of Dreams passage, Vergil appears to propose that the false doctrine of the Underworld is the necessary foundation of the best or at any rate the most praiseworthy man.

iii. Lucretius' Critique of Piety

The unsuitableness of piety to heroism is thought to lie in piety's emphatic acknowledgment of man's dependency or insufficiency. The pious man is "abject," "prostrate;"[15] he lacks the impressive self-reliance and self-assertion that characterizes the hero. The reproach that he raises his arms to heaven when he "ought" to be fighting[16] means that he is *mistaken* in relying on the gods rather than on himself: he ought to rely on himself either because it is an error to think that gods give victories or because, even if gods do give victories, it is still possible, and since possible therefore more creditable, for men to get their victories on their own. Piety reduces the heroism of a man's deeds by just so much as the man has depended on divine support in doing those deeds. Such a judgment of piety rests, then, on the judgment that the dependency or insufficiency expressed by it is either untrue or unnecessary: it is not *true* that men are dependent on gods (as for example because there are no gods), or, it is not *necessary* for men to be dependent on gods (as for example because some men can achieve on their own the same things that other men can achieve only with the help of gods). Whether piety's acknowledgment of dependence on gods is manly or not depends on the nature of things, the truth of things. If the truth of things is that men are on their own, then to acknowledge dependence on gods is unmanly because it is foolish. But if the truth is that men *are* dependent on gods, then men's vaunting their independence is unmanly because *it* is foolish.

The opinion that piety as reliance on gods is unmanly is the poetic[17] teaching above all of Lucretius' *De Rerum Natura*. It is Lucretius' poem that, in presenting Epicurus as the true exemplar of heroism, makes an explicit and powerful case for understanding piety as incompatible with manliness, as indeed the specific sign of human folly and cowardliness. *Pietas* is devotion to fathers, fatherland, and fathers' gods. In the *De Rerum Natura*, Lucretius offers an analysis of piety as men's false opinion of their indebtedness to fathers, fatherland, and fathers' gods; it is the falseness of the opinion that makes the attitude of reverence or devotion weak or unmanly. According to Lucretius, Epicurus' superiority to Achilles and Odysseus lies in the superiority of his defiance of gods over their defiance of enemies and hardships. The gods are the true enemies and hardships of the human race; it is in asserting himself against them, against Religion looming from the skies, that the Epicurean philosopher is the true exemplar of manliness.

Piety is promoted by terror-talking priests who frighten men into believing that whatever religion requires of them is pious; but the truth is that what religion requires of men is not only craven and foolish but, in the true sense, actually impious. True piety (5.1198 ff.) is something altogether different from what priests and poets mean by the term. Lucretius expects the announcement that Epicurus has trampled religion beneath the feet to frighten Memmius away from the study of Epicurus' doctrine, as tending to impiety and criminality:

> illud in his rebus vereor, ne forte rearis
> inpia te rationis inire elementa viamque
> indugredi sceleris. Quod contra saepius illa
> Religio peperit scelerosa atque impia facta.

> What I fear in these matters is that you perchance may think you are entering
> upon the elements of impious reasoning and starting on the path of crime. But
> all to the contrary, it has more often been religion itself that has given rise to
> criminal and impious deeds.

> (1.80–83)

Lucretius' exemplary proof of this claim is the sacrifice of Iphigenia at Aulis (1.84 ff.). Everyone can see the evil in this deed (101), and since piety, whatever it is, is at any rate something good, this deed shows the power of religion to give rise to impious deeds under the color of piety. How can the Greeks at Aulis have believed that the sacrifice of Iphigenia was anything but an impious crime? The foundation of this belief was the prior belief that the gods are angry and punitive gods; and this prior belief they got from the terror-talking words of seers (102–103). The requirements of religion, which have got the popular reputation of "piety," cannot be truly pious because they are based on a false understanding of the gods themselves. Under cover of religion, priests make human beings act against the human good—not by way of renouncing their private good in favor of something greater or higher, but by way of being bullied into craven and outright wicked deeds in pursuit of a false notion of their private good as residing in the propitiation of the angry gods. Men do impious deeds in the name of piety because, not knowing the nature of the soul, they do not know there is a determinate end to sufferings. With this knowledge they would have the strength to stand up against religion and the threats of priests; without it they have no defense against the fear that subjects them to priests, the fear of eternal punishment by the gods after death (111). Impious deeds are such deeds as anyone can see by human reasoning are harmful to the human good, like the sacrifice of Iphigenia, not such deeds as terror-talking priests claim are displeasing to angry gods, like the study of Epicurean doctrine. Religion is cowardly, foolish, and impious; irreligion is courageous, wise, and, in the true sense, pious.

Priests frighten the people not only by threatening the gods' eternal punishment for deeds displeasing to them, but also by accusing the people of ingratitude in their hearts. In his account of the worship of Cybele, Lucretius portrays the incredible power of her unmanned priests to terrify men: the very flints with which they have castrated themselves are held up by the *galli* in their processions as symbols of the punishment in store for the multitude from the gods. These flints, when wielded in this way, have the power to confound the "ungrateful minds and impious hearts of the multitude" (*ingratos animos atque impia pectora uolgi*) with terror of the divinity of the goddess (2.622–623). In this way, the *galli* are thought to warn that those who are found to have violated the divinity of the goddess-Mother and to be ungrateful to parents are unworthy to bring forth offspring of their own (614–617).[18] The peculiar union in piety of submission to gods and submission to fathers and fatherland is illustrated here by Lucretius very emphatically: gods, parents, and fatherland are inextricably bound together by priests as the sources of our being to which we owe a gratitude wholly beyond our power to discharge. Once we are made aware of this by the priests' accusation of our nothingness—our total dependence, our total inability to pay for our arising or make ourselves our own masters—we must be forever accessible to fear of punishment for the infinite insufficiency of our gratitude. The castrate priests are able to make themselves the masters of men because men are impressed by the accusation that their ungrateful hearts are impious. When the farmers compare the difficulty of getting a living out of the earth in the present with the ease of it in the past, they imagine this must be because the men of the past ages were full of piety (2.1170). Thus piety as gratitude to fathers becomes piety as reverence for ancestors. Because the ancestors were in some (certainly not all, and not the most important) ways better off, men mistakenly imagine that the ancestors were being rewarded for virtues from which the present generation has declined. They do not realize that all things, the earth included, gradually waste away, worn out by the passage of time (2.1173–1174). The earth, so far from being an immortal goddess as the terror-talking priests claim, is itself heading for the tomb in accordance with the fixed laws of nature—not by way of punishment for men's impiety.

In the vulgar understanding, piety preserves men from criminality by making them fear eternal punishment for their crimes after death. But not only is there no such punishment, but the fear of it, so far from restraining men from crime, actually encourages them to violate shame, break the bonds of friendship, and overthrow piety itself (3.82–84). For men have often betrayed their fatherland and their dear parents in the attempt to avoid the realms of Acheron (3.85–86).

Men are mistaken in believing that they owe a boundless debt of gratitude to gods, fathers, and fatherland. Not gods but the natural concatenation of the atoms has given all men their being; gratitude is not owing for it because there was no intention to benefit us; the natural concatenation of the atoms is accidental. Besides this, our being is not much to be grateful for; for our being as given to us lacks the reasoning about life that is now called wisdom (5.8–9), without which our lives are passed in a misery of terror and anger. The nature of the world as given to us is far too faulty to have been divinely created (2.177–181, 5.156–234). The gratitude men imagine is due to the gods for our life, and for such improvements to it as the invention of grain and wine, is due in truth only to the one who invented the reasoning about life that is now called wisdom; it is he rather than the gods who is our benefactor; indeed if one is to speak as the known majesty of things demands, one must say that *he* was a god (5.7–12). As for our fathers, they are no more our true fathers than the gods are the true gods; for life as we have got it from them is no better than life as we have got it from the gods; Epicurus is not only the true god but also our true father:

> tu, pater, es rerum inventor, tu patria nobis
> suppeditas praecepta. . . .

> You, father, are the inventor of things, you furnish us with paternal precepts. . . .
>
> (3.9–10)

Nor is it to our fatherland that we are indebted for such life as would deserve our gratitude. It is not Rome but Athens that gave us the sweet solaces of life (6.4), when she gave birth to the man who saw that life as given to men by gods, fathers, and fatherlands—life with such provisions, more or less, as are needed to sustain it, with such security as is possible, with wealth and honors and praises—is hardly worth living. For he saw that with all this everyone's heart is nonetheless anguished. It was he therefore who purged the hearts with truth-speaking words, established an end of desire and fear, set forth the highest good to which we all incline, and showed the way, the little path, by which we can make for that good by a straight course; and as for the evils that there are in mortal things whether by chance or by force, he showed how to meet each one (6.9–32).

The grateful reverence to gods, fathers, and fatherland that is popularly understood by piety is due then rather to Epicurus; but even this is only in a manner of speaking, for in very truth the nature of things as revealed to us by Epicurus is such as to give no footing for any such grateful reverence. You realize that the world is mortal when you consider how the greatest members of the world (the elements) naturally fight with one another in a war that is not in any way pious (5.380–383). You see that the outcome of this war will not be victory for the pious or punishment for the impious but the ultimate destruction of the world itself, according to the fixed laws of nature. Epicurus' having shown us the nature of things is what suggests, in a manner of speaking, that our piety ought to be directed to him as our true god and father and fatherland; but the nature of things that he has shown us lacks any basis at all for piety understood as grateful reverence. If we understand properly what we owe to Epicurus, what follows from it is not piety understood as devotion to our benefactor Epicurus but piety newly understood as devotion to the greatest good as he has revealed it: the divine pleasure of contemplating the nature of all things (5.1198–1203; cf. above, p. 116). The true piety is peace of mind in the face of the impious war of the greatest members of the world. The true piety is not prostrate and craven but bold and potent; it is the ability to attain this masterful peace of mind that distinguishes the truly pious from the conventionally pious. The conventionally pious, both peoples and kings, are frightened by the evidences of the impious war of the elements into believing these are punishments for their own misdeeds; they cower with vows and prayers before gods they believe are intending to punish them (5.1204 ff.)—to such an extent does some hidden force grind down human affairs, and seem to trample down the beautiful rods and fierce axes and hold them up to ridicule (5.1233–1235). *Quid mirum, si se temnunt mortalia saecla*

(5.1138)? What wonder is it, then, that the generations of mortals, being despicable in their piety, actually despise themselves?

Piety, then, in Lucretius' presentation—conventional piety, devotion to gods, fathers, fatherland—is so far from complementing courage as a part of heroic virtue that it is in fact a symptom of man's utmost abjectness,[19] his false belief in his own dependence, all-indebtedness. Indeed heroic courage itself is only courage conventionally understood; in truth what is regarded as courage in the Homeric heroes is only a reflex of those heroes' fear of death. The actions that are conventionally regarded as displaying heroic contempt of death actually stem from abject terror of death. Men die for glory, for "statues and a name" (3.78), not because they have overcome their fear of death but because in their frantic effort to preserve their lives at any cost they become self-forgetful. Dying for glory is like committing suicide (3.79 ff.): men are driven to it because in the confusion of their fears they forget that death is what they are chiefly trying to avoid; their attempts to avoid it make their lives so miserable that they hurl themselves finally into the very death they are fleeing from. Heroic courage is not true courage. True courage springs from true liberation from the fear of death, and nothing but Epicurean doctrine can effect this liberation. A true understanding of the heroes shows that they, like all non-Epicurean men, are like boys afraid of the dark (3.87 ff.). The way of overcoming this fear is not to hurl oneself senselessly into ecstatic attempts to master or escape death but to accept the necessity of death in peace of mind; this can be achieved only by understanding this necessity from first principles, by devoting oneself to knowledge of the nature of things. The heroes were living vilely until Epicurus displayed the true courage, the courage to resist the reputation of the gods; heroic courage had misidentified the true enemy of human beings, the enemy against whom it is truly courageous to resist. The gods, so far from being the proper objects of piety, are the proper objects of courageous defiance. The many virtues converge in one: true piety and true courage coincide in the ability to contemplate all things with a mind at peace. For it is the mark of true, Epicurean courage to be able to see with a mind at peace that all things do not include any gods.

CHAPTER THIRTEEN

～

Aeneas and the Heroes

Vergil recommends Aeneas as the true type of the hero by displaying his superiority to *the* heroes Achilles, Odysseus, and Epicurus. Vergil's intention of winning men's hearts and minds to Aeneas' brand of heroism as the object of the fullest or loftiest human aspiration means winning men's hearts and minds away from the charms and claims of the heroes of Homer and Lucretius. The *Aeneid* is so conceived as to spoil forever the impressiveness of Achilles, Odysseus, and Epicurus, showing them by contrast with Aeneas to be fundamentally small, incomplete, misguided: their heroism is based in each case on a mistaken view of the nature of things. But Vergil's claim of Aeneas' heroic superiority is undertaken in full consciousness of the reasons to suspect that Aeneas' piety disqualifies him for heroism altogether. Vergil shows the seriousness of his intention to vindicate piety as heroic virtue by putting into the mouths of Aeneas' enemies the real reasons to doubt that piety could be compatible with manliness. It is thus against the background of the fullest receptiveness to the imputations against piety as heroic virtue that Vergil develops the character of Aeneas as the supreme exemplar of heroism.

In a preliminary and very schematic way it may be said that Aeneas' superiority to Achilles is established in Book 2, where Aeneas rejects the heroism of immortal glory; his superiority to Odysseus and Epicurus in Book 4, where he rejects the heroism of love and of science; and his superiority to all three in Book 6, where he learns directly the falsity of their views on the nature of things and on the fate of the human soul. Thus the first half of the

Aeneid may be said to be the negative half of the establishment of Aeneas' claim through the rejection or refutation of the claims of the contending heroes. The second half of the *Aeneid*, on the other hand, may be viewed as the positive treatment of Aeneas' heroic virtue, the unfolding of his great deeds in critical times. Put otherwise, one may say that the first half of the *Aeneid* shows the education (or reeducation) of Aeneas, the second half his achievements.

The present chapter offers an account of the three types of heroism rejected by Aeneas, so as to establish a foundation for an understanding of the position from which Aeneas' heroism can claim to have exposed the inadequacy of Achillean, Odyssean, and Epicurean heroic virtue in turn. This account aims to illuminate the specific character of each brand of heroic virtue by following what may be called the "method" of the epic poets themselves. Homer established this method by presenting heroism under two mutually contradictory aspects that he reveals through their explicit contest with one another, in the persons of Achilles and Odysseus. Lucretius followed Homer in this method by presenting Epicurus' heroism in contest with both that of Achilles and that of Odysseus. Vergil's Aeneas, in the tradition of this method, is presented in contest with Achilles, Odysseus, and Epicurus as his rivals.

The centrality of piety in the heroic character of Aeneas emerges most directly in the rivalry Vergil portrays between Aeneas and Epicurus, for it is Lucretius' critique of piety that Vergil's praise of Aeneas' piety most directly answers. While vindicating Aeneas' pious heroism against the charges of Lucretius, however, Vergil offers his own critique of piety, which throws under a melancholy shadow the triumph of Aeneas' heroic virtue. Vergil presents the basis of Aeneas' heroism in Aeneas' direct experience of the gods and the dead; but he presents this very experience of the gods and the dead as an experience of images whose conformity to the things themselves, the truth of things, is at least profoundly dubious if not simply false. Thus the famous sadness of Vergil's poem, its evocation of the "tears of things," is found to have its root in the ultimate incongruity between heroism and science; Vergil's vindication of Aeneas includes the judgment that Aeneas "rejoices in an image while being ignorant of reality" (*rerumque ignarus imagine gaudet*, 8.730). But the tension between Aeneas' ignorant rejoicing and Vergil's knowing sadness appears also within Aeneas himself, in the tension between his own joy and his own sadness, in such a way that Aeneas shows forth not only the grandeur of what must finally be judged a heroic delusion but also an opening, however ambiguous, to the fullness of Vergil's own understanding.

i. Achilles vs. Odysseus

According to the teaching of the *Iliad*, the courage of heroism is the courage to defy Fate or Necessity by refusing to accept the limitations on human beings that bar them from enjoying the perfect happiness of the gods. The perfect happiness of the gods resides in their superhuman strength and pleasure and, especially, in their immortality. The gods are lovers, friends, and parents to men, and as such they sometimes give men brief experiences of divine strength (as on the battlefield) or pleasure (as in love). But the gods are not omnipotent: they cannot make men into gods. Nor do they wish to: their sadness at the suffering or death of the men they love is fleeting, and is in any case mitigated by their recognition of the contemptible nature of these mortals. As Zeus puts it to the immortal horses of Achilles when they weep for the death of Patroclus,

> Ah, wretches, why did we give you to King Peleus, a mortal, while you are ageless and immortal? Or was it so that you might have sorrows among unhappy men? For there is not anything at all more miserable than a man, of all things whatever that breathe and creep upon earth.
>
> (*Iliad* 17.443–447)

The specifically divine pleasure of the gods is marked by their contemplation of the world from a standpoint from which the painfulness of human affairs vanishes into the pleasurableness of their appearance. As Zeus puts it to Poseidon:

> I care about them, even though they perish.
> But even so, I shall stay sitting upon the peak of Olympus
> where I shall pleasure my heart by watching.
>
> (*Iliad* 20.21–23)

From the lofty vantage point of the gods, the pleasurableness of the human scene is connected to its essential likeness to other scenes, scenes that from the human point of view look very different from, even opposed to, the human scenes as viewed by the gods. The scene on the plain before Troy appears to Greeks and Trojans colored by the highest stakes for which the combatants are fighting the war. But to the gods the scenes before Troy—the flashing of bronze armor in the sunlight, the waving of pointed objects, the surging to and fro of the massed armies—sometimes appear no more like a distant war than like a distant forest fire, a distant stormy ocean, or a distant field of waving grain; and the gods take pleasure in these appearances.[1]

Athene and the lord of the silver bow, Apollo,
assuming the likeness of birds, of vultures, settled
aloft the great oak tree of their father, Zeus of the aegis,
pleasuring themselves in looking at the heroes whose ranks, dense-settled,
shuddered into a bristle of spears, of shields and of helmets.
As when the shudder of the west wind suddenly rising
scatters across the water, and the water darkens beneath it,
so darkening were settled the ranks of Achaians and Trojans
in the plain.

(Iliad 7.58–66, Lattimore translation)

It is not exactly that the gods are cruel, that they take pleasure in the sufferings of men. It is rather that what the gods see from the divine point of view is not the sufferings of men, or anything humanly significant at all, but only the pleasurable beauty of the appearances. From the gods' most comprehensive point of view, the aspirations and sorrows of mortal men do not appear at all; the action of the war appears simply and pleasurably beautiful.

Men, meanwhile, are unhappy with a tragic unhappiness. Men, and especially the greatest men, who consort with the gods, can see vividly their own inferiority to the gods: their strength and pleasure are limited, and they themselves die. Men's unhappiness is tragic in the sense that it reflects a tragic necessity in the nature of things: men naturally long to be gods, and the greatest men the most intensely; but this longing is unalterably unrealizable. When men die, their souls enter a mindless existence in the house of Hades; after death their mindless souls are no longer capable of any kind of happiness, or of unhappiness either. As Achilles exclaims after the soul of Patroclus visits him in the night:

> Oh alas, even in the house of Hades, then, there is some soul and image, but there is no mind in it at all.

(Iliad 23.103–104)

The incongruity of men's loftiest longings on the one hand and their irremediable weakness and insignificance on the other is the tragic truth about human life at its greatest, and although men's nothingness escapes their notice in the heat of action, they are capable of recognizing it in certain moods:

> High-hearted son of Tydeus, why ask of my generation?
> As is the generation of leaves, so is that of humanity.
> The wind scatters the leaves on the ground, but the live timber

burgeons with leaves again in the season of spring returning.
So one generation of men will grow while another dies.

                 (*Iliad* 6.145–50, Lattimore translation)

As the nature of things in the *Iliad* is such as to bar men by necessity from achieving the greatest desire that is by nature implanted in them, so heroic courage in the *Iliad*—Achilles' heroism—is the intransigent refusal to accept the mortal, anonymous leaf-existence of men, the loathsome fate appointed for them at their very coming-into-being (κήρ . . . στυγερή, ἥ περ λάχε γιγνόμενόν περ, 23.78–79). Achilles' heroism is defiance of necessity. His quest for immortal glory is a quest to refute the necessity of the mere leaf-existence or species-existence of the human being, to show that the human limitations that had appeared to be fixed in the nature of things had appeared that way only because insufficient efforts had so far been made to overcome them. What if a man's supreme efforts should enable him to perform deeds so far exceeding the supposed limits of human nature that his name will be forever remembered in speech as showing the potential of the *best* man to encroach upon the domain of the gods? Such deeds as could lead to immortal glory would have to be manifestly beyond the known abilities of men, manifestly superhuman, very like the deeds of gods. Heroic courage is the courage, in the face of the evidence of men's incorrigible weakness, to strive after superhuman feats that are as close as possible to godlike, and that will secure one's immortal fame among the generations to come. But this very striving brings it about that for the hero there are ecstatic experiences, in which he rises above himself, above what is ordinarily possible for a man, and becomes something on the verge of being a god, of enjoying divine strength and pleasure. Thus, though immortal glory is only second-best to immortality itself, the quest for immortal glory may enable the hero to experience for himself in his own life the closest possible likeness to divine happiness. In the *Iliad*, Homer holds up for men's emulation both Achilles' claim to immortal glory and the ecstatic inner godlikeness of Achilles in his *aristeia*, his human necessity annihilated in the beautiful, more-than-human deed by which he also wins immortal glory.

    Insofar as Achilles' heroic virtue consists in defiance of necessity, its glamour is shadowed by the suspicion that defiance of necessity may be rather the depth of folly than the height of greatness. Homer brings this shadowy uneasiness about Achilles' heroic character into the light of day in the mouth of Odysseus, whose heroic virtue is self-consciously conceived in opposition to that of Achilles. The praiseworthiness of Achilles' heroism stands or falls with the opinion that nothing is better than to be a god, and second best is to be as like a god as possible. Odysseus for his part holds that the finest thing is when good cheer takes hold of people, and feasters in the halls listen to a singer, and the tables are full of bread and meat, and the winebearer draws wine from the bowl and pours it into the cups (*Od.* 9.5–11);[2] or as he puts it on another occasion,

> nothing is finer and better
> than when two agreeing together in their thoughts keep house,
> a man and his wife: great sorrows to their enemies,
> joys to their friends; and they themselves have the best reputation.
>
> (*Odyssey* 6.182–184)

The best object of human aspiration is the perfect enjoyment of the domestic pleasures. Thus Odysseus' highest aspiration is for his homecoming, and the *Odyssey* celebrates his successful attainment of it. His homecoming is his return in his proper person to his own household and city, his own father and son, and, preeminently, his own wife, the woman who agrees harmoniously with him in her thoughts. On the way to achieving his homecoming, Odysseus is offered outright what Achilles devoted his life to wresting from unyielding necessity. The beautiful goddess Calypso offers him immortality if he will give up his homecoming to remain with her:

> If you knew in your heart how many troubles fate has stored up for you before you reach your fatherland, you would stay here with me and keep this house and be an immortal. . . .
>
> (*Odyssey* 5.206–209)

But Odysseus loves his own better than he loves the condition of the gods, and he rejects outright and without hesitation the object of Achilles' heroic aspiration:

> I myself well know all this, that circumspect Penelope is inferior to you in looks and stature; for she is mortal, while you are immortal and ageless; and yet even so, throughout all the days I wish and yearn to go home and to see my day of homecoming.
>
> (*Odyssey* 5.215–220)

Odysseus' love of his own gains in respectability from his being preeminently the man who has knowledge of the other possibilities: "Many were they whose cities he saw, whose mind he learned" (1.3). In his travels Odysseus comes to know the whole range of what is possible for human beings, from the self-forgetfulness of the Lotus Eaters to the autonomy of the god-defying Cyclopes, to the divine craftsmanship of the Phaiakians, to the Sirens' promise of knowledge of all things, to the immortality of a life with the beautiful Calypso. In particular, in his visit to the house of Hades he comes to know at first hand the dismal fate of the dead, as it is explained to him by his dead mother Antikleia:

> This is . . . what happens, when they die, to all mortals.
> The sinews no longer hold the flesh and the bones together,
> and once the spirit has left the white bones, all the rest
> of the body is made subject to the fire's strong fury,
> but the soul flitters out like a dream and flies away. Therefore
> you must strive back toward the light again with all speed. . . .
> (*Odyssey* 11.217–223, Lattimore translation)

or by the dead Achilles himself:

> O shining Odysseus, never try to console me for dying.
> I would rather follow the plow as thrall to another
> man, one with no land allotted him and not much to live on,
> than be a king over all the perished dead.
> (*Odyssey* 11.488–491, Lattimore translation)

The heroic courage of Odysseus is the courage to reject everything, even immortality, that can only be bought at the cost of what he loves as his own, and to reject it without illusions as to the end in store for him as a mortal man; "keeping a stubborn spirit in his breast" (5.222), to outwit, reject, endure, or overcome every challenge to the perfect desirability of his homecoming.

The difference between the heroic courage of Odysseus and that of Achilles is related to the fundamental difference between the nature of things as represented in the *Odyssey* and in the *Iliad*. In the *Iliad* the character of heroic courage sprang from defiance of a tragic necessity, the necessary disjunction between the gods who enjoy their strength and pleasure forever and the men who appear and vanish like the leaves on the trees. In the *Odyssey*, in place of this absolute barrier between the divine and the human, there appears not only an unbroken continuum from inanimate objects to brutes, men, and gods, but a state of permanent flux in which the different kinds of beings can metamorphose into one another with ease. Proteus, who transforms himself into water, tree, serpent, lion, represents this flux, which also emerges in the transformation of Odysseus' crew into swine and back to men, the dwelling of mind in the ships of the Phaiakians and the transformation of those same ships into immobile stone, the transformation of the mortal woman Ino into the immortal goddess Leukothea (5.334–335), the prophesied transportation of Menelaus to the Elysian Fields rather than the house of Hades, the transformation of the suitors' laughter into lamentation. In the world of the *Odyssey* everything is potentially something else, higher or lower, and shows a tendency, even an attraction, toward actually becoming something else. Whereas in the *Iliad* the sphere of heroism was the defiant project of leaping impossibly across the boundaries of necessity so as to become a god, the sphere of heroism in the *Odyssey* is the project of stubbornly preserving the germ of one's own mortal being against the pressure of all temptations to become something else, and especially against the temptation to become a god. The charm of Odysseus' heroism lies in the stubbornness, resourcefulness, and duplicity with which he preserves against all foreign temptations the "seed of fire" (5.490) within himself, the germ of his own being, which he carries to its proper hearth before kindling it into a blaze of full self-revelation as master of his own Ithaca and like-minded husband of his own Penelope.

The *Iliad* and the *Odyssey* together constitute the whole of Homer's teaching, and the heroic courage of Achilles and Odysseus have in common that they display themselves as defiance against the way of things. But the *Iliad* and the *Odyssey* contradict each other in every essential point regarding what the way of things is, and therefore Achilles and Odysseus contradict one another regarding the supreme exemplar of heroic virtue. In the tragic world of the *Iliad*, the different kinds of beings are strictly delimited by Necessity or Fate, and the greatest mortals have by nature an aspiration to immortality that is by nature unrealizable. Human concerns and achievements are merely transient intrusions into a divine world that is ultimately indifferent to human things. The gods take pleasure from the spectacle of human affairs as from the spectacle of ocean storms or forest fires. The roaring sea washed against the shores of Troy before there was such a city, and will do so again when there is no longer any vestige of the war that "the race of half-god men" once fought there (12.12–33). The immortal things, the gods and the world, are alien and terrible in their ultimate indifference to human thoughts and aspirations. The courage of the greatest hero in his quest for immortal glory is the courage of his contemptuous rejection of all merely human pleasures as insipid distractions from the only truly great object. The great object is to burst altogether out of the sphere of the familiar and lovable mortal beings into the infinitely higher, though alien and indifferent, sphere of the immortal beings. But in the comic world of the *Odyssey*, all the

different kinds of beings merge into one another by degrees; nothing pro-
hibits, and much promotes, the transformation of kind into kind. The
courage of the greatest hero is the courage to resist the pull of what is alien
to him, however superior; to choose the inferior woman who is his own, his
known and like-minded wife, the choice of whom condemns him to a mindless afterlife among the dead, over the superior goddess who offers him immortal participation in her divinity.

Odysseus' attachment to his own is represented with especial insistence as
his attachment to his own belly, that belly that has what the goddess who
loves him contemptuously calls "such needs as yours" (5.189), clamorous
needs for "such things as mortal people feed upon" (5.197). Odysseus introduces himself to Alkinoos, who thinks he may be a god, by declaring that he
is in no way like the immortals, but only like the most wretched of mortal
men, men so wretched that even their own contemplation of their own
wretchedness is overcome by the needs of the belly:

> But leave me now to eat my dinner, for all my sorrow,
> for there is no other thing so shameless as to be set over
> the belly, but she rather uses constraint and makes me think of her,
> even when sadly worn, when in my heart I have sorrow
> as now I have sorrow in my heart, yet still forever
> she tells me to eat and drink and forces me to forgetfulness
> of all I have suffered, and still she is urgent that I must fill her.
>
> (*Odyssey* 7.215–222, Lattimore translation)

Odysseus, in full consciousness of the disgraceful needs and dismal destinies
of men who are mortal, chooses homecoming over immortality.

The *Iliad* and the *Odyssey* together represent a profound quarrel between
Achilles and Odysseus as to the true object of heroic courage. That quarrel
between the two poems is already adumbrated within the *Iliad* itself, in a con-
densed and therefore exceptionally vivid form, in the quarrel of Achilles and
Odysseus in Book 19. Here, after the death of Patroclus and the consequent
decision of Achilles to put aside his anger at Agamemnon and reenter the
war to avenge his friend, Achilles and Odysseus quarrel over whether the
army should engage the enemy at once or should have dinner first. According to Odysseus, food and wine "is" battle-spirit and prowess (τό γὰρ μένος
ἐστὶ καὶ ἀλκή, 19.161), and therefore the battle must wait on the feeding of
the troops; but according to Achilles, battle-spirit comes from the consciousness of unavenged outrage, and therefore the army must fight at once
and unfed, under the pressure of retribution alone (19.199–214). Odysseus
regards it as weak-minded (19.218 ff.) to ignore or deny the needs of the

belly, and Achilles regards it as contemptible to acknowledge them. In Odysseus' eyes Achilles is the victim of a dangerous delusion, the delusion of taking himself for a god; for it is the gods who "eat no food, nor do they drink of the shining / wine, and therefore they have no blood and are called immortal" (5.340–342), while for mortal Achaians it is not possible to show their grief for the dead by denying the needs of the belly (19.225–233). But in Achilles' eyes, Odysseus and his likes take men for mere cattle, urging them to meet the greatest crisis of the spirit by seeing to the care and feeding of their bodies. Patroclus lies slain by Hector, "and you think of eating"!

> No, but I would now
> drive forward the sons of the Achaians into the fighting
> starving and unfed, and afterwards when the sun sets
> make ready a great dinner, when we have paid off our defilement.
> But before this, for me at least, neither food nor drink shall
> go down my throat, since my companion has perished. . . .
> . . . Food and drink mean nothing to my heart
> but blood does, and slaughter, and the groaning of men in the hard work.
> (*Iliad* 19.205–14, Lattimore translation)

It is hard to say who, according to Homer, is in the right in this quarrel. Odysseus wins, as far as the feeding of the army goes. Zeus himself appears to endorse the truth of Odysseus' argument: he acknowledges that soldiers must eat to fight, and that even Achilles himself, if "unfed and fasting," would be overtaken by the weakness of hunger (19.342–348). But Achilles does not eat. His claim that his fighting spirit is independent of food and drink is absolutely vindicated. The gods in fact infuse nectar and ambrosia into his breast, so that he enters the battle "unfed," like something more than a man (19.340–356). At the opening of Book 19, Achilles' pleasure in the divine armor made by Hephaistos had been briefly shaken by his horror of the flies that might feed on Patroclus' rotting flesh (21–27). By the end of Book 19, Achilles appears to have proved that, while men like Odysseus urge prudent submission to what they claim is an iron necessity, a sufficiently great man can reveal this supposed necessity to be merely weakness: it is not necessary that men's bodies be food for flies, or that meat and wine be food for men.

One might formulate the complete teaching on heroism of the *Iliad* and the *Odyssey* together as follows: the quarrel between Odysseus and Achilles is undecidable. Heroism has, and must have, two mutually contradictory forms. Man is so constituted that his whole desire is to enjoy the love of his own immortally, but the world is so constituted that man must choose between the love of his own and the love of the immortal. The immortal life of the gods for which man yearns because it is higher, better, than he, is alien and indifferent to mortal beings; to strive after it is to renounce one's moorings in the domestic life of men. His own beloved things, his city and home and wife and family, for which man yearns because they are his own and love him in return, are mortal, thus defective, and in some ways disgraceful. The life of striving for the alien immortal and the life of striving for the mortal beloved are as necessarily the two exemplars of heroism as the immortal and the beloved are necessarily the two objects of men's desire. But since men's desire has two incompatible objects, the man striving for either of them is forever indicted by the man striving for the other; the quarrel between Achilles and Odysseus can never be settled. The complete teaching of Homer points to the conclusion that there is no adequate resolution in the heroic life to the human problem; man is a being who cannot become whole or happy through heroism.

ii. Epicurus vs. Achilles and Odysseus

Since Lucretius' intention is to win for philosophy the hearts of men who are already enchanted by Homer's portrayal of heroic virtue, he presents Epicurus as a hero who outshines both of them on their own ground. Epicurus outshone Achilles' *virtus animi* (DRN 1.70) by seeking to smash in not the gates of a walled city but the gates of walled nature; and he outshone Odysseus' *vis animi* (1.72) by travelling not beyond the furthest reaches of human habitation in ships but altogether beyond the flaming walls of the world in mind and spirit. He was victorious not over Agamemnon, Hector, Troy; not over storms, cannibals, his wife's suitors; but over Religion itself, which until his victory had terrorized the whole human race.

In truth, though, it is not that Epicurus outshone Achilles' and Odysseus' heroic virtue on its own ground but that he undermined altogether the very ground of their heroic virtue. Although at the outset the reader of the *De Rerum Natura* may envision Epicurus as a greater version of or the consummation of Homeric heroism, in the end he must come to see that Epicurus is the destroyer of Homeric heroism. In the light of the Epicurean teaching, the Homeric heroes appear as confused, frightened, puerile beings; their supposed virtues are not lesser versions of Epicurean virtue, but vices. In the light of Epicurus' daring defiance of Religion, it becomes clear that all of human life before him had been lived vilely, in abject submission to Religion; the Homeric heroes lacked the courage and insight to stand up against the only true enemy of human beings, the reputation of the gods. The achievements of

Achilles and Odysseus looked good to men who were deluded about the true conditions of human life; they can never look good again to men enlightened as to those conditions by Lucretius' poem.

Achilles appears great because of his intransigent quest for divine pleasure. Lucretius too of course endorses divine pleasure (*divina voluptas*, 3.28) as the one worthy object of human desire, and promises it to his readers, while showing that Achilles was radically mistaken about what divine pleasure is. Achilles identified it with immortality, but the quest for immortality, which appears at first as the greatest man's masterful claim on the greatest good, is exposed finally by Lucretius as nothing but an involuntary, terrified flight from imaginary evils, the imaginary evils of death. The understanding of human greatness that guides Achilles' life is based on a vulgar error about the nature of things. Achilles, under the influence of Religion like all men before Epicurus, believed that the world and the gods are immortal and that human souls survive the bodies in a dismal existence in the house of Hades. The "anger of Achilles," so far from pointing to Achilles' heroic greatness, is merely the symptom of his false beliefs. It is from his false belief that there are immortal gods that Achilles derives his anger at not being immortal himself, and his resolution to exact immortal glory in compensation for his mortality, as if that were an injury to him (*Iliad* 1.352–354). Like the most deluded of the vulgar, Achilles is indignant at having been born mortal (*indignatur se mortalem esse creatum*, DRN 3.884); like them, he is indignant at the prospect that after death his flesh will rot or be consumed by fire or by wild beasts (3.870–872). It is from his false belief that the world is immortal that Achilles derives his deluded lust for immortal glory: he devotes himself to achieving deeds that will cause him to be praised eternally among men because he does not see that men and their world will soon come crashing down. It is from his false belief that human souls survive the bodies in a dismal existence in the house of Hades that Achilles derives his craven, childish terror of death, pathetically disguised as a valiant quest for immortality.

In truth the "divine pleasure" that is the proper object of men's desire is the pleasure of the philosophers, the pleasure of contemplating all things with a mind at peace (3.28–30; cf. 5.1203). For the attainment of divine pleasure nature, our nature, clamors for nothing but the absence of pain from the body and the enjoyment, secluded from anxiety and fear, of pleasant sensation in the mind (*DRN* 2.17–19). But neither luxurious wealth nor the greatest deeds of martial valor can ever secure divine pleasure (2.20–61). For divine pleasure requires the removal of anxiety and fear, but anxiety and fear themselves are not frightened away by arms. Lucretius ridicules the heroic warriors who appear to attain divine pleasure through supreme feats of arms:

they are like nothing so much as children terrified in the dark of things that are in reality not terrible. Through his ridicule Lucretius makes his readers envision with contempt the Achillean heroes blindly bent on hiding from themselves through heroic deeds of mastery the childish terror that in fact is mastering and driving them. The true masters are not these warriors who are like children in the shadows (2.55), but the philosophers who look down on them from above much as the gods in the *Iliad* are thought to look down on the human world from Mt. Olympus.

For Lucretius borrows from Homer, though with crucial modifications, the idea that the specifically divine pleasure lies in the contemplation of the world from a divine height. According to Lucretius the gods who enjoy this pleasure are the philosophers, and the pleasure itself arises not from the beauty of the appearances but from their comforting truth. The philosophers look down on the life of heroes not from Mt. Olympus but from the well-fortified temples of the wise, and accordingly what they see is not beautiful likenesses of forest fires and fields of grain but pathetic struggles for worthless supremacies. The philosophers can see from their temples that they themselves are free of the anxieties and fears that they can see are driving other men, and thus they take pleasure in their full consciousness of their own happiness.

> But nothing is sweeter than to occupy the well-fortified temples raised up by the serene doctrine of the wise, whence you could look down on others and see them straying here and there and, in their wanderings, seeking the path of life: competing in talents, contending in nobility, striving night and day with surpassing labor to rise up to the summit of wealth and get mastery over things.
>
> (2.7–13)

When the philosopher hears the nature of things proclaimed by Epicurus' reasoning that arises from his divine mind, the terrors of the spirit take flight, the walls of the world part asunder, and he sees everything being done throughout all space (3.14–17). From this supreme vantage point, from which the earth no longer bars his complete perception of everything, he sees that the abodes of the gods are inviolate and, climactically, that nowhere are there any realms of Acheron (3.18–27). At this sight he is seized by a certain divine pleasure and shuddering, since by Epicurus' power nature has been exposed so openly in every direction (3.14–16, 25–30).

It is only the philosopher who occupies this standpoint who can hope to cast out headlong the fear of Acheron that muddies human life from the bottom up, suffusing everything with the blackness of death and leaving no pleasure clear and pure (3.35–40). As for the pleasures of heroes, they are, like the pleasures of all unenlightened human beings, blackened by the false terror that coerces them to flee the things, like poverty and dishonor, that remind them of their mortality. In their desperate wish to master death some, in search of immortal glory, perish "for statues and a name;" some are seized by such a hatred of a life lived in terror of death that they themselves kill themselves to escape it (3.59–82). For one who can see the world from the point of view of the philosophers, Achilles' heroic virtue, his courage in defying the necessity that bars men from attaining the immortality of the gods, is utterly exploded. It is only his ignorant terror of death that drives him to waste his life in deluded hopes of a nonexistent immortality rather than devoting it to the quest for the one truly divine pleasure, which is happily accessible to human beings.

Odysseus, on the other hand, had appeared great not because of any quest for immortality but because of his unswerving devotion to the love of his own, and in particular to the love of his own wife. The heroic character of this love appears in Odysseus' courage to fight through all obstacles and overcome all temptations that would prevent his homecoming. The exemplary deed of Odysseus' heroism is his deliberate choice of the mortal Penelope over immortality with Calypso. Odysseus' devotion appears to be vindicated by his triumph over his enemies, his reestablishment in the kingship of Ithaca, and especially by the answering love of Penelope herself.

Lucretius' teaching debunks the heroic devotion of Odysseus: his life, like Achilles', is ruled by a vulgar error about the nature of things. This vulgar error is the erotic delusion, the common, entirely unheroic imagination that one's happiness is bound up in the possession of one particular woman. Lucretius' analysis of love, in Book 4 of the *De Rerum Natura*, categorizes this passion as one of the phenomena caused by wrongly interpreted images. Sense perception and mental perception take place through the impingement of the atoms of images on the atoms of our organs of perception. The images themselves are perfectly real in the sense that they are composed of matter; all our sensations are true in this sense, but our interpretation of them is often faulty (4.379–521) both because of the imperfection of our reasoning and because of our tendency to wishful thinking. Some of our misinterpretations arise spontaneously, without any intention on our part (as when a square tower looks curved to us when we see it from a great distance, 4.353–365). But other misinterpretations of ours are caused or promoted by our desire not to be thought to inhabit waste places deserted even by the gods. It is this desire that leads us to boast of miracles—or there is some other reason, since the whole human race is too greedy for miracles (4.590–594). By "some other reason" Lucretius seems to mean that even if we are not moved to lies by our concern for what others think of our situation, our own greed for miracles moves us to deceive ourselves.

Love is one of these delusions caused by our tendentious misinterpretation of images. Our sexual need is real enough, and, like hunger and thirst, easily enough satisfied; its satisfaction no more requires a specific woman than the satisfaction of hunger requires a specific piece of meat; and he who avoids love gets the fruits of Venus "without punishment" (*sine poena commoda sumit*, 4.1074). But in love, the lovers are deluded by images (*in amore Venus simulacris ludit amantis*, 4.1101): the image of the chance object of their erotic desire is endowed by them with altogether imaginary properties. Nature punishes their delusion, for the imaginary need of one specific woman is, because imaginary, unfulfillable; indeed, while natural needs are marked by their capacity to be satisfied, love is the one thing of which the more we have, the more our heart is inflamed by relentless desire (4.1088–1090).

At the heart of the erotic delusion, as of the glory-seeking delusion, is the fear of death. Unenlightened men cannot bear their own insignificance or nothingness as mortal beings; they crave not to be thought to inhabit places deserted by the gods. The lover attributes imaginary virtues to his beloved because, wishing to be affirmed in his vain self-esteem, he wants to be loved by gods; thus he aggrandizes himself by attributing to his beloved "more than is right to grant to a mortal" (4.1183–1184).[3] The deluded lover could be brought to condemn himself for his stupidity in making such attributions if it could be brought home to him vividly enough that his beloved makes as foul smells as other women (4.1175–1182), or if he could be brought to see her sexual responsiveness to him not as a confirmation of his unique worthiness of a unique love but as having no other reason than the reason why we see the dogs coupling in the streets (4.1192–1205).

If ever there was a man who attributed more to his beloved than it is right to grant to a mortal, Odysseus stands self-confessed as that deluded lover:

> Goddess and queen, do not be angry with me. I myself know
> that all you say is true and that circumspect Penelope
> can never match the impression you make for beauty and stature.
> She is mortal after all, and you are immortal and ageless.
> But even so, what I want and all my days I pine for
> is to go back to my house and see my day of homecoming.
>
> (*Odyssey* 5.215–220, Lattimore translation)

Odysseus could be taken for an exemplar of heroic virtue only by men who share his delusion about the nature of things, a delusion that Epicurus alone has been able to explain and from which he has thus potentially liberated us. Odysseus' homecoming had appeared as a triumph: after the victory over Troy, after his travels beyond the known boundaries of human habitation and his success in meeting every danger that had faced him there, Odysseus returns to reclaim his kingship, acknowledge his son, destroy his enemies, repair his property, and see his love returned by his like-minded wife, in whose arms and to whose delight he gives an account of what he has seen in his travels. What he has seen is that men are in danger of letting themselves be changed into pigs or into immortal gods unless with heroic courage and endurance they remember their homecoming (23.310–343). But Odysseus' apparent triumph vanishes in the light of Epicurus' triumph:

> Thus the lively force of his mind triumphed, and he advanced beyond the far-flaming walls of the world and traversed in mind and thought the immeasurable whole. From there he brings back to us in his triumph [an account of] what can come into being and what cannot, and for what reason the power of each thing and its deeply inhering boundary is delimited. Thus Religion in its turn is overmastered and trampled beneath his feet: his victory makes us equal to heaven.
>
> (*DRN* 1.72–79)

Epicurus' victory has enabled us to overcome the charms of Odysseus: he has shown us the reason why it is impossible for men to turn into pigs or into immortal gods, why it is false that the souls of the dead live a dismal afterlife in the house of Hades, and why it is a self-deception to seek our happiness in the love of a mortal being.

iii. Aeneas vs. Achilles, Odysseus, and Epicurus

The opening words of the first book of the *Aeneid, arma virumque cano,* pit Aeneas against Achilles and Odysseus, as its conclusion with the song of Iopas pits him against Epicurus. Vergil proposes a hero superior not only to both Homeric heroes but also to that hero whom Lucretius has already proposed as surpassing both Homeric heroes. The superiority of Aeneas to Achilles and Odysseus lies in his combining the spheres of both of them in one. Such a combination would suggest that the human incompletion of each of the Homeric heroes is not necessary after all, that Homer was mistaken in presenting man as compelled in the best case to choose between tragic devotion to immortality and comic devotion to his own. Aeneas' superiority to Epicurus is surely not superiority in Epicurus' own sphere; in no sense is Aeneas a philosopher. On the contrary, Aeneas outranks Epicurus as a hero by making it manifest that the philosopher as such is defective as a model for the emulation of men as such. Lucretius had poetically represented Epicurus as a hero in order to make Epicurus' way of life attractive to men whose taste was formed by heroic poetry. But this poetic way of speaking is false, and Lucretius employed it not for the wise reasons for which the poets (like Vergil) employ poetic falsehoods but because he was in error about the nature of things, and particularly about human nature. From the truth that the philosophic life is the supreme peak of human happiness he erroneously concluded that human happiness could be promoted by turning the generality of men to emulation of the philosopher. The true conclusion, however, is that only through emulation of the pious founder can the generality of men achieve such happiness as they are capable of, and only through a previous provision for the general happiness of men can the special happiness of the philosopher be secured.

As for Achilles and Odysseus, in the first half of the *Aeneid* Aeneas performs great travels that inevitably challenge comparison with the travels of Odysseus, and in the second half he wages great wars that inevitably challenge comparison with the martial exploits of Achilles. But any attempt to pursue these comparisons soon leads to the recognition that this cannot be done without a more fundamental comparison of the meaning of everything in the *Aeneid* with the meaning of everything in the *Iliad* and the *Odyssey*. For by what standard is one to judge whether Aeneas' meeting in the Underworld with the unburied Palinurus (6.336–383) is greater or lesser than Odysseus' meeting in the Underworld with the unburied Elpenor (11.51–83), or whether Aeneas' human sacrifice of eight Latins (10.517–520) is greater or lesser than Achilles' human sacrifice of twelve Trojans (21.26–33)? Aeneas' purpose in his travels is not homecoming, and his purpose in his wars is not the attainment of immortal glory. Above all, the fate of the human soul in the *Aeneid* is not eternal misery in the house of Hades; and it is only in the light of the truth about the fate of the human soul that one could reach any conclusion from comparing the heroic deeds of Achilles and Odysseus with those of Aeneas.

Before it shows the great founding deeds of Aeneas, the *Aeneid* shows the education of Aeneas; it educates its reader by inducing him to participate, in imagination and in thought, in the education of its hero. Aeneas, like the reader, is in need of this education because he is in the first place drawn to form himself in emulation of Achilles, Odysseus, and Epicurus. In the course of Aeneas' education he is induced to renounce each of these exemplars of heroism so as ultimately to become himself the exemplar of a new type of heroism. The *Aeneid* "forms the mind to heroic virtue by example"[4] insofar as it draws its readers first into the experiences that lead

Aeneas to make these renunciations and then into his founding achievements themselves.

Aeneas' fundamental break with Achillean heroism takes place during the fall of Troy as described in his own narrative in Book 2. At the beginning of the battle Aeneas in his furor is animated by an opinion that is the fruit of his entire heroic education: it is noble to die under arms, *pulchrum mori in armis* (2.317). By the end he has renounced any hope of such a noble death under arms, together with the possibility of immortal glory belonging to it, by doing what is, according to his initial opinion, the preeminently base thing: fleeing the burning city. But along the way, and in the midst of the terrific and pathetic confusion of the battle, he learns by degrees to revise his initial opinion in accordance with a more comprehensive point of view from which his self-preservation is seen to be not ignominious but supremely virtuous. His reformed opinion is by no means the same opinion that temporarily leads Achilles in *Iliad* 9 to the decision to preserve his own life by abandoning the war, the opinion that, compared with the difference between being alive and being dead, there is nothing to choose between honor and dishonor (9.318–320). Aeneas' reformed opinion has in common with Achilles' that it arises from a point of view not normally accessible to human beings, closer than usual to the more comprehensive view of the gods. But in Aeneas' experience, the more comprehensive view is not one from which honor is exposed as a human illusion, but one from which the gods' commands point to something yet higher than honor, which, while not yet or not ever fully intelligible, is at least clearly connected with the founding of a new city. This more comprehensive view is at first far more intelligible to the reader of the *Aeneid* than to Aeneas himself, since that reader has heard Jupiter's prophecy to Venus in Book 1 and since he sees before his eyes, as it were, outside the poem altogether, the fruits of Aeneas' founding in the greatness of Rome itself. During the fall of Troy Aeneas comes to risk not his life but his self-esteem. In order to die nobly in battle, Aeneas needed only to have followed the habits and opinions in which he had been educated; in order to flee alive he needed to renounce his habits and opinions at the critical moment for which his entire education had prepared him as for its consummation. And he needed to do this in obedience to commands from the gods and from the shades of the dead, commands whose status could only be obscure to him.

After the account of Aeneas' renunciation of Achillean heroism in Book 2, his attraction to and then his crucial break with both Odyssean and Epicurean heroism follow in Book 4, where, again in immediate obedience to commands of the gods and the dead, he renounces Dido and Carthage. Dido is, as it were, both Aeneas' Calypso and his Penelope: like Calypso, she offers him, if he will give up his journey, a happiness he cannot look for with the wife who awaits him at the end of that journey; like Penelope, she agrees with him harmoniously in her thoughts.[5] Aeneas in his sojourn with Dido is drawn to putting his highest hopes in the mutual love of a woman who is his soul mate; he attempts to remake with Dido the home and family and kingdom that he had lost with Creusa's death and the fall of Troy. This inclination of Aeneas, though later minimized by him in his denial to Dido that he had ever married her (4.338–339), is noticed in Mercury's reproach to Aeneas "*tu nunc . . . uxorius urbem / exstruis*" (4.265–267).

The form of heroism to which Aeneas is tempted by Dido and Carthage is not, however, only that of mutual love but also that of wisdom; Aeneas' love of Dido as his own Calypso/Penelope is entangled with his love of Carthage as the city of science. Aeneas' forgetfulness of his divinely appointed kingdom during his sojourn at Carthage shows the uncertainty of his piety. The visions and oracles that require him to go to Italy deserve his obedience only if they are real; but Aeneas is confronted at Carthage with the pure teaching of Iopas and the popular opinions of Dido and the Carthaginians to the effect that those visions and oracles are illusions. As it will not be until his visit to the Underworld in Book 6 that Aeneas will learn the grounds of the gods' claims on his obedience, his exposure to Carthaginian opinion charms him, as it charms us, with the prospect of a self-sufficient human empire liberated from the harsh demands of ruling and punishing gods.

The trouble with Achillean and Odyssean heroism, the two poles of Homeric heroism, is that they are jointly based on a wrong understanding of the nature of things. Each appears both praiseworthy in itself and totally irreconcilable with the other only when the nature of things is erroneously understood. Achillean heroism is worthy of emulation only if being born mortal is an injury to a human being; Odyssean heroism is worthy of emulation only if, in the limitless flux of things, nothing is more desirable than one's own. Epicurean heroism has the merit of being grounded in the truth about the nature of things: death is not an indignity to human beings, and in the limited, orderly flux of things nothing is more desirable than the greatest, the purest, pleasure, the philosophic pleasure of contemplating the true nature of things without fear. But the merit of Epicurean heroism is altogether outweighed by the fact, inadequately grasped by Lucretius, that emulation of Epicurus is a futile and, even more important, a harmful enterprise for almost all men. For in almost all cases the emulation of Epicurean heroism comes down to the defiance of the reputation of the gods without an understanding of the whole nature of things from first principles. Men in general cannot rationally dismantle their fear of death and thus disarm their anger as Lucretius imagined. The emulation of Epicurus' resistance to the reputation of the gods, instead of making men shudder with divine pleasure without harm to one another, emancipates men from any restraint on the fullest expression of their anger in bestial cruelty and in demented efforts at self-protection against the object of their fears. The emulation of Epicurus' proud independence of the gods naturally follows from the view that Epicurus' victory has made us the equals of heaven and thus that there is nothing above the highest man, nothing to which man as such must bow. This view, though, does not lead most men to a sober acceptance of their mortality; it leads them rather to throw off, together with fear of divine punishment, any restraint in the self-aggrandizement to which they are helplessly, involuntarily driven by their incorrigible terror of death. Contempt of the gods without contempt of death, the perverted form of Epicureanism alone accessible to nonphilosophers, produces not peaceable Epicuruses shuddering with harmless pleasure but suicidally distracted Didos and atrociously tyrannical Mezentiuses, seeking to take against themselves or against the others an unattainable revenge for their mortality.

For almost all men, the truth that death is not an indignity to us and that nothing is more desirable than the purest pleasure can be brought into practical connection with their lives, made a practical guide of their lives, not in its direct and undiluted form but only in a poetic, i.e., untrue, form. That death is not an indignity to us emerges for Lucretius' hero directly from the truth that our souls are mortal, but for Vergil's hero indirectly from the opinion that our immortal souls are justly rewarded and punished in the next life for our conduct in this life. And from this opinion of the ultimately just destiny of souls emerges also a view of what the greatest or purest pleasure is: not the pleasure of contemplating the nature of things, but the pleasure of divine bliss in the next life, the faithful expectation of which casts its glow back over our present actions as these accord with the requirements of divine justice.

CHAPTER FOURTEEN

~

The Education of Aeneas: I

By the education of Aeneas is meant those experiences and reflections by which Vergil shows his transformation from a Homeric hero into the Roman hero whose leading virtue is his piety. This education begins on the night of the fall of Troy, when Aeneas' flight from the falling city opens the crucial breach with Homeric heroism; continues throughout Aeneas' travels to Italy; and is completed with Aeneas' visit to the Underworld, where he learns the whole of what can be learned about the divine truths that justify his piety and thus vindicate his manliness.

i. Aeneas' Narrative of the Fall of Troy

'immo age et a prima dic, hospes, origine nobis
insidias' inquit 'Danaum casusque tuorum
erroresque tuos; nam te iam septima portat
omnibus errantem terris et fluctibus aestas.'

"But come, guest, and tell us from the first origin the treachery," she said, "of the Greeks and the misfortunes of your men and your own wanderings; for it is now the seventh summer that carries you in your wanderings over all lands and seas."

(1.753–756)

In response to Dido's urging, Aeneas tells in Book 2 of the treachery of the Greeks and the defeats or misfortunes of his men, and in Book 3 of his wanderings. The "first origin" from which he begins is the final day and night of Troy's existence, the day on which the Trojans brought the horse into the

253

city and the night on which the Greeks emerged from the horse and took the city. On the night of Troy's fall, Aeneas himself, he says, saw very pitiable things and was a great part of them (2.5–6). The meaning of Troy's fall, the cause of it, was obscure to Aeneas during the battle, partly because he could not at the time see the things of which he was a part, and partly because the things he did see presented variously false appearances and suggested correspondingly false interpretations. In the seven years that have passed since then, Aeneas has come to "see" in memory or thought the things of which he was a part, and has come to know that some of the things he saw on that night were false appearances. Vergil makes Aeneas' way of narrating the story raise into prominence the difference between his blindness or deceived state at the time and his better knowledge now. Nevertheless, still now, with everything he has at his disposal for interpreting in retrospect the fall of Troy, the central question for him, the question that guides and organizes his narrative of the defeat, is whether its cause was (divine) fate or (human) fraud. His narrative suggests that what happened was in accordance with a divine plan for him, his family, and the surviving Trojans, and that it happened somehow in accordance with human deserts. But it also prompts the opposite interpretation, that what happened was that the Greeks, practicing a godless deception on the god-fearing Trojans, simply got away with it. Aeneas himself is inclined to take the first view; it is the view he is acting on in seeking Italy. But he tells his story in such a way that Dido, who assumes from the outset that the misfortunes of Aeneas' men and the treachery of the Greeks are the whole story, is not simply being closed-minded in seeing this interpretation supported by Aeneas' narrative.

To all appearances, the Greek defeat of Troy arose not from superior Greek military virtue and not from the justice of the Greek cause but from the perjury of Sinon, to which he swore by the inviolable divinity of the eternal fires (2.154–155). In retrospect, Aeneas knows that Sinon was lying (*Talibus insidiis periurique arte Sinonis*, 2.195). This means in the first place that he was lying about the purpose of the horse; but once his story is examined in the knowledge of his willingness to perjure himself, other questions come up too about his account of the Greeks' affairs. For the whole premise of Sinon's story, the "truth" to which he so artfully ties the false part,[1] is the notion that the Greek cause, or the Greeks' understanding of their cause, is tied to the requirements of divine favor and anger. But on the face of it, this premise appears to be simply false.

What really happened during the fall of Troy is of central importance to our understanding of Aeneas' heroic character because his character was formed by it: one may say that he entered those events as a complete Homeric hero and emerged from them as a rudimentary Vergilian hero. That is, he entered with the view that when one's city is falling the noble action is to die under arms and (thus) not unavenged; in the end, though, he saved himself alive. The question whether his flight from Troy was an act of vile cowardice or an act of heroic piety is still the burning question for Aeneas at the time when he narrates the story to Dido. At the beginning of the *Aeneid*, Aeneas' Roman heroism has not yet become second nature to him as his Homeric heroism had been until the catastrophic night; his first words in the *Aeneid*, during his shipwreck off the shore of Carthage, reflect his readiness to regret what he has done, and his envy of his fellows who fell nobly in the battle in the way that he himself, before the transforming events of that night, would have chosen as of course for himself:

> o terque quaterque beati
> quis ante ora patrum Troiae sub moenibus altis
> contigit oppetere! o Danaum fortissime gentis
> Tydide! mene Iliacis occumbere campis
> non potuisse tuaque animam hanc effundere dextra,
> saevus ubi Aeacidae telo iacet Hector, ubi ingens
> Sarpedon, ubi tot Simois correpta sub undis
> scuta virum galeasque et fortia corpora volvit!

O thrice and four times blessed, to whom it fell to die before the faces of the fathers beneath the lofty walls of Troy! O Tydides, bravest of the race of Danaans! Why could I not have fallen upon the Ilian fields and poured forth this soul by your right hand—where fierce Hector lies fallen by the spear of Aiacides, where huge Sarpedon lies, where Simois churns beneath its waves so many swept-off shields of men, so many helmets and brave bodies!

(1.94–101)

Aeneas' regretful prayer is pressed from him at a moment when any possible high purpose of his flight from the falling city, and thus any possible approving interpretation of what he has done, appears about to be cut off forever by his senseless death at sea.[2] Having been saved from that event, when he recounts his actions to Dido at her feast he is no longer so directly exposed to extreme self-doubt about their meaning, and his way of telling his story is very open to the view that he behaved well. But it is only *open* to that view, without compelling it. The meaning of the events during the fall of Troy is still uncertain to Aeneas and thus to us as well.

Book 2 unfolds in two movements: the story of Sinon and the horse, and the story of Aeneas' experiences during the final battle. The story of Sinon shows how the Greeks took Troy through fraud, by presenting to the pious

Trojans a false appearance of piety; the story of Aeneas' experiences in the battle shows how the apparent truth behind the Greeks' false piety is only another appearance, behind which lies the deeper truth that Troy fell not through human fraud but through a beneficent plan of the gods. It may be said that the lesson of the first movement is that the truth of things is human force and fraud, so that human beings ought to look out for themselves without reliance on any gods. This lesson discloses itself by entirely natural means, through a comparison of Sinon's speeches with the actions of the Greeks. The lesson of the second movement is that the truth of things is divine providence, so that human beings ought to abandon all reliance on their own understanding of their situation in favor of obedience to the gods. This lesson is disclosed only by divine revelation, by supernatural images seen and heard by Aeneas during the battle. The Trojans were susceptible to the Greeks' fraud because of their belief in divine government of the human world; the exposure of the Greeks' fraud implies that there is no divine government of the human world; but this implication is refuted in its turn by the teaching of the gods as communicated in dreams and visions.

ii. Sinon and the Trojan Horse (2.13–267)

Sinon's story is as follows. He had been sent to Troy by his father as a follower of his kinsman Palamedes (86–87); and as long as Palamedes was strong among the kings at Troy, Sinon himself had been respected (88–90). But Palamedes tried to stop the war (*bella vetabat*, 84). Palamedes' motive in this was somehow not disloyal to the Greek cause (Sinon does not explain the matter), but the Greeks' response to Palamedes' attempt was to frame him on a false charge of treason (83–84); and, through the envy of the wicked Ulysses, Palamedes was put to death (90–91). Sinon loyally, if somewhat imprudently, protested Palamedes' death and threatened to take vengeance for it after the war (94–96), thus attracting against himself the further scheming of Ulysses (97–99). Ulysses wanted to deal with Sinon as he had with Palamedes, and was on the lookout for some charge that could be brought against Sinon. It was in these circumstances, according to Sinon's story, that Diomedes and Ulysses performed an impious deed that caused the collapse of the Greek forces through divine punishment. This deed was the capture of the Palladium. From the start, all the Greeks' hopes in the war had always rested on Pallas' support (162–163). But the capture of the Palladium from its temple in the Trojan citadel by the impious Diomedes and Ulysses the inventor of crimes (163–165), so far from securing or demonstrating Pallas' support of the Greek cause, caused Pallas to become angry. Whether because it violated the sanctity of her temple (165), or because of the murder of the sentries (166), or because Diomedes and Ulysses touched her virginal fillets while their hands were bloodied by that murder (167–168)—from that time the hopes of the Greeks ebbed and their strength was broken; the mind of the goddess was set against them (169–170). The goddess made her displeasure evident through monstrous apparitions once her statue was placed in the Greek camp: flames blazed from its eyes, sweat broke out on its limbs, she herself flashed forth three times bearing shield and spear (171–175). The Greeks' seer Calchas interpreted all this to mean that the Greeks could never take Troy unless they first returned to Argos with the Palladium to take the omens anew, and then brought the Palladium back to Troy under these new omens (176–178); and this, explains Sinon, is what they in fact have sailed off to do (179–182). Furthermore, Calchas instructed the Greeks to build the wooden horse, to be left at Troy as an expiatory offering to the offended Pallas; if the Trojans should harm it, it would insure the destruction of Priam's kingdom, but if they should bring it into their city, it would insure the destruction of Greece by Troy (183–194). But after the Greeks had built the horse and were prepared to set sail on their mission to take new omens, thunderstorms prevented their departure from Troy, as stormy weather had often previously prevented them from fleeing when they were exhausted by the long war (108–113). Therefore the Greeks sent Eurypylus to the oracle of Apollo to inquire. Eurypylus returned with a terrible reply: as the Greeks had sailed from Aulis at the cost of Iphigenia's blood, so they must sail from Troy at the cost of Argive blood (116–118). The oracle however had not named the person whose blood must pay for this sailing. Calchas, though hard pressed by Ulysses, was unwilling for a long time to name the victim intended by the oracle. Sinon implies that Calchas was having a long struggle with his conscience: Ulysses wanted him to name Sinon, out of resentment at Sinon's having protested the execution of Palamedes, but Calchas was at first reluctant to do this; it took him ten days to reconcile himself to acting as Ulysses' minister in this business (*donec Calchante ministro,* 100). Then at the very last minute, when everything was prepared for the sacrifice of Sinon, Sinon himself escaped. His plan was to wait in hiding until the Greeks had set sail, as they now have (132–136; Sinon does not mention whether they had sacrificed a stand-in for him, or how they had satisfied the gods' demand for Argive blood). Realizing that it will never be safe for him to return to his country, Sinon has now emerged from hiding to throw himself on the mercy of the Trojans (137–144).

Sinon's art of perjury, as observed by all commentators, rests on his ability to make the plausible falsehoods depend on known truths. His story appeals to the following truths: 1) the execution of Palamedes by the Greeks; 2) the capture of the Palladium by the Greeks, with their murder of the Trojan sentries; 3) the thunderstorms; 4) the sacrifice of Iphigenia at Aulis; and 5) the visible absence of the Greek fleet from Troy, and the presence there of Sinon and the wooden horse. Of these truths, numbers 2, 3, and 5 are known to the Trojans by their own experience, numbers 1 and 4 by report only.

It turns out that Sinon is lying about the purpose of the Trojan horse. So far from being the innocent victim of the impious Ulysses, Sinon is the brazen mouthpiece of an elaborate perjury concocted by the Greeks in common in order to gain entrance into Troy. What took in the Trojans was the familiarity in Sinon's story of all its assumptions about divine favor and anger and the lengths to which the Greeks were willing to go in order to win the one and avoid or conciliate the other. If we rehearse Sinon's story in the light of events, and particularly in the light of our knowledge that its perjury was the deliberate product of Greek counsel, we see that the truth was something like the following.

Sinon had nothing to do with Palamedes. Whatever the cause of the Greeks' injustice against that hero, there is no reason to think that either Sinon or any human being or any god punished or threatened to punish the Greeks for it. The capture of the Palladium by Diomedes and Ulysses, so far from being an offense to the goddess, was simply an instance of the Greeks' superior daring. It did not mean that the Greeks were exposed to divine punishment. It meant that just as Diomedes and Ulysses had penetrated the citadel by stealth to capture the statue that the Trojans regarded as safeguarding their city, and thus undermined the confidence of the pious Trojans, so the whole Greek army would soon penetrate the citadel by stealth—as indeed that very night they proceeded to do. The goddess whom the Trojans regard as their protectress in the form of the Palladium does not punish those who violate her temple, her sentries, her virginal fillets. After capturing the Palladium in token of their superior daring and intelligence, the Greeks, encouraged by this success, planned how they could open the city to themselves through an even more brazen fraud. In accordance with their plan they built the horse, retired to Tenedos (after waiting out an unplanned thunderstorm), and left Sinon to deceive the Trojans with his elaborate story (a story that cleverly transforms the thunderstorm from a chance nuisance into a significant piece of plot). Calchas was never at any point consulted about propitiating any gods; the oracle of Apollo was never consulted about the meaning of any thunderstorm; the Greeks were never of the opinion that they had offended or might offend any gods, and no gods ever gave them reason for such an opinion. The Greeks' object was to penetrate Troy by any means; they succeeded in this by perjury, and with impunity; they won the war as a result of it. Troy fell because the Trojans took Sinon's oaths seriously, believing as they did that the gods punish perjury. But so far from being punished for abusing the good faith of the Trojans in the name of the gods, Sinon and the Greeks were rewarded with victory in the war.

Sinon's story is framed in Aeneas' narrative by the story of Laocoon, the Trojan priest whose sound advice against trusting the horse is rejected by the Trojans, to whom he appears to be punished by the goddess before their very eyes. In retrospect, Aeneas interprets the Trojans' fatal rejection of their priest's counsel as stemming from either the fates of the gods or the Trojans' own folly of mind: *si fata deum, si mens non laeva fuisset . . . Troia . . . nunc staret* (54–56). Before Sinon's appearance on the scene, the Trojans had been divided in counsel about the horse. Thymoetes led a party urging that the horse be brought into the city, and Capys a party urging that the horse be destroyed or investigated, i.e., opened; the uncertain multitude (*incertum vulgus*) was divided between the two counsels (32–39). Aeneas himself appears to have been "a part of these things" (6) in the sense of being a part of the uncertain multitude; but now, in retrospect, he characterizes Thymoetes' view as arising from either fraud or fate, *sive dolo seu iam Troiae sic fata ferebant* (34), while Capys' view arose from better judgment of mind, *melior sententia menti* (35). That Thymoetes may have been a traitor to Troy reminds us that the split among the Trojans regarding the disposition of the horse will have been one of many, of continuous splits among them regarding the prosecution of the war. Thymoetes may have had a personal score to settle with Priam,[3] but many Trojans will have had doubts about the plausibility of their own cause and the prospects of victory—like Palamedes on the Greek side, there will always have been Trojans who "tried to stop the war."[4] If Thymoetes' counsel aimed at treachery, it was well fashioned to that end; if from the fates, then dullness of human thought must be one of the ways in which the fates operate. Still, fate or no fate, Capys and his party had taken a perfectly clear-headed approach to the question of dealing with the horse; and at the moment before Sinon's entry upon the scene, Laocoon's speech and actions seemed almost certainly to have carried the day for their view.

The whole controversy about the horse resides in the question whether it is to be understood as a *religio* or as a *machina belli* (151). Whatever Thymoetes' real motive, his view finds sympathy because the horse is assumed by many Trojans to be a *religio*, a votive offering to Athene, and is therefore thought to be able to cause Athene's favor and disfavor. Capys' party, on the other hand, regard the horse as purely a product of human artifice that would have to be understood humanly in terms of the Greeks' probable intentions not toward

Athene but toward the Trojans. The priest Laocoon, with all the advantage of his priestly knowledge, does not include any sort of *religio* among the possible interpretations of the horse that he offers: either there are Greeks hidden inside it, or it is an engine of war, or there is some deception somewhere (45–48); "whatever it is, I fear the Greeks even when they bring gifts" (*quidquid id est, timeo Danaos et dona ferentis*, 49). Laocoon is much wiser than his fellow Trojans about the difference between human and divine things. Knowing the Greeks, knowing in particular Ulysses, he is not taken in by the popular report that the horse is a *religio*. Knowing the Trojans, he tries with consummate art to open their eyes to the need to deal with the horse strictly as an instrument of Greek guile; he regards the Trojans' openness to the religious interpretation as *insania* (42).[5] As Servius observes, Laocoon chooses his words carefully so as to emphasize to them the naturalness of the horse, its being "just a piece of wood," and thus weaken their susceptibility to religious imaginings.[6] Indeed Vergil has made him rap out his list of alternative explanations of the horse in a strikingly Lucretian manner, "whether x, or y . . . whatever it is . . ." where the prosey *quidquid id est* is Lucretius' familiar tag.[7] As Lucretius in his account of the causes of motions of the heavenly bodies (5.509–770) raps out alternative possible causes to emphasize the overriding point that although *the* cause of any of these motions cannot be known for sure, all the possibilities are natural and not divine, so Laocoon here argues that although *the* cause of the horse cannot be known for sure, it is certain that this cause is human and not divine. But however close he comes to persuading them of the truth, the popular report that the horse is a *religio* fits in with their idea that the Greeks would certainly be driven to expiate somehow their impious removal of the Palladium in order to avoid divine punishment; so when Laocoon's appeal is interrupted by the entrance of Sinon, the Trojans are predisposed to believe Sinon's religious explanation of the horse.

Aeneas' narrative makes it seem that the Trojans—*pium genus*, as Ilioneus had characterized them to Dido (1.526)—may be somewhat too inclined to take a religious view of things; and Aeneas seems to include himself, *pius Aeneas*, in the Trojan multitude taken in by Sinon's story (2.195–198). When Sinon finished speaking, Laocoon was in the act of sacrificing a bull to Neptune (201–202)—apparently he had not stayed around to listen to Sinon's story, but had got on with his own business, perhaps hoping that what he could not achieve by argument to the Trojans he might achieve by the authority of his office. Aeneas shudders to recall (204) how at that very moment, when the Trojans, who had successfully resisted ten years of siege and a thousand ships, had fallen to Sinon's art of perjury, a pair of serpents suddenly appeared in the sea making from Tenedos. As the Trojans had just been

confirmed in their predisposition to perceive the wooden horse as a *religio*,
now they are even more predisposed to see the serpents in this light: they are
in the frame of mind to fall in with Greek wiles by seeing every unusual
occurrence as a display of purposeful divine forces.[8]

When the serpents came ashore they made straight for Laocoon while the
crowd scattered in terror (212–213). Actually they didn't make straight for Laocoon but straight for Laocoon's two small sons (213–215), who may not have
been able to flee as quickly as the adults, and presented therefore an obvious tar-
get; the serpents did not attack Laocoon until he attacked them in defense of
his sons (216–217); no one came to Laocoon's defense. In effect Laocoon lived
out in earnest among the Trojans the sacrificial part that Sinon had lyingly as-
cribed to himself as a tale plausible to Trojans. The Trojans did not kill Laocoon
themselves, but they watched him die like a sacrificial bull:

> ille simul manibus tendit divellere nodos
> perfusus sanie vittas atroque veneno,
> clamores simul horrendos ad sidera tollit:
> qualis mugitus, fugit cum saucius aram
> taurus et incertam excussit cervice securim.

While he strained to tear away their coils with his hands, with his fillets
drenched in gore and black venom, he raised horrendous shouts to the stars:
like the lowing when a wounded bull flees the altar and shakes loose from his
neck the axe that has missed its true mark.

(2.220–224)

They watched him die in the belief that he deserved punishment for his
impiety in attacking the wooden horse. Indeed they believed that his death
was punishment, divine punishment, for that deed, and that they themselves
would escape punishment and win favor by bringing the horse into the goddess's shrine:

> et scelus expendisse merentem
> Laocoonta ferunt, sacrum qui cuspide robur
> laeserit et tergo sceleratam intorserit hastam.
> ducendum ad sedes simulacrum orandaque divae
> numina conclamant.

They said that Laocoon had paid deservedly for the crime of injuring the sacred oakwood with his spear and boring his criminal shaft into its back. They
all shouted that the image must be brought home and the divinity of the goddess invoked in prayer.

(229–233)

Aeneas tells this entire story in the knowledge that, as events showed, the wooden horse was not a sacred thing, Laocoon's hurling his spear at it was not an impious deed, and thus Laocoon's death was not a divine punishment for impiety. While he refrains from drawing the inference explicitly, the whole thrust of his story is to the effect that either the fate of Laocoon was an accidental natural event having nothing whatsoever to do with Laocoon's stance towards the horse (and possibly could have been averted if the Trojans had not abandoned him to the serpents), or, if the fate of Laocoon was brought about by gods, its purpose was not to punish him for any wrong he had done but to complete by divine fraud the human fraud practiced on the Trojans by Sinon. Either there are no gods seeing to the deserts of men, and things happen by chance and necessity; or the gods are actually hostile to the welfare of pious men,[9] and promote fraud and injustice.

It is noteworthy that Aeneas himself frankly includes himself, by his use of the first person plural, in the crowd of Trojans acting in concerted folly under the influence of Sinon's speeches: he fled with the others at the sight of the serpents (212); he participated in opening the city gates (234) and forcing the horse through them (including himself in his judgment that they were all "senseless and blind with furor") (244); he joined the others in setting up the horse in the citadel (245) and in decking out the shrines of the gods with festal wreaths (248–249) as if in celebration of a great national deliverance. But in the midst of this narrative of his participation in the crowd's deeds, he distances himself from the crowd's judgment of Laocoon, and their consequent decision to bring the horse into the citadel, by using for it the third person plural (*ferunt* 230, *conclamant* 233). This manner of narration[10] compels us to envision Aeneas, while sharing generally in the Trojan folly after the appearance of the serpents, as nonetheless observing the fate of the priest in some division of mind, hanging back from joining in the others' condemnation of him as justly punished, wondering about the meaning of it.

Aeneas then saw and was a part of all these events, from the Trojans' inspection of the abandoned Greek camp to the festal decoration of the shrines. What he describes next, 250–267, neither he nor any Trojan saw: the return of the Greek fleet, Sinon's release of the picked Greek warriors from the horse, their opening the city gates to the whole Greek army. Aeneas describes these things as he has come to visualize them in the light of his later knowledge. In particular, he conceives the approach of the Greek ships from Tenedos in the image of the approach of the serpents from Tenedos.

The first movement of Book 2 has contrasted the fates of Laocoon and Sinon in such a way as to make it deeply questionable whether there is any divine oversight of human affairs, and in particular whether Greek victory is not due to godless perjury and Trojan defeat to god-fearing honesty: it would seem that the impiety of its citizens, so far from being liable to bring down divine punishment on a city, is rather rewarded—whether by gods or by nature—with success and prosperity. Dido undoubtedly, hearing this opening movement of the story, is confirmed in her views, and may expect Aeneas to see in his own narrative the evidence for them: the Trojans were defeated not because of any lack of valor but because, unlike the Greeks and the Carthaginians, they were not able to put aside considerations of the requirements of piety when the needs of their city called for this. Laocoon, the devoted father, faithful priest, and wise counselor of his fellow citizens, is destroyed in agony after watching the cruel deaths of his children and seeing himself abandoned by his people; he is disgraced in death by the judgment of the Trojans he tried to save. Sinon, swearing to lies by the eternal fires' inviolable divinity (154–155), saves himself and the Greeks, sees the complete triumph of his undertaking and the destruction of the enemy, and not only gets away with it but is somehow protected by the inequitable or iniquitous fates of the gods (*fatisque deum defensus iniquis*, 257). Fraud and perjury bring success to men and nations; truthfulness and god-fearingness bring destruction that oddly wears the look of punishment—either because through folly of mind accidental events are mistaken for the consequences of human deeds, or because in truth piety is against nature and necessarily brings upon itself nature's punishment. The heavenly bodies by whose divinity Sinon mockingly swears, and to which Laocoon raises his horrendous cries, are either blind and deaf to human deserts or actually favor impious fraud over pious just dealing.

iii. The Dream-Vision of Hector: 2.268–297

Although in the Sinon episode Aeneas saw pitiable things and was a part of them, he was not a great part of them (2.6); it was only after the entry of the Greeks into the city, only when it was a matter of giving battle rather than counsel, that Aeneas himself in his own right became a great part of events. In his narrative to Dido, he portrays himself beginning the night of battle as the Homeric Aeneas; being shaken in the course of it by supernatural visions claiming his obedience to demands for such conduct as nothing in the education of the Homeric Aeneas had ever prepared him for; and leaving Troy as the bearer of a new view of life. His experience during the final battle is marked by a sequence of three visions that successively transform him from the old Homeric to the new Roman hero: the dream vision of Hector, the revelation of Venus, and the apparition of Creusa's shade. These visions cumulatively turn him from the resolve to seek a noble death in battle to the resolve to save himself. It is difficult for him to make this turn without coming to despise himself as base; his action in the battle is indistinguishable from cowardice[11] except by the standard of the three visions that he alone sees.[12] In the course of the battle, the apparent lesson of the Sinon episode is revealed to Aeneas as yet another false appearance. For behind it, according to his visions, lies the truth of a divine plan in which all the evidences of the gods' absence or injustice turn out to have a different meaning, a plan in the light of which the shocking fates of Laocoon and Sinon are after all justified.

Aeneas incongruously characterizes the time of night at which the vision of Hector appeared to him as the time when first sleep begins for afflicted mortals (*mortalibus aegris*) and creeps into them most pleasingly by the gift of the gods (268–269). As he had three lines earlier described the Greeks as entering a Troy already buried—"buried in sleep and wine" (265)—this "gift of the gods" that had buried the city seems to be intelligible as a gift only insofar as death is the proper remedy of the mortals' affliction.[13] Aeneas' words have an uncharacteristic edge of bitterness or even self-parody: he had welcomed sleep on the fatal night, comforted by the delusion that the gods provide for afflicted mortals and had provided for Troy.

> in somnis, ecce, ante oculos maestissimus Hector
> visus adesse mihi largosque effundere fletus.

> In my sleep, lo! before my eyes most mournful Hector seemed to be present to me, and to pour forth copious tears.

> (270–271)

Hector appeared as when being dragged by Achilles' chariot: black with bloody dust and with thongs piercing his swollen feet (272–273). To make the appearance of Hector imaginatively vivid to Dido, Aeneas connects it both to the representation of the scene he had seen earlier on Dido's temple (*ter circum Iliacos raptaverat Hectora muros*, 1.483; *raptatus bigis ut quondam*, 2.272) and to the description he had heard earlier, from Venus, of the appearance to Dido of her murdered husband in dream (*crudelis aras traiectaque pectora ferro / nudavit*, 1.355–6; *aterque cruento / pulvere perque pedes traiectus lora tumentis*, 2.272–3). This emphasis on the familiar in Hector's appearance is Aeneas' editorial addition in retrospect; within the dream itself, the striking thing had been how changed Hector appeared (*quantum mutatus*, 274). The familiar Hector was Hector triumphantly wearing Achilles' armor, triumphantly hurling fire into the Greek ships (275–276), whereas this dream-

Hector had a filthy beard and hair stiffened with blood, and wore in place of Achilles' armor the many wounds he had received around the ancestral walls (277–279). The dreaming Aeneas had forgotten what had happened to Hector after the death of Patroclus. Seeing this strangely disfigured Hector pouring forth copious tears, Aeneas in his dream seemed to weep too and to address the hero in mournful speech (*maestas expromere voces*, 280, to suit *maestissimus Hector*, 270). Aeneas in his dream had forgotten what he "knew" when he went to sleep: that the war was over and the Greeks had gone home. It seemed to him rather that Hector had unaccountably been away while the Trojans, exhausted by hard battles and many casualties, had been awaiting him as their most reliable hope. Aeneas in his dream-tears addressed Hector as the missing savior of Troy with words compounded of praise, need, and reproach; until, brought up short by the strangeness of Hector's appearance—the incongruity between the Hector he is addressing and the assumptions on which he is addressing him—he changed course and asked about the cause of Hector's appearance (281–286).

To all this Hector said nothing; but neither did he allow Aeneas to continue asking empty questions: he cut off the stream of Aeneas' sad words by groaning deeply and speaking words that immediately showed him more radically "changed from that former Hector" than anything in his appearance had shown. For the change in Hector's appearance that is so unaccountable to the dreaming Aeneas is in fact an outer change that took place during Hector's lifetime, and that Aeneas remembered before he fell asleep and will remember again after he awakens; but the change reflected in the words Hector now speaks is an inner change that took place between Hector's death and the present crisis, and that Aeneas could have no way of knowing about except for the evidence of this dream itself. *"Heu fuge,"* Hector says, cutting off as inconsequential all Aeneas' confused dream-thoughts to present Aeneas with something truly amazing: Hector urging flight, Hector urging the Trojan hero to give up the falling city for lost and escape alive.

For the familiar Hector, the Homeric Hector, stands for an unequivocal opinion about heroic virtue. The known Hector is he who, when Andromache pleaded with him not to widow her and orphan their child for the glory of a noble death, had explained himself as follows:

> All these
> things are in my mind also, lady; yet I would feel deep shame
> before the Trojans, and the Trojan women with trailing garments,
> if like a coward I were to shrink aside from the fighting;
> and the spirit will not let me, since I have learned to be valiant

and to fight always among the foremost ranks of the Trojans,
winning for my own self great glory, and for my father.
. . . some day seeing you shedding tears a man will say of you:
"This is the wife of Hektor, who was ever the bravest fighter
of the Trojans, breakers of horse, in the days when they fought about Ilion."
(*Iliad* 6.440–446, 459–461, Lattimore translation)

The known Hector is he who, when the seer Poulydamas urged a prudent with-
drawal of the army on the basis of his interpretation of a bird sign from Zeus, re-
torted: "One bird sign is best: to fight in defense of our country" (*Iliad* 12.243).

It is from this known Hector, the champion of the Achillean glory of a
self-disregarding death against all considerations of the preservation of city,
family, and self, that Aeneas' dream-Hector is most shockingly changed. The
dream-Hector, dismissing all Aeneas' thoughts and puzzlements, perempto-
rily charges him:

'heu fuge, nate dea, teque his' ait 'eripe flammis.
hostis habet muros; ruit alto a culmine Troia.
sat patriae Priamoque datum: si Pergama dextra
defendi possent, etiam hac defensa fuissent.

O flee, goddess-born, and save yourself from out of these flames. The enemy
occupies our walls; Troy is falling from its lofty summit. You have given enough
to your fatherland and to Priam; if Troy could be defended with the right hand,
it would have been defended by this of mine.

(2.289–292)

Hector's calculation of what is enough to have given to king and fatherland
before saving oneself is clear: it is enough to have given everything up to the
point where the city could still be saved by one's sacrifice. It is not required
to die for a lost cause; Troy is a lost cause. Hector rejects the shame that had
prevented him from accepting any such calculation himself: he urges Aeneas
to be reasonable. Aeneas, like Hector, was ashamed to shrink aside from the
fighting because, like Hector, he had "learned to be valiant and to fight always among the foremost ranks of the Trojans, winning for his own self great
glory, and for his father," so that even after the destruction of his city he himself will still be renowned as "ever the bravest fighter of the Trojans, breakers of horses, in the days when they fought about Ilion." Aeneas' dream-
Hector, by exhorting Aeneas to flee and save himself, conveys that since his
death he has changed his most fundamental conviction: he now sees the
shame that was the foundation of their common education, their bulwark
against the inclination to unmanly deeds, as misplaced.

To this point, Hector's shocking speech urging this shameful action is a mere command that has nothing to recommend it to Aeneas but the authority of Hector himself; but now Hector adds a consideration that suggests how Aeneas can carry out this apparent counsel of cowardice without viewing himself as a coward, how he can replace the foundation of his education in heroic shame or pride with a new foundation in obedient piety. When thinking of "Troy" he must think that the city itself, the essence of the city, resides not in its ancestral walls, and not in the assembly of living and dead ancestors represented by those walls, but in the city gods as separable from those walls:

> sacra suosque tibi commendat Troia penatis;
> hos cape fatorum comites, his moenia quaere
> magna, pererrato statues quae denique ponto.

> Troy commends to you her sacred things and her penates. Take these as the companions of your fates, with these seek the great walls that you will ultimately establish after crossing the sea.

> (2.293–295)

Hector here provides his exhortation to self-preservation with an end beyond itself, that of preserving Troy's gods and settling them in different walls. No such consideration had ever been offered to Hector himself in the *Iliad* by those who urged him to avoid death: Poulydamas had urged calculation of the best chance of saving Troy; Andromache, Priam, and Hecuba had urged their own interest in his preservation as their own husband or son. The reason for self-preservation that Hector presents to Aeneas is one that he himself had never rejected in his lifetime. The purport of this reason is to dignify the apparently craven action it recommends, so as to outweigh the force of the uncalculating shame that opposes that action. In the dream, Hector illustrates what he has just said by putting into Aeneas' hands the Vesta and the eternal fire drawn from the innermost shrine (296–297). With these in his charge, Aeneas is to envision himself as motivated by the highest rather than the lowest ends in fleeing the falling city: he is commissioned not to save himself but to save the city by removing its gods from its walls.

Vergil has cast Aeneas' account of his dream of Hector in such terms as to recall Lucretius' account of sleep and dreams (*De Rerum Natura* 4.722 ff. and 1.124 ff.). The most striking thing about Aeneas' condition in his dream, his having forgotten that Hector was dead and the war was (as he thought) over, illustrates the fundamental Lucretian doctrine of dreams. When we are asleep our minds are struck by the same streams of atoms as when we are awake, but what differentiates sleep from waking is that in sleep all the senses and the memory are inactive and cannot refute falsehood with known truth, with the result that

> we seem to see him whose life has been lost and whom death and earth already have in their power. . . . And withal the memory is at rest and heavy with sleep, and does not object that the one whom the mind believes it is seeing alive is already long since in the power of death and oblivion.
>
> (DRN 4.760–761, 765–767)

Aeneas' narrative emphasis on this typical forgetfulness of the dreaming subject will then have had the ring of verisimilitude to his Lucretian audience at Carthage. And the content of his dream, the mournful Hector pouring forth copious tears, will have reminded them of Lucretius' most vivid presentation of a dream, Ennius' dream of Homer. This passage is the climax of Lucretius' introductory argument against religion that leads up to his exposition of the first principles of Epicurean physics. Having illustrated through the Greeks' sacrifice of Iphigenia[14] the evils to which religion can persuade men (101), Lucretius argues that the reason why seers have got such a hold on men's hearts through threats of punishment after death is that men are ignorant of the true nature of the soul, its origin and its fate, whether it survives the body at death and thus whether it is possibly subject to eternal punishment (102–116). Men are not just neutrally ignorant about the soul, but they have a partiality toward imagining it surviving the body in one way or another—going to dwell in the shadows of Orcus, or insinuating itself by divine agency into other animals. This partiality is due to the influence on men of the great poets such as our own Ennius, who presented a whole teaching about the fate of our souls based on his interpretation of a dream he had had in which Homer seemed to appear to him and instruct him in words about the nature of things (117–126).

In Ennius' dream Homer appeared to him pouring forth salty tears (*lacrimas ecfundere salsas*, 1.125, as Hector had appeared to Aeneas *largos effundere fletus*, *Aen.* 2.271). Hector's tears were the visible sign of his knowledge of what Aeneas was ignorant of, the fall of Troy; so too Homer's tears were the visible sign of his knowledge, or rather his opinion, of what Ennius had been ignorant of, the nature of things: for according to Homer it is the lamentable nature of things that after death neither our bodies nor our souls are perduring, but only certain shadows of ourselves, pale in wondrous ways (122–123). Therefore, concludes Lucretius—because, that is, we do not know the true nature of the soul and are inclined to be impressed by such poetic reports as that of Ennius—therefore we must get a rational account both of the things in the heavens and, especially, of the nature of the soul. In order to understand and therefore be able to reject Ennius' dream-vision of Homer, we must find out what it is that terrifies us, coming before our minds when we are awake but ill and when we are buried in sleep,[15] in such a way that we seem to see and hear face-to-face those who are already dead.

Vergil has composed Aeneas' account of his dream-vision of Hector so as to put before us as vividly as possible the question raised by the dream. Was it a direct revelation to Aeneas of a truth that supercedes his education in Achillean heroism, showing on superhuman authority that Aeneas has a higher end than immortal glory, and thus that his flight from Troy is not cowardly but heroic? Or was it an all-too-natural illusion arising from the inactivity of his senses and memory during sleep, and later misinterpreted by him in harmony with his all-too-natural wish to justify his base action?

iv. The Revelation of Venus (2.298–633)

Perhaps the most amazing thing about Aeneas' dream of Hector is that although he remembers it so vividly now, seven years later, when he is narrating it to Dido and her court, he did not remember it at all when he awakened from it, or at any time during the events of that critical night.[16] Aeneas was awakened from sleep not by his dream but by an external noise, which he now knows was the noise of the real-world battle coming ever closer to where he lay in his father's house. Shaken from sleep by this noise, Aeneas climbed onto the rooftop and stood there with his ears pricked up (298–303). Having thus put himself in the best attitude to see and hear, and thus to figure out the meaning of the noise, Aeneas at first could make nothing of it. Vergil makes him express his condition in a remarkable simile:

> in segetem veluti cum flamma furentibus Austris
> incidit, aut rapidus montano flumine torrens
> sternit agros, sternit sata laeta boumque labores
> praecipitisque trahit silvas: stupet inscius alto
> accipiens sonitum saxi de vertice pastor.

> Just as when a fire falls upon the crops when the south winds are raging, or the violent torrent of a mountain stream razes the fields, razes the fertile plantings and the oxen's labors, and drags off the forest trees headlong: a shepherd, perceiving the sound from the lofty summit of a cliff, is dumbstruck with incomprehension.

> (2.304–308)

This simile refers to Homer's similes in such a way as to drive home an essential difference between the Homeric and the Vergilian hero. In the *Iliad*, as here, distance from the scene of battle is the matrix of similes. It is typically from great heights, and preeminently from Mt. Olympus itself, that the scenes of battle look like something other than scenes of battle; and it is therefore preeminently the gods, and heroes only when in the most godlike of states, who see the battle as looking like forest fires, storms at sea, fields of grain, rivers in flood, the reaping of grain, and so on. The distant view of the battle yields not only a characteristic cognition of the likeness in the appearances of things, but also a characteristic feeling of godlike pleasure in the beauty of the appearances. The cumulative lesson of the Iliadic similes is that divine insight and pleasure arise from the peculiar perspective that brings into view the beautiful likeness of all things.

Vergil makes Aeneas surprise us, by contrast, with the characterization of the distant viewer not as delighting his heart in the beautiful surface of things but as being dumbstruck at the menacing unintelligibility of things. His high vantage point gives not a purchase on divine pleasure but a sinister intimation of men's inability to grasp the natural disaster of things, the leveling of all their works by fire and flood. Vergil's reversal of the Homeric simile of the distant viewer here is mediated by Lucretius' illustrations of the primacy of the sense of touch, and thus the inadequacy of our senses operating at a distance. Just as from a distance a flock of sheep in varied activity looks like a still white patch on a green background, just as from someplace high in the mountains a battle looks like a still patch of brightness in the fields, so the things around us look like stable, immobile objects when in truth they are, far below the threshold of our poor vision, battlefields of purposelessly colliding atoms in the ceaseless process of composition and decomposition (*DRN* 2.308–333).

After Aeneas' initial stupefaction at the overall scene, its particulars gradually brought the truth home to him. In his progress from uncomprehending stupefaction to the realization that the Greeks had taken Troy, it did not once occur to Aeneas that Hector had just told him this in his dream (*hostis habet muros, ruit alto a culmine Troia*, 290); and when he had realized by natural means what had just been revealed to him in supernatural vision, he did not remember that Hector had just bidden him flee from these flames with the Trojan penates. Instead, he responded unthinkingly, automatically, as his and Hector's common education had taught them to respond:

> arma amens capio; nec sat rationis in armis,
> sed glomerare manum bello et concurrere in arcem

cum sociis ardent animi; furor iraque mentem
praecipitat,[17] pulchrumque mori succurrit in armis.

Mindlessly I take up arms; nor is there enough reason in arms, but my spirits burn to collect a troop for war and rush upon the citadel with my companions; furor and rage send my mind rushing headlong, and it occurs to me how it is noble to die under arms.

(2.314–317)

Aeneas' experience upon taking up arms (318 ff.) shows that the gods of Troy have been conquered by the perjured Greeks (320); savage Jupiter has given over everything to the Argives (326–327); Sinon has triumphed with impunity in his perjury (329–330); the Trojans' gods have abandoned the city (351–352); Trojan corpses are piled up not only in the streets but also on the religious thresholds of the gods (365);[18] the heavens were unaffected by Cassandra's raising her eyes to them (405); Coroebus was cut down at the altar of Athene (424–426); the justest man in Troy fell because somehow the gods saw things otherwise (426–428); many Trojans were mistakenly cut down by their own troops in the ghastly outcome of a Trojan attempt to imitate the enemy's fraud (390, 411, 428–429); and the priest Panthus' great piety and fillets of Apollo were no protection to him (429–430). Throughout these events, the dream vision of Hector is for Aeneas as if it had never happened; in retrospect he swears by the ashes of Troy that if it had been in his power to do so he would have fallen gloriously on that battleground (431–434) without a thought of Hector's charge to him.

The question about the gods raised first by the contrast between the cruel death of Laocoon and the cool triumph of Sinon, and then by Aeneas' experiences in the battle, is brought to yet a higher pitch, if that is possible, by the exchange Aeneas witnesses between Priam and Neoptolemus. The noncombatants of the royal family—the aged Priam and Hecuba, and their daughters—have taken refuge at the palace altar (513) when Neoptolemus bursts upon the scene in pursuit of the wounded Polites, and cuts him down there before his parents' eyes. Priam, as he shows in his indignant protest to Neoptolemus (535–543), thinks there is a relevant difference between killing a man on the field of battle and killing that same man at the altar of the gods before the eyes of his aged parents. He thinks the latter is an offense to the gods, and that one ought therefore, if there is in heaven any piety that cares about such things, to restrain oneself in fear of the gods' condign punishment; he thinks that one should be restrained also by the fear of disgracing one's father through such deeds, and the more so if one's father was the great Achilles who "blushed at the rights and trust of a suppliant" (540–542).

It is true that Priam omits to mention Achilles' desecration of Hector's body, an outrage that the gods themselves saw as the destruction of shame and a dishonor to the earth (*Iliad* 24.44–45, 54); but it is also true that Achilles had finally been accessible to the claims made by men and gods on behalf of shame and the earth, and had beaten down his anger.

Achilles' son, though, is full of scorn for Priam's talk of gods in heaven and fathers in the Underworld; he vaunts his freedom from such outmoded terrors in the sarcastic words with which he dispatches Priam to the next life:

> referes ergo haec et nuntius ibis
> Pelidae genitori. illi mea tristia facta
> degeneremque Neoptolemum narrare memento.
> nunc morere.

> So you will go as my ambassador and report these things to my father Pelides! Don't forget to recite my dreadful deeds to him, and tell him how Neoptolemus has degenerated from him! Now die.

> (2.547–550)

The encounter between the pious old king and the impious young warrior ends in total triumph for the latter. Aeneas sees Priam die at the altar, falling in the blood of his son and with the sight of his burning city before his eyes; and he sees Neoptolemus ("new-style war") behead the old man's corpse so as to leave it not only dead but "nameless" (550–558). The restraints of old-style war had kept the battle for Troy undecided for ten years; new-style war, throwing over those restraints, brings victory at last to men and nations. "If there is in heaven any piety that cares about these things," it is not in evidence in anything that Aeneas has seen so far during the fall of Troy.

Aeneas' next great experience on that night seems to confirm that whatever piety there may be in heaven, Priam was mistaken in thinking it exacts what any human being would regard as condign punishment (537–8); the human indignation that looks to the gods for support must come to terms with the truth that "the gods see it differently" (428). Until witnessing Priam's death, Aeneas has given all his thought to his city and king, none to his family. But now, when he sees the old king die so cruelly, an image of his dear sire steals upon him—*subiit cari genitoris imago*, 560—and then also the thought of his wife, house, and son (562–3). These images awaken Aeneas to the plight of his family, as the sounds of battle had earlier awakened him to the plight of his city: he now suddenly looks about him as if he had been in a trance until this point. Looking at the scene now from the roof of the palace, as earlier from the roof of his father's house, he notices that he is alone, his troops fallen or scattered; and in the glare of the conflagration of Troy he notices Helen cowering at the shrine of Vesta.[19]

With the images of his own family as the undercurrent[20] of his feelings and thoughts, Aeneas' reaction to the sight of Helen in the protection of the shrine repeats his earlier reaction to the sight of the Greeks invading Troy: a blaze of fury and the thought of what is beautiful or praiseworthy. But whereas in the earlier scene Aeneas' anger against the Greek enemy had been in perfect harmony with the beauty of dying under arms, here what his anger urges is not beautiful; for there is no glorious name in punishing a woman (583–584). But Aeneas overcomes this inhibiting effect of thought upon anger by arguing to himself that such punishment would be praiseworthy *if* undertaken not in the spirit of defeating an enemy but in the spirit of extinguishing sin (*nefas*) and satisfying one's ancestors' ashes (585–587)—if, that is, one performs it on behalf of the gods and the dead.[21] Aeneas, having persuaded himself that in this way—as the agent of divine punishment—he could act laudably on his anger without losing his self-respect, was being borne along by his infuriated mind when suddenly his mother appeared before his eyes in her full divinity, more vividly than she ever had done before (588–592), to show him that he is totally mistaken about what merits punishment: "the gods see it differently."[22]

Venus restrained Aeneas bodily and also with speech from her rosy lips (592–593). Her rosy lips, the mention of which in this place is defended by Servius and modern commentators as conventional,[23] seem rather to be remarked here because of what Aeneas has just been thinking about Helen. For if Helen deserved punishment because her desertion of her husband was the cause of the war (572), Venus, exactly in the erotic character represented by those rosy lips, was surely the cause of Helen's desertion of her husband. The incongruity of Aeneas' observation of his mother's rosy lips at this moment is already an unsettling intimation of the solemn words she presently speaks to him from those lips about crime and punishment:

> non tibi Tyndaridis facies invisa Lacaenae
> culpatusve Paris, divum inclementia, divum,
> has evertit opes sternitque a culmine Troiam.

> Not the hated face of Spartan Helen or the guilt of Paris, but the gods' inclemency, the gods', has overthrown these forces of yours and pulled down your Troy from its summit.

> (2.601–603)

With these words Venus introduces a divine revelation to Aeneas that is based on Athene's revelation to Diomedes in the *Iliad*: she removes the mist that obscures his mortal sight (604–606, cf. *Iliad* 5.127–128), so that he can see the divine reality that lies behind the human appearances and belies the human opinions about crime and punishment.

Venus offers her revelation in support of her urging Aeneas to think "first" of his father, wife, and son, and only afterwards, if at all, of his rage (594–598): his anger and his urge to punish the wrongdoers must yield to his care for preserving the objects of his love. Love first, fighting afterwards. In order to defuse Aeneas' anger, Venus begins by exculpating Helen and Paris: the hatred and blame heaped on Helen and Paris by Trojans and Greeks alike is misplaced; not they but the gods are responsible for the war. Venus' claim recalls the words of Priam to Helen in *Iliad* 3: "I am not blaming you: to me the gods are blameworthy / who drove upon me this sorrowful war against the Achaians" (3.164–165, Lattimore translation). Whatever combination of royal manners and insight into the causes of things had led Priam to his exoneration of Helen,[24] Venus here supports her exoneration of Helen by demonstrating *ad oculos* her claim that what appear to men to be tragic events compounded of human intention, action, and responsibility or guilt are in truth mere appearances, the reality behind which is the unexplained and intractable inclemency of the gods. Where clouded human vision shows the Greeks leveling the city of Troy, divine insight shows quite another scene:

hic, ubi disiectas moles avulsaque saxis
saxa vides, mixtoque undantem pulvere fumum,
Neptunus muros magnoque emota tridenti
fundamenta quatit totamque a sedibus urbem
eruit.

Here, where you see great buildings split apart and stones torn from stones and billowing smoke mingled with dust, it is Neptune who is shaking the walls and moving the foundations with his great trident and uprooting the entire city from its seat.

(2.608–612)

Where Aeneas sees Greeks leading the invasion of Troy, Venus shows him it is most savage Juno who is urging them on (612–614). Where Aeneas sees the citadel in flames, Venus urges him to look more carefully (*respice*): it is savage Pallas who is causing the flashing with her Gorgon head (615–616). Where Aeneas sees spirited Greeks assailing Trojan arms, Venus shows him it is really the Father himself, *ipse pater*, inciting gods against Troy

(617–618). From this revelation, Venus instructs Aeneas, he is to draw the inference that he must cease struggling and flee: *eripe, nate, fugam finemque impone labori* (619). Her exhortation recalls Hector's first words in Aeneas' earlier dream: *heu fuge, nate dea, teque his . . . eripe flammis* (289). Hector had justified his exhortation by asserting that the enemy (not the gods) had occupied Troy and charging Aeneas with the preservation of the Trojan penates; Venus justifies it by showing that it is the gods (not the enemy) who have Troy in their power; instead of Aeneas' duty to preserve the penates, she speaks of his duty to preserve his family, and promises to escort him safely back to his father's house.

When Athene in *Iliad* 5 removed the mist from Diomedes' eyes, she made him godlike by enabling him to distinguish, as normally only gods are able to distinguish, between gods and men. The result of this revelation to Diomedes is, by making him godlike in vision, to encourage him to surpass the usual limits of human achievement by doing battle against gods. When Venus here removes the mist from Aeneas' eyes, she likewise enables him to distinguish between gods and men—but in such a way as not to encourage heroic combat but to prove that the enemy is inexpugnable, and thus to justify flight. The truth made accessible by Athene's divine revelation to Diomedes in the *Iliad* is that the closer man comes to seeing the gods as the gods see themselves, the closer he comes to imitating them. Vergil's education of Aeneas requires him to reject the teaching of the *Iliad* as superceded by Venus' revelation: the truth is that the closer man comes to seeing the gods as the gods see themselves, the closer he comes to bowing before their inexpugnable power and turning to the preservation of himself and his own.[25] As a result of the revelation of Venus, what Aeneas sees after her departure is no longer Greeks at war with Trojans or the hated face of Spartan Helen, but the dreadful faces and great divinities of the gods in their enmity to Troy: *apparent dirae facies inimicaque Troiae / numina magna deum* (2.622–623).

Up to this point, the lessons conveyed to Aeneas by his experience during the fall of Troy may be summed up as follows. First, from the experience of Sinon's triumph, it seems that fraud and perjury are the way to victory, while justice and piety are unrewarded, not to say punished. And then, from the appearances of Hector's shade and of Venus in her full divinity, it seems that Aeneas is required to renounce the heroic deed of dying nobly under arms in favor of self-preserving flight. Hector has justified such flight in the name of preserving Troy's gods; Venus had appealed to Aeneas' love of his family as the only motive remaining after the revelation that not human guilt but divine inclemency is at work in the wars of men. One further lesson remains for Aeneas during the fall of Troy.

v. The Shade of Creusa (2.634–804)

Aeneas returns to his father's house with the intention of fleeing the burning city with his family, in accordance with Venus's instructions (and in accordance with Hector's too, though at the time he did not have this in mind). But his father refuses to leave. The speech Vergil here puts in Anchises' mouth is beautifully calculated to impress upon us how radically Aeneas' opinions are changed from the ancestral Trojan or heroic mores he shared with his father before his experiences during this night. In Anchises' remarkable speech he appears to approve Aeneas' own intention to flee, while excusing himself from flight by appealing to the weakness of old age. But while he tactfully says that the crucial difference between himself and Aeneas is age, he clearly means that the crucial difference is between his own fidelity to ancestral opinions and ways and the young people's fickleness or, frankly, cowardice: "I, the trembling old man, will of course go down in battle; you young people, go right ahead and save your skins; no, of course I don't mind about not getting buried, don't stay around just for that; treat me as dead already; the gods already hate me, Jupiter has already struck me with lightning; why shouldn't I now be abandoned by my strong young son so as to have no hope even of burial" (638–649). Everything Anchises says is calculated to undermine Aeneas' reliance on Venus' precepts and shame him into a resolution to stay and fight. Anchises succeeds: as a result of his speech, Aeneas returns to the resolution he had taken at the outset (314–317), to take up arms and die nobly in battle:

> arma, viri, ferte arma; vocat lux ultima victos.
> reddite me Danais; sinite instaurata revisam
> proelia. numquam omnes hodie moriemur inulti.

> Arms, men, take up arms! Their last light summons the conquered! Let me back at the Greeks, let me see the battles renewed again! Never will all of us die unavenged today.

> (2.668–670)

Surprisingly, Aeneas lets Anchises' speech change his mind without making any effort to explain to Anchises, who is so respectful of divine signs, the two divine visions that had led him to his resolution to flee. Instead of telling Anchises about Hector's peremptory charge to preserve the Trojan penates, or about the vision of the gods' inclemency that Venus has just showed him in justification of her command to flee, Aeneas limits himself to bitter reflection on the likelihood that Venus' safe conduct has enabled him to reach home only to see repeated there the slaying of the child before the father's eyes that he has just witnessed in the palace of Priam (657–667). For Anchises, the atrocities of the Greeks are reason to seek death in resisting them, not reason to flee; and Aeneas does not tell him the reasons for flight that would have weight with him. Why is Aeneas so ready to give up his own intention to obey the divine behests sooner than tell Anchises about them? Vergil suggests in this scene that the familiarity of Anchises' views of the requirements of manliness is still much more powerful in Aeneas than the plausibility of the strange divine commands. Perhaps he feels that an account of what has been revealed to him would not be believable to someone who had not seen it himself; perhaps, in the face of his father's stern reminder of the ancestral opinions, he can no longer summon up his own conviction of the truth of what he has seen.

What changes Anchises' mind is a miraculous sign, the appearance of a harmless flame about the temples of the young Ascanius (680–686). Anchises, who has despaired of Jupiter's favor ever since the time when Jupiter touched him with fire (648–649), thinks that this touching of his grandson with fire may presage the return of the divine favor, and prays for confirmation (687–691). When his prayer is immediately followed by thunder and a falling star, Anchises understands this as meaning that Jupiter, whom Venus has just revealed to Aeneas as bent on inspiriting the Greeks and the gods in their destruction of Troy, is after all swayed by the deserts of "our" piety. Thus he is "conquered" and "yields" (*victus* 699, *cedo* 704); he believes that the star's path toward Ida is an indication from the ancestral gods (*di patrii*, 702) that he is to follow it out of the city.

Anchises seems to understand the sign as follows. Before the sign, he understood "Troy" to be inextricably "in" the gods, families, and city walls of Troy, in such a way that with the destruction of the material city there could be no preservation of its gods and families. After the sign he thinks that after all "Troy" is "in" the gods themselves: *vestroque in numine Troia est* (703); the material city is dispensable; burial in the ancestral ground is dispensable.[26] Anchises' new understanding is in harmony with Hector's charge to Aeneas to take the penates and find walls for them; indeed Anchises' speech expresses even more clearly than Hector's had that the city resides in the city gods, not in the city walls. According to this view, fleeing with the gods is not abandoning the city but preserving the city: the city may have these walls or those walls, but the same gods make it the same city. Having come around to Aeneas' new view of things, Anchises is prepared to flee from Troy on Aeneas' shoulders, with the sacred things and the ancestral penates in his hands. It is now from Anchises' own mouth that Aeneas hears, for the third time during this night, the exhortation to flee: *nate, fuge, nate* (733).[27]

The shade of his wife Creusa, who vanishes during the flight out of the city, is the third and last of the visions of Aeneas during the fall of Troy. In her speech she offers him the strange consolation that no fault of his but the will of the gods, of Jupiter himself, is responsible for her death (776–779, 785–789); and she instructs him, implicitly in the name of Jupiter, to seek the kingdom that has been appointed for him in the Hesperian land (780–784). Creusa's words confirm and complete the messages of Hector and Venus. Regarding the great walls Hector had instructed Aeneas to establish for the penates, Creusa adds their location in Italy. Where Hector had left the impression that Aeneas was required to establish the new city on his own, Creusa adds that a kingdom and royal consort have already been appointed for him there (783–784); and she implies that the appointer of this kingdom, as well as the source of her prophetic knowledge of it, is Jupiter himself (779).[28] With regard to Jupiter, Creusa's speech complements Venus's revelation in an as yet mysterious way. Creusa assures Aeneas that it is not without the will of the gods, and of Jupiter in particular, that all these things are coming about (777). Aeneas had had no more reason to think that these things were coming about without the will of the gods than that they were coming about with the malign will of the gods. Creusa, with her prophetic insight from the other world, vindicates the gods: it was their will that Aeneas lose her, but rather than being taken captive by the Greeks she has been taken under the protection of the great mother of the gods (788); it was Jupiter's will that Aeneas not have Creusa as companion of his flight (778–779), but Jupiter's purpose is not to punish Aeneas but to provide for the "happy affairs and kingdom and royal consort" appointed for him in the Hesperian land. Apparently, in the eyes of a departed soul that can see further or understand more deeply than Aeneas himself, Jupiter's tearing down the city of Troy, inspiriting the Greeks and the gods in their destruction of Troy, was after all not simply *"inclementia"* (602) but part of the working out of a beneficent divine providence.

Aeneas' experiences during the fall of Troy have irreparably discredited for him the Achillean heroism of his Homeric past. On the one hand, his natural experience during the fall has led to the conclusion that fraud and perjury are better favored by gods or nature than courage and nobility; on the other hand, three purportedly divine revelations have instructed him that the preservation of Troy's gods for some future city is a higher motive than honor and immortal glory in defense of Troy's walls. These two refutations of Achillean heroism are incompatible with one another. At the time when he narrates all this to Dido, seven years after the events, Aeneas is inclined to believe that the authority of the divine revelations outweighs everything else, and that the apparent triumph of Greek wickedness in the fall of Troy is explainable by the gods' beneficent purposes. His purpose in telling Dido these things is, in large part, to explain to her why he cannot accept her invitation to settle in Carthage: he regards himself as bound by divine commands to establish a city for the Trojan gods in Italy. That this is his conviction emerges from his telling her so; that his conviction is weak emerges from his then forgetting it and settling in Carthage with Dido. His conviction is weak because his education is incomplete: he does not yet know, as we do, the meaning of Jupiter's plan for the new Trojan/Italian city; and he does not yet know whether the divine revelations that have appeared to him are true.

CHAPTER FIFTEEN

The Education of Aeneas: II

The education of Aeneas begins, during the fall of Troy, with the irruption into his experience of direct revelations from the dead and the gods. Aeneas is not the first man to have experienced this. But the credibility of the communications that other men have received from the gods and the dead was vouched for by their agreement with what men already knew from poetry and from ancestral tradition. The peculiarity of Aeneas' experience is that what the dead and the gods tell him is at odds with all of poetry and ancestral tradition. It requires him to renounce at once the striving for immortal glory, and afterwards the striving for domestic and intellectual bliss—every human aspiration to greatness or happiness known to mankind from poetry and tradition—in favor of actions that seem ignominious and ends that seem arbitrary and uncertain. But it is not only their unorthodox content that makes the divine admonitions questionable. The very experience of them is dubious, and easily forgotten or discounted under the influence of mundane experience—as Aeneas forgets or is silent about his visions of Hector and Creusa.

In order for Aeneas to act with reasonable confidence of the reality and divine source of his visions, he would have to know things that he does not know. Are the dead really alive, and privy to the prophetic wisdom of the gods, solicitous for the living and able to communicate with them? Do the gods really exist, care for and have power to promote the human good, and give revelations and guidance to human beings, reward and punish their souls? Is there really a human good for which glory, love, and science could all be reasonably renounced as inferior? Aeneas' visions during the fall of Troy could not be true unless the answer to all these questions is yes; but Aeneas does not have the knowledge from which this answer could be given. In Books 3–6 Vergil represents the progress of Aeneas' education with a view to this knowledge, the consummation of which occurs in his visit to the Underworld.

i. Polydorus

Like Achilles and Lucretius, Aeneas is shown that the familiar appearance of things is a human illusion, that a different reality comes into view from the perspective of the gods: things appear "otherwise" to the gods (*dis aliter visum*, 2.428). But for Aeneas the truth behind the appearances of things is such as to arouse shudderings not of divine pleasure but of sinister terror. The reality of things is not the beautiful likeness or unity of the appearances, not the intelligible regularity of the laws of nature, but the ugly and unintelligible doings of the gods and the dead. What if Lucretius' portrayal of pre-Epicurean man cowering in terror of incomprehensible divinities is the portrayal not of ignorant folly but of the human conduct most appropriate to the truth of things? What if pleasing the gods, winning the gods' favor, is not a matter of vile subjection to self-imposed, imaginary tyrants, but of acknowledging the truth of things and bowing to its necessity?

In Book 3 Aeneas tells Dido and her court that after the gods decided to overturn Priam's innocent nation (*evertere gentem / immeritam visum superis*, 3.1–2), the Trojans were driven on their journey by the auguries of those very gods (5): the mystery of the gods' apparent injustice was accompanied by the springing hope of the gods' guidance. The remnant of the nation overturned by the gods sets forth into exile with the penates and great gods as all their guide. As Aeneas had not told Anchises about his visions of Hector and Venus on the night of Troy's fall, so he keeps his counsel about his vision of Creusa: the notion that the Trojan refugees are to seek a kingdom in Italy is not publicly in play. Only the events of the journey itself, and especially the divine visions and prophecies that unfold during it, will gradually guide the Trojans toward acting in accord with the original injunction of Creusa[1]—just as during the battle only the unfolding of events had gradually guided Aeneas toward acting in accord with the original injunction of Hector. The injunctions of the dead and the gods are hard to interpret and easy to forget; only in retrospect, with the accumulation of events into a pattern, does their real significance come into view.

Aeneas at first understood his mission as the resettlement of the Trojan remnant in a new city, and naturally thought of resettling them in a land whose penates were allied with the penates of Troy. Thus he located his first walls in Thrace, in the land once ruled by Lycurgus, an ancient ally of Troy (13–18). Here, while sacrificing a bull to the supreme king of the celestial gods, Aeneas saw a miraculous sign, *mirabile monstrum*, when he tried to gather some shrubbery with which to wreathe the altar: the stems he pulled dripped blood. At this, frigid horror shook his limbs, and his freezing blood congealed with terror (19–30). But his terror was overcome by his desire to know, so he pulled up the stem of another shrub in order to find out the deeply hidden causes, *causas penitus temptare latentis* (32).

What he seems to mean is something like this. He knows that his breaking the stem cannot in itself be the cause of the stem's bleeding, because he has broken other stems without thereby causing them to bleed. The deeply hidden causes, then, may be discernible somewhere between the pulling up of the stems and their bleeding, if Aeneas is more attentive to what happens in this interval than he was the first time, when he was not expecting anything unusual to happen. Accordingly, Aeneas' second uprooting is slow and deliberate (*lentum, convellere, insequor*); but again dark blood "follows" (*sequitur*, 33) without the cause becoming manifest to Aeneas.

At this point, turning over many things in his mind, Aeneas adores the rural Nymphs and father Gradivus, praying that they may make the vision favorable and mitigate the omen. One of the many things Aeneas turned over in his mind[2] must have been the possibility that his effort to find the hidden causes might be displeasing to the gods. For in the first uprooting, Aeneas' pious intention to wreathe the altars was what led him to the act that was followed by the bleeding stem, but in the second uprooting it was the intentional exploration of the hidden causes of this monstrous phenomenon that was followed by a repetition of the phenomenon.[3] Aeneas in his prayer does not ask the gods to explain the causes to him, but to "mitigate the omen." By this he seems to mean that they should insure that when Aeneas discovers the deeply hidden causes by his own efforts, those causes may turn out not to be menacing to him, e.g., not to be warning him of some bloody event for himself or his people. After his prayer, accordingly, he returns to his experiment; and for the third time, with even greater effort, straining on his knees against the resisting sand, he attempts the stems. This time he hears a voice:

quid miserum, Aenea, laceras? iam parce sepulto,
parce pias scelerare manus.

Why, Aeneas, do you torment a poor wretch? Spare the buried man, forbear to incriminate your pious hands.

(3.41–42)

The speaker identifies himself as Polydorus and explains that the blood is not coming from the stem but from him, Polydorus, who was struck down here by many spears from which the spiky shrubs have grown up (41–46). It must be said that this revelation of the deeply hidden causes, so far from expelling the terror from Aeneas' mind, only heightens it:

tum vero ancipiti mentem formidine pressus
obstipui steteruntque comae et vox faucibus haesit.

Then truly, oppressed in mind with ambiguous fear, I was struck dumb, my hair stood on end, and my voice stuck in my throat.

(3.47–8)

As soon as the paralyzing terror left his bones, Aeneas consulted the leaders of the people, and especially his father, about the *monstra deum*, and followed their unanimous counsel to flee from this land of polluted hospitality. "Therefore" (62) they gave Polydorus the traditional funeral rites so as to bury his soul in the tomb (57–68).

In this Polydorus episode Vergil puts into Aeneas' own mouth a narrative version of the "beatitudes" of the second *Georgic*, the comparison of the happiness of the pious man with that of the knower of causes. There Vergil's first desire, to know the causes of things, is prevented by the cold blood around his heart; so he settles for the second, inglorious desire of loving the rural things. His consolation is that while he who is able to find out the causes of things is happy, and tramples under foot all fears and the din of greedy Acheron, also fortunate is he who knows the country gods, Pan and Silvanus and the sister Nymphs. So also Aeneas. His first desire is to find out the deeply hidden causes; but the coldness of his blood (*frigidus horror gelidusque sanguis*, 29–30[4]) disables him. Therefore he settles for venerating the rural Nymphs and father Gradivus, and finally paying the due of the greedy Underworld with libations of milk and blood. Knowledge of causes and veneration of the Underworld, natural science and traditional religion, are *the* alternatives. Exploration into the deeply hidden causes of things incriminates pious hands.

In the unfolding of the journey from Troy in Book 3, a series of visions and oracles cumulatively recalls and confirms the divine revelations of Book 2, and supplements them with additional elements. The principal contents of Hector's, Venus', and Creusa's communications to Aeneas—that Aeneas is divinely commanded to flee Troy with the Penates and found a new city for them in Italy—are variously repeated, clarified, and confirmed by prophecies of Apollo (94–98), the Penates (154–171), Celaeno (247–257), and Helenus (374 462). To these contents are added the information that Aeneas' new city in Italy is to be the seat from which his descendants will rule all lands forever (97–98), and that hardships and wars await the Trojans in Italy (254 ff., 458–460). In the seven years between the fall of Troy and his arrival in Carthage, Aeneas has gradually come to grasp the contents of the various visions and oracles so that they fit together into a coherent course of action. Aeneas narrates these things to Dido so as to show her, as fully as he understands it himself, that it is because the gods require him to settle his Trojans in Italy that he must decline her invitation to settle them in Carthage. But the coherence of the contents of the various visions and oracles is not yet an explanation, not to say a guarantee, of the reality of their divine source. Although Aeneas represents himself to Dido as having already renounced his craving to know the deeply hidden causes of things in favor of obedience to the gods' will, it is only at Carthage that the strength of that renunciation will be put to the test.

ii. Carthage

Although Aeneas in his narrative to Dido thus lays forth for her in detail the divine commands and revelations that prevent him from accepting her invitation to settle the Trojans in Carthage, his stay in Carthage exposes the weakness of his own belief in his divinely appointed mission; under the influence of Dido's love and Carthage's science, he becomes oblivious to the kingdom appointed for him in Italy, and inattentive to the turbid image of his father Anchises admonishing him in the night (351–353).[5] Only under the immediate terror (279–280) of Mercury's appearance and disappearance in broad daylight does Aeneas recall himself and carry out the departure for Italy, which was the aborted conclusion of his narrative in Books 2–3. For Aeneas, the decisive event of Book 4 is Mercury's appearance to him. Aeneas does not know, as we do, that Mercury's appearance is the refutation of Iarbas' explicit skepticism about Jupiter's existence and justice. For Aeneas it seems to be decisive because he experiences it with his own senses in broad daylight. Until the appearance of Mercury, Aeneas' conduct at Carthage has shown him oblivious to or ignoring the commands of the gods in favor of love and science. After Mercury's appearance, Aeneas' self-understanding, and his resolution to repent, is shown not only by his conduct but also by his speeches, and especially by his long speech to Dido at 333–361.

Aeneas explains himself as follows. If it had been open to him to guide his life by "his own" free will (*sponte mea*, 341), he would never have abandoned Troy—the walls of Troy—in its defeat. "His own" will was the will formed by his traditional Homeric education, the will that he began to replace on the night of Troy's fall with a will formed by the revelations and commands of the gods. Instead of living and dying in the walls of Troy by his own free will, he is making for Italy in obedience to divine will: *Italiam non sponte sequor* (361). He renounced his own will in favor of the gods' will;[6] and it was this and only this that gave his flight from Troy the inner meaning of a heroic action rather than a deed of craven cowardice. But the inner meaning of his flight would be confirmed only by his completion of the mission for which he undertook that flight. During his stay in Carthage, the image of his father Anchises has been bringing him terrible warnings in his dreams (351–353);[7] and he has been conscious that by remaining in Carthage he is robbing his son Ascanius of the Italian kingdom appointed him by the fates (354–355). It has been only by ignoring all this that Aeneas has brought himself to remain with Dido in Carthage.[8]

If things had remained like this, the meaning of Aeneas' life would have been that, after fleeing Troy in the uncertain belief that gods were commanding him to save the penates and found a new city for them in Italy, he had discovered in Carthage the falsity of that belief. He had learned that images have a strictly natural interpretation and that, however lifelike and terrifying they may appear, they do not arise from any divine source. His desire to learn the deeply hidden causes of things had triumphed, after seeming to have been trampled down by veneration of the gods and the dead. He had learned that natural pleasure, the pleasure of thought and friendship, rather than supernatural will ought to be the guide of human conduct. The proper end of his flight from Troy was not self-renunciation in favor of the will of the gods but self-fulfillment in the happiness of a mutual love with a like-minded wife; not self-subordination to the gods' requirements for a mysterious "fatherland" across the seas (347) but active works on behalf of the natural (godless) fatherland for all the peoples. If things had remained so, Aeneas' life would have been a declaration of the truth formulated by Iarbas: that behind the thunderbolt is not an omnipotent and just Jupiter but blind fire in the clouds— that Jupiter is an empty rumor (4.206–218). Aeneas would have succeeded in heroically trampling the fear of Acheron under foot, and satisfied the critics who complain of his cowering before the gods. From a cringing, superstitious, dependent, frightened, dumbstruck fellow he would have made himself over into a scientific, autonomous, self-assertive, skeptical one striking out for the humanly knowable human good, the real goods: not the ambitious delusions of empire recommended by other people's words, but the pleasures recommended by the senses themselves (*De Rerum Natura* 5.1130–1134).

Up to this point in his speech, Aeneas has conceded all to Dido by conceding the criterion of "the senses themselves." But now everything has been suddenly changed, according to Aeneas' account of himself, by the manifestation to him of a god whom he himself saw in broad daylight and whose speech he himself heard with "these" ears, so that he swears this god was a messenger sent by Jupiter himself:

> nunc etiam interpres divum Iove missus ab ipso
> (testor utrumque caput) celeris mandata per auras
> detulit: ipse deum manifesto in lumine vidi
> intrantem muros vocemque his auribus hausi.

> And now a messenger of the gods sent by Jupiter himself (I swear it by your head and mine) has brought down commands through the swift breezes: I myself saw the god entering the walls in broad daylight, and heard his voice with these very ears.

> (4.356–359)

Aeneas at Carthage has learned to be skeptical of whatever recommends itself by other evidence than one's own senses. But as he presents it to Dido, it is this very lesson that now requires him to deem true the fundamental claim of the previous revelations as well: that there are gods whose providential will it is that Aeneas go to Italy. Dido scornfully denies that there is any essential difference between Apollo's oracles and Mercury's appearance (376–378). But Aeneas' argument suggests that to reject the evidence of Mercury's manifest appearance and speech is to deny the gods no longer on the basis of the canon of sense but out of mere self-will or rigid dogmatism, against the evidence of the senses themselves.

At this juncture, where Vergil portrays Aeneas' decisive turn from Epicurean self-assertion and self-will to Roman piety, he puts in the mouth of Dido (4.365–387) the most explicit form of the critics' censure of Aeneas' character: he is no hero but a moral and intellectual weakling. In so doing, Vergil suggests that Aeneas' critics are moved not by reasonable judgment but by wishful thinking and self-will, while Aeneas' turn from Carthage is moved not by coldness of heart or weakness of mind but by reasonable repentance:

> At pius Aeneas, quamquam lenire dolentem
> solando cupit et dictis avertere curas,
> multa gemens magnoque animum labefactus amore
> iussa tamen divum exsequitur.

> But pious Aeneas, however much he wishes to ease her grief with comfort and remove her cares with words, however much he groans, however much he is shaken in spirit by love—nevertheless follows the commands of the gods.

> (4.393–396)

When Mercury appears to Aeneas for a second time in Book 4 (556 ff.), he appears in the dream form that had compromised the certainty of the source of Aeneas' earlier visions. But now Aeneas' confidence in the divine authority of Mercury's commandments is secured by the broad-daylight evidence with which this dream-appearance is in accord. Thus he distinguishes his ignorance of Mercury's identity from his certainty of Mercury's divine authority:

> deus aethere missus ab alto
> festinare fugam tortosque incidere funis
> ecce iterum instimulat. sequimur te, sancte deorum,
> quisquis es, imperioque iterum paremus ovantes.

> A god sent from highest heaven again urgently bids us speed our flight and cut the twisted cables. We follow you, holy one of the gods, whoever you are, and again joyfully obey your command.

> (4.574–577)

iii. Palinurus

The principal content of Book 5 is Aeneas' conduct of the funeral games in honor of Anchises. Through the funeral games Vergil presents Aeneas as ruler of men, confronting the great problem to be faced by Rome as ruler of cities: men who are spirited enough to subdue Italy in the name of Aeneas' founding mission (5.751) are also liable to be moved by envy and love of victory to injustice among themselves. The most elaborately narrated of the games is the ship race, and the book as a whole is framed by the nautical episode of Palinurus.[9] The ship race and the Palinurus episode have in common the odd feature of a ship's captain taking the helm after his pilot has been thrown overboard. In the race, the Chimaera's captain Gyas throws his pilot Menoetes overboard because he believes that Menoetes' cautious navigation will cost his ship the victory; as a result the Chimaera comes in third: "she loses because she has been deprived of her master" (cedit, quoniam spoliata magistro est, 224). In the actual navigation of the Trojan fleet, the loss of the pilot has quite another outcome. On the very last night of the seven-year journey from Troy, in calm waters and under a clear sky, just before the fleet must negotiate the dangerous rocks of the Sirens, the pilot Palinurus is lost overboard, taking the rudder and part of the stern with him in his fall. Aeneas, suddenly sensing that his ship is adrift and pilotless, steers it himself (ipse ratem . . . rexit, 868); though shaken in spirit by the loss of his friend, he navigates perfectly without either pilot or rudder.

The piloting of ships is a celebrated image for the government of cities, and Vergil's pilot-overboard stories seem to refer to the most celebrated discussion of this image in Book 6 of Plato's *Republic* (488A–489D). According to Socrates' interpretation there, the true pilot (ἀλήθινος κυβερνήτης) is the philosopher who ought by rights to rule, the ship owner (ναύκληρος, corresponding to Vergil's ship captains) is the actually ruling part of the city, and the sailors are the citizens at large, who aspire to rule. The image as a whole, Socrates says, represents "the cities in their disposition toward the true philosophers" (489A): as things are, it is not surprising that the citizens and rulers conspire to kill or throw out the philosopher, though he is the only one who has the true art of piloting/government and thereby the only one fit to govern them well.

In the *Chimaera's* fate in the ship race, Vergil offers what appears to be an orthodox illustration of the Socratic image of the ship of state. Menoetes is the true pilot, master of the true art of piloting: his concern is for the whole good of the ship and crew, which involves some combination of glory and preservation, and which he alone knows how to secure. Gyas is the ignorant, ambitious ship owner or captain: his concern is only for glory or victory, but although he has the passion for it in abundance, he lacks the art of acquiring it.[10] By rejecting the moderation of the true pilot as a barrier to victory and throwing Menoetes overboard, Gyas disgraces the ship whose glory he hoped to promote. Through this orthodox use of the ship-of-state image in the body of the funeral games, Vergil prepares us to be all the more impressed by the unorthodox outcome of the Palinurus episode.

The art of piloting stands for government because it involves steering or guiding,[11] and for philosophy because it derives from astronomy: knowledge of the year, the seasons, the heaven, the stars, the winds, and everything else belonging to this art (*Republic* 489d). In the *Aeneid* Vergil too has represented philosophy as derived from astronomy, through the philosopher Iopas whose teacher was the astronomer Atlas;[12] Iopas' Lucretian song is mainly a song of the heavenly bodies (1.740 ff.). Among the Trojans, the only man who shares part of Iopas' philosophic knowledge, namely knowledge of the constellations, is the pilot Palinurus. Vergil emphasizes this connection between Iopas and Palinurus by repeating an entire line from the song of Iopas in his description of Palinurus' scanning of the heavens:

sidera cuncta notat tacito labentia caelo,
Arcturum pluviasque Hyadas geminosque Triones
armatumque auro circumspicit Oriona.

He takes note of all the constellations passing in the silent heaven, Arcturus and the rainy Hyades and the twin Triones, and he examines Orion armed with gold.

(3.515–517; 516 = 1.744)

In Iopas at Carthage and Palinurus in the Trojan fleet Vergil represents opposite arrangements for the relationship of science and rule in the cities. At Carthage science is sovereign: Iopas instructs Dido in the nature of things so as to set for her the political project of universal enlightenment that flows from nature—nature as understood by Lucretian natural science. Carthage is the "ship of state" according to nature, in this view: "for it is not natural for a pilot to beg the sailors to be ruled by him" (*Rep.* 489B).[13] In the Trojan fleet Vergil represents the pre-Carthaginian city, where the pilot or scientist puts his art at the disposal of the political ruler who sets the destination. Unlike Iopas, Palinurus does not seek to know the whole nature of things or to determine his ship's proper destination; he regards his knowledge of the constellations as instrumental to reaching the destination set by Aeneas. The claim of the Carthaginian city, the city in which science rules, to be "king of the nations" has been exploded in Book 4; in Book 5, it emerges that the defect of Carthage cannot be supplied by a return to the pre-Carthaginian city. As the fate of the *Chimaera* shows, the pilot's art is only apparently self-subordinating to the rule of the captain. In ordinary situations, Menoetes willingly puts his art at the service of his captain's ends, and the conflict between them is invisible; but in an emergency, it turns out that the pilot's art has its own ends. Precisely when he is being a true pilot, Menoetes is insubordinate: he follows the requirements of the art of piloting where these diverge from the ambitions of rule. The pilot is intolerable to his captain precisely in the emergencies in which his science is most needed. The scientist is both indispensable and intolerable to the ruler of the pre-Carthaginian city.

As Aeneas approaches the site of Rome, Vergil adumbrates the way in which Rome is to supply the defect of Carthage without attempting to return to pre-Carthage. Menoetes' science was indispensable to Gyas, but on the final night of the journey to Italy Aeneas learns that Palinurus' science is entirely dispensable to him: it is in fact replaced by the direct guidance of divine providence:[14]

currit iter tutum non setius aequore classis
promissisque patris Neptuni interrita fertur.
iamque adeo scopulos Sirenum advecta subibat,
difficilis quondam multorumque ossibus albos
(tum rauca adsiduo longe sale saxa sonabant),
cum pater amisso fluitantem errare magistro
sensit, et ipse ratem nocturnis rexit in undis . . .

The fleet plies a safe path through the sea all the same, and is carried fearlessly along in accordance with the promises of father Neptune. And now it was approaching the Sirens' rocks, once so dangerous and white with the bones of many men (even then the noisy rocks were incessantly resounding far over the sea), when the father sensed that his ship was wandering adrift with its master lost, and himself steered it through the nocturnal waves. . . .

$$(5.862–868)^{15}$$

As all of Aeneas' experience since the fall of Troy has suggested, the foundation of Rome is to replace natural knowledge with inspired or prophetic knowledge; the Siren song of science[16] is harmless to the divinely guided ruler who can dispense with science. If the arts of astronomy can be yielded to "others" while Rome cultivates the arts of ruling the peoples with empire (6.849–853), that is because the arts of ruling can be guided directly by divine providence or divine revelation without depending on astronomical-philosophic science.

What foundation is there for the dispensability of the pilot's art, for the possibility that divine revelation could replace science as the source of the arts of ruling the peoples with empire? Just before the final voyage in which Aeneas replaces Palinurus, the shade of Anchises instructs Aeneas to visit the Underworld in order to "learn" his entire race and what walls are granted (*tum genus omne tuum et quae dentur moenia disces*, 737). If anything can be learned about the conditions for the possibility of divine revelation, as opposed to the contents of divine revelation, it is in the Underworld that Aeneas might expect to learn it.

iv. Catabasis

The truth about the Underworld is the key to the truth about the nature of things and about heroism. The crucial question about the nature of things, the issue between science and religion, is whether the world has three parts or four: are heaven, earth, and ocean the whole of the world, or is the Underworld the fourth part? Since courage is a stance of the soul towards death, the decisive question about heroism is what effect the prospect of death ought to have on men's souls. Achilles' heroism rests on the view that men's souls are destined to a dismal phantom-like existence after death; Odysseus' on the view that there are only arbitrary exceptions to that destiny; Epicurus' on the view that men's souls perish with their bodies. Only if these views are untrue is the heroism that rests on them exposed as illusory. Only if it is true that men have immortal souls, justly rewarded and punished after death for their conduct in this life, could Aeneas' piety be vindicated as the stance of true courage in the face of human destiny.

The content of what Aeneas learns in the Underworld demonstrates that the pious hopes on which he has pinned his renunciation of Troy, Dido, and Carthage are justified by the nature of things; but the form in which he learns it is such as to put its truth in doubt again. The content may be summarized under three heads: the fate of souls, the nature of the cosmos, and the political destiny of mankind. Human souls are immortal, and are judged, rewarded, and punished after death. Mind rules the cosmos, so that it is in accordance with the universal order of mind that the human souls are judged. The city Aeneas is commissioned to found in Italy is to be the germ of a universal empire that will permanently restore the Golden Age to earth. The apparent success of force, fraud, and defiance of the gods is ultimately corrected: the man who spurns justice and the gods is finally punished, and the nations that achieve great successes through injustice and contempt of gods are finally conquered and ruled by universal Rome.

From what Aeneas learns in the Underworld it follows both that his founding efforts are to provide the greatest possible benefit to the human race in the distant future, and that he himself is to enjoy the eternal bliss of those who have merited the remembrance of others (*quique sui memores alios fecere merendo*, 6.664). What he learns fires his spirit with love of fame to come (889)—not such fame as is furnished by unsupported human memory to humanly admirable deeds, but such fame as is guaranteed by the Mind that rules the Whole to deeds whose worthiness may not be easily or immediately manifest to men. Glorious deeds are defined not by what human beings independently admire, but by what universal mind ordains. In the light of what Aeneas learns in the Underworld, the heroism of Achilles, Odysseus, and Epicurus crumbles to nothing. Achillean glory-seeking, as compensation for the nothingness of human life, as human assertion of greatness in the teeth of human insignificance, is wiped out by the knowledge that men, like gods, may enjoy eternal bliss for themselves; to extort men's acknowledgment of one's godlikeness in poetry is as nothing compared with enjoying that superiority forever oneself in the next life. Odyssean rejection of the immortal happiness of gods in favor of one's own—one's own belly, wife, son, house, kingdom—is paltry when one can reasonably be devoted to the salvation of the human race for all time. Epicurean contempt of great practical deeds in favor of god-defying words, the Epicurean quest for divine happiness as the wisdom of understanding that no gods rule the nature of things, that philosophic insight is the only true godlikeness of man—this is contemptible delusion, not heroic courage, if the truth is that immortal souls are judged by just and powerful gods in accordance with the dictates of universal mind.

Vergil introduces the catabasis of Aeneas with the interwoven episodes of the funeral rites of Misenus and Aeneas' plucking of the Golden Bough, which together hark back to the funeral rites of Polydorus and the plucking of the bleeding stems in Book 3.[17] In the Polydorus episode as narrated by Aeneas himself, Aeneas renounced his desire to find out the deeply hidden causes of the bleeding stems in favor of venerating the gods and the rites of the Underworld. In his experience, it had been as if finding out causes and cultivating piety through funeral rites were mutually exclusive; and he had chosen in favor of piety. But in the prelude to the catabasis, it appears that the performance of Misenus' funeral rites is not to replace but to be accompanied by knowledge of the deeply hidden causes of things: the Golden Bough, like the bleeding stem in its miraculous character, is unlike it in presaging access to the fullest insight rather than exclusion from it. Piety is not a bar to knowledge but the key to it.[18] The Sibyl wins Aeneas' entrance to the Underworld, his passage in Charon's boat, by presenting the Golden Bough and Aeneas' piety as tokens of each other: "if the image of such great piety does not move you, yet acknowledge this bough" (*si te nulla movet tantae pietatis imago, at ramum hunc . . . agnoscas*, 6.405–407). The particular knowledge in question here is that of the efficacy of funeral rites, and it is brought to the fore by the characterization of Misenus' rites as offered to "thankless ashes," *cineri ingrato* (6.213). As the issue between science and piety is whether there are three parts of the world or four, so the performance of funeral rites is *the* act of piety, while *the* scientific question is whether the dead are benefited by such rites or are, as Anna's Lucretian speech to Dido had suggested,[19] only "thankless ashes." Until the catabasis, funeral rites are *the* act of piety because they replace or exclude *the* scientific knowledge of causes. But the prelude to the catabasis suggests that the fullest knowledge of causes will turn out to vindicate the efficacy of the funeral rites. Aeneas' obedience to the gods is after all to be completed by his knowledge of the nature of the whole within which that obedience is practiced.

Aeneas sees with his own eyes, immediately upon his arrival at the bank of the Cocytus, that the souls survive death; and he learns from the Sibyl (325–330) how the dead are benefited by funeral rites: they have a longing to cross the Cocytus, but without burial they are denied passage. The Sibyl does not disclose why they have this longing. In response to her explanation, Aeneas has many thoughts, pitying in his mind the unfair lot (*sortemque animo miseratus iniquam*, 332). The unfairness appears to reside in the fact that the natural longing of the dead is fulfilled or not, and thus the dead are happy or miserable, regardless of anything that could be seen as their own deserts: their happiness depends on burial, but they cannot bury themselves. The fate of men's souls is unjust. Leucaspis and Orontes, the captains who went down bravely with the ships Aeneas lost off Carthage through the unjust persecutions of Juno, are now wretched for lack of funeral rites (333–336). Aeneas' own pilot Palinurus, thrown overboard by a malignant divinity, is now in the same case (337 ff.). The Sibyl offers Palinurus comfort for his hard misfortune (*duri solacia casus*, 377) in the prophesy that his bones will ultimately be buried in a place that will keep his name "eternal" (378–381); but for Leucaspis and Orontes, no end to their misery is in store. One cannot hope to turn aside by prayer the fates of the gods (376); and the fates of the gods are unjust.

If men can know that the souls survive into another life where they are at the mercy of the unjust fates of gods, then it is understandable that men fear the gods, but hardly heroic. If the fate of men's souls is unjust, defiance rather than piety would be the heroic stance for a man who has found this out: heroism would be the stance of an Achilles, seeking to wrest the justice of recognition from men, rather than to accept the common lot imposed by unjust gods.

Aeneas learns, however, as his education in the Underworld proceeds, that ultimately the souls are justly rewarded and punished. He sees Minos judging those condemned to death on false charges (430–433); he hears the groans of those suffering torments in Tartarus (557–558), and hears the Sibyl's account of the judgment and punishment of wrongdoers (562–627); and he sees the happiness of the blessed in Elysium (637–665). That the souls are "justly" rewarded and punished means that the standards by which they are judged in the next life are the same standards that are discernible in just laws in this life. The foremost injustice for which souls are punished is defiance of the divinity of Jupiter (580 ff.); it is followed by violations of duty toward kin, client, and fatherland (608–627), but here too the central violation is contempt of the gods, exemplified in the speech that constitutes and explains the punishment of Phlegyas: "Be warned to learn justice and not contemn the gods" (*discite iustitiam moniti et non temnere divos*, 620). The center of justice is submission to the gods. This is confirmed in the list of the types of men rewarded with the bliss of Elysium, where priests have the central place between soldiers and artists:

> hic manus ob patriam pugnando vulnera passi,
> quique sacerdotes casti, dum vita manebat,
> quique pii vates et Phoebo digna locuti,
> inventas aut qui vitam excoluere per artis,
> quique sui memores aliquos fecere merendo.

Here the band who suffered wounds in fighting for their fatherland; and those who were chaste priests as long as their life lasted, and those who were pious seers and spoke things worthy of Phoebus; or those who enriched life through the invention of arts, and those who made some remember them deservedly.

(6.660–664)

The fate of souls after death shows, in the case of the soldier and the priest, that what appears to be the renunciation of one's own enjoyment of the goods of life ultimately earns a reward far exceeding those goods. The case of the inventor of arts is somewhat different, though, since his enrichment of life enriches his own life as well.[20] This question of the arts points forward to the lines in which Anchises suggests that the Roman art of ruling the peoples with empire is to be in the service of preserving and promoting the arts of the "others"—sculpture, rhetoric, and philosophy (847–853). The reward of the artists after death is to be represented in life by Rome's invention of the art that promotes the invention and cultivation of all the other arts.

Aeneas' knowledge of the survival of souls and their just reward and punishment in the next life still leaves open the question how this provision for human beings fits into the whole nature of things. Anchises' speech at 724 ff., purporting to answer Aeneas' question (721) as to how the blessed souls in Elysium could have so fierce a desire for life on earth, gives all the account Aeneas will receive of the principle of the whole. This principle is expressed in distinctly (anti-)Lucretian terms, in a passage that should be compared with the Lucretian song of Iopas that Aeneas heard at Dido's feast at the end of Book 1. According to Anchises, the principle of the whole is that mind moves all (724–727); but the details are certainly perplexing. The whole that is moved by mind consists of heaven, earth, and ocean, but not the Underworld (724–725). The origin of the race of men in celestial fire does not distinguish them from beasts (728–729). Grief and joy belong to the bodies, but it is the souls that suffer punishment and enjoy reward (733, 736 ff.).[21] Aside from the spirit that nourishes the whole inwardly and the mind that moves it, the only divine being mentioned is the god who assembles purified souls in order to induce them through forgetfulness to want to return to bodies (748–751); Anchises does not explain how the ruling, judging, rewarding, and punishing gods fit into mind's moving of all things; in particular, he does not answer the thematic question of the Aeneid, "Is there such anger in celestial spirits?"

Apparently the general drift of Anchises' teaching, to the effect that it is not chance or necessity but mind that rules all, is only obscurely accessible, and only in the most general terms, to human beings who are still, like Aeneas, shut up in the shadows and the blind prison of the body (734). The fact that even a partial insight into the highest truth can pierce the mist in which men live is not only a pledge of the full understanding they can hope to have after liberation from the body, but also a suggestion of the ground in nature for such divine revelation as Aeneas has received on earth from shades and gods. In Book 1, Vergil had made Aeneas express bitter despair of the truth of Venus' appearance and communication to him:

> quid natum totiens, crudelis tu quoque, falsis
> ludis imaginibus? cur dextrae iungere dextram
> non datur ac veras audire et reddere voces?

> Why do you so often delude your son—you cruel as well!—with false images? Why is it not granted to join right hand with right hand, and hear and exchange true voices?

> (1.407–409)

Aeneas' meeting with Anchises in the Underworld shows him that his despair of divine revelation is at least partially to be replaced by confidence. Although the joining of the hands turns out to be out of reach (6.697–702), the sights and sounds of encounter between the embodied and the disembodied are truly perceptible:

> datur ora tueri,
> nate, tua et notas audire et reddere voces.

> It is granted to see your face, my son, and to hear and exchange known voices.
> (6.688–689)

Anchises' account of the nature of things, then, includes an implicit account of how the nature of things can be made accessible, though only partially, to living human beings. The nature of things is such as to prevent men from knowing it directly or completely, while allowing them to know it indirectly and incompletely through divine revelation.

Up to this point in the catabasis (751), what Aeneas has learned of the fate of human souls and the principle of the whole is such as to vindicate the respectability of his flight from Troy and his abandonment of Dido and Carthage. His pious obedience to the strange commands of the dead and the gods is shown not to have been weak or cowardly or deluded; it was based rather on the soberest insight into the truth of things and the manliest self-mastery, the renunciation of the conventional or traditional human aspirations to glory, love, and science in favor of a higher end accessible only through divine revelation. What is still lacking is the explanation of the actual content of that end. In accordance with the mind that moves the whole, the gods and the dead have commanded Aeneas to renounce all else for the sake of founding a city in Italy. But Aeneas does not know what purpose is to be served by the fulfillment of this commandment. This purpose has been known to us since Book 1, where Vergil displayed it in Jupiter's prophecy to Venus (1.257–296). The burden of Anchises' remaining speeches in Book 6 is to convey this purpose to Aeneas. For only with an insight into this purpose could Aeneas carry out his founding mission not only in obedience to the will of the gods but also in comprehension of the goodness of the end proposed by that will.

Thus while the bulk of the Show of Heroes (756–790, 808–846) points to such great deeds of Aeneas' descendants as might have characterized the rulers of any great nation, its centerpiece is Anchises' account of the unique end of Aeneas' founding mission in the restoration of the Golden Age, and its conclusion is his formulation of the specific end of the Romans in contradistinction to all other rulers. The centerpiece is the prophecy of the rule of Augustus Caesar. Anchises startlingly seems to introduce Augustus as the man "whom you so often hear promised to you" (hic vir, hic est, tibi quem promitti saepius audis, 791). But since no "man" has ever been promised to Aeneas, perhaps Anchises' words suggest that this man is "that which" Aeneas so often hears promised to him, namely, some intelligible good to be set in motion by the act of founding new walls for the Trojan penates in Italy. Anchises' account of Augustus—that he is to be the offspring of a god (792); that he is to refound the Golden Age where Saturn first founded it, but extend it to the ends of the earth (792–797); that the distant nations of the world are already receiving divine intimations of Augustus' future coming (798–800); that Augustus' benefits to the human race are to outshine those of Hercules and Bacchus (801–805)—constitutes Aeneas' whole[22] education about the purpose of the deed he has been commanded to do. The charged rhetorical question with which Anchises concludes his prophecy of Augustus suggests that this knowledge has hitherto been lacking, but has been the only knowledge lacking, to Aeneas' ability to form a resolve sufficient to the founding labors that now face him in Italy. Anchises expects that any hesitations and fears that may still have weakened Aeneas when he already knew the fate of souls and the principle of the whole will be resolved by his now knowing the ultimate political purpose that the gods have in view for him and for all humanity:

et dubitamus adhuc virtutem extendere factis,
aut metus Ausonia prohibet consistere terra?

Can we then still hesitate to extend our virtue by our deeds, or can fear still
bar us from occupying the Ausonian land?

(6.806–807)

The doubts Vergil has compelled us to feel about the worthiness of Aeneas' pious brand of heroism are resolved by the knowledge he shows Aeneas
acquiring for himself in the catabasis. The manliness of Aeneas' conduct is
guaranteed by the truths that had been inaccessible to former heroes: that
the immortal souls are justly rewarded and punished in the next life, that the
whole is governed by mind, and that there is a providential plan for the salvation of the human race. In the light of these truths, Aeneas' flight from
Troy was not an act of cowardly self-preservation, and his flight from Dido
was not a craven rejection of the offices of love, and his flight from Carthage
was not a superstitious shrinking from the rigors of scientific knowledge.
These deeds were not flights from the arenas of human greatness and happiness but advances towards a twofold end—the political salvation of humanity and the beatitude of the pious soul's reward—higher than anything that
the heroes of glory, love, and science ever proposed to themselves. But although the content of Aeneas' education in the Underworld robustly supports this conclusion, the manner of that education throws it into question
all over again.

For Aeneas' experience in the Underworld is the experience of images whose
uncertain status Vergil is at pains to bring home to us. In particular, Vergil continually calls to our attention, in emphatically Lucretian phrases, the Epicurean
analysis of the images perceived by Aeneas. The persuasiveness of Vergil's account of the Underworld lies partly in the directness of Aeneas' experience of
it through his own senses. But at the same time, Vergil's account calls vividly to
mind the hierarchy of the senses, all descending from the sense of touch.[23] Aeneas is twice deluded by his assumption that what he sees and hears arises from
what he can touch: first when he draws his sword against the vain dreams that
occupy the dark tree at the entrance to the Underworld,[24] only to be instructed
by the learned Sibyl that they are "without body" (290–294); then when he
finds that the desire to embrace Anchises, which follows upon seeing and hearing him, is unfulfillable since Anchises' image slips through his hands very like
a dream (697–701). But not only are the sights and sounds of Aeneas' experience without basis in touch. Vergil repeatedly characterizes the things Aeneas
sees as doubtful in themselves. The entry through the "empty and void realms
of Dis" (269) is like a path in the woods lit with malignant light by an uncertain moon, when Jupiter has buried the heaven in shadow and dark night has
taken the color away from things (270–272). Aeneas' encounter with the still-

angry shade of Dido, who had doubted and caused him to doubt that the dead survive or care about the living, silently settles in Aeneas' favor the great issue between them. But precisely Dido—who is silent, so that Aeneas must rely entirely on what he sees of her—is seen by him "obscurely through the shadows, like a moon one sees rising through clouds at the beginning of the month—or thinks one has seen" (452–455). And as for the sounds that Aeneas hears, most of them are words, the words of the Sibyl and of Anchises; "and we know," as Servius remarks on the concluding lines of the catabasis, "that the things we say can be false, while the things we see are true without doubt" (*ad* 6.893).

The sound other than words that Aeneas hears in the Underworld is the fearful din of Tartarus:

hinc exaudiri gemitus et saeva sonare
verbera, tum stridor ferri tractaeque catenae.
constitit Aeneas strepitumque exterritus hausit.

From here groans were heard and fierce lashings sounded, and the clash of iron and chains being dragged. Aeneas stopped and took in the din in terror.

(6.557–559)

This is the fearful sound that is trampled beneath the feet by the happy man who has come to know the causes of things (*Geo.* 2.490–492). Vergil had promised in the *Georgics* that in his own future poem with Caesar at its center, he would restore through dramatic images the fearfulness of the Underworld punishments that the happy knower of causes had trampled beneath the feet (*Geo.* 3.16–39). In the invocation to the catabasis at the center of the *Aeneid* (6.264–267), the poet asks not for knowledge of the causes of divine anger, as in the invocation to the *Aeneid* as a whole, but for authorization to speak "things heard" (*sit mihi fas audita loqui*, 266).[25] Vergil presents the consummation of Aeneas' education as his exposure to the images provided by Vergil himself for the express purpose of making fear of the Underworld the foundation of the political salvation of mankind.

Notes

Introduction

1. For an overview of contemporary Vergil interpretation see S. J. Harrison, "Some Views of the *Aeneid* in the Twentieth Century," in Harrison, S. J., ed., *Oxford Readings in Vergil's Aeneid* (New York and Oxford: Oxford University Press, 1990), 1–20; also W. R. Johnson, *Darkness Visible: A Study of Vergil's Aeneid* (Berkeley: University of California Press, 1976), 8–16.

2. According to Diogenes, Epicurus holds that "only the wise man would converse rightly about music and poetry, but in actuality he would not compose poems" [μόνον τε τὸν σοφὸν ὀρθῶς ἂν περί τε μουσικῆς καὶ ποιητικῆς διαλέξεσθαι· ποιήματά τε ἐνεργείᾳ οὐκ ἂν ποιῆσαι]. (Diogenes Laertius 10.120).

3. On the preparatory stage of this project carried out in the *Georgics* cf. Eve Adler, "The Invocation to the *Georgics*," *Interpretation* 11 (1983): 25–41.

4. Cf. especially W. A. Merrill, "Parallels and Coincidences in Lucretius and Virgil," *University of California Publications in Classical Philology* 3 (1918): 135–247; Cyril Bailey, "Virgil and Lucretius," *PCA* (1931): 21–39 ("an incredibly close acquaintance on Virgil's part with his predecessor's work and a marvelously retentive memory," 39); A. Rostagni, "Virgilio e Lucrezio," *RFIC* (1931): 289–315; E. Paratore, "Spunti Lucreziani nelle Georgiche," *Atene e Roma*, S. 3 7–8 (1939–40), 177 ff.; Herta Klepl, *Lukrez und Virgil in ihren Lehrgedichten* (Darmstadt, 1967); G. Castelli, "Echi lucreziani nelle ecloghe virgiliane," *RSC* 14 (1966), 313–342, and 15 (1967), 14–39; Diskin Clay, *Lucretius and Epicurus* (Ithaca, N.Y.: Cornell University Press, 1983), 251; Richard Jenkyns, *Virgil's Experience. Nature and History: Times, Names, and Places* (New York and Oxford: Oxford University Press, 1998), 290, "Virgil reflects the influence of Lucretius in countless details of style and language"; Joseph Farrell, *Vergil's Georgics and the Traditions of Ancient Epic: The Art of Allusion in Literary History* (New York, Oxford: Oxford University Press, 1991), 169–206.

5. According to one extreme formulation, "one line in twelve of Virgil consciously or unconsciously echoes Lucretius." D. E. W. Wormell, "The Personal World of Lucretius," in D. R. Dudley, *Lucretius* (New York: Basic Books, 1965), 67, n. 23.

6. For a useful bibliography on this matter cf. J. S. Clay, "The Argument of the End of Vergil's Second *Georgic*," *Philologus* 120 (1976), 236–237, n. 18.

7. W. Y. Sellar, *The Roman Poets of the Augustan Age: Virgil* (New York and Oxford: Oxford University Press, 1877), 199–257.

8. Sellar, *The Roman Poets*, 199. So Philip R. Hardie, *Virgil's Aeneid: Cosmos and Imperium* (New York and Oxford: Oxford University Press, 1986), 46, on "the peculiarly involved mixture of attraction and repulsion that Virgil feels towards his Roman predecessor: attraction for the grandiose cosmic afflatus that pervades the *De Rerum Natura*, intellectual attraction to the resounding certainties of the Lucretian world-picture; but repulsion from the accompanying demand that the emotional ties to Rome and Italy, and perhaps to irrationality itself, must be cut once and for all."

9. Sellar, *The Roman Poets*, 204–205; cf. also 212–214, 225.

10. Sellar, *The Roman Poets*, 226.

11. Arthur Stanley Pease, *Publi Vergili Maronis Aeneidos Liber Quartus* (Darmstadt: Wissenschaftliche Buchgesellschaft, 1967), "Introduction" and *passim*, with bibliography on the question, 37–38; "Some Aspects of the Character of Dido," *Classical Journal* 22 (1926–1927): 243–252. See also L. Alfonsi, "L'epicureismo nella storia spirituale di Virgilio," *Epicurea in Memoriam Hectoris Bignone* (Genoa: Istituto di Filologia Classica, Università di Genova, 1959): 167–178.

12. Pease, *Publi Vergili Maronis*, 38 n. 289.

13. Pease, *Publi Vergili Maronis*, 37–38. Cf. Wendell Clausen, *Vergil's Aeneid and the Tradition of Hellenistic Poetry* (Berkeley: University of California Press, 1987), 49: "Dido, it seems, is an Epicurean, Aeneas a Stoic—a Roman Stoic."

14. Johnson, *Darkness Visible*, 141 ff.

15. Johnson, *Darkness Visible*, 151.

16. For the biographical evidence of Vergil's philosophic concerns cf. J. S. Clay, "The Argument," 237.

17. E. O. Wallace, *The Notes on Philosophy in the Commentary of Servius on the Eclogues, the Georgics and the Aeneid of Vergil* (New York: Columbia University Press, 1938) explains the "unusual" "presence of so strong a strain of Epicureanism" (183) in Servius' notes as due on the one hand to Servius' own "open-mindedness" (166) and inclination to "make neo-Platonism, Platonism, Stoicism, and Epicureanism lie down together and not war" (86), and on the other hand to "the fact that Servius is aware of the fact that Vergil is so greatly inspired by Lucretius" (183). Although Wallace's study treats Servius' notes as showing Servius' own philosophical opinions without reference to Servius' interpretation of Vergil's opinions, it does bring out admirably the "surprising . . . presence . . . of Lucretius' influence" (146) as something in need of explanation. Cf. Émile Thomas, *Scoliastes de Virgile: Essai sur Servius et son Commentaire sur Virgile* (Paris: E. Thorin, 1880); Don Fowler, "The Virgil Commentary of Servius," 73–78 in *Cambridge Companion to Virgil*, ed. Charles Martindale (Cambridge University Press, 1997); David B. Dietz, "Historia in the Commentary of Servius", *TAPA* 125 (1995): 72–73, 80, 94.

18. Cf. his comments on the following: *Aeneid* 2.502; 3.138, 577, 587; 4.34, 210, 705; 5.527; 6.264, 272, 282, 376, 719, 885, 893; 7.4, 60; 8.187; 10. 467, 487, 861.

19. *ad.* 4.210.

20. *ad.* 893; cf. *ad.* 6.282: "Et intelligimus hanc esse eburneam portam, per quam exiturus Aeneas est. Quae res haec omnia indicat esse simulata, si et ingressus et exitus simulatus est et falsus." Cf. Lucretius, *De Rerum Natura* 4.453–521. Servius' comment is taken seriously by Tenney Frank, who calls it "the blunt statement of Servius

. . . that the portal of unreal dreams refers the imagery of the sixth book to fiction" ("Epicurean Determinism in the *Aeneid*," *American Journal of Philology* 41 [1920]:126); but explained away by Wallace: "Servius believes that he has perceived that in his figure of the twin Gates of Sleep, Vergil has declared that he has seen through the glass darkly and would not claim to have revealed the truth. Vergil has presented the poet's conception which approaches the truth, but it is not the truth" (Wallace, *The Notes on Philosophy*, 173).

21. A. K. Michels, "Lucretius and the Sixth Book of the *Aeneid*," *American Journal of Philology* 65 (1944), 135–148. For related views cf. M. E. Hirst, "The Gates of Virgil's Underworld: A Reminiscence of Lucretius," *Classical Review* 26 (1912): 82–83 (cited by Michels, 135); Tenney Frank, *Vergil. A Biography* (New York: Henry Holt, 1922), 182–192, and "Epicurean Determinism," 115–126 (". . . hypothesis that the eschatological scene of the sixth book . . . was adopted as a mythos for purposes of plot," 116).

22. Michels, "Lucretius and the Sixth Book," 135.

23. Michels, "Lucretius and the Sixth Book," 147–148.

24. Michels, "Lucretius and the Sixth Book," 148.

Chapter 1: The Theme of the *Aeneid*

1. *Quasi amborum Homeri carminum instar.* Donatus, *Vita* 21. For an exhaustive demonstration of the completeness with which Vergil has incorporated the *Iliad* and the *Odyssey* into the narrative of the *Aeneid*, see G. N. Knauer, *Die Aeneis und Homer: Studien zur poetischen Technik Vergils mit Listen der Homerzitate in der Aeneis* (Göttingen, Germany: Hypomnemata, 1964); and "Vergil's Aeneid and Homer," *Greek, Roman, and Byzantine Studies* 5 (1964), 61–84.

2. Servius *ad* 1.11: *Animis caelestibus: dis superis, nam apud inferos constat esse iracundiam, ubi sunt Furiae.*

3. *arma, insignem pietate* (1, 10); cf. *Aeneas . . . quo iustior alter / nec pietate fuit, nec bello maior in armis* (1.544–5); and *Troius Aeneas, pietate insignis et armis* (6.403).

Chapter 2: The Song of Iopas and the Song of Vergil

1. Cf. the Trojan bard Cretheus, *amicum Crethea Musis, / Crethea Musarum comitem, cui carmina semper / et citharae cordi numerosque intendere nervis, / semper equos atque arma virum pugnasque canebat*: "dear to the Muses; Cretheus, companion of the Muses, who always had songs and lyres at heart and the plucking of the numbers on the strings; he always used to sing of horses and the arms of men and battles" (9.774–777). Vergil delicately alludes to the *Aeneid* in the phrase *arma virum*.

2. Cf. Richard Heinze, *Virgils Epische Technik* (Leipzig: B. G. Teubner, 1903), 488; W. Kranz, "Das Lied des Kitharoden von Jaffa," *Rheinisches Museum* 96 (1953):38; L. Alfonsi, "L'epicureismo nella storia spirituale di Virgilio," (Genoa: Istituto di Filologia Classica, Università di Genova, 1959), 176; and J. S. Clay, "The Argument of the End of Virgil's Second Georgic," *Philologus* 120 (1976): 239.

3. Cf. Empedocles, αἷμα γὰρ ἀνθρώποις περικάρδιόν ἐστι νόημα (DK, fr. 105). Cf. Hardie, *Cosmos and Imperium*, 42–43.

4. For Vergil's Lucretian language, cf. especially *DRN* 1.78–79: *quare Religio pedibus subiecta vicissim / opteritur*; and 3.37: *et metus ille foras praeceps Acheruntis agendus.* On the

reference of the passage to Lucretius, cf. Clay, "The Argument": 239; R. D. Williams, *The Aeneid of Vergil, Books 1–6* (New York: St. Martin's Press, 1972), *ad* 1.742 f.; M. C. J. Putnam, *Virgil's Poem of the Earth: Studies in the* Georgics (Princeton N.J.: Princeton University Press, 1979), 149–151; Gary B. Miles, *Virgil's Georgics: A New Interpretation* (Berkeley: University of California Press, 1980), 154–155; Guy Lee, "Imitation and the Poetry of Virgil," *Greece and Rome* 28 (1981): 12–14; and Frances Muecke, "Poetic Self-Consciousness in *Georgics* II," *Ramus* 8 (1979): 98.

Cf. Matthew Arnold, "Memorial Verses" ll. 29–33 (on Goethe):

And he was happy, if to know
Causes of things, and far below
His feet to see the lurid flow
Of terror, and insane distress,
And headlong fate, be happiness.

Cf. on these lines the note of Kenneth Allott in *Poems of Matthew Arnold,* ed. Kenneth Allott (London: Longmans, 1965), 227–228, who takes Arnold's contrast of Goethe and Wordsworth in this poem to refer to Vergil's contrast of Lucretius and himself at *Geo.* 2.490 ff.

5. J. S. Clay, "The Argument": "Perhaps Vergil's choice of these minor woodland divinities points to an attempted compromise between traditional religious views and Lucretius' condemnation of religion" (241).

6. On *felicitas* vs. *fortuna,* cf. Augustine, *De Civitate Dei* 4.18.

7. Cf. R. W. Johnson, "The Broken World: Virgil and his Augustus," *Arethusa* 14 (1981): 52.

8. Cf. M. O. Lee, *Fathers and Sons in Virgil's Aeneid* (Albany, N.Y.: State University of New York Press, 1979), 9 and n. 5.

9. Cf. Adler, "The Invocation to the *Georgics*," *Interpretation* 11 (1983): 29–33.

10. Vinzenz Buchheit, *Der Anspruch des Dichters in Vergils Georgika* (Darmstadt: Wissenschaft Buchgesellschaft, 1972), 45 ff. and esp. 76. Buchheit's argument that *Geo.* 2.475 ff. is a conventional *recusatio* is decisively laid to rest by J. S. Clay, "The Argument": "[W]hat is praised as the highest cannot be rejected on the basis of what is second best" (240).

11. Cf. Hardie, *Cosmos and Imperium,* 63, for the view that "the discrepancy between the scientific subject matter of the Song of Iopas and the legendary matter of the body of the *Aeneid,* a serious problem if we hold that Iopas is in some sense a figure of Virgil the epic poet . . . can be circumvented in a number of ways." Marco Girolamo Vida, *De Arte Poetica,* indicates that the song of Iopas is the teaching of Vergil himself:

Haud sum animi dubius, magnos memorare poetas
Interdum Solisque vias, Lunaeque labores,
Astrorumque ortus: qua vi tumida aequora surgant,
Unde tremor terris, quamvis illi orsa sequantur
Longe alia, aut duri cantantes proelia Martis,
Aut terrae mores varios, cultusque docentes.
At prius invenere locum, dein tempore capto
Talia subjiciunt parci, nec sponte videntur
Fari ea. Rem credas hoc ipsam poscere; ita astum
Dissimulant, aditusque petunt super omnia molles.

(II 205–214)

12. Cf. Pease, *Publi Vergili Maronis*, 36 n. 284: "It is not impossible that Dido's epithet *infelix* . . . may point to her dependence on a fortune which was in the outcome to play her false."

13. On Vergil's intention to instruct Augustus and the Romans in political principles, cf. R. S. Conway, "Poetry and Government," *Proceedings of the Classical Association* (1928): 21–22.

14. Cf. Hardie, *Cosmos and Imperium*, 57–60.

15. Cf. Servius *ad* 1.741; Pease *ad* 4.247; and Austin, *Aeneidos Liber Primus*, *ad* 1.741. M. C. J. Putnam, "Mercuri, facunde nepos Atlantis," *Classical Philology* 69 (1974): 215–217, collects evidence for the representation of Atlas as astronomer/philosopher and for the view that "Homer is the initial source for the interpretation of Atlas as prototype of the natural scientist" (216).

16. Cf. Charles Segal, "The Song of Iopas in the *Aeneid*," *Hermes* 99 (1971): 344–345.

17. *DRN* 1.41–43, 943–950. Cf. James Nichols, *Epicurean Political Philosophy* (Ithaca, N.Y.: Cornell University Press, 1976), 19–20 and 41–45.

18. Cf. Richard Monti, *The Dido Episode and the* Aeneid (Leiden, Netherlands: Brill, 1981): 1.

19. Servius' reference (*ad* 1.738) to a tradition that Iopas was one of the suitors of Dido (*Iopas vero rex Afrorum, unus de procis Didonis, ut Punica testatur historia*) recalls also Lucretius' account of how he was induced to the labor of putting his teaching in poetry by the hoped-for pleasure of sweet friendship (1.140–145).

20. In Lucretius' simile the child is deceived by the physician's honey *labrorum tenus*, as far as the lips, and thus drinks the bitter wormwood down to the last drop (*DRN* 1.939–941). In the drinking immediately preceding Iopas' song, Dido swallows the wine *summo tenus ore*, only as far as the lips, while Bitias drinks deeply, followed by the other lords (1.737–739). Dido's fastidious manner of drinking, which Servius *ad loc.* attributes to her Roman sense of feminine modesty, may be Vergil's allusion to the fatal incompleteness of Dido's Lucretian education. Lucretius, as the story of Dido brings out, has not provided for the case of a pupil who just tastes the honey without going on to swallow the medicine (who throws off the fear of gods and adopts the standard of pleasure without coming to know the nature of things from first principles, or philosophizing).

21. Cf. summary contents of *DRN* 5 at 5.64–81.

22. Cf. T. E. Kinsey, "The Song of Iopas," *Emerita* 47 (1979): 79–80. The connection here between natural science and world-unifying gold or commerce is indicated by Montesquieu, who gives "*maximus quae docuit Atlas*" as the motto at the head of his "Invocation to the Muses," which opens Part IV, on commerce, of *De l'Esprit des Lois*. That Montesquieu regards Vergil's Iopas as standing for Lucretius is suggested by his invoking the Muses to beautify his own presentation of Atlas' teaching: "Vous n'êtes jamais si divines que quand vous menez à la sagesse et à la verité par le plaisir;" "si vous ne voulez pas adoucir la rigueur de mes travaux, cachez le travail même"; cf. *DRN* 1.921 ff. The suggestion is strengthened by Montesquieu's going on to introduce Book 23 (on population) with a translation of the proem to the *DRN* (105). Cf. D. Lowenthal, "Montesquieu," in *History of Political Philosophy*, ed. Leo Strauss and Joseph Cropsey (Chicago: Rand McNally, 1972), 504; and Leo Strauss, *Natural Right and History* (Chicago: University of Chicago Press, 1953), 188–189.

23. Cf. Charles Segal, "Iopas Revisited (*Aeneid* 1.740 ff.)," *Emerita* 49 (1981): 21.

24. A view attributed by Gauthiez to Augustus himself: "*Ipse praesertim Augustus Caesar, utqui, propter illiberalem animum, ad superstitionem maxime proclivis esset, mire perspexerat 'Inferorum, quamvis fictae essent, fabulas, maxima efficitate hoc efficere, ut metum erga*

superos atque inter homines justitiam servarent'; *nec vim ac potentiam tantam omiserat, ut homines certius regere posset.*" Pierre Gauthiez, *De Virgilii Philosophia* (Paris, 1895), 10.

25. Cf. Pease, "Some Aspects," 251, treating Dido's Epicureanism as a reflection of Vergil's own youthful beliefs: ". . . that state whose philosophy is the hedonistic self-expression typified by its foundress Dido, however attractive or brilliant it may be, must fall before that more sober and self-controlled civilization represented by Aeneas, which builds its actions upon the foundation of fidelity to divine purpose."

26. "As he discloses the true character of the true doctrine, he discloses his true motive: if the true doctrine were simply gratifying, his love of Memmius would be a sufficient motive for writing the poem; but since it is not simply gratifying, it is not certain that Memmius or any other man known to the poet will be gratified by it; he can reasonably hope only for praise, that is, for praise by indeterminate readers." Leo Strauss, "Notes on Lucretius," in *Liberalism Ancient and Modern* (New York: Basic Books, 1968), 92.

Chapter 3: The Carthaginian Enlightenment

1. Cf. Austin, *Aeneidos Liber Primus, ad* 1.422 on the Lucretianism *strata viarum*.

2. . . . *bene ergo miratur Aeneas, ubi fuerant magalia illic esse legitimam civitatem; nam et portas et vias videbat et mox templum Iunoni ingens (ad* 1.422).

3. "Temples were the most prominent landmarks in the city." John E. Stambaugh, *The Ancient Roman City* (Baltimore: Johns Hopkins University Press, 1988), 215, citing Vitruvius 1.7.1–2. Cf. Pierre Grimal, *Roman Cities*, trans. and ed. G. M. Woloch (Madison: University of Wisconsin Press, 1983), 14–15, who argues that temples were thought to belong on high points because the gods protect what they can see of the city from their temples.

4. Among men, too, according to Evander's account in *Aeneid* 8, *amor habendi* arose under the regime of Jupiter; but in the case of men it led away from the peaceable consorting under laws that Saturn had formerly taught them, "until gradually a degenerate and deformed era succeeded, with war-madness and love of having" (8.324–327). Why it is that *amor habendi* welds together bee communities but splits apart human communities seems to be indicated by the fact that the bees' love of having is accompanied by a custom you will find amazing (*mirabere*, Geo. 4.197): they get their offspring without the erotic love of other bees (197–202). In accordance with this, they have no self-love; they spontaneously (*ultro*, 204) lay down their lives for the glory (!) of the common honey-production, *generandi gloria mellis* (205). Cf. Pufendorf, *De Jure Naturae et Gentium*, VII.II.4, "How a swarm of bees differs from a state."

5. Thus when Dido is overtaken by religious terrors in Book 4, Vergil likens the scenes of her nightmares to scenes on the tragic stage (4.469–473). That passage, which has so troubled critics by the supposed inappropriateness of its theatrical references, in fact fulfills or explains this first characterization of Carthage. Cf. Debra Hershkowitz, *The Madness of Epic: Reading Insanity from Homer to Statius* (New York and Oxford: Oxford University Press, 1998), 28.

On the Roman Senate's ban on construction of a permanent stone theatre as contrary to Roman virtue, see Valerius Maximus 2.4.2; on censure of Pompey for finally constructing one, Tacitus, *Annales*, 14.20; cf. W. Warde Fowler, *Social Life at Rome in the Age of Cicero* (New York: Macmillan, 1909), 309–311.

6. "What, precisely, is Aeneas so happy about? Presumably the glory of what was done and suffered in the last days of Troy boosts his spirits in the somewhat conventional antique way: he thinks of the immortality conferred by art. But even this positive view of his situation and state of mind is subject to certain reservations. First, he is standing by the temple of his archenemy, and the meaning of this enmity eludes him here as it constantly eludes him elsewhere in the poem. In a way that also eludes him (and some readers), the frescoes that amaze and hearten him are a kind of victory monument to Juno: they depict crucial, pathetic moments in the ruin of Troy, a ruin in which Juno, of course, takes a savage, ineffable delight." W. R. Johnson, *Darkness Visible*, 103. See also N. M. Horsfall, "Dido in the Light of History," *Proceedings of the Virgil Society* 13 (1973–1974): 1–13.

7. Cf. R. D. Williams, "The Pictures on Dido's Temple (*Aeneid* 1.450–493)," *Classical Quarterly* n.s. 10 (1960): 145–151.

8. R. D. Williams, *The Aeneid of Vergil*. In response to Aeneas' self-presentation (*sum pius Aeneas*, 1.378 ff.), Venus had addressed him as *quisquis es* (1.387)—"a cruel touch of irony, as Venus affects not to be aware of the names Troy or Aeneas."

9. Cf. also: *veterisque memor Saturnia belli,/ prima quod ad Troiam pro caris gesserat Argis*, "Saturnian [Juno], remembering the old war which she had been the chief in waging against Troy on behalf of her dear Greeks" (1.23–24).

10. Cf. Monti, *The Dido Episode*, 20: "Despite the subjective quality of the ecphrasis, it is clear that Vergil wants Aeneas' opinion to remain as the reader's impression of Dido as she arrives and has the interview with Ilioneus."

11. On Dido's temple of Juno as indicative of philosophic enlightenment cf. F. Klingner, *Virgil. Bucolica, Georgica, Aeneis* (Zürich, Artemis, 1967), 398–399.

12. Cf. Machiavelli, *Discorsi* I.11 (*"Della religione de' Romani"*): *"E veramente mai fu alcuno ordinatore di leggi straordinarie in uno populo che non ricorresse a Dio. . . ."*

13. Cf. Monti, *The Dido Episode*, 18: "The attribution of *iustitia* is for Ilioneus not the statement of a fact, but rather a prescription, cloaked in the words of a diplomat, for the modes of civilized conduct."

14. *Sane opportune post blanda principia ista ponuntur; prodest enim nonnumquam subtiliter obiurgare quem roges (ad 1.543).*

15. "To those who pass through a country, by water or by land, it ought to be permissible to sojourn for a time, for the sake of health, or for any other good reason; for this also finds place among the advantages which involve no detriment. So in Virgil, when the Trojans were forbidden to sojourn in Africa, Ilioneus dared to appeal to the gods as judges." Grotius, *De Jure Belli ac Pacis Libri Tres*, trans. F. W. Kelsey (Indianapolis: Bobbs-Merrill, 1962), book 2, chapter 2, XV.1.

16. Niccolò Machiavelli, *The Prince*, trans. Harvey C. Mansfield, Jr. (Chicago: University of Chicago Press, 1985), 66. Cf. Servius *ad* 1.540 ff., cited in Grotius, *De Jure*, book 2, chapter 2, XV.1, note 1.

17. Perhaps her statement reminds them of the part played in the fall of Troy by their king's imprudent hospitality to the apparently harmless Sinon, 2.57–198.

18. On the historical realities reflected by this rule cf. N.D. Fustel de Coulanges, *The Ancient City: A Study on the Religion, Laws, and Institutions of Greece and Rome* (English trans. of *La cité antique*) (Baltimore: Johns Hopkins University Press, 1980), 118–150 and 185–190.

19. *Non ait Siculos, sed quos Acestes colit.* Servius *ad loc.*

20. P. T. Eden, *A Commentary on Virgil: Aeneid VIII* (Leiden, Netherlands: E. J. Brill, 1975): "'the god of us both', Greeks and Trojans, now in alliance; similarly at A. 12.118 Rutulians and Trojans prepare altars for the *di communes* to ratify the general truce during the duel of Aeneas and Turnus. In both contexts Virgil is thinking solely of the necessity of having a commonly recognised god for the solemnity to be available and binding for both parties . . . what gods the Trojans and a primitive Italian tribe could in fact have had in common is difficult to see; and here there is no reason to believe that the Trojans were particularly devoted to Hercules who is commemorated in the Salian hymn (290 f.) as the destroyer of Troy" (94, *ad* 8.275, *communem . . . deum*).

21. *Dicendo 'utinam' et humanitatem suam ostendit et Aeneae se cupidam*, Serv. *ad* 1.575.

22. Cf. Monti, *The Dido Episode*, 35: "The emotional aspect of the Dido-Aeneas relationship does not obliterate its initial political character, but rather is an intensification and extension of it"; but Monti understands Dido as "the ideal Roman dynast" (37).

23. Cf. 5.77–8: *hic duo rite mero libans carchesia Baccho / fundit humi*; 1.215, 1.177.

24. Lucretius himself uses the phrase *rapax vis solis equorum*, *DRN* 5.398; and cf. *Aen.* 5.104–5.

25. Cf. *DRN* 5.79, 5.693, 5.1437, 6.737.

26. *urbe, domo socias* (600). How has Dido offered to associate "us" with her *house?* She spoke of her kingdom and city (572–573). Aeneas' addition of her house seems to respond to her unspoken or at any rate allusive wish for the union of Trojan king and Carthaginian queen. Cf. 4.318, *miserere domus labentis*.

27. For *mens sibi conscia recti* as a second subject with *di* rather than with *iustitia*, cf. R. D. Williams, *The Aeneid of Vergil, ad loc.*

28. Cf. Servius *ad* 5.687 ff.: *bene autem "si" ubique interponit: hic enim est optimus ductus, qui agentis voluntatem latenter ostendit.*

29. On *honos* in Aeneas' speech, cf. Monti, *The Dido Episode*: "*Honos* has religion as its proper sphere of application since it means the homage paid to the gods and usually indicates a sacrifice or ritual offering. . . . Transferred to the political sphere, *honos* is used to designate the payment of the debt that results from receiving an *officium* or a *beneficium. . . .*" (26).

30. Also like Lucretius, Dido later explains that what she means by "race of the gods" is "very great man," which for her is as much as to say, "very strong and courageous man" (4.11–13); when she changes her view of his character she says that no goddess was his mother but the rough Caucasus bore him and Hyrcanian tigers suckled him—for why dissimulate any longer? (4.365–368).

31. Cf. Nausikaa to Odysseus, in the Homeric model of this scene, *Od.* 6.187–190.

32. On *honos*, cf. n. 29 above.

33. Cf. the Homeric exemplar of the hospitable man (Eumaios), *Odyssey* 13.56 ff., 83 ff., 387 ff.

34. "The invocation must have rung strangely in Trojan ears: and Dido is unconsciously calling on the goddess of marriage." Austin, *Aeneidos Liber Primus, ad* 1.734.

35. The commentators point to the parallel to Dido's feast in Book 8.154–369 in order to harmonize Dido's conduct with Evander's (e.g. Eden, *A Commentary, ad* 8.184 ff.); but that entire passage serves on the contrary to point up by vivid contrast the connection of luxury and irreligion at Dido's court. Where Dido speaks of what "people say" about Jupiter, Evander opens his ceremony with the declaration "It is not vain superstition that has enjoined upon us these solemnities. . . ." (8.185–189). And where Dido's palace is

characterized by gold, silver, and purple, Evander lives in pious poverty ("Dare, my guest, to despise wealth. . . ." 8.359–365). Vergil's intention is to heighten, not to level out, the contrasts between the Carthaginian and the old Italian mores.

36. Macrobius, *The Saturnalia.* Trans., intro. and notes by Percival Vaughan Davies (New York: Columbia University Press, 1969), III.xi.4–7.

37. Cf. chapter 2, n. 20.

38. Cf. Milton, *Ad Patrem* 41–49: it was before luxury came in that royal bards, when singing of the beginnings or foundations of the world, used to include heroes and gods in their songs. Milton's language, esp. at lines 43 and 45, refers to *Aeneid* 1.738–746 and points the contrast with Iopas' post-luxury song, which does not refer to heroes and gods.

39. For example, Cicero, *De Rep.* II 7–8; Polybius VI 52, 56.

40. So Montesquieu; cf. above, chapter 2, n. 22.

41. Cf. Pease, *Publi Vergili Maronis*, 8–9: "two distinct philosophies are also contrasted [in the Dido episode], the pleasure-loving, self-expressive Epicurean on the one hand and on the other the self-restrained Stoic, subordinating his own impulses to the good of his people," and 36: "Pleasure-loving, craving friendship, prone to emotion and to individual self-expression, skeptical of the intervention of divine beings in human concerns and emphasizing the power of fortune, Dido exhibits not a few characteristics of the typical Epicurean. . . ."; also Pease, "Some Aspects," *Classical Journal* 22 (1927): 243–252.

42. Cf. *DRN* 3.832–837:
et velut anteacto nil tempore sensimus aegri,
ad confligendum venientibus undique Poenis,
omnia cum belli trepido concussa tumultu
horrida contremuere sub altis aetheris oris,
in dubioque fuere utrorum ad regna cadendum
omnibus humanis esset terraque marique. . . .
and Livy 29.17.6: *in discrimine est nunc humanum omne genus, utrum vos an Carthaginienses principes orbis terrarum videat.*

43. Cf. Hannah Arendt, *On Revolution* (Penguin, 1986), 191, quoting from John Adams, *Discourses on Davila*, in *Works* (Boston, 1851), vol. 6, 281: "Is there a possibility that the government of nations may fall in the hands of men who teach the most disconsolate of all creeds, that men are but fire flies, and this *all* is without a father? Is this the way to make man as man an object of respect? Or is it to make murder itself as indifferent as shooting plover. . . ?"

Chapter 4: Was There a Roman Enlightenment?

1. "General Introduction," in *T. Lucreti Cari De Rerum Natura Libri Sex*, ed. W. E. Leonard and S. B. Smith (Madison: University of Wisconsin Press, 1970), 76. Cf. Philip R. Hardie, *Virgil's Aeneid: Cosmos and Imperium* (New York and Oxford: Oxford University Press, 1986): "whereas in Lucretius this cosmic vision is made the servant of a philosophically developed view of a materialist universe, in Virgil the divine is restored to the central place; here Virgil shows a truly Augustan conservatism" (330).

2. Cf. Introduction, nn. 4 and 5 above (301); also Arthur Stanley Pease, *Publi Vergili Maronis Aeneidos Liber Quartus* (Darmstadt: Wissenschaftliche Buchgesellschaft, 1967), 37–38; and W. Y. Sellar, *The Roman Poets of the Augustan Age: Virgil.* 3rd ed. (Oxford: Oxford, 1897), 199 ff.

3. W. E. Leonard and S. B. Smith, *De Rerum Natura*, 76. Cf. Alan Wardman, *Religion and Statecraft among the Romans* (Baltimore: Johns Hopkins University Press, 1982) 56–57.

4. Eve Adler, "The Invocation to the *Georgics*," *Interpretation* 11 (1983), 33.

5. W. E. Leonard and S. B. Smith, *De Rerum Natura*, 76.

6. Benjamin Farrington, *Science and Politics in the Ancient World* (New York: Oxford University Press, 1940), 184.

7. Montesquieu, *Considérations sur les Causes de la Grandeur des Romains et de leur Decadence* (Paris: Flammarion, 1900), 98.

8. Montesquieu, *Considérations*, 96.

9. Life of Pyrrhus, XX.3–4.

10. Montesquieu, *Considérations*, 96.

11. Polybius VI 56.12: διόπερ οἱ παλαιοὶ δοκοῦσί μοι τὰς περὶ θεῶν ἐννοίας ὑπὲρ τῶν ἐν ᾅδου διαλήψεις οὐκ εἰκῇ καὶ ὡς ἔτυχεν εἰς τὰ πλήθη παρεισαγαγεῖν, πολὺ δὲ μᾶλλον οἱ νῦν εἰκῇ καὶ ἀλόγως ἐκβάλλειν αὐτά.

12. Polybius VI 56.9.

13. Montesquieu, *Considérations*, 97.

14. Cicero, *Letters to Atticus* IV.17.

15. Cf. J. D. Minyard, *Lucretius and the Late Republic: An Essay in Roman Intellectual History*. (Leiden, Netherlands: Brill, 1985), 75–76; and Charles Norris Cochrane, *Christianity and Classical Culture: A Study of Thought and Action from Augustus to Augustine* (New York: Oxford University Press, 1944), 35–42.

16. Cf. Norman Wentworth De Witt, *Epicurus and his Philosophy* (Minneapolis: University of Minnesota Press, 1954), 329–331, 340–344.

17. Cf. *De Finibus* II 49–50: *Philosophus nobilis, a quo non solum Graecia et Italia sed etiam omnis barbaria commota est, honestum quid sit, si id non sit in voluptate, negat se intellegere, nisi forte illud quod multitudinis rumore laudetur.* . . .

18. Cf. *DRN* 5.50, *dictis non armis*.

19. On the meaning of *mali* cf. *De Republica* III 26: *qui minime sunt in disserendo mali, qui in ea causa eo plus auctoritatis habent, quia, cum de viro bono quaeritur, quem apertum et simplicem volumus esse, non sunt in disputando vafri, non veteratores, non malitiosi.* . . .

20. διέγνωκας ὁποῖόν ἐστι τὸ ἑαυτῷ φιλοσοφῆσαι καὶ οἷον τὸ τῇ Ἑλλάδι· συγχαίρω σοι. "Sententiae Vaticanae" LXXVI, in *Epicurus: The Extant Remains*. Ed. Cyril Bailey (Oxford: Clarendon Press, 1926): 118.

21. "Sententiae Vaticanae" LVIII, in *Epicurus: The Extant Remains*, 114–115.

22. *DRN* 5.1129–1130.

23. Nichols, *Epicurean Political Philosophy*, 192. Pierre Boyancé, *Lucrèce et l'Épicurisme* (Paris: Presses Universitaires de France, 1963), 9, proposes a related distinction between Amafinian "moral" Epicureanism and Lucretian "physical" Epicureanism.

24. Farrington, *Science and Politics*, 129; so Hardie, *Cosmos and Imperium*, 171: "But Lucretius' universal vision is still more closely tied to his overriding didactic intention of releasing men's minds from superstitious fear. The final goal of the poem is the construction of an ethic valid for all mankind." Cf. Boyancé: "Amafinius . . . en s'adressant à la foule, répondait à une des préoccupations du fondateur: rechercher avant tout la clarté et permettre l'accès de la sagesse même aux gens sans culture." *Lucrèce et l'Épicurisme*, 9–10. Cf. Cicero, *De Fin*. II 15.

25. Farrington, *Science and Politics*, 193; cf. also 126, 130, 184–5.

26. Cf. Cicero, De Fin. II.102: Haec non erant eius qui innumerabiles mundos infinitasque regiones, quarum nulla esset ora, nulla extremitas, mente peragravisset, with Lucretius, De Rerum Natura 1.74: omne inmensum peragravit mente animoque.

27. W. E. Leonard and S. B. Smith, T. Lucreti Cari De Rerum Natura, 11; cf. Farrington, Science and Politics, 191–2.

28. Cf. DeWitt, Epicurus: "If decent citizens of small towns chose to study Epicurus in bad translations, this was tolerable; it was tolerable also if a section of the nobility chose to adopt such an idle philosophy; but when a new Epicurean literature written in Latin of the highest excellence began to threaten the supremacy of Ennius and the other classics, the limit of endurance was drawing near" (322). "Against Lucretius was inaugurated a tacit conspiracy of silence" (345).

29. Cf. Neal Wood, Cicero's Social and Political Thought (Berkeley: University of California Press, 1988), 63.

Chapter 5: Lucretius' Teaching

1. DRN 3.322.

2. Κενὸς ἐκείνου φιλοσόφου λόγος, ὑφ' οὗ μηδὲν πάθος ἀνθρώπου θεραπεύεται· ὥπερ γὰρ ἰατρικῆς οὐδὲν ὄφελος μὴ τὰς νόσους τῶν σωμάτων ἐκβαλλούσης, οὕτως οὐδὲ φιλοσοφίας, εἰ μὴ τὸ τῆς ψυχῆς ἐκβάλλει πάθος. Epicurus, Fragment D.54, in Epicurus: The Extant Remains, 132.

3. =1.936–950 with differences in 949–950. Cf. D. Clay, Lucretius and Epicurus (Ithaca, N.Y.: Cornell University Press, 1983), 184. Tali ratione in 23 is parallel to tali pacto in 17 but cannot mean simply "by such means" after the emphatic use of ratio in 18 and 21. The physician's pactum is the scheme of disguising the medicinal wormwood's bitterness, but Lucretius' ratio is both the medicinal reasoning itself and the scheme of disguising its bitterness. The physician's scheme, that is, is not a product of the wormwood itself, while Lucretius' scheme somehow is or is a product of the very reasoning which it is designed to mask.

4. Cf. Nichols, Epicurean Political Philosophy (Ithaca, N.Y.: Cornell University Press, 1976), 44; W. E. Leonard and S. B. Smith, T. Lucreti Cari De Rerum Natura (Madison: University of Wisconsin Press, 1970), 71.

5. Plato, Republic, 606E.

6. On ancient assignments of the De Rerum Natura to the epic genre, cf. Clyde Murley, "Lucretius, De Rerum Natura, Viewed as Epic," Transactions of the American Philological Association 78 (1947): 337–338.

7. Cf. P. H. Schrijvers, Horror ac divina voluptas: Études sur la poésie de Lucrèce (Amsterdam: A. M. Hakkert, 1970), 14–26; and Bernard Frischer, The Sculpted Word: Epicureanism and Philosophical Recruitment in Ancient Greece (Berkeley: University of California Press, 1982), 71 n. 7, 80–83, 127: ". . . verbal and plastic secondary imagery function in exactly the same way, a fact of great importance for understanding Lucretius' creation of a protreptic poetic language, perhaps more in line with Epicurean theoretical and practical precedents than many literary critics have been willing to grant."

8. Cf. Hardie, Cosmos and Imperium, 194 ff.

9. On the reading tendere, cf. Leonard and Smith, T. Lucreti Cari, ad loc.; also David West, The Imagery and Poetry of Lucretius (Edinburgh: Edinburgh University Press, 1969),

61–62: "*Tendere oculos* is a surprising phrase. . . . I think it should surprise us, at the beginning of this military context, into thinking of the stretching of the bow. . . ."

10. Cf. Hardie, *Cosmos and Imperium*, 188–189.

11. *Odyssey* 5.203–210, 10.237–240.

12. Cf. D. Clay, *Lucretius and Epicurus*, 217: "[Lucretius] makes of [Epicurus] a Roman *triumphator*, and thereby reverses the values placed upon the active and the contemplative lives."

13. Denique Tyndaridem raptam belloque subactas
Troiugenas gentis cum dicunt esse, videndumst
ne forte haec per se cogant nos esse fateri.

$$(1.464–466)$$

Lucretius calls attention here to the atomic compounding of the perfect passive system from words, as above (196–198) and below (823–827, 912–914) he discusses the compounding of words from letters. It is as misleading to see *esse* in *raptam esse* as to see *se* in *esse*.

14. For example, 1.72, 75, 79; 3.13; 5.3, 8, 22ff.; 6.5, 8.

15. Cf. Lucretius' use of the myth of Phaethon, 5.395–406.

16. Cf. Hardie, *Cosmos and Imperium*, 173–175.

17. Cf. Cicero, *De Natura Deorum* I.43.

18. Cf. Epicurus, *Letter to Menoeceus* 135.7–9: ζήσεις δὲ ὡς θεὸς ἐν ἀνθρώποις. οὐθὲν γὰρ ἔοικε θνητῷ ζῴῳ ζῶν ἄνθρωπος ἐν ἀθανάτοις ἀγαθοῖς. "You shall live as a god among human beings. For a human being who lives among immortal goods does not appear like a mortal living being." *Epicurus: The Extant Remains*, 92.

19. As Vergil indicates in the *Georgics* (cf. above, 11).

20. Cf. Strauss, "Notes on Lucretius," 92, 113, 134, but also 94, 131. Also Nichols, *Epicurean Political Philosophy*, 19, 40–41.

21. Cf. Nichols, *Epicurean Political Philosophy*, 78.

22. "He comes close to suggesting that . . . by freeing men from the fear of death, one does not emancipate crime from a powerful restraint; one rather contributes to the abolition of crime." Strauss, "Notes on Lucretius," 105.

23. Cf. Samuel Stern, *Aristotle on the World State* (Columbia: University of South Carolina Press, 1970), 58–59.

24. So Leonard and Smith, *T. Lucreti Cari De Rerum Natura, ad loc.*

25. Cf. 3.870 ff.:

proinde ubi se videas hominem indignarier ipsum,
post mortem fore ut aut putescat corpore posto
aut flammis interfiat malisve ferarum. . . .

and 3.1045: tu vero dubitabis et indignabere obire?

26. Cf. D. Clay, *Lucretius and Epicurus*, 225.

Chapter 6: Furor

1. Cf. A. K. Michels, "Lucretius and the Sixth Book," *American Journal of Philology* 65 (1944): 135–148.

2. *Geo.* II 483–484.

3. Cf. Joe Sachs, "The Fury of Aeneas," *St. Johns Review* 33 (82): 75–82.

4. "The root of Juno's animosity is her thwarted love for Carthage." Brooks Otis, *Virgil: A Study in Civilized Poetry* (Oxford: Clarendon Press, 1964), 129.

5. On the connection of this scene with Homer and Lucretius, cf. V. Buchheit, *Vergil über die Sendung Roms* (Heidelburg, 1963), 61–67; and Hardie, *Cosmos and Imperium*, 90 ff. and 180 ff.

6. Cf. Buchheit, *Vergil über die Sendung Roms*, 67.

7. Cf. Philip R. Hardie, *Virgil's Aeneid: Cosmos and Imperium* (New York, Oxford: Oxford University Press, 1986), 180 ff. and 237 ff.

8. For example, *magno indignantur murmure*, DRN 6.197, *indignantes magno cum murmure*, Aen. 1.55; *magnos montis ... insuper*, DRN 6.191–2, *montis insuper altos*, Aen. 1.61.

9. Cf. Hardie, *Cosmos and Imperium*, 227 ff.

10. Cf. K. Quinn, *Vergil's Aeneid: A Critical Description* (Ann Arbor: University of Michigan Press, 1968), 101: "Conway describes these lines as a fanciful, humorous expansion of Lucretius 6.189–203. A better way of putting it is to say that what Lucretius presents as a series of formal similes (his clouds only *look* like caves, his winds only *sound* like wild beasts) Virgil restates as a fantasy in which the words that are evocative of imagery are to be taken at their full value."

11. Cf. Hardie, *Cosmos and Imperium*, 95.

12. Cf. M. C. J. Putnam, *The Poetry of the Aeneid: Four Studies in Imaginative Unity and Design* (Cambridge, Mass.: Harvard University Press, 1965), 131.

13. "Just as the blowing of the winds preserves the sea from the foulness which would be the result of a prolonged calm, so also corruption in nations would be the product of prolonged, let alone 'perpetual,' peace." Hegel, *Philosophy of Right*, trans. T. M. Knox (Oxford: Clarendon Press, 1967), 210.

14. Cf. J. Conington in *P. Vergili Maronis opera*, 3rd ed. (London: Whittaker & Co., 1872–1876), *ad loc.*: "This simile . . . is remarkable as an illustration of Nature from man, the reverse of which is the general rule in Virgil as in Homer." V. Pöschl, in *The Art of Vergil: Image and Symbol in the Aeneid* (Ann Arbor: University of Michigan Press, 1962), claims that "a natural event explained by means of a political event serves to show that nature is a symbol of political organization," and thus that "Roman order is founded in the same divine whole from which it derives its grandeur" (23), but this is to ignore the implications of Vergil's striking reversal, which rather makes political organization the symbol of nature, thus demoting the stature of "the divine whole" as much as raising the stature of politics.

15. Cf. Servius *ad* 3.57: *sane sciendum, latenter Aenean hoc agere, ut Troianos Didoni ex infelicitatis similitudine commendat: nam et eius marito auri causa intulit necem.*

16. On Vergilian/Lucretian usage of *modis miris*, cf. Austin, *Aeneidos Liber Primus, ad loc.*

17. On the transitive usage of *celerare*, only in Lucretius 2.231 before Vergil, cf. Austin, *Aeneidos Liber Primus, ad loc.*

18. Cf. Numa Denis Fustel de Coulanges, *The Ancient City: A Study on the Religion, Laws, and Institutions of Greece and Rome* (Baltimore: Johns Hopkins University Press, 1980), 137.

Chapter 7: Dido in Love

1. Hannah Arendt, commenting on the role of the Book of Exodus and the *Aeneid* as foundation legends for the American Revolution, observes that "these tales seem to

contain an important lesson; in strange coincidence, they both insist on a hiatus between the end of the old order and the beginning of the new. . . . The revolution—so at least it must have appeared to these men—was precisely the legendary hiatus between end and beginning, between a no-longer and a not-yet." *On Revolution*, 205. What Arendt suggests about Vergil's presentation of the founding of Rome is even more true of his presentation of the founding of Carthage.

2. Arthur Stanley Pease, *Publi Vergili Maronis Aeneidos Liber Quartus* (Darmstadt: Wissenschaftliche Buchgesellschaft, 1967), *ad* 4.209, *caeci*: "In 4.2 . . . the *caeci ignes* are of a different and figurative sort, but our passage is imitated by Sil. 12.628–629 (in describing the disbelief of Hannibal): *Caecum e nubibus ignem / murmuraque a ventis misceri vana docebat*; cf. also Statius, *Theb.* 4.742–743: *omnia caecis / ignibus hausta sedent*."

3. J. Henry, *Aeneidea; or, Critical, exegetical, and aesthetical remarks on the Aeneis* (London: Williams and Norgate, 1873–1892), *ad loc.*

4. Cf. Pease, *Liber Quartus*, *ad* 4.14, *fatis*: "Virgil often alludes to fate or the fates . . . and in Aeneas' own narration to Dido he frequently uses the terms in connection with his own experiences (e.g., in Book 3, lines 7, 9, 17, 182, 337, 375, 395, and 494), so that Dido may merely, in her use of the word, be quoting him. It is noticeable that while Aeneas constantly uses 'fate(s),' in the fashion of the Stoic sage to whom he has been likened, Dido, on the other hand, prefers to speak of *casus* . . . or, again, of *fortuna*."

5. "What does Dido mean? . . . perhaps she feels that any marriage may bring like disappointment to that of her first; perhaps the words are simply part of her own self-deception, an attempted defence against desire." R. G. Austin, *Aeneidos Liber Primus* (Oxford: Clarendon Press, 1971) *ad loc.*

6. Pease, *Liber Quartus*, *ad loc.* Cf. Austin, *Aeneidos Liber Quartus* (Oxford: Clarendon Press, 1955), *ad loc.*: "This vivid, unexpected line throws a clear light on Dido's character. . . . her tears show that she is unstable and irresolute, for all her bravery—a foreshadowing of what is to follow."

7. Cf. *DRN* 4.757–776.

8. "Anna does not know how Juno hated Aeneas, and her words are full of tragic irony," Austin, *Aeneidos Liber Quartus*, *ad loc.* Anna as well as Dido had heard Aeneas' song with its clear references to Juno's hatred towards Aeneas (e.g., 2.612–614, 3.433–440); Anna's speech about Juno is based not exactly on ignorance but on a certain coloring of Aeneas' narrative in the light of Lucretius' teaching.

9. ". . . it might well be argued that her later determination is taken because the persuasions of Anna reenforced her waking decision to neglect the supernatural warnings of the night. . . ." Pease, *Liber Quartus*, *ad* 4.9, *insomnia*.

10. Austin, *Aeneidos Liber Quartus*, *ad loc.*, points out that Dido's ritual here "corresponds closely to that followed by Aeneas later in his sacrifice to the chthonic powers" at 6.243 ff., but without noting how the correspondence brings out by contrast the excessive character of Dido's observance.

11. On the inner connections between atheism and superstition cf. Plutarch, *De Superstitione*. "The atheist thinks there are no gods; the superstitious man wishes there were none, but believes in them against his will; for he is afraid not to believe. And yet, as Tantalus would be glad indeed to get out from under the rock suspended above his head, so the superstitious man would be glad to escape his fear by which he feels oppressed no less than Tantalus by his rock, and he would call the condition of the atheist happy because it is a state of freedom. But, as things are, the atheist has neither part nor lot in supersti-

tion, whereas the superstitious man by preference would be an atheist, but is too weak to hold the opinion about the gods which he wishes to hold" (170F). "For thus it is that some persons, in trying to escape superstition, rush into a rough and hardened atheism, thus overleaping true religion which lies in between" (171F) (Babbitt translation). On *superstitio* vs. *religio*, cf. Cicero, *De Natura Deorum* II 72; and Varro, cited in Augustine, *De Civitate Dei* 6 9.

12. The exclamation also suggests 1) Vergil's authorial exclamation over the inadequacy of priests to soothe or restrain an impassioned woman through customary rituals; and 2) Vergil's authorial exclamation over the impermeability of Dido's mind to the potential assistance to her of the priests' advice, i.e., his blame of Dido for not taking to heart the priests' negative interpretations of the entrails (taking *vatum* as an objective genitive with *ignarae*, "minds ignorant of the seers," as of Vulcan, *haud vatum ignarus venturique inscius aevi*, 8.627).

13. *Multaque praeterea vatum praedicta priorum / terribili monitu horrificant* (4.464–465); cf. *nec vates Helenus, cum multa horrenda moneret, / hos mihi praedixit luctus, non dira Celaeno* (3.712–713).

14. Cf. *eque tuo pendet resupini spiritus ore*, of Mars' attitude towards Venus when smitten by the wound of love, *DRN* 1.37.

15. Cf Lucretius' account: *Nam si abest quod ames, praesto simulacra tamen sunt / illius, et nomen dulce obversatur ad auris* (4.1061–1062).

16. *Interea magno misceri murmure caelum / incipit*, 4.160–161; cf. Neptune's perception of the storm in Book 1, *interea magno misceri murmure pontum / emissamque hiemem sensit*, 1.124–125.

17. "[Dido's] complaint of the ingratitude of Aeneas parallels that by Iarbas against Dido herself (4.211–214), who, like Aeneas, was an outcast without a city of her own, to whom he had granted a foothold on the coast . . . and who had, in turn, declined his advances." Pease, *Liber Quartus, ad* 4.373.

18. Cf. Gordon Williams, *Technique and Ideas in the* Aeneid (New Haven, Conn.: Yale University Press, 1983), 27.

19. *Latenter secundum Epicureos locutus est*, Serv. *ad* 4.210. Pease, *Liber Quartus, ad loc.*, compares the line-ending *in nubibus ignes*, 4.209, with *DRN* 2.214, *abrupti nubibus ignes*, and notes the rare Lucretian word *terrificant* in *Aen.* 4.210 (cf. *DRN* 1.133, 4.34).

20. Pease, *Liber Quartus, ad* 4.237, cites Donatus: *si omnia Iovis ipsius verba considerentur, nihil Hiarbae contemplatione invenietur mandasse Mercurio nec ad illius aliquam culpam pertinere poterit qui Carthaginis finibus excludi praeceptus est*.

21. And like Aristophanes' Strepsiades, whose response to Socrates' doctrine of Zeus' non-existence is to thumb his nose at Zeus, *Clouds* 380–381, 827–828.

22. The most striking links between Vergil's presentation of Iarbas and Dido:

Dido	Iarbas
per aras (56), ante ora deum . . .	centum aras (200), ante aras
ad aras (62)	media inter numina divum (204)
pinguis . . . ad aras (62), pecudum- que reclusis / pectoribus (63–4)	pecudumque cruore / pingue solum (202)
His dictis . . . animum flammavit (54)	incenditque animum dictis (197)
oath by "pater omnipotens" (25)	prayer to "Iuppiter omnipotens" (206)

23. Cf. Bacon, "Of Revenge," in *The Essays*, ed. John Pitcher (New York: Penguin, 1985): "The most tolerable sort of revenge is for those wrongs which there is no law to

remedy: but then let a man take heed the revenge be such as there is no law to punish. . . . Cosmus, Duke of Florence, had a desperate saying against perfidious or neglecting friends, as if those wrongs were unpardonable: *You shall read* (saith he) *that we are commanded to forgive our enemies; but you never read that we are commanded to forgive our friends"* (72).

24. Cf. *Geo.* 2.458–459, *O fortunatos nimium, sua si bona norint, / agricolas!* The condition on the farmers' fortunateness is knowledge (cf. J. S. Clay, "The Argument of the End of Virgil's Second *Georgic,*" *Philologus* 120 [1976]: 234); Dido speaks as if the condition on her own felicity had been chance.

25. "If an appeal cannot be made to an oath, on what does Dido base her claim?"— Monti, *The Dido Episode,* 3. Monti's own suggestion is "the assumption of obligations in political relationships" (6), but he does not take up the question what the sanction of such obligations could be.

26. Cf. 4.266, *fundamenta locas,* with 1.428, *fundamenta locant.*

27. Cf. R. D. Williams, *The Aeneid of Vergil* (New York: St. Martin's Press, 1972), *ad* 4.331 ff.: "When Aeneas makes this final statement about Mercury he seems to be certain that Dido will see that he must obey; but she sees nothing except her own terrible predicament. Everything to her is personal between herself and Aeneas—she accepts no other considerations, indeed understands none."

28. Cf. Pease, *Liber Quartus,* 34: "her reluctance to be as confidential as she is devoted leads to a complete misunderstanding. . . ." Cf. Servius *ad* 4.365: *non est sola in Aeneam vituperatio, sed etiam in se obiurgatio, quia dixerat* (4.12) *"credo equidem, nec vana fides, genus esse deorum."* Cf. Gordon Williams, *Technique and Ideas,* 39, on the "use by Lucretius of divine machinery, subverted and defined by later stages of the text," as "a model for Virgil's very much more complex and extensive adaptation of his generic inheritance."

29. Cf. R. D. Williams, *The Aeneid of Vergil, ad* 4.362 f.: "This speech is highly rhetorical, frighteningly remote from the give-and-take of human behaviour; the frustration of hope and pride has led to an elaborately formalised and grandiose concentration of all the hatred of her outraged heart;" W. Clausen, *Virgil's Aeneid and the Tradition,* 49: "She lapses into the third person, as if turning away from Aeneas and appealing to an imaginary audience, as characters in drama occasionally do in moments of intolerable exasperation or anger."

30. "Donat.: *si ista vera sunt, cur non extiterunt ante beneficia mea?* The repetition also suggests, but in an ironical way, that of *nunc* in the speech of Aeneas (4.345; 4.356)." Pease *ad* 4.376, *nunc.*

31. *DRN* 1.44–49 (=2.646–651), 5.82, 6.58–79.

32. Cf. Gordon Williams, *Technique and Ideas in the Aeneid* (New Haven, Conn.: Yale University Press, 1983), 27: ". . . as if to confirm Dido's subversion of this account, the next time Mercury appears to Aeneas it is in a dream and, again, what he says follows exactly the line of argument that would naturally occur to a man in Aeneas' situation. . . ."

33. "The sarcastic word *scilicet* and the hissing of *s*'s are pointers for the bitterness of her words about the gods; both *labor* and *sollicitat* are ironical as applied to the gods, and her statement immediately associates her with Epicurean ideas; the word *quietus* is used by Lucretius of the Epicurean deities (e.g. 6.73). Dido is not prepared to believe that anyone should sacrifice his personal life to requirements supposed to be imposed by the gods. It is a conflict between belief in a man-centred universe and belief in a divinely controlled world." R. D. Williams, *The Aeneid of Vergil, ad* 4.379 f. Cf. also Clausen, *Virgil's Aeneid and the Tradition,* 49.

34. "Similarly the reference to her death may suggest, though she does not say so, that it will be the means of her vengeance." R. D. Williams, *The Aeneid of Vergil, ad* 4.384f.

35. "Whether Dido here and in 4.323 (*moribundam*) means more than hyperbole may be queried, but Virgil interestingly shows how the thought, once introduced, develops and comes to possess her mind. . . ." Pease, *Liber Quartus*, ad 4.308.

36. With *turicremis . . . aris*, 4.453, cf. *DRN* 2.353, *turicremas . . . aras*.

37. Cf. Charles P. Segal, "Iopas Revisited (*Aeneid* 1.740 ff.)," *Emerita* 49 (1981): 20.

38. Austin, *Aeneidos Liber Quartus*, ad 4.590.

39. Austin, *Aeneidos Liber Quartus*, ad 4.614. Cf. *DRN* 1.77, 1.596, 2.1087–1088, 5.90, 6.66.

40. Cf. Arendt, *On Revolution*, 203: "When Madison speaks of the 'successors' on whom it will be 'incumbent . . . to improve and perpetuate' the great design formed by the ancestors, he anticipated 'that veneration which time bestows on every thing, and without which the wisest and freest government would not possess the requisite stability.'"

41. Cf. Pease, *Liber Quartus*, ad 4.14, *fatis*: In 4.614 and 4.651, "there may be detected a sneering reference to the religiosity of Aeneas, as expressed in 4.340–341 and 4.356, just as she has already sneered at it in 4.376–380, and we are consequently not justified in inferring from the use of the word any sincere belief on her part in fate. This is all an indication—though the point should not be pressed too far—of the contrast between Dido's essential Epicureanism and the typical Stoicism of Aeneas." Cf. also Pease, *Liber Quartus*, ad 4.450.

Chapter 8: The Theme of the *Aeneid* Again

1. *TU QUOQUE sicut Misenus, Palinurus etiam*. Servius *ad* 7.1; Paratore *ad loc*. argues that Vergil refers only to Misenus. Cf. Richard Jenkyns, *Virgil's Experience. Nature and History: Times, Names, and Places* (New York and Oxford: Oxford University Press, 1998), 465.

2. "Caieta may be said to have conferred fame on a single spot on the Italian coast: the coast itself rather conferred fame on her." John Conington, *P. Vergili Maronis opera* (London: Whittaker & Co., 1872–76), ad 7.1.

3. Cf. Servius *ad* 6.234: '*aërium*' *autem alii altum dicunt, alii nomen montis antiquum volunt: unde est 'qui nunc Misenus ab illo dicitur'*. Cf. 6.776: *haec tum nomina erunt, nunc sunt sine nomine terrae*.

4. The nurse of Aeneas, or of Aeneas' son? *hanc alii Aeneae, alii Creusae, alii Ascanii nutricem volunt*. Servius *ad* 7.1.

5. And cf. *DRN* 1.831–2, 3.260.

6. Cf. Vinzenz Buchheit, *Vergil über die Sendung Roms* (Heidelberg: Gymnasium, 1963), 174 n. 4.

7. Cf. C. Connolly, "Who Was Palinurus?" In *The Unquiet Grave* (New York and London: Harper & Brothers, 1945), 144–145.

8. *Bene autem interest funeri postquam ab inferis rediit, sicut interfuit antequam descenderet, ut medium actum ostenderet* (*ad* 7.4.). K. W. Gransden, *Virgil's Iliad: An Essay on Epic Narrative* (Cambridge, Eng. and New York: Cambridge University Press, 1984), 32–33, emphasizes rather the framing not of the catabasis by the two burials but of Book 6 by the two deaths, the death of Palinurus in Book 5 and the death of Caieta in Book 7.

9. "Tutti i commentatori interpretano nel senso di *quae magna est gloria*. Servio è fuor di strada, perché si rifà alla dottrina epicurea, e quindi prende la frase alla lettera come testimonianza di scetticismo riguardo alla gloria terrena." E. Paratore, *Eneide* (Milano: A. Mondadori, 1985), *ad loc*.

10. In Book 10, confronting the body of Lausus, whom he has just slain, Aeneas himself expresses doubt: *"quid pius Aeneas tanta dabit indole dignum? / arma, quibus laetatus, habe tua; teque parentum / manibus et cineri, si qua est ea cura, remitto"* (10.826–828).

11. The other relevant funeral is that of Polydorus, 3.13–72, which Aeneas performs implicitly as an alternative to seeking the deeply hidden causes of things (3.32; cf. Servius *ad* 3.30) and which, like the funeral of Caieta, is followed by the departure of the fleet from the burial site.

12. *gemitus irascentium leonum*, ἐν διὰ δυοῖν, Servius *ad loc.*

13. Cf. *Geo.* 2.493–4 on the triumph of the Epicurean philosopher over all fears and the din of the Underworld.

14. Cf. *DRN* 1.15–16: *ita capta lepore / te [Venus] sequitur cupide.*

15. For example, *Nunc age, quo motu . . . /expediam. tu te dictis praebere memento* (*DRN* 2.62–66); *nunc age, quo pacto . . . / . . . expediam* (*DRN* 6.495–497); *nunc age, Averna tibi quae sint loca cumque lacusque / expediam* (*DRN* 6.738–739); *nunc age, iam deinceps cunctarum exordia rerum . . .* (*DRN* 2.333); *exordia prima animai* (3.380); *causarum exordia prima* (*DRN* 5.677); and *sic volvenda aetas commutat tempora rerum* (*DRN* 5.1276).

16. "But Erato, as the Muse of Love, is more appropriately invoked to rehearse the loves of Jason and Medea than the present theme, though Germ. thinks that the war in Italy may be said to have been kindled by the love of Lavinia's suitors," Conington, *P. Vergili Maronis opera, ad* 7.37. Servius: *"vel pro Calliope, vel pro qualicumque musa posuit,"* *ad* 7.37.

17. "It is . . . as if two different aspects of Saturn have descended down to Aeneas' time. . . ." William S. Anderson, "Juno and Saturn in the *Aeneid*," *Studies in Philology* 55 (1958): 528.

18. Juno is called *"Saturnia"* four times in Books 1–6 (1.23; 3.380; 4.92; 5.606), twelve times in Books 7–10 (7.428, 560, 572, 622; 9.2, 745, 802; 10.659, 760; 12.156, 178, 807); Saturn is referred to once in Books 1–6 (6.794), six times in Books 7–12 (7.49, 180, 203; 8.319, 357; 12.830); Italy is called Saturnian once (by Dido) in Books 1–6 (1.569), three times in Books 7–12 (8.329, 358; 11.252). In the last reference to Saturn in the *Aeneid*, Jupiter hints that Juno's characteristic anger is related to her being the offspring of Saturn (12.830; Jupiter himself is called *Saturnius pater* by Dido, 4.372, and Neptune is referred to as *Saturnius domitor*, 5.799; Dis is nowhere explicitly connected with Saturn). Cf. L. A. MacKay, "Saturnia Juno," *Greece and Rome* 2nd Ser. 3 (1956): 60: ". . . the name *Saturnia* is applied to Juno chiefly in the part of the poem where her chief activity is the direct defence of the old order, the native traditions, the indigenous element of the *Saturnia tellus*"; for another view, cf. C. W. Amerasinghe, "Saturnia Juno: Its Significance in the *Aeneid*," *Greece and Rome* 22 (1953): 61–69.

Chapter 9: The Golden Age

1. *"Nam primi sex ad imaginem Odyssiae dicti sunt, quos personarum et adlocutionum varietate constet esse graviores, hi autem sex qui sequuntur ad imaginem Iliados dicti sunt, qui in negotiis validiores sunt: nam et ipse hoc dicit 'maius opus moveo.' et re vera tragicum opus est, ubi tantum bella tractantur."* Servius *ad* 7.1.

2. ". . . grander, that is, than what he has hitherto related, if measured by the standard of importance in the *Aeneid*, for otherwise they could hardly be grander than the fall of

Troy. But Virg. may mean to contrast generally the narrative of wars with the narrative of wanderings, the *Iliad* with the *Odyssey*." John Conington, *P. Vergili Maronis opera* (London: Whittaker & Co., 1872–76), *ad* 7.44. Cf. Duncan F. Kennedy, "Virgilian Epic," in *Cambridge Companion to Virgil*, ed. Charles Martindale (Cambridge and New York: Cambridge University Press, 1997), 147.

3. 1.456–493; all of Book 2; 3.86–87, 301–305; 4.215; 5.755–757; 6.88–94.

4. Cf. Jacob Klein, "The Myth of Virgil's *Aeneid*," *Interpretation* 2 (1971): 13–20.

5. Aeneas has at no other time heard this man promised to him, nor will he after this speech, though he will see Vulcan's representation of him on the shield in Book 8.

6. "As it is expressed elsewhere, 6.792, E. 4.8, the iron age will pass into the golden." Conington, *P. Vergili Maronis opera, ad* 1.291.

7. Cf. Hesiod, *Works and Days* 111; Ovid, *Metamorphoses* 1.113–114.

8. *Works and Days* 109–110; *Metamorphoses* 1.89.

9. *Works and Days* 112–120; *Metamorphoses* 1.89–112.

10. Monti, *The Dido Episode and the* Aeneid: *Roman Social and Political Values in the Epic* (Leiden, Netherlands: Brill, 1981), 87, observes justly that Latinus' words do not necessarily mean that the Latins themselves have no laws: "To state that a people is just not because of the restraint imposed by laws, but of their own free will is not the same as to assert that they have no laws;" he compares Sallust's comment on the early Romans, *ius bonumque apud eos non legibus magis quam natura valebat* (Cat. 9.1). But clearly Latinus regards the *original* regime of Saturn as having been characterized by the absence of laws, and his own contemporary Latins as reflecting that original regime precisely insofar as they are restrained not by whatever laws they may have but by the *veteris dei more*. Latinus' understanding of Saturnus' *mos* cannot be identified with the laws given to the Latins according to Evander (*leges dedit*, 8.322), since Latinus is at pains to distinguish between laws on the one hand and this *mos* on the other (7.203–204).

11. "*Ac si diceret, aurei saeculi imagine vivimus.*" Servius *ad* 7.204.

12. In *Hesiod, the Homeric Hymns and Homerica*, ed. and trans. Hugh G. Evelyn-White (Cambridge, Mass.: Harvard University Press, 1974).

13. Cf. William S. Anderson, "Juno and Saturn in the *Aeneid*," *Studies in Philology* 55 (1958): 526: ". . . Latinus insists that his people have observed the habits of their great ancestor Saturn. . . . And yet everything goes wrong. . . . Anarchy prevails in the city. . . . *Latinus may be mistaken about the character of Saturn's reign*, as he clearly is about the Italian observance of the ancient customs." (Emphasis added.)

14. For example, Conington, *P. Vergili Maronis opera, ad* 8.315: "The view of primitive society which follows agrees generally with the well-known descriptions of Aesch. Prom. 447 foll., Lucr. 5.925 foll., and with the notions formed by such writers as Sallust and Tacitus. . . . The idea of a golden age, which Virg. attempts to incorporate with it, is really antagonistic to it." Also Gransden, *Virgil's Iliad*, 63: "Virgil, in his characteristically syncretistic and assimilative style, conflated two accounts of primitive man: an evolutionary one, found in Lucretius, in which early man was nomadic, living off the land, ignorant of fire, in conflict with the wild beasts, without laws; later man developed into a social being, able to make fire and shelter; and a Hesiodic account, in which a 'golden' race lived in peace under Saturn: for them 'the fruitful earth brought forth in abundance of its own accord.'" Eden, *A Commentary, ad* 8.314–332, calls the passage "a combination of elements from four sources: Lucretius, folk-etymology, Hesiod, and

Roman antiquarianism." Cf. Richard Jenkyns, *Virgil's Experience*, 493–499 ("Virgil's synthesis, then, is distinctively his own," 496).

15. Cf. Dido's invocation to Jupiter, "*hospitibus nam te dare iura loquuntur*" (1.731).

16. Cf. Paratore, *Eneide*, ad 8.324: "*l'espressione, che indica la frequenza con cui si parla dell'età dell'oro, sembra adoperata da Virgilio per accennare al fatto che egli adduce una particolare figurazione di quell'età; e la formulazione ha tutta l'energia d'una affermazione definitiva.*"

17. For example, οἳ μὲν ἐπὶ Κρόνου ἦσαν, ὅτ' οὐρανῷ ἐμβασίλευεν (*Works and Days* 111).

18. R. J. Clark notes the tension between Evander's account and the tradition: "Here Vergil has not solved the difficulty that Saturn was both the Bad Ruler exiled by Zeus in the Battle of the Gods and the King of a bygone Golden Race, who after his release from Tartarus presided over a distant Wonderland of departed heroes." R. J. Clark, *Catabasis: Vergil and the Wisdom-Tradition* (Amsterdam: Grüner, 1979), 175. Cf. Paratore, *Eneide*, ad 8.321: "*gli aurea saecula sono presentati come una creazione di Saturno sempre dopo l'avvento di Giove.*"

19. For example, *Aurea prima sata est aetas* (in Ovid, *Metamorphoses* 1.89).

20. For example, Χρύσεον μὲν πρώτιστα γένος μερόπων ἀνθρώπων / ἀθάνατοι ποίησαν (*Works and Days* 109–110).

21. For example, *non galeae, non ensis erat: sine militis usu / mollia securae peragebant otia gentes* (*Metamorphoses* 1.99–100).

22. For example, *At vetus illa aetas, cui fecimus aurea nomen, / fetibus arboreis et, quas humus educat, herbis / fortunata fuit nec polluit ora cruore* (*Metamorphoses* 15.96–98). Cf. *Georgics* 1.125–128, 2.536–540.

23. For example, *vindice nullo, / sponte sua, sine lege fidem rectumque colebat* (*Metamorphoses* 1.89–90).

24. "The idea of a golden age, which Virg. attempts to incorporate with [Evander's view of primitive society], is really antagonistic to it." Conington, *P. Vergili Maronis opera*, ad 8.315.

25. And differing significantly from the treatment of the Golden Age in both the *Eclogues* and the *Georgics*; cf. Adler, "Invocation," 29.

26. On the contradiction between Latinus' version and Evander's cf. Monti, *The Dido Episode*, 86–87 and, for bibliography, n. 6, 109. Monti correctly observes that in the context of the *Aeneid* it is Latinus' version, not Evander's, that is anomolous: "To attribute to Latinus' assessment of the Saturnian character of his people a reference to the traditional mythical golden age of a Hesiod or an Ovid would be to posit an anomaly in a conception that is both clearly distinct from the standard notion and elsewhere consistent in the *Aeneid*" (87); for this reason among others he deems it "unlikely that Vergil wishes to evoke the memory of this traditional golden age with Latinus' proclamation that the Latins observe the institutions of Saturn" (86). The persuasiveness of Monti's interpretation depends on believing that the evocation of the traditional Golden Age which all readers have felt in Latinus' words was not intended by Vergil.

27. This connects the myth of the *Aeneid* with the Fourth Eclogue. On the untraditional character of the prophecy that the Golden Age will return, cf. Ch. Fantazzi, "Golden Age in Arcadia," *Latomus* 33 (1974): 280–305; and Adler, "Invocation to the *Georgics*."

28. Hesiod's Heroic Age (*Works and Days* 156–173) interrupts the linear decline of the Ages but not the overall motion downwards from Gold to Iron. On the interpretation of

Hesiod's account of the five ages, cf. Leo Strauss, "The Liberalism of Classical Political Philosophy," in *Liberalism Ancient and Modern* (New York: Basic Books, 1968), 34–37.

29. On ancient versions of the origins and vicissitudes of the human race, cf. Arthur O. Lovejoy and George Boas, *Primitivism and Related Ideas in Antiquity* (New York: Octagon, 1965).

30. As implied in Iopas' Lucretian song at Carthage, *unde hominum genus et pecudes*, 1.743.

31. On the ambiguous character of the development of the arts in Lucretius, cf. Leo Strauss, "Notes on Lucretius," in *Liberalism Ancient and Modern* (New York: Basic Books, 1968), 133; James Nichols, *Epicurean Political Philosophy* (Ithaca, N.Y.: Cornell University Press, 1976), 172–176. Cf. the discussion of Eric Voegelin, *The Ecumenic Age* (Baton Rouge: Louisiana State University Press, 1974), 307–308, pointing to Lucretius' "sensitiveness for the questionable character of a process which culminates, in his own experience, both in the philosopher's meditation on the *natura rerum* and in the concupiscential atrocities of the imperial wars" (308).

32. Cf. R. W. B. Lewis, "Homer and Virgil—The Double Themes," *Furioso* 5 (Spring 1950): 57: "a poetic account of the founding of Rome must see in its foundation the quality of a return. . . . Anchises speaks of 'cycles,' but Virgil's fundamental outlook is not cyclical in any simple sense. The return is not to the *same* thing from which the departure was first made. . . ."

33. "We have learned by tradition" that Latinus' parents were Faunus and the Nymph Marica (*Aen.* 7.47–48). Evander's story suggests that the origin of this tradition is a wishful aggrandizing of men's true birth from the earth like the beasts, as Lucretius speaks of the earliest men, among the other *sitientia saecla ferarum*, discovering potable water in the precincts of the "Nymphs" (5.949), after having explained how lonely and miracle-mongering country folk make up stories of Fauns and Nymphs: *haec loca capripedes Satyros Nymphasque tenere / finitimi fingunt, et Faunos esse loquuntur* (4.580–581). Cf. Hardie, *Cosmos and Imperium*, 218–219.

34. *Metamorphoses* 1.101–110, 15.96–98. Cf. Dante: Io secol primo quant'oro fu bello; / fè savorose con fame le ghiande, / e nettare con sete ogni ruscello. *Purg.* xxii.148–150.

35. Referred to by Vergil, *Geo.* 2.536–538; cf. Ovid, *Metamorphoses* 15.96–98; Plato, *Politicus* 271 D–E.

36. Homer, *Odyssey*, trans. R. Lattimore (New York: Harper & Row, 1967). Cf. also *Od.* 9.188–192. Servius perhaps has the Cyclopes in mind when he explains Evander's *truncis et duro robore nati: hoc figmentum ortum est ex antiqua hominum habitatione, qui ante factas domos aut in cavis arboribus aut in speluncis manebant. qui cum exinde egrederentur aut suam educerent subolem, dicti sunt inde procreari* (ad 8.315).

37. On ancient vegetarianism, cf. Arthur O. Lovejoy and George Boas, *Primitivism and Related Ideas in Antiquity* (New York: Octagon, 1965), 32–34.

38. Homer connects Cyclopean cannibalism with lawlessness and godlessness, *Od.* 9.275 ff.

39. Greek Teucer, Trojan Teucer, Dido, Sinon, Dardanus, Helenus, Mezentius, Metabus, Evander, Aeneas.

40. P.T. Eden, *A Commentary on Virgil: Aeneid VIII* (Leiden: E. J. Brill, 1975), xxiii, comments on "symbolic links" in Book 8: "Saturn, Evander and Aeneas, all foreign immigrants, are the past, present and future colonisers and civilizers of Latium. . . ."; and, *ad* 8.333 *pelagique extrema sequentem*, points out that "Evander (like Aeneas) found the voyage so long that it seemed that the shores he was looking for must be receding from him."

41. *ad* 7.204.

42. On *amor habendi* cf. chapter 3, n. 4 above.

43. Vergil follows Lucretius in making law rather than speech the distinctively human or humanizing element. In the *De Rerum Natura*, the first compacts among men were made with sounds and gestures, *vocibus et gestu* (5.1022): agreement on the equity of commiserating the weak preceded knowledge of the words to express it. The sounds made by the early men were, like the sounds still made by the brutes, the natural expressions of their primary passions (5.1056–61). In Evander's account of the origins, Saturn's giving of names (8.322–3) is secondary to his giving of laws. The dissolution of the Saturnian Golden Age is accompanied by the loss of true names (8.329–332), but this is secondary to the breakdown of Saturn's laws.

44. Although Lucretius does not explicitly derive fear of gods from law, he seems to show his meaning by making belief in gods (fear of gods) appear for the first time in human history simultaneously with acceptance of law (*legibus uti*, 5.1144; *divom genus*, 5.1156). Thus his account of the origin of religion (5.1161 ff.) follows immediately upon his discussion of the origin of law (5.1136–1160). Cf. Strauss, "Notes on Lucretius," 127–128; Nichols, *Epicurean Political Philosophy*, 143–149.

45. Cf. Plato, *Rep.* 546A: χαλεπὸν μὲν κινηθῆναι πόλιν οὕτω ξυστᾶσαν· ἀλλ' ἐπεὶ γενομένῳ παντὶ φθορά ἐστιν, οὐδ' ἡ τοιαύτη ξύστασις τὸν ἅπαντα μενεῖ χρόνον, ἀλλὰ λυθήσεται. "Certainly it is difficult for a city so constituted to be changed; but since everything that comes into being has a passing away, not even such a constitution will remain for all time, but it will be destroyed."

46. *DRN* 3.806–818 = 5.351–363.

47. *Fortuna gubernans*, *DRN* 5.107.

48. *DRN* 5.91 ff.; cf. *explicat ut causas rapidi Lucretius ignis, / casurumque triplex vaticinatur opus. . . .* Ovid, *Tristia* 2.425–426.

49. *sed res quaeque suo ritu procedit, et omnes / foedere Naturae certo discrimina servant.* *DRN* 5.923–924.

Chapter 10: Aeneas' Founding of Rome

1. This episode is linked with the Carthaginian hunt in several ways. The phrase *quae prima laborum causa fuit* (7.481–2), while making the hunting the cause of the war, links the episode to the day of the ambiguous wedding of Dido and Aeneas, *primusque malorum causa fuit* (4.169–70), which flowed from the scattering of the hunters by the storm. At Carthage Ascanius had ambitiously hoped for a boar or a lion rather than a deer (*pecora inertia*, 4.158), as in Latium it was his dogs rather than he himself that made for Silvia's deer; Ascanius' own unconsciousness of his prey and its fate recalls the figure of Aeneas in 4.68–73, the shepherd who has unconsciously wounded the deer that represents Dido.

2. Paratore, *Eneide*, remarks on *agrestis*, 482: "in accordo con quello che sarà il quadro bucolico dell'episodio del cervo, il poeta torna alla figurazione degli aborigeni come pacifici contadini," though he thinks this characterization is contradicted by *duri* at 504.

3. "*Telum ira facit*" recalls "*furor arma ministrat*" in the simile in Book 1 in which Vergil compares Neptune's calming of the storm winds with the calming of a seditious mob by a man grave with piety. This verbal reference to the simile is preparation for the double reversal of it in 7.586–600, where the rioting Latins are compared with a stormy

sea and where Latinus' pious speech has no calming effect on them. Although the two phrases seem at first to argue rather vividly against the efficacy of disarmament (as Machiavelli cites *furor arma ministrat, Discorsi* II.24, to this effect), nonetheless in both situations the people armed in this manner are in fact defeated, in the one case by the calming words of the grave man and in the other by the military superiority of the Trojans.

4. "Di nuovo la caratterizzazione dell'Ausonia come pacifica, che contraddice ad altre notizie." Paratore, *Eneide, ad loc.*

5. These expressions are picked up in Book 11 by Diomedes' response to the Latin embassy: *o fortunatae gentes, Saturnia regna, / antiqui Ausonii, quae vos fortuna quietos / sollicitat suadetque ignota lacessere bella?* (11.252–254).

6. W. Warde Fowler, *Virgil's "Gathering of the Clans"* (Oxford: B. H. Blackwell, 1916): "As a king of pacific policy he reminds us of Numa" (63); but cf. of Tullus in the show of heroes: *qui rumpet patriae residesque movebit / Tullus in arma viros et iam desueta triumphis / agmina* (6.812–815). And cf. of Dido, 1.721–722.

7. Cf. Paratore, *Eneide, ad loc.*

8. So Eden, *A Commentary, ad loc.*, though not for this reason but because of the disagreement with 7.45–6.

9. Cf. John Conington, *P. Vergili Maronis opera* (London: Whittaker & Co., 1872–1876), *ad* 7.423: "It is implied v. 426 that Turnus had assisted Latinus in war against the Tyrrhenians. How this is to be reconciled with the long peace spoken of v. 46 does not appear: we can scarcely suppose that Turnus fought the battles of the Latins without their help. In 8.55 the Arcadians (who *may* be meant by the Tyrrhenians here, though this is hardly probable) are said to be constantly at war with the Latins."

10. "This line is in favour of the supposition that in v. 55 'Latina' is used loosely for Rutulian. Probably we are meant throughout more or less to identify the two nations." Conington, *P. Vergili Maronis opera, ad loc.*

11. *Sic agit, ut et ipse praestare videatur; nam et supra ait "socia arma rogantes,"* Servius *ad* 7.146. "Like his opponents (vv. 13, 17), Aeneas seems to think it part of diplomatic policy to exaggerate facts and attribute motives"—Conington, *P. Vergili Maronis opera, ad* 7.147. C. J. Fordyce, *P. Vergili Maronis Aeneidos, Libri VII–VIII* (New York and Oxford: Oxford University Press, 1977), *ad loc.*, indignantly: "In these lines Aeneas' diplomacy rests its case on total misrepresentation: for the Italians have done no more than repel the Trojan incomers and there has been no suggestion that they even have designs on anything that is not their own."

12. Cf. Paratore, *Eneide, ad* 7.46, on the information of Dionysius of Halicarnassus "che Latino era in guerra coi rutuli."

13. So Machiavelli: "che non solamente in Lacedemonia nascevano gli uomini da guerra, ma in ogni altra parte dove nascessi uomini, pure che si trovasse chi li sapesse indirizzare alla milizia, come si vede che Tullo seppe indirizzare i Romani. E Virgilio non potrebbe meglio esprimere questa opinione, né con altre parole mostrare di accostarsi a quella, dove dice, 'Desidesque movebit Tullus in arma viros.'" Nicolò Machiavelli, *Discorsi sopra la Prima Deca di Tito Livio* (Milan: Biblioteca Universale Rizzoli, 1984), I.21; on Machiavelli's *desides*, cf. Harvey Mansfield, *Machiavelli's New Modes and Orders* (Ithaca, N.Y.: Cornell University Press, 1979), 92.

14. As Servius points out, there is even rather a presumption of alliance between Turnus and Evander as "Greeks": *et bene praestandorum auxiliorum exprimit causam, ne magis Turno, quasi Graeco, favere credantur (ad 8.55).*

15. So Servius ad 8.570.

16. Compare the situation of Dido before Aeneas' arrival, when it appeared that she was proof against the flame of love but only because, by a fortunate accident, none of her suitors happened to please her.

17. The prophet means "from the same direction and in the same direction" as the bees of the portent; but his words also suggest that the Trojans are to attack the same land from which they themselves originally came.

18. Servius observes of Amata's argument for Turnus' foreignness (ad 7.367): *per quod duas res agit latenter: nam dicendo originem considerandam, docet et Turnum Graecum esse ab Inacho et Acrisio, et Aenean Latinum a Dardano.*

19. Cf. Cicero, *De Legibus* I 24–25: *. . . animum esse ingeneratum a deo. ex quo vere vel agnatio nobis cum caelestibus vel genus vel stirps appellari potest. . . . ex quo efficitur illud, ut is agnoscat deum, qui unde ortus sit quasi recordetur et agnoscat.*

20. *Quod autem dicit verum est: nam et Suetonius ait in vita Caesarum <II 94>, responsa esse data per totum orbem, nasci invictum imperatorem.* Servius ad 6.798.

21. As, for example, T. E. Page *ad loc.* speaks of the "splendid arrogance of these famous lines," *The Aeneid of Virgil* (London: Macmillan, 1962); Austin, *Aeneidos Liber Sextus* (Oxford: Clarendon Press, 1977), *ad* 852, says that the parenthetically introduced *hae artes* are "finer than all the accomplishments that Virgil is content to assign to '*alii.*'" Other commentators take Vergil to suggest more of a parity in the worthiness of the Greek and Roman arts. Eduard Norden, *P. Vergilius Maro, Aeneis Buch VI* (Stuttgart: B.G. Teubner, 1957) speaks of "der Gegensatz der beiden, jeder in ihrer Eigenart grossen und vereint dem Ziel einer Weltkultur zustrebenden Nationen," (334) and of "beide Nationen mit den ihnen von der Natur verliehenen Gaben . . . der Römer real zum Segen des Staates, der Grieche ideal zum Segen der Kultur" (337); similarly, Paratore, *Eneide, ad loc.*, "Si afferma decisamente l'ideale di una civiltà mondiale, che si ripartisce in cultura artistica, letteraria, filosofica e scientifica, in cui prevalgono i greci, e sapienza giuridica, amministrativa, politica e militare, in cui predominano i romani."

22. On the reading *paci* or *pacis*, see Eduard P. Norden, *Vergilius Maro, Aeneis Buch VI* (Stuttgart: B. G. Teubner, 1957), *ad loc.*; Paratore, *Eneide, ad loc.* If the dative is read, it emphasizes all the more strongly the status of peace as the end of the Roman rule of the peoples.

23. The allusion of "regere imperio" to Lucretius, *DRN* 5.1129–30, remarked by all commentators, refers polemically to the question of the true relationship between ruling and studying the nature of things. Lucretius argues that because philosophizing is intrinsically (*sensibus ipsis*) worthwhile and rule is considered desirable only by hearsay (*alieno ex ore, ex auditis,* 1133–4), it is much more satisfactory to obey quietly than to rule with empire and hold kingdoms. The teaching that Vergil puts into Anchises' mouth here is in effect that Lucretius was so impressed by the intrinsic superiority of philosophy over rule that he forgot to notice that the conditions for pursuing philosophy can be secured only by rule.

24. The emphatic division between what Aeneas claims and what he foregoes is noted by W. Warde Fowler, *The Death of Turnus: Observations on the Twelfth Book of the Aeneid* (Oxford: B. H. Blackwell, 1919), 62: "Aeneas is conceived as more deeply concerned with religion than with any other part of the life of the community; in other words, the *ius divinum* is his share of the task, the *ius civile* is that of Latinus. . . . He is to undertake the solemn religious duty of founding a new city common to both peoples; to Latinus was as-

signed the headship of the political and military elements in the State." But this formulation does not capture the subsumption of the "political" under the "religious" (the specifically Roman task being "*populos regere imperio*"), or the identity between marrying Lavinia and succeeding Latinus, i.e. becoming the political head of the Latins.

25. Servius *ad* 12.192 emphasizes the gift-character of Aeneas' words (*captat gratiam populi*) without explaining why a vanquished people would find the worship of the victor's gods entirely welcome. Paratore, *Eneide, ad loc.* appears to take *sacra deosque dabo* as meaning no more than that Aeneas will settle his gods within his own walls: "Questa era la principale missione che Enea sentiva essergli stata affidata e a cui teneva particolamente: trasferir i culti patrii nella nuova sede." This does not explain what Aeneas means by "*dabo*"; and see below on Jupiter's restatement of Aeneas' terms.

26. Paratore, *Eneide, ad* 839: "questo [nuovo culto] non potrà essere se non quello dei Penati di Troia."

27. Aeneas invokes "*pater omnipotens*," 12.178; Latinus picks this up with "*genitor qui foedera fulmine sancit*," 12.200.

28. Juno's sense of being insufficiently honored was the root of her anger, 1.48–49.

29. *Aen.* 1.50–64.

Chapter 11: World Empire

1. The reading *omni* is preferred by some editors, including Servius, who explains "*melius 'omni' quam 'omnis,' ut significet 'omni potestate,' id est pace, legibus, bello.*" Thus Venus complains to Jupiter, after the shipwreck at Carthage, that the "whole circle of lands," *cunctus terrarum orbis* (233), has been closed off to the Trojans.

2. *Haec autem Iovis allocutio partim obiecta purgat partim aliquid pollicetur.* Servius *ad* 1.286.

3. *Nulla terra est, quae non subiaceat sideribus.* Servius *ad* 6.795.

4. On the practical world map projects of Julius Caesar and Agrippa, cf. O. A. W. Dilke, *Greek and Roman Maps* (Ithaca, N.Y.: Cornell University Press, 1985), 40–44 and Appendix I.

5. Cf. *Geo.* 1.1–42, where Vergil elaborates the idea of Augustus' rule of the four quarters of the world. On the relation of the earthly *oecumene* with divine cosmography cf. Voegelin, *The Ecumenic Age*, 197–211. An exhaustive treatment of Vergil's expressions for "the whole world" as pointing to "future universal rule of the Romans" is provided in Philip R. Hardie's chapter on "Universal Expressions," *Virgil's* Aeneid: *Cosmos and Imperium* (New York and Oxford: Oxford University Press, 1986), 293–335; Hardie attributes Vergil's use of these "cosmic" expressions to "a truly Augustan conservatism" in which "it is the political or ideological level that is ultimately determinative" (330); Venus' words "could be taken straight from official Augustan propaganda" (334).

6. Cf. also the prophecy of the Penates: *idem venturos tollemus in astra nepotes / imperiumque urbi dabimus*, 3.158–159. On the dependence of eternal empire on universal empire, cf. Apollo's prophecy at 3.97–8. Based on Poseidon's prophecy at *Iliad* 20.302–308, it extends Poseidon's temporal reference to Aeneas's "sons' sons and those who are born of their seed hereafter" by specifying that these will rule over "all shores" (*cunctis oris*).

7. Further developed in Anchises' speech by the comparison of Rome with *Berecyntia mater* (6.784–787), on which Servius comments, *per hanc autem comparationem nihil aliud ostendit, nisi Romanos duces inter deos esse referendos.* Hardie, *Cosmos and Imperium*,

297–298, emphasizes the "qualified" character of Vergil's "assertion of the universal extension of Roman power;" at 1.287 and 6.782 Vergil "stops short of the ultimate expression of royal power, possession of the Heavens (which would necessitate a fully divinized ruler), but the mention in both passages of a word for the Heavens has the illogical effect of making it seem as if the empire spanned both Heaven and Earth" (334–335).

8. Indeed world empire goes even beyond this: Anchises in his prophecy to Aeneas suggests that Augustus will extend the reach of the restored Golden Age from Latium not only to "the stars" but "beyond the stars": . . . *iacet extra sidera tellus,* / *extra anni solisque vias,* 6.795–796.

9. Cf. *Ecl.* 5.56–57: *"Candidus insuetum miratur limen Olympi* / *sub pedibusque videt nubes et sidera Daphnis."*

10. Cf. Servius *ad* 7.100, *"SUB PEDIBUS. sub imperio suo ac potestate."* Cf. John Conington, *P. Vergili Maronis opera* (London: Whittaker & Co., 1872–76), *ad loc.*: "The Caesars (*'nepotes'*) and especially Augustus are here spoken of in terms applicable at once to universal empire and divinity. . . . *'Verti,'* which denotes the natural movement of the universe . . . is more appropriate to the god; *'regi'* recalls the emperor."

11. Cf. Cicero, *De Legibus* I.61: *idemque [animus] cum caelum, terras, maria rerumque omnium naturam perspexerit. . . . seseque non <omnis> circumdatum moenibus popularem alicuius definiti loci, set civem totius mundi quasi unius urbis agnoverit, in hac ille magnificentia rerum atque in hoc conspectu et cognitione naturae, dii inmortales, quam se ipse noscet, quod Apollo praecepit Pythius!*

12. Conington, *P. Vergili Maronis opera, ad* 4.229: ". . . the temper of the Italian nations at the time of Aeneas' arrival was a matter of infinitely small moment compared with the destiny in store for them: at the same time it was the imperious and unbridled character of those nations which marked them out as instruments in the conquest of the world after they should have been conquered themselves, first by Aeneas and eventually by Rome, so that Italy could be said to be not only the future mother of empire, but actually teeming with it at the moment when Jupiter was speaking."

13. For the distinction between *consistere* and *considere* cf. Conington, *P. Vergili Maronis opera, ad loc.*

14. Recalling 1.281–282, where Jupiter had prophesied the day when Juno *mecumque fovebit* / *Romanos, rerum dominos, gentemque togatam.* Cf. Plutarch, *On the Fortune or the Virtue of Alexander,* in *Plutarch's Moralia,* translated by F. C. Babbitt, vol. 4 (Cambridge, Mass.: Harvard University Press, 1936), 329F–330D, for a discussion of the importance of matters of national costume to world empire. "As a philosopher what he wore was a matter of indifference, but as sovereign of both nations and benevolent king he strove to acquire the goodwill of the conquered by showing respect for their apparel, so that they might continue constant in loving the Macedonians as rulers, and might not feel hate toward them as enemies" (330A).

15. Cf. Voegelin, *The Ecumenic Age,* 117–133, on the relative strength of practical and theoretical motivations in Polybius' account of Roman imperialism.

16. Cf. Plato, *Republic* 460A; *Laws* 737C–738E, 740D–741A; Aristotle, *Politics* 1265a12–1265b17, 1325b33–1326b26.

17. Cf. Plato *Republic* 466e–471b, *Timaeus* xx, *Laws* 625E–631B; Aristotle *Politics* 1256b23–27, 1333a31–1334b4.

18. Or, "reared by a common law" (νομῷ [νόμῳ] συντρεφομένης).

19. Or, "well-pastured state" (εὐνομίας).

20. W. W. Tarn, *Alexander the Great. Vol. II, Sources and Studies* (Cambridge: Cambridge University Press, 1950), 417ff., argues that the "politeia" referred to by Plutarch is not Zeno's treatise of that name, written before he came under the influence of Alexander's career, but the *idea* of a "cosmopolitan World-State" (419) that Zeno later derived *from* Alexander: it was not that Alexander "gave effect to Zeno's idea", but that Alexander supplied the deed which "lay behind" or gave rise to Zeno's word.

21. Cf. Plutarch, *Life of Alexander* VIII.4.

22. "Tyranny and Wisdom," in Leo Strauss, *On Tyranny* (Ithaca, N.Y.: Cornell University Press, 1963), especially 180–184.

23. Alexandre Kojève, "Tyranny and Wisdom," in Leo Strauss, *On Tyranny* (Ithaca, N.Y.: Cornell University Press, 1963), 143–188. Kojève here defines the idea of universal empire as including, minimally, the rejection of *a priori* geographic or ethnic limits and the consequent rejection of a geographically or ethnically predetermined capital. Cf. W. Warde Fowler, *Death of Turnus: Observations on the Twelfth Book of the* Aeneid (Oxford: B. H. Blackwell, 1919),140, on the question of Augustus' views (and Vergil's) on the location of the "capital of the Roman Empire."

24. This and the preceding quotations from Kojève, "Tyranny and Wisdom," 181–182.

25. Kojève, "Tyranny and Wisdom," 180.

26. Kojève, "Tyranny and Wisdom," 183.

27. Kojève, "Tyranny and Wisdom," 181. Tarn's argument for the philosophic basis of Alexander's project fails to take account of the Socratic foundations of the idea of the human race (see esp. Appendix 25, 399–449, in Tarn, *Alexander the Great).* A critique of Tarn's views which seeks to demonstrate that it is idle to look for a "consciously held intellectual theory" behind Alexander's deeds is H. C. Baldry, *The Unity of Mankind in Greek Thought* (Cambridge: Cambridge University Press, 1965), 114 ff. Voegelin's treatment of Alexander in *Order and History* (Baton Rouge: Louisiana State University Press, 1974), 153–165 and 205–207, discerns as the foundation of Alexander's deeds "the power drive of the conqueror blended with the curiosity of the explorer, and with the deadly concupiscence of reaching the 'horizon.'" Voegelin's account of the coincidence of the horizon of empire and the horizon of knowledge in the "concupiscence of conquest" (208) has in common with Kojève's argument its grounding of the impetus to world empire in a *philosophic* striving ("the meaning of imperial expansion as an attempt to represent universal humanity visibly through the organized social unity of mankind in its cosmic habitat," 208); but Voegelin evaluates this philosophic drive itself as founded on a hubristic and futile error.

28. Kojève, "Tyranny and Wisdom," 182.

29. Cf. Cicero, *De Natura Deorum* I.10–11.

30. Dante Alighieri. *Monarchia.* Foreword, introduction, translation, and comments by Gustavo Vinay (Florence, Italy: Sansoni, 1950). *Est ergo temporalis Monarchia, quam dicunt Imperium, unicus principatus et super omnes in tempore vel in hiis et super hiis que tempore mensurantur* (I.2).

31. For a comprehensive treatment of the *Monarchy,* see Etienne Gilson, *Dante the Philosopher* (London: Sheed and Ward, 1948), chap. 3, 162–224; also Donna Mancusi-Ungaro, *Dante and the Empire* (New York: Peter Lang, 1987). Colin Burrow ("Virgils, from Dante to Milton." In *Cambridge Companion to Virgil,* ed. Charles Martindale [Cambridge: Cambridge University Press, 1997]) argues that Dante saw in Vergil "the poet of an ideal polity" not in the sense that Vergil conceived such a polity, but in the sense that he already lived in it (82).

32. On the "human race," cf. Dante, *De Vulgari Eloquentia* I.vi.3: *Nos autem, cui mundus est patria velut piscibus aequor, quanquam Sarnum biberimus ante dentes et Florentiam adeo diligamus ut, quia dileximus, exilium patiamur iniuste. . . ."*

33. Dante purports to deduce this from a principle of Aristotle; cf. *Politics* 1254a28 ff. G. Vinay discusses Dante's probable source for this attribution in Dante, *Monarchia*, 34–35, n. 4.

34. Cf. II.6: nature necessarily produces a multiplicity of human beings, differing in aptness for each of the activities required to nature's end; and "not only individual human beings, but also peoples, are some of them by nature apt to rule, while others are by nature apt to be subjects and to serve."

35. As also on the basis of his explicit appeal to the authority of Averroes by name for his account of the potential intellect in I.3. Cf. Etienne Gilson, *Dante the Philosopher*, translated by David Moore (London: Sheed and Ward, 1948), 168–171 and 212–224; Ernest Fortin, *Philosophie et Dissidence au Moyen Age* (Montreal: Bellarmin, 1981), 99–103; "Dante and Averroism," *Actas del V° Congreso de Filosofia Medieval*, Vol. II (Madrid, 1979), 739–746; and Mancusi-Ungaro, *Dante and the Empire*, 130 ff.

36. "No peace, no philosophy. Therefore universal peace, if not our beatitude, is at any rate the loftiest of its concomitants" (Gilson, *Dante the Philosopher*, 174). But "our beatitude" here means the beatitude of "the human race," not that of the human being: it is not universal peace on which the salvation of souls is dependent.

37. '*Deus et natura nil otiosum facit*', *sed quidquid prodit in esse est ad aliquam operationem*, I.3.

38. *Nullam rem e nihilo gigni divinitus umquam*, DRN 1.150.

39. Cf. *irarum tantos volvis sub pectore fluctus*, 12.831.

40. Cf. Juno's expression *magnanimi Iovis ingratum . . . cubile*, 12.144, and Conington, P. *Vergili Maronis opera, ad loc.*: "'Magnanimi Iovis' . . . seems to be used in a bad or half-ironical sense."

41. Cf. Gilson, *Dante the Philosopher*, 69, 141; *The Spirit of Medieval Philosophy* (Notre Dame, Ind.: University of Notre Dame Press, 1991), 269–288; and Mancusi-Ungaro, *Dante and the Empire*, 174. Dante's claim in *De Monarchia* I.11 that possession of the world is the term of cupidity consorts ill with both Christian doctrine and classical philosophy.

42. Thus Henry's reading of 12.831 as an "exclamatory question"—as if Jupiter were claiming that Juno's fury is incompatible with her kinship to the celestial gods—misses Jupiter's acknowledgement of the ineradicable fury in the celestial gods as such. James Henry, *Aeneidea; or, Critical, Exegetical, and Aesthetical Remarks on the Aeneis*, vol. 1 (London: Williams and Norgate, 1873–92), 196–7.

43. Cf. Herodotus 3.80: καίτοι ἄνδρα γε τύραννον ἄφθονον ἔδει εἶναι, ἔχοντά γε πάντα τὰ ἀγαθά. τὸ δὲ ὑπεναντίον τούτου ἐς τοὺς πολιήτας πέφυκε . . . νόμαιά τε κινέει πάτρια καὶ βιᾶται γυναῖκας. . . . Cf. Michael Davis, "Aristotle's Reflections on Revolution," *Graduate Faculty Philosophy Journal*, New School for Social Research, Vol. 11, No. 2 (1986): 58; and Vittorio Alfieri, *Della Tirannide (Of Tyranny)*, trans. Julius A. Molinaro and Beatrice Corrigan (Toronto: University of Toronto Press, 1961): "I can already hear the objection raised that the tyrant cannot desire the wives of all men; and that it is even a rare occurrence in the present state of society for him to try to seduce two or three; and that he will accomplish this with promises, gifts, and honours bestowed on the husband, never with open violence. These are the wicked reasons which reassure the hearts of modern husbands. . . ." (I.14, 74).

44. Cf. D. Comparetti, *Vergil in the Middle Ages*, trans. E. F. M. Benecke (London: Allen and Unwin, 1966), 230.

45. Represented especially by astronomy: *caelique meatus / describent radio et surgentia sidera dicent*, 6.849–50.

Chapter 12: Piety and Heroic Virtue

1. John Dryden, "Dedication of the Aeneis," in *Essays of John Dryden*, sel. and ed. W. P. Ker, vol. 2 (Oxford: Clarendon Press, 1926), 154, 179.

2. Numa Denis Fustel de Coulanges, *The Ancient City: A Study on the Religion, Laws, and Institutions of Greece and Rome* (Baltimore: Johns Hopkins University Press, 1980), 136. Cf. James Henry, *Aeneidea; or, Critical, Exegetical, and Aesthetical Remarks on the Aeneis*, vol. 1 (London: Williams and Norgate, 1873–92), 288–9: "But which of us has ever yet sympathized with Aeneas? Who, except his own mother, would ever have lifted a hand to save him, had it been possible, from his persecutress—would not rather have said he deserved all he got and should have got more. And more he assuredly would have got had the poet lived, not under Augustus, but under the Republic and before the fall of Carthage, while Juno was still the enemy of Rome, while heroes still bore some faint resemblance to Hector and Achilles, while Dido's were oftener ravished than seduced, and men parleyed with their gods face to face, eye to eye, and hard word for hard word—not beating their breasts and blubbering, abject on their knees, or prostrate in the dust moaning." Cf. John Conington, *P. Vergili Maronis opera* (London: Whittaker & Co., 1872–76), xxviii: "We are wearied, it must be confessed, by being continually reminded of his piety." Cf. also C. M. Bowra, "Aeneas and the Stoic Ideal," *Greece and Rome* 3 (33): 8.

3. W. Y. Sellar, *The Roman Poets of the Augustan Age: Virgil*, 3rd ed. (Oxford, Eng.: Oxford University Press, 1897), 389–90 and 391: "The impression produced by the superiority of Aeneas to ordinary passion is like the impression produced by the superior tolerance and enlightenment of some of Scott's heroes, when contrasted with the more animated impulses and ruder fanaticism of the other personages in his story."

4. Dryden, "Dedication," 179.

5. Dryden, "Dedication," 179–184. Henry Nettleship, "Suggestions Introductory to a Study of the Aeneid," in *Lectures and Essays on Subjects Connected with Latin Literature and Scholarship* (Oxford: Clarendon Press, 1885), 104: "His distinguishing epithet (*pius*) suggests not one heroic quality merely, but the character of the son who loves his father, of the king who loves his subjects, of the worshipper who reverences the gods."

6. R. G. Austin, *Aeneidos Liber Primus* (Oxford: Clarendon Press, 1971), *ad* 1.92 ff.

7. R. D. Williams, *Virgil* (Oxford, London: Clarendon Press, 1967), 31.

8. Viktor Pöschl, *The Art of Vergil: Image and Symbol in the Aeneid*. Trans. Gerda Seligson. (Ann Arbor: University of Michigan Press, 1962), 50–53. Aeneas "represents a new type of hero, the 'unheroic' hero," R. D. Williams, *Virgil* (Oxford, London: Clarendon Press, 1967), 31; cf. Wendell Clausen, "An Interpretation of the Aeneid," *Harvard Studies in Classical Philology* 68 (1964): 140; and Brooks Otis, *Virgil: A Study in Civilized Poetry* (Oxford: Clarendon Press, 1964), 231 ff.

9. For example, Henry, *Aeneidea*, vol. 1, 175–187: "Pietas, the Greek eusebeia, is softness, gentleness and goodness of heart, mercifulness, meekness and kindness of disposition" (175–6); "tenderness, pity" (177–181); "The virtue therefore for which Aeneas was

so remarkable (*insignem*), the virtue which it was the scope of Virgil's poem to recommend and inculcate by the example of his hero, was not piety, or devotion to heaven, but pietas (*pitié*), or tenderness and brotherly love to mankind, that same noble, generous, kindly, charitable, self-sacrificing feeling which is inculcated and set forward in every sentence of Christ's preaching, and of which Christ afforded in his own person so illustrious an example" (184). For discussion of the relation of piety and pity in Aeneas' *pietas*, see W. R. Johnson, "Aeneas and the ironies of pietas," *Classical Journal* 60 (1965): 359–364; M. Owen Lee, *Fathers and Sons in Virgil's* Aeneid (Albany, N.Y.: State University of New York Press, 1979), 180, n. 15, provides a bibliography on the view that Aeneas' *pietas* is pity.

10. Fustel de Coulanges, *The Ancient City*, 136. Cf. Servius *ad* 8.552: *Aeneam ubique pontificem ostendat. . . . Aeneam non tantum pontificii iuris, sed omnium sacrorum et peritum et primum fuisse.*

11. Cf. H. P. Stahl, "Aeneas—An 'Unheroic' Hero?" *Arethusa* 14 (1981), 157–178, and esp. 174 on Vergil's interest in portraying Aeneas as a successful rival of Achilles.

12. For example, Otis, *Virgil: A Study in Civilized Poetry*, 304.

13. *Positis externorum periculorum curis ne luxuriarent otio animi, quos metus hostium disciplinaque militaris continuerat, omnium primum, rem ad multitudinem imperitam et illis saeculis rudem efficacissimam, deorum metum iniciendum ratus est. Qui cum descendere ad animos sine aliquo commento miraculi non posset, simulat sibi cum dea Egeria congressos nocturnos esse; eius se monitu, quae acceptissima diis essent sacra instituere, sacerdotes suos cuique deorum praeficere.* I.xix.4–5. Vergil puts in the mouth of Anchises the criticism that Numa's policy, while contributing "laws" to the imperium of Rome, still left the country weakened by *otia*, and disaccustomed the men to arms (6.809–815).

14. Cf. Livy VIII.31.

15. James Henry, *Aeneidea*, 289; cf. *DRN* 1.62, *foede cum vita iaceret*.

16. Fustel de Coulanges, *The Ancient City*, 136.

17. "Poetic" because manliness itself is ultimately exposed by Lucretius as a false standard; cf. above, pp. 59–61.

18. On the connection between self-castration and fear of death cf. 6.1208–1209, *metuentes limina Leti / vivebant ferro privati parte virili*, and context.

19. On the abjectness of conventional piety, cf. also 2.14–61, 3.48–93, 1076–1094, 4.1236–1239, 6.50–67, 86.

Chapter 13: Aeneas and the Heroes

1. For the gods' pleasure in the beautiful appearances of the war, cf. also 13.11–14, 21.388–390. The pleasurable likenesses of the war to other things are for the gods what the similes are for Homer's listeners. On the pleasure in the contemplation of such likenesses cf. Aristotle, *Rhetoric* 1410b12 ff.: "For easy learning is by nature pleasant to all, and words signify something, so that the most pleasant words are those that cause us to learn. . . . But it is metaphor that most does this. . . . For when the poet calls old age "stubble," he causes learning and knowledge through the genus. . . . And the similes (εἰκόνες) of the poets do the same." Cf. also *Poetics* 1448b9 ff.: "We enjoy looking at the most accurate likenesses (εἰκόνες) of things which are in themselves painful for us to see . . . because it befalls those who look at the likenesses to learn and reason out what each thing is."

2. Quoted in reproach by Plato's Socrates, *Republic* 390A–B, as an example of Homer's attributing immoderate speech to the "wisest" man; and with approbation by Aristotle, *Politics* 1338a28 ff., as belonging to Odysseus' representation of the liberal and noble use of leisure.

3. On Lucretius' account of love, cf. James Nichols, *Epicurean Political Philosophy* (Ithaca, N.Y.: Cornell University Press, 1976), 97–100.

4. John Dryden, "Dedication of the Aeneis," in *Essays of John Dryden*, selected and edited by W. P. Ker, vol. 2, 151–195 (Oxford: Clarendon Press, 1926), 179.

5. As, for example, in their sharing the experience of fleeing their fatherlands to found new cities, and in a certain taste (an eastern, a Phoenician/Trojan taste) for luxury and leisure (4.259–264).

Chapter 14: The Education of Aeneas: I

1. Cf. Servius *ad* 81, *utitur bona arte mendacii; ad* 83 *Sinon callide quasi ignorantibus quae vera sunt dicit, ut fidem sequentibus faciat; ad* 162 *more suo a veris incipit.*

2. Cf. Gary B. Miles, "Glorious Peace: The Values and Motivation of Virgil's Aeneas," *California Studies in Classical Antiquity* 9 (1976): 142–3.

3. Cf. Servius *ad* 2.34.

4. Indeed according to Livy's account Aeneas himself, along with Antenor, was recognized by the victorious Greeks as deserving special consideration for his efforts to stop the war: *Iam primum omnium satis constat Troia capta in ceteros saevitum esse Troianos, duobus, Aeneae Antenorique, et vetusti iure hospitii et quia pacis reddendaeque Helenae semper auctores fuerant, omne ius belli Achivos abstinuisse* (I.1.1).

5. And cf. Austin, *Aeneidos Liber Secundus* (Oxford: Clarendon Press, 1980), *ad* 2.49, on a remark of St. Jerome: "can a 'gift-horse' have had a special significance in primitive belief, and was Laocoon flouting superstition?"

6. *Bene "ligno" quasi dissuasorie, non simulacro . . . nam in suasione vel dissuasione tam sensus quam verba considerantur; adfectavit tapinosin dicens "ligno": infirmare enim vult fictam eorum religionem* (*ad* 46).

7. E.g., *DRN* 3.135, 5.577, 1252.

8. *Hac autem re ostendit, ex accidentibus dolos Graecorum esse firmatos* (Servius *ad* 199).

9. Cf. Vergil's invocatory question to the Muse, 1.8–11.

10. Cf. Wendell Clausen, *Virgil's* Aeneid *and the Tradition of Hellenistic Poetry* (Berkeley: University of California Press, 1987), 32: ". . . Virgil's Aeneas does not involve himself personally in the story of the Horse: he speaks in the first- or third-person plural only, more as a spectator than as a participant." The plurals do emphasize that Aeneas takes no position of leadership in these events; but surely the *first*-person plurals make him a participant.

11. Cf. Hans-Peter Stahl, "Aeneas—An 'Unheroic' Hero?" *Arethusa* 14 (1981): 165–168. "Can we really expect Virgil to make Aeneas leave his city right away without any attempt at conquering the invaders? In case he did, would we not perhaps gain the impression that the Emperor's ancestor was happy to receive orders to leave—similar to a coward?" (165).

12. Though the omens that appear later to his father (2.679–704) offer some confirmation to Aeneas that his experience is not merely the delusion of a self-excusing imagination.

13. Cf. 6.719–721: O pater, anne aliquas ad caelum hinc ire putandum est / sublimis animas iterumque ad tarda reverti / corpora? quae lucis miseris tam dira cupido?

14. DRN 1.84–100; this passage has already been recalled by Sinon's story of the Greeks' attempt to make a sacrificial victim of him.

15. Somnoque sepultis, DRN 1.133; cf. somno vinoque sepultam, Aen. 2.265.

16. Contrast Dido's awakening from her dream-vision of Sychaeus, his commota, 1.360; Achilles' awakening from his dream-vision of Patroclus, ταφὼν δ' ἀνόρουσεν, Iliad 23.101.

17. With praecipitat, cf. just above, in the simile, the torrent's uprooting of the trees (praecipitis 307); and with ardent just above, in Aeneas' view of the invaded city, the burning house of Ucalegon (ardet 311). In retrospect, Aeneas disapproves his heroic actions by describing them as passions.

18. Recalling Lucretius' account of the disposal of the dead when the exigencies of the plague had made men forget about religio divum, DRN 6.1272–1279.

19. On the question of the authenticity of the Helen passage, cf. R. G. Austin, Aeneidos Liber Secundus, 219 ff.; G. P. Goold, "Servius and the Helen Episode," Harvard Studies in Classical Philology 74 (1970): 101–168; C. E. Murgia, "More on the Helen Episode," California Studies in Classical Antiquity 4 (1971): 203–217; Kenneth J. Reckford, "Helen in Aeneid 2 and 6," Arethusa 14 (1981): 85–99; and G. B. Conte, The Rhetoric of Imitation: genre and poetic memory in Virgil and other Latin poets. (Ithaca, N.Y.: Cornell University Press, 1986): 196–207.

20. Emphasized in the repetition of subiit (560, 562), as previously the opinion "pulchrum mori in armis" had stolen upon him as the undercurrent (succurrit, 317) of his actions in battle; and cf. subit ira, 575.

21. Aeneas justifies his slaying of Turnus in the last lines of the poem with a similar argument, that Turnus is not an enemy to be defeated but a criminal to be punished on behalf of the dead; Aeneas claims to act as the agent of the dead Pallas (12.945–949).

22. Dis aliter visum, 2.428.

23. "Perpetuum epitheton," Servius ad loc.; cf. e.g. Austin, Aeneidos Liber Secundus, ad loc.

24. His exoneration is confirmed in a way by the later scene between Helen and Aphrodite, 3.383 ff.

25. Vergil's revision of Athene's revelation to Diomedes in Venus' revelation to Aeneas is mediated by the account of Epicurus' revelation to Lucretius in De Rerum Natura 3.1–31. In Lucretius' version, human sight is human intellect: the mist that obscures human sight consists of the "terrors of the mind" (16), and when these are removed by the divine (15) revelation of Epicurus' paternal precepts and golden words (9–13), the truth revealed to Lucretius is that the gods are inaccessible to pain (18–22), Nature supplies everything needed for peace of mind (23–24), and there are no realms of Acheron (25–27). The result of the revelation for Lucretius is that he is seized by shudders of divine pleasure (28–30). Vergil's references to Lucretius in his account of the revelation of Venus include: parentis . . . praeceptis (604–605; DRN 3.9–10 patria . . . praecepta); apparent dirae facies inimicaque Troiae / numina magna deum (622–623; DRN 3.18, apparet divum numen sedesque quietae).

26. On the constitution of Aeneas' piety (εὐσέβεια) by father and father's (and mother's) gods, rather than father, father's gods, and fatherland, cf. Xenophon Cyn. I.15: Αἰνείας δὲ σώσας μὲν τοὺς πατρῴους καὶ μητρῴους θεούς, σώσας δὲ καὶ αὐτὸν τὸν πατέρα δόξαν εὐσεβείας ἐξηνέγκατο, ὥστε καὶ οἱ πολέμιοι μόνῳ ἐκείνῳ ὧν ἐκράτησαν ἐν Τροίᾳ ἔδοσαν μὴ συληθῆναι.

27. Hector: *heu fuge, nate dea* (289); Venus: *eripe, nate, fugam* (619).

28. Curiously, just as Aeneas had not remembered Hector's instructions during the battle, so he does not remember Creusa's during the navigation in Book 3.

Chapter 15: The Education of Aeneas: II

1. Cf. R. B. Lloyd, "Aeneid III: A New Approach," *American Journal of Philology* 78 (1957): 133–151.

2. Servius *ad loc.* speculates in some detail on what the many things would have been.

3. Cf. M. C. J. Putnam, "The Third Book of the *Aeneid*: from Homer to Rome," *Ramus* 9 (1980): 3.

4. So Servius *ad loc.* points out the rational physiology of Aeneas' coldness of blood in words recalling the second *Georgic*: *physice loquitur et rationabiliter; nam hinc et pallor nascitur, cum se ad praecordia fugiens contrahit sanguis.* (For *praecordia*, cf. *Geo.* 2.484).

5. Anchises in the Underworld refers back to the danger that Aeneas might have abandoned his mission at Carthage: *quam metui ne quid Libyae tibi regna nocerent*, 6.694.

6. Cf. *invitus . . . iussa deum*, 6.460–1.

7. Cf. 6.694–696.

8. Cf. Gary B. Miles, "Glorious Peace: The Values and Motivation of Virgil's Aeneas," *California Studies in Classical Antiquity* 9 (1976): 149–50.

9. The opening of Book 5 recalls the opening of Book 3. As in Book 3 deeply hidden causes (*causas penitus latentis*, 3.32) connected with the pollution of hospitality (*pollutum hospitium*, 3.61) had led to the veneration of the Underworld and the rites of the dead, so in Book 5 the hidden cause of the conflagration at Carthage (*causa latet*, 5.5), connected with the pollution of love (*amore polluto*, 5.5–6), introduces the funeral games of Anchises.

10. On the conflict between art and glory, cf. also Iapyx the physician, descended like Palinurus from Iasus, who chose *mutas agitare inglorius artis* (12.397); and cf. *Geo.* 2.486 of Vergil's own georgic art, *flumina amem silvasque inglorius*, and *Geo.* 4.564, *studiis florentem ignobilis oti*. David Quint, *Epic and Empire: Politics and Generic Form from Virgil to Milton* (Princeton, N.J.: Princeton University Press, 1993), 83–96, argues that the Palinurus episode "stands . . . for the sacrifice that Aeneas . . . must make of his own individuality, even of his heroic agency" (84).

11. Vergil uses the verb *rego* and the noun *rector* indifferently of piloting ships and ruling gods and men (*rector* of a pilot, 5.161, 176; of Jupiter's kingship, 8.572; *rego* of piloting, 5.868, 6.350, 10.218; of divine and human kingship, 1.230, 340, 4.230, 6.851, 7.46, 8.325); and he makes the captain Mnestheus, exhorting his crew to its ultimate effort, address them as *cives* (5.196).

12. As also at 6.849–850.

13. On the "pre-Socratic" character of the pilot in Socrates' own discussion of the image of the ship of state, see Seth Benardete, *Socrates' Second Sailing* (Chicago: University of Chicago Press, 1989), 145–146.

14. Cf. 10.246–250, where Aeneas at the helm (218) is sped on by the skilled power of Cymodoce: *stupet inscius ipse / Tros Anchisiades, animos tamen omine tollit.*

15. For verbal references to the Menoetes/Gyas episode, cf. *saxa timens* 164, *pete saxa* 166, *scopulosque sonantis* 169, *exarsit . . . dolor ossibus ingens* 172, *ipse gubernaclo rector subit, ipse magister* 176, *cedit quoniam spoliata magistro est*, 224.

16. *Odyssey* 12.184–191.

17. The Sibyl prophesies that the two things Aeneas must do in order to gain admission to the Underworld are to pluck the Golden Bough and to bury Misenus (6.133–155). Phrases linking this passage to the Polydorus episode are *lento vimine* (6.137), *lentum vimen* (3.31); *convellere* (6.148, 3.24, 31; also *vellitur* 3.28); *conde sepulcro* (6.152), *sepulcro condimus* (3.67–8).

18. Cf. Anchises' greeting to Aeneas, *tuaque exspectata parenti / vicit iter durum pietas*, 6.687–8.

19. *Id cinerem aut manis credis curare sepultos?* 4.34.

20. The line recalls Lucretius' praise of Epicurus as a greater benefactor of mankind than the gods of poetry, *DRN* 5.9–12.

21. The blessed have the same pleasure in arms and care for their horses that they had when alive (653–655).

22. Supplemented later by the prophetic pictures on the Shield, 8.626–728.

23. *DRN* 4.230–822.

24. On the emphatic Lucretian references in the introductory section of the catabasis, esp. 268–294, see A. K. Michels, "Lucretius and the Sixth Book of the *Aeneid*," *American Journal of Philology* 65 (1944): 135–148.

25. For *audita*, cf. Lucretius on the delusion of those ambitious for rule: *sapiunt alieno ex ore petuntque / res ex auditis potius quam sensibus ipsis*, *DRN* 5.1133.

building, other kids pulled fire alarms and generally caused bedlam.

now must
gents exams to earn
high school diploma, and
they can ill afford to be

soc
Ed

Canal-deal probers to seize developer's files

By **KENNETH LOVETT**
and **FREDRIC U. DICKER**

ALBANY — An investigation into the state Canal Corp. heated up yesterday as subpoenas were served on a private developer who secured a potentially lucrative contract for a paltry sum.

State Attorney General Eliot Spitzer and the state inspector general have subpoenaed records dating back to 1995 from the sole bidder for development along the 500-mile Erie Canal.

Investigators were seeking telephone records, files and e-mails from Richard Hutchens, who won the $30,000 contract for exclusive Erie Canal development rights.

State Comptroller Alan Hevesi canceled the controversial deal after concluding "false and misleading" statements were used to "steer" it to the developer.

Meanwhile, Gov. Pataki ducked questions yesterday about Hevesi's finding last week that the Long Island Power Authority paid $582,217 to Anastasia Song, a former Pataki aide, to serve as its acting chief financial officer.

Hevesi has demanded that most of the money be returned.

"I know that LIPA officials and the comptroller's office are talking and they're looking at it, so we'll see what they come up with," Pataki said.

Pataki denied the mega-salary — which had not first been submitted to Hevesi for approval, as required by state law — was evidence of widespread patronage that some Democrats charge exists.

"Questions have been raised that in certain cases have called for investigations, and in those cases, I supported it," he said.

B
t

y
fi
p
b
th
v
th

a
v
s
c
a
t

l
s
b
s
h

Correspondent

GALVESTON, Texas — Robert Durst said repeatedly yesterday that he didn't remember how he butchered his neighbor Morris Black — including whether he cried as he carried out the carving.

Speaking in a nasal monotone, the cross-dressing millionaire was mostly cool and calm while being cross-examined by Galveston District Attorney Kurt Sistrunk.

"Did you cry when you were cutting up your best friend?" Sistrunk asked pointedly.

The eccentric millionaire claims he killed the 71-year-old Black accidentally before using two saws and an ax to chop him up.

"We're talking about a big ax," Durst said.

But his memory failed when Sistrunk asked how long it took.

"I don't remember," he said.

"Can you tell me where you started?" Sistrunk continued. "The arms? Legs? Head?"

Again, "I don't remember."

Durst, who posed as a

the hall from had a memory whether he Black before carve him up o stuck each li bage bag as he

Sistrunk als drinking a fifth iels before sta zarre act caus problems.

This time, member, and I

The prose Durst, the c scion of one o wealthiest rea lies, killed Bla drifter with h

Sporey details: 120 sq. fee

By DAREH GREGORIAN

Paint it blech.

City inspectors found that the mold condition in Bianca Jagger's Park Avenue apartment is "immediately hazardous" to human health, and that there's a ton of it — 120 square feet in just one room.

"It's unconscionable and it should be illegal," Jagger — the ex-wife of Rolling Stone Mick Jagger — said of the conditions inside her $4,600-a-month Midtown apartment. The wild-

child-turned-human-rights-activist spoke out about the spores after a hearing in Manhattan Housing Court, where she's getting sued for having not paid rent since April.

Bradley Silverbush, the lawyer for landlord Katz Park Avenue, accused Bianca — who coughed throughout the hearing and afterward — of having blown the problem out of proportion in an attempt to get her rent reduced.

"This is no This is about verbush told Hoyos.

Jagger la Wagner sai from the cit of Housing and Develop Jagger's apar 17, and foun olations, wh ered "imme ous."

Carol Abr woman for found eight

~

Bibliography

Adler, Eve. "The Invocation to the Georgics." Interpretation 11 (1983): 25–41.

Alfieri, Vittorio. Of Tyranny. Translated by Julius A. Molinaro and Beatrice Corrigan. Toronto: University of Toronto Press, 1961.

Alfonsi, L. "L'epicureismo nella storia spirituale di Virgilio." In Epicurea in memoriam Hectoris Bignone, 167 ff. Genoa: Istituto di Filologia classica, University di Genova, 1959.

Alvis, John. Divine Purpose and Heroic Response in Homer and Virgil: The Political Plan of Zeus. Lanham, Md.: Rowman and Littlefield, 1995.

Amerasinghe, C. W. "Saturnia Juno: Its Significance in the Aeneid." Greece and Rome 22 (1953): 61–69.

Anderson, William S. "Juno and Saturn in the Aeneid," Studies in Philology 55 (1958): 519–532.

———. The Art of the Aeneid. Englewood Cliffs, N.J.: Prentice-Hall, 1970.

Arendt, Hannah. On Revolution. New York: Penguin, 1986.

Arnold, Matthew. Poems of Matthew Arnold. Edited by Kenneth Allott. London: Longmans, 1965.

Augustine. De civitate Dei. Cambridge, Mass.: Harvard University Press (Loeb Classical Library), 1957–1972.

Austin, R. G. Aeneidos Liber Quartus. With commentary. Oxford: Clarendon Press, 1955.

———. Aeneidos Liber Primus. With commentary. Oxford: Clarendon Press, 1971.

———. Aeneidos Liber Sextus. With commentary. Oxford: Clarendon Press, 1977.

———. Aeneidos Liber Secundus. With commentary. Oxford: Clarendon Press, 1980.

Bacon, Francis. The Essays. Edited by John Pitcher. New York: Penguin, 1985.

Bailey, Cyril. "Virgil and Lucretius," Proceedings of the Classical Association (1931): 21–39.

———. Religion in Virgil. Oxford: Clarendon Press, 1935.

Baldry, H. C. The Unity of Mankind in Greek Thought. Cambridge University Press, 1965.

Benardete, Seth. Socrates' Second Sailing: On Plato's Republic. Chicago: University of Chicago Press, 1989.

Bowra, C. M. "Aeneas and the Stoic Ideal." *Greece and Rome* 3 (1933): 8–21.

Boyancé, Pierre. *Lucrèce et l'Épicurisme*, Paris: Presses Universitaires de France, 1963.

Brisson, J. P. "Le pieux Ené." *Latomus* 31 (1972): 379–412.

Buchheit, Vinzenz. *Vergil über die Sendung Roms*. Heidelberg, 1963.

———. *Der Anspruch des Dichters in Vergils Georgika. Dichtertum und Heilsweg*. Darmstadt: Wissenschaftliche Buchgesellschaft, 1972

Büchner, Karl. P. *Vergilius Maro, der Dichter der Römer*. Stuttgart: A. Druckenmuller, 1961.

Burrow, Colin. "Virgils, from Dante to Milton." In *Cambridge Companion to Virgil*, 79–90. Edited by Charles Martindale. Cambridge: Cambridge University Press, 1997.

Cairns, Francis. *Virgil's Augustan Epic*. Cambridge: Cambridge University Press, 1989.

Castelli, G. "Echi lucreziani nelle ecloghe virgiliane," *Rivista Storia Classica* 14 (1966): 3–3–342; and 15 (1967): 14–39 and 176–216.

Cicero. *Letters to Atticus, Books I–VI*. Translated by E. O. Winstedt. Cambridge, Mass.: Harvard University Press, 1980.

Clark, Raymond J. *Catabasis: Vergil and the Wisdom-Tradition*. Amsterdam: Grüner, 1979.

Clausen, Wendell. "An Interpretation of the Aeneid," *Harvard Studies in Classical Philology* 68 (1964): 139–147.

———. *Virgil's Aeneid and the Tradition of Hellenistic Poetry*. Berkeley: University of California Press, 1987.

Clay, Diskin. *Lucretius and Epicurus*. Ithaca, N.Y.: Cornell University Press, 1983.

Clay, Jenny Strauss. "The Argument of the End of Virgil's Second Georgic." *Philologus* 120 (1976): 232–245.

Cochrane, Charles Norris. *Christianity and Classical Culture: A Study of Thought and Action from Augustus to Augustine*. New York: Oxford University Press, 1944.

Comparetti, Domenico. *Vergil in the Middle Ages*. Translated by E. F. M. Benecke. London: Allen and Unwin, 1966.

Conington, John, commentary, and Henry Nettleship, editor. *P. Vergili Maronis opera*. 3rd edition. London: Whittaker & Co., 1872–76. 3 vols.

Connolly, Cyril. "Who Was Palinurus?" In Cyril Connolly, *The Unquiet Grave*, 134–147. New York and London: Harper & Brothers, 1945.

Conte, G. B. *The Rhetoric of Imitation: Genre and Poetic Memory in Virgil and other Latin Poets*. Edited by Charles Segal. Ithaca, N.Y.: Cornell University Press, 1986.

Conway, R. S. "Poetry and Government." *Proceedings of the Classical Association* (1928): 19–38.

Dante Alighieri. *Monarchia*. Foreword, introduction, translation, and comments by Gustavo Vinay. Florence, Italy: Sansoni, 1950.

Davis, Charles T. *Dante and the Idea of Rome*. Oxford: Clarendon Press, 1957.

Davis, Michael. "Aristotle's Reflections on Revolution." *Graduate Faculty Philosophy Journal* 11, no. 2 (1986): 49–64.

De Witt, Norman Wentworth. *Epicurus and his Philosophy*. Minneapolis: University of Minnesota Press, 1954.

Dietz, David B. "Historia in the commentary of Servius." *Transactions of the American Philological Association* 125 (1995) 61–97.

Dilke, O. A. W. *Greek and Roman Maps*. Ithaca, N.Y.: Cornell University Press, 1985.

Donatus. *Vita*. In *Vitae Vergilianae Antiquae*, edited by C. G. Hardie. London: Oxford University Press, 1966.

Dryden, John. "Dedication of the Aeneis." In *Essays of John Dryden*, selected and edited by W. P. Ker, vol. 2, 151–195. Oxford: Clarendon Press, 1926.

Dudley, D. R. *Lucretius*, New York: Basic Books, 1965.

Eden, P. T. *A Commentary on Virgil: Aeneid VIII*. Leiden: E. J. Brill, 1975.

Epicurus. *Epicurus: The Extant Remains*. Edited by Cyril Bailey. Oxford: Clarendon Press, 1926.

Fantazzi, C. "Golden Age in Arcadia." *Latomus* 33 (1974): 280–305.

Farrell, Joseph. *Vergil's Georgics and the Traditions of Ancient Epic: The Art of Allusion in Literary History*. New York and Oxford: Oxford University Press, 1991.

Farrington, Benjamin. *Science and Politics in the Ancient World*. New York: Oxford University Press, 1940.

Feeney, D. C. *The Gods in Epic: Poets and Critics of the Classical Tradition*. Oxford: Clarendon Press, 1991.

Fordyce, C. J. P. *Vergili Maronis Aeneidos, Libri VII–VIII*. With commentary. New York and Oxford: Oxford University Press, 1977.

Fortin, Ernest. *Dissidence et philosophie au moyen âge*. Montreal: Bellarmin, 1981.

Fowler, Don. "The Virgil Commentary of Servius." In *Cambridge Companion to Virgil*, edited by Charles Martindale, 73–78. Cambridge: Cambridge University Press, 1997.

Fowler, W. Warde. *Social Life at Rome in the Age of Cicero*. New York: Macmillan, 1909.

———. *Virgil's "Gathering of the Clans."* Oxford: B. H. Blackwell, 1916.

———. *The Death of Turnus: Observations on the Twelfth Book of the Aeneid*. Oxford: B. H. Blackwell, 1919.

Frank, Tenney. "Epicurean Determinism in the *Aeneid*." *American Journal of Philology* 41 (1920): 115–126.

———. *Vergil, A Biography*. New York: Henry Holt, 1922.

Frischer, Bernard. *The Sculpted Word: Epicureanism and Philosophical Recruitment in Ancient Greece*. Berkeley: University of California Press, 1982.

Fustel de Coulanges, Numa Denis. *The Ancient City: A Study on the Religion, Laws, and Institutions of Greece and Rome*. English translation of *La cité antique*. Baltimore: Johns Hopkins University Press, 1980.

Gauthiez, Pierre. *De Virgilii Philosophia*. Paris, 1895.

Gilson, Étienne. *Dante the Philosopher*, translated by David Moore. London: Sheed and Ward, 1948.

———. *The Spirit of Medieval Philosophy*. Translated by A. H. C. Downes. Notre Dame, Ind.: University of Notre Dame Press, 1991.

Goold, G. P. "Servius and the Helen Episode." *Harvard Studies in Classical Philology* 74 (1970): 101–168.

Gransden, K. W. *Virgil's Iliad: An Essay on Epic Narrative*. Cambridge and New York: Cambridge University Press, 1984.

Grimal, Pierre. *Roman Cities*. Translated and edited by G. Michael Woloch. Madison: University of Wisconsin Press, 1983.

Grotius, Hugo. *The Law of War and Peace: De Jure Belli ac Pacis Libri Tres*. Translated by F. W. Kelsey. Indianapolis: Bobbs-Merrill, 1962.

Hardie, Philip R. *Virgil's Aeneid: Cosmos and Imperium*. Clarendon: Oxford University Press, 1986.

———. "Virgil and Tragedy." In *Cambridge Companion to Virgil*, edited by Charles Martindale, 312–326. Cambridge: Cambridge University Press, 1997.

———. *Virgil*. New York and Oxford: Oxford University Press, 1998.

Harrison, S. J., editor. *Oxford Readings in Vergil's Aeneid*. New York and Oxford: Oxford University Press, 1990.

———. "Some Views of the *Aeneid* in the Twentieth Century." In *Oxford Readings in Vergil's* Aeneid, edited by S. J. Harrison, 1–20. New York and Oxford: Oxford University Press, 1990.

Hegel, G. W. F. *Philosophy of Right*. Translated by T. M. Knox. Oxford: Clarendon Press, 1967.

Heinze, Richard. *Virgils Epische Technik*. Leipzig: B. G. Teubner, 1903

———. *Virgil's Epic Technique*. Translated by Hazel and David Harvey and Fred Robertson. Berkeley: University of California Press, 1993.

Henry, James. *Aeneidea; or, Critical, exegetical, and aesthetical remarks on the Aeneis*. 2 vols. London: Williams and Norgate, 1873–92.

Hershkowitz, Debra. *The Madness of Epic: Reading Insanity from Homer to Statius*. New York and Oxford: Oxford University Press, 1998.

Hesiod. *Works and Days*. In *Hesiod, the Homeric Hymns and Homerica*, edited and translated by Hugh G. Evelyn-White. Cambridge, Mass.: Harvard University Press, 1974.

Hirst, M. E. "The Gates of Virgil's Underworld: A Reminiscence of Lucretius." *Classical Review* 26 (1912): 82–3.

Homer. *Iliad*. Translated by Richmond Lattimore. Chicago: University of Chicago Press, 1963.

———. *Odyssey*. Translated by Richmond Lattimore. New York: Harper & Row, 1967.

Horsfall, Nicholas M. "Dido in the Light of History." *Proceedings of the Virgil Society* 13 (1973–4): 1–13.

———. *A Companion to the Study of Virgil*. Leiden, Netherlands: E. J. Brill, 1995.

Jenkyns, Richard. *Virgil's Experience. Nature and History: Times, Names, and Places*. New York and Oxford: Oxford University Press, 1998.

Johnson, W. R. "Aeneas and the Ironies of *Pietas*," *Classical Journal* 60 (1965): 359–364.

———. *Darkness Visible: A Study of Vergil's Aeneid*. Berkeley: University of California Press, 1976.

———. "The Broken World: Virgil and His Augustus." *Arethusa* 14 (1981): 49–56.

Kennedy, Duncan F. "Virgilian Epic." In *Cambridge Companion to Virgil*, edited by Charles Martindale, 145–155. Cambridge: Cambridge University Press, 1997.

Kinsey, T. E. "The Song of Iopas." *Emerita* 47 (1979): 77–86.

Klein, Jacob. "The Myth of Vergil's Aeneid." *Interpretation* 2 (1971): 10–20.

Klepl, Herta. *Lukrez und Vergil in ihren Lehrgedichten*. Darmstadt,1967; reprinted from Dresden edition, 1940.

Klingner, Friedrich. *Virgil. Bucolica, Georgica, Aeneis*. Zürich: Artemis, 1967.

Knauer, G. N. *Die Aeneis und Homer: Studien zur poetischen Technik Vergils mit Listen der Homerzitate in der Aeneis*. Göttingen: Hypomnemata, 1964.

———. "Vergil's Aeneid and Homer." *Greek, Roman and Byzantine Studies* 5 (1964): 61–84.

Kojève, Alexandre. "Tyranny and Wisdom." In Leo Strauss, *On Tyranny*, 143–188. Ithaca, N.Y.: Cornell University Press, 1963.

Kranz, W. "Das Lied des Kitharoden von Jaffa." *Rheinisches Museum* 96 (1953): 30–38.

Lee, Guy. "Imitation and the Poetry of Virgil." *Greece and Rome* 28 (1981): 10–22.

Lee, M. Owen. *Fathers and Sons in Virgil's Aeneid*. Albany: State University of New York Press, 1979.

Leonard, W. E., and S. B. Smith. *T. Lucreti Cari De Rerum Natura Libri Sex*. Madison: University of Wisconsin Press, 1970.

Lewis, R. W. B. "Homer and Virgil—The Double Themes." *Furioso* 5 (Spring 1950): 47–59.

Lloyd, R. B. "*Aeneid* III: A New Approach," *American Journal of Philology* 78 (1957): 133–151.

Lovejoy, Arthur O. and George Boas. *Primitivism and Related Ideas in Antiquity*. New York: Octagon, 1965.

Lowenthal, D. "Montequieu." In *History of Political Philosophy*, edited by Leo Strauss and Joseph Cropsey, 487–508. Chicago: Rand McNally, 1972.

Machiavelli, Nicolò. *Discorsi sopra la Prima Deca di Tito Livio*. Milan: Biblioteca Universale Rizzoli, 1984.

———. *The Prince*. Translated by Harvey C. Mansfield, Jr. Chicago: University of Chicago Press, 1985.

MacKay, L. A. "Saturnia Juno." *Greece and Rome* 2nd Ser. 3 (1956): 59–60.

Macrobius. *The Saturnalia*. Translated, introduction, and notes by Percival Vaughan Davies. New York: Columbia University Press, 1969.

Mancusi-Ungaro, Donna. *Dante and the Empire*. New York: Peter Lang, 1987.

Mansfield, Harvey C. *Machiavelli's New Modes and Orders*. Ithaca, N.Y.: Cornell University Press, 1979.

Martindale, Charles, editor. *Cambridge Companion to Virgil*. Cambridge: Cambridge University Press, 1997.

Merrill, W. A. "Parallels and coincidences in Lucretius and Virgil," *University of California Publications in Classical Philology* 3 (1918): 135–247.

Michels, A. K. "Lucretius and the Sixth Book of the *Aeneid*." *American Journal of Philology* 65 (1944): 135–148.

Miles, Gary B. "Glorious Peace: The Values and Motivation of Virgil's Aeneas." *California Studies in Classical Antiquity* 9 (1976): 133–164.

———. *Virgil's Georgics: A New Interpretation*. Berkeley: University of California Press, 1980.

Minyard, J. D. *Lucretius and the Late Republic: An Essay in Roman Intellectual History*. Leiden, Netherlands: Brill, 1985.

Montesquieu, Charles de Secondat, baron de. *Considérations sur les Causes de la Grandeur des Romains et de leur Decadence*. Edited by G. Franceschi. Paris: Flammarion, 1900.

———. *De l'Esprit des Lois*. Edited by Victor Goldschmidt. Paris: Garnier-Flammarion, 1979.

Monti, Richard C. *The Dido Episode and the Aeneid: Roman Social and Political Values in the Epic*. Leiden, Netherlands: Brill, 1981.

Muecke, Frances. "Poetic Self-Consciousness in *Georgics* II." *Ramus* 8 (1979): 87–107.

Murgia, C. E. "More on the Helen Episode." *California Studies in Classical Antiquity* 4 (1971): 203–217.

Murley, Clyde. "Lucretius, *De Rerum Natura*, viewed as Epic." *Transactions of the American Philological Association* 78 (1947): 336–346.

Nettleship, Henry. "Suggestions Introductory to a Study of the *Aeneid*." In *Lectures and Essays on Subjects Connected with Latin Literature and Scholarship*, 85–141. Oxford: Clarendon Press, 1885.

Nichols, James. *Epicurean Political Philosophy*. Ithaca, N.Y.: Cornell University Press, 1976.

Norden, Eduard. *P. Vergilius Maro, Aeneis Buch VI*. Stuttgart: B. G. Teubner, 1957.

Otis, Brooks. *Virgil: A Study in Civilized Poetry* . Oxford: Clarendon Press, 1964.

Page, T. E. *The Aeneid of Virgil*. 2 vols. London: Macmillan, 1962, 1970.

Paratore, Ettore. "Spunti Lucreziani nelle Georgiche," *Atene e Roma*, S. 3 7–8 (1939–40): 177–204.

——. *Eneide*. Translated by Luca Canali, commentary by Ettore Paratore. Milan: A. Mondadori, 1985.

Pease, Arthur Stanley. "Some Aspects of the Character of Dido." *Classical Journal* 22 (1926–7): 243–252.

——. *Publi Vergili Maronis Aeneidos Liber Quartus*. Darmstadt: Wissenschaftliche Buchgesellschaft, 1967. Reprinted from the Harvard edition of 1935.

Plutarch. *De Superstitione*. In *Plutarch's Moralia*. Vol. 2. Translated by F. C. Babbitt. Cambridge, Mass.: Harvard University Press, 1971.

——. *On the Fortune or the Virtue of Alexander*. In *Plutarch's Moralia*. Vol. 4. Translated by F. C. Babbitt. Cambridge, Mass.: Harvard University Press, 1936.

Polybius. *The Histories of Polybius*. Translated from the text of F. Hultsch, by Evelyn S. Shuckburgh. Westport, Conn.: Greenwood Press, 1974.

Pöschl, Viktor. *The Art of Vergil: Image and Symbol in the Aeneid*. Trans. Gerda Seligson. Ann Arbor: University of Michigan Press, 1962.

Pufendorf, Samuel. *De Jure Naturae et Gentium Libri Octo*. Translated by C. H. Oldfather and W. A. Oldfather. New York and Oxford: Oxford University Press, 1934.

Putnam, M. C. J. "Mercuri, facunde nepos Atlantis," *Classical Philology* 69 (1974): 215–217.

——. *Virgil's Poem of the Earth: Studies in the Georgics*. Princeton, N.J.: Princeton University Press, 1979.

——. "The Third Book of the Aeneid: from Homer to Rome." *Ramus* 9 (1980): 1–21.

——. *Virgil's Aeneid: Interpretation and Influence*. Chapel Hill: University of North Carolina Press, 1995.

Quinn, Kenneth. *Virgil's Aeneid: A Critical Description*. Ann Arbor: University of Michigan Press, 1968.

Quint, David. *Epic and Empire: Politics and Generic Form from Virgil to Milton*. Princeton, N.J.: Princeton University Press, 1993.

Rawson, E. *Intellectual Life in the Late Roman Republic*. Baltimore: Johns Hopkins University Press, 1985.

Reckford, Kenneth J. "Helen in Aeneid 2 and 6." *Arethusa* 14 (1981): 85–99.

Ross, David O., Jr. *Virgil's Elements: Physics and Poetry in the Georgics*. Princeton, N.J.: Princeton University Press, 1987.

Rostagni, A. "Virgilio e Lucrezio." *Rivista di Filologia* (1931): 289–315.

Sachs, Joe. "The Fury of Aeneas." *St. John's Review* 33 (1982): 75–82.

Schrijvers, P. H. *Horror ac divina voluptas: Études sur la poésie de Lucrèce*. Amsterdam: A. M. Hakkert, 1970.

Segal, Charles P. "The Song of Iopas in the Aeneid," *Hermes* 99 (1971): 336–349.

——. "Iopas Revisited (*Aeneid* 1.740 ff.)." *Emerita* 49 (1981): 21 ff.

Sellar, W. Y. *The Roman Poets of the Augustan Age: Virgil*. 3rd ed. Oxford: Oxford, 1897.

Servius. *Servii Grammatici qui feruntur in Vergilii Carmina Commentarii*. Edited by G. Thilo and H. Hagen. 3 vols. Hildesheim: G. Olms, 1961.

Stahl, Hans-Peter. "Aeneas—An 'Unheroic' Hero?" *Arethusa* 14 (1981): 157–178.

Stambaugh, John E. *The Ancient Roman City*. Baltimore: Johns Hopkins University Press, 1988.

Stern, Samuel M. *Aristotle on the World State*. Columbia: University of South Carolina Press, 1970.

Strauss, Leo. *Natural Right and History*. Chicago: University of Chicago Press,1953.

———. "Notes on Lucretius." In Leo Strauss, *Liberalism Ancient and Modern*, 76–139. New York: Basic Books, 1968.

———. "The Liberalism of Classical Political Philosophy." In Leo Strauss, *Liberalism Ancient and Modern*, 26–64. New York: Basic Books, 1968.

Tarn, W. W. *Alexander the Great. Vol. II: Sources and Studies*. Cambridge: Cambridge University Press, 1950.

Tarrant, R. J. "Poetry and Power: Virgil's Poetry in Contemporary Context." In *Cambridge Companion to Virgil*, edited by Charles Martindale, 169–187. Cambridge, Eng.: Cambridge University Press, 1997.

Thomas, Émile. *Scoliastes de Virgile: Essai sur Servius et son Commentaire sur Virgile*. Paris: E. Thorin, 1880.

Vida, Marco Girolamo. *De Arte Poetica*. Edited, translated, and commentary by Ralph G. Williams. New York: Columbia University Press, 1976.

Voegelin, Eric. *The Ecumenic Age*. Vol. 4 of *Order and History*. Baton Rouge: Louisiana State University Press, 1974.

Wallace, Edith Owen. *The Notes on Philosophy in the Commentary of Servius on the Eclogues, the Georgics and the Aeneid of Vergil*. New York: Columbia University Press, 1938.

Wardman, Alan. *Religion and Statecraft among the Romans*. Baltimore: Johns Hopkins University Press, 1982.

West, David. *The Imagery and Poetry of Lucretius*. Edinburgh: Edinburgh University Press, 1969.

Williams, Gordon W. *Technique and Ideas in the Aeneid*. New Haven, Conn.: Yale University Press, 1983.

Williams, R. D. "The Pictures on Dido's Temple (*Aeneid* 1.450–93)." *Classical Quarterly*, n.s. 10 (1960): 145–151.

———. *Virgil*. Oxford and London: Clarendon Press, 1967.

———. *The Aeneid of Virgil, Books 1–6*. With commentary. New York: St. Martin's Press, 1972.

Wood, Neal. *Cicero's Social and Political Thought*. Berkeley: University of California Press, 1988.

Wormell, D. E. W. "The Personal World of Lucretius." In *Lucretius*, edited by D. R. Dudley. New York: Basic Books, 1965.

Index

Passages Index